Keep this book. You will
need it and use it throughout
your career.

PURCHASING for HOSPITALITY OPERATIONS

Educational Institute Courses

Introductory

INTRODUCTION TO THE HOSPITALITY INDUSTRY
Fourth Edition
Gerald W. Lattin

AN INTRODUCTION TO HOSPITALITY TODAY
Third Edition
Rocco M. Angelo, Andrew N. Vladimir

TOURISM AND THE HOSPITALITY INDUSTRY
Joseph D. Fridgen

Rooms Division

FRONT OFFICE PROCEDURES
Fifth Edition
Michael L. Kasavana, Richard M. Brooks

HOUSEKEEPING MANAGEMENT
Second Edition
Margaret M. Kappa, Aleta Nitschke, Patricia B. Schappert

Human Resources

HOSPITALITY SUPERVISION
Second Edition
Raphael R. Kavanaugh, Jack D. Ninemeier

HOSPITALITY INDUSTRY TRAINING
Second Edition
Lewis C. Forrest, Jr.

HUMAN RESOURCES MANAGEMENT
Second Edition
Robert H. Woods

Marketing and Sales

MARKETING OF HOSPITALITY SERVICES
William Lazer, Roger Layton

HOSPITALITY SALES AND MARKETING
Third Edition
James R. Abbey

CONVENTION MANAGEMENT AND SERVICE
Fifth Edition
Milton T. Astroff, James R. Abbey

MARKETING IN THE HOSPITALITY INDUSTRY
Third Edition
Ronald A. Nykiel

Accounting

UNDERSTANDING HOSPITALITY ACCOUNTING I
Fourth Edition
Raymond Cote

UNDERSTANDING HOSPITALITY ACCOUNTING II
Third Edition
Raymond Cote

BASIC FINANCIAL ACCOUNTING FOR THE HOSPITALITY INDUSTRY
Raymond S. Schmidgall, James W. Damitio

MANAGERIAL ACCOUNTING FOR THE HOSPITALITY INDUSTRY
Fourth Edition
Raymond S. Schmidgall

Food and Beverage

FOOD AND BEVERAGE MANAGEMENT
Second Edition
Jack D. Ninemeier

QUALITY SANITATION MANAGEMENT
Ronald F. Cichy

FOOD PRODUCTION PRINCIPLES
Jerald W. Chesser

FOOD AND BEVERAGE SERVICE
Second Edition
Ronald F. Cichy, Paul E. Wise

HOSPITALITY PURCHASING MANAGEMENT
William P. Virts

BAR AND BEVERAGE MANAGEMENT
Lendal H. Kotschevar, Mary L. Tanke

FOOD AND BEVERAGE CONTROLS
Fourth Edition
Jack D. Ninemeier

General Hospitality Management

HOTEL/MOTEL SECURITY MANAGEMENT
Raymond C. Ellis, Jr., Security Committee of AH&MA

HOSPITALITY LAW
Third Edition
Jack P. Jefferies

RESORT MANAGEMENT
Second Edition
Chuck Y. Gee

INTERNATIONAL HOTEL MANAGEMENT
Chuck Y. Gee

HOSPITALITY INDUSTRY COMPUTER SYSTEMS
Third Edition
Michael L. Kasavana, John J. Cahill

MANAGING FOR QUALITY IN THE HOSPITALITY INDUSTRY
Robert H. Woods, Judy Z. King

CONTEMPORARY CLUB MANAGEMENT
Edited by Joe Perdue for the Club Managers Association of America

Engineering and Facilities Management

FACILITIES MANAGEMENT
David M. Stipanuk, Harold Roffman

HOSPITALITY INDUSTRY ENGINEERING SYSTEMS
Michael H. Redlin, David M. Stipanuk

HOSPITALITY ENERGY AND WATER MANAGEMENT
Second Edition
Robert E. Aulbach

PURCHASING for HOSPITALITY OPERATIONS

William B. Virts, CPA

Contributing author: Jack D. Ninemeier, Ph.D., CHA

EDUCATIONAL INSTITUTE
of the American Hotel & Motel Association

Disclaimer

This publication is designed to provide accurate and authoritative information in regard to the subject matter covered. It is sold with the understanding that the publisher is not engaged in rendering legal, accounting, or other professional service. If legal advice or other expert assistance is required, the services of a competent professional person should be sought.
  —From the *Declaration of Principles* jointly adopted by the American Bar Association and a Committee of
    Publishers and Associations

The author, William B. Virts, is solely responsible for the contents of this publication. All views expressed herein are solely those of the author and do not necessarily reflect the views of the Educational Institute of the American Hotel & Motel Association (the Institute) or the American Hotel & Motel Association (AH&MA).

Nothing contained in this publication shall constitute a standard, an endorsement, or a recommendation of the Institute or AH&MA. The Institute and AH&MA disclaim any liability with respect to the use of any information, procedure, or product, or reliance thereon by any member of the hospitality industry.

©Copyright 1987, 1996
By the EDUCATIONAL INSTITUTE of the
AMERICAN HOTEL & MOTEL ASSOCIATION
1407 South Harrison Road
P.O. Box 1240
East Lansing, Michigan 48826

The Educational Institute of the American
Hotel & Motel Association is a nonprofit
educational foundation.

Printed in the United States of America
    5 6 7 8 9 10 00 99

Library of Congress Cataloging-in-Publication Data
Virts, William B.
  Purchasing for hospitality operations.

Bibliography: p.
Includes index.
  1. Hotels, taverns, etc. 2. Restaurants, lunch rooms,
etc. 3. Food service. 4. Purchasing. I. Ninemeier,
Jack D. II. Title
TX911.3.P8V57 1987 647'.95'0687 86-29196
ISBN 0-86612-033-5
ISBN 0-86612-114-5 (pbk.)

Editor: Kent F. Premo

Contents

Congratulations. . .

You have a running start on a fast-track career!

Developed through the input of industry and academic experts, this course gives you the know-how hospitality employers demand. Upon course completion, you will earn the respected American Hotel & Motel Association certificate that ensures instant recognition worldwide. It is your link with the global hospitality industry.

You can use your AH&MA certificate to show that your learning experiences have bridged the gap between industry and academia. You will have proof that you have met industry-driven learning objectives and that you know how to apply your knowledge to actual hospitality work situations.

By earning your course certificate, you also take a step toward completing the highly respected learning programs—Certificates of Specialization, the Hospitality Operations Certificate, and the Hospitality Management Diploma—that raise your professional development to a higher level. Certificates from these programs greatly enhance your credentials, and a permanent record of your course and program completion is maintained by the Educational Institute.

We commend you for taking this important step. Turn to the Educational Institute for additional resources that will help you stay ahead of your competition.

Preface

Purchasing comprises a complex series of management activities designed to maximize value for the hospitality operation and its guests. The importance of purchasing is clear and unmistakable in its contribution to bottom-line profits, continuity of supply, efficient operation, and guest satisfaction.

This textbook is intended for hospitality professionals interested in methods of increasing buying power, as well as for students and instructors. In writing this textbook, the purpose has been to cover the most innovative techniques available to hospitality purchasers, including cost-plus and forward contracting. The idea is to shift the buying system from the routine maintenance of supply levels to a forward-thinking, cost-saving program.

Most other books give the reader a one-dimensional view of purchasing. Some reduce purchasing to a theoretical discussion; others dwell on its technical side. This book offers the reader a well-rounded approach to both the principles and the practices of purchasing. Part I introduces management concepts essential to successful purchasing. Part II applies these concepts to specific techniques used to purchase commodities.

Many people should be thanked for their contributions to the text. Outstanding industry professionals offered their personal insights into the concept of value presented in Chapter 1. Taken as a whole, their comments in this book reflect the essence of hospitality purchasing.

A debt of gratitude is owed to Donna Lynes, President of Arcop, Inc., and James Ratliff, Corporate Director of Procurement at Hilton Hotels Corporation. They invested substantial amounts of time and effort in reviewing the text with the express purpose of making it more valuable to you, the reader.

I also wish to thank Robert Krump, Regional Sales Manager with L. J. Minor, and Robert L. Barker, Jr., Vice President of Purchasing with Szabo Food Service, Inc., who both contributed to the textbook's outline. Richard Weil, Manager of Major Accounts with Kraft-Westman Food Service, offered insightful comments on the concept of value featured in Chapter 1.

Helmut Maass, Regional Manager, Motor Lodge Division of Howard Johnson's, is gratefully acknowledged for his review of several early chapters. E. H. "Sonny" Dellinger of Carver & Associates provided much appreciated assistance in reviewing Chapter 17, "Equipment, Services, and Supplies."

Every hospitality operation—whether it is part of a vast organization or a small, independent property—can benefit from a thorough examination of the purchasing system. Regardless of the resources at its disposal, progressive purchasing practices will help a hospitality operation achieve a significant competitive edge.

William B. Virts, President
William Virts Associates, Inc.
Bethesda, Maryland

Study Tips for Users of
Educational Institute Courses

Learning is a skill, like many other activities. Although you may be familiar with many of the following study tips, we want to reinforce their usefulness.

Your Attitude Makes a Difference

If you want to learn, you will: it's as simple as that. Your attitude will go a long way in determining whether or not you do well in this course. We want to help you succeed.

Plan and Organize to Learn

- Set up a regular time and place for study. Make sure you won't be disturbed or distracted.

- Decide ahead of time how much you want to accomplish during each study session. Remember to keep your study sessions brief; don't try to do too much at one time.

Read the Course Text to Learn

- *Before* you read each chapter, read the chapter outline and the learning objectives. If there is a summary at the end of the chapter, you should read it to get a feel for what the chapter is about.

- Then, go back to the beginning of the chapter and *carefully* read, focusing on the material included in the learning objectives and asking yourself such questions as:

    —Do I understand the material?

    —How can I use this information now or in the future?

- Make notes in margins and highlight or underline important sections to help you as you study. Read a section first, then go back over it to mark important points.

- Keep a dictionary handy. If you come across an unfamiliar word that is not included in the textbook glossary, look it up in the dictionary.

- Read as much as you can. The more you read, the better you read.

Testing Your Knowledge

- Test questions developed by the Educational Institute for this course are designed to measure your knowledge of the material.

- End-of-the-chapter Review Quizzes help you find out how well you have studied the material. They indicate where additional study may be needed. Review Quizzes are also helpful in studying for other tests.

- Prepare for tests by reviewing:
  —learning objectives

  —notes

  —outlines

  —questions at the end of each assignment

- As you begin to take any test, read the test instructions *carefully* and look over the questions.

We hope your experiences in this course will prompt you to undertake other training and educational activities in a planned, career-long program of professional growth and development.

Part I
Purchasing Management

The theme of this book is **value** and its intent is to provide tools which enable operators, both small and large, to manage the purchasing function effectively. Price and quality are the primary determinants of guest satisfaction. The most successful operations grasp every opportunity to meet or surpass their guests' expectations.

Purchasing, in its broadest sense, includes a full range of management tasks, from listing supply needs to controlling inventory. A purchasing program must guard against excessive costs, poor quality products, and unavailability of needed products. Managers should attempt to move the purchasing program from routine order-placing to cost-effective buying.

A hospitality operation must tailor a purchasing program to meet its individual needs. As an operation grows, it may enjoy cost advantages simply as a result of its size. Distribution charges may be lower due to consolidation of orders or suppliers may offer discounts based on greater purchase volume. Regardless of an operation's size, cost-saving measures should be explored: innovative purchasing can pay dividends.

Distribution is the means by which goods are transferred through a series of intermediaries to the hospitality operation. Value should be added at every link in the transfer chain. With distribution costs escalating at a much faster rate than food costs, this area represents an opportunity for maximizing profits.

A hospitality operation requires suppliers who meet product quality and price concerns while providing dependable service. Today's manager can usually choose from among a number of suppliers offering products of comparable quality. A good supplier consistently provides the best value and fosters a long-term relationship.

Every purchase involves negotiation to some extent. The key to success is to identify and organize sources of authority to the negotiator's advantage. From an ethical standpoint, purchasers must conduct themselves so as to be beyond reproach. Purchasers must ensure that none of their actions can be construed as limiting competition, conspiring with others to set prices, or in any way inhibiting competition through monopolistic means.

A hospitality operation depends on the orderly flow of information, records, and documents to control and monitor each of its many functions. Managers use control tools to determine whether the system is working properly and to identify the need for corrective action. Close cooperation between the purchasing and accounting departments is necessary to ensure the effectiveness of the overall purchasing system.

How does management know whether the purchasing system is effective? This may be accomplished through a three-step process of evaluation. The first step is to identify specific and measurable goals, usually involving such concerns as price, quality, quantity, and supply source. The second step is to assess performance through established procedures which allow managers to determine whether goals have been met. The final step is to improve the purchasing system by correcting any problems revealed in the second step.

Chapter Outline

Historical Development
Focus on the Guest
Value: An Essential Concern
Goals of Purchasing Systems
The Task of Purchasing
The Role of Purchasing Personnel
The Need for Effective Purchasing Practices
Purchasing Options

Learning Objectives

1. Describe how the concept of purchasing has changed in recent years.

2. Explain the key points of value.

3. Describe the goals and benefits of effective purchasing.

4. Summarize the management activities related to purchasing.

5. Explain the relationship of line managers to staff members.

6. Compare and contrast available purchasing options.

Purchasing Systems: An Overview

IN RECENT YEARS, the role of purchasing has developed into a sophisticated function in most successful hospitality operations. Purchasing currently commands considerable attention from hospitality professionals as a means to ensure product supply and increase profit margins. Management has responded to the changing needs, desires, and expectations of guests while recognizing the need to consider both cost and quality aspects of purchasing decisions.

Historical Development

Historically, the purchasing function was classified as a service activity in most hospitality businesses. Hotel/motel, restaurant, and institutional managers traditionally viewed purchasing as a support function required to purchase those products, supplies, and services needed for production and service activities. As a result, purchasing consisted of little more than fulfilling a need for a particular product in a routine manner.

Until recently, purchasing received minimal emphasis and little recognition for its role in helping to attain profit objectives and cost containment goals. Some considered purchasing "just picking up the telephone and calling in an order." Others delegated responsibility to supplier representatives for such important matters as quality, quantity, and price.

In small single-unit properties, this lack of concern has been understandable, if not defensible. The busy manager with many responsibilities besides purchasing simply has not had the time to undertake the steps necessary to implement a cost-effective purchasing system.

In larger multi-unit properties, the traditional concern has been to control product costs after items reach the facility, not necessarily before that point. While many operators in the hospitality industry have always been concerned about quality, other aspects of purchasing, such as negotiation, creative pricing plans, and detailed knowledge about the markets, have been overlooked at times.

Lately, managers have recognized the need to maximize value for the hospitality company and its guests. Purchasing should no longer be considered a simple matter of ordering needed products; the economic and operational benefits derived from effective purchasing are too great to disregard the complexities of modern purchasing systems.

Focus on the Guest

The guests' search for value is apparent when today's strong emphasis on the price/quality relationship is considered. Excellent hospitality companies closely monitor the changing needs of their target markets. The winners continually aim to meet or exceed their guests' expectations.

The purchasing system used by an operation has a direct bearing on the value received by the business. This, in turn, affects the total dining experience as perceived by guests; price and quality are primary determinants of a positive experience.

It is management's responsibility to define its target markets as accurately and precisely as possible. In selecting products and services to offer, management must continually answer the following questions:

1. Will the products/services sell and at what price?

2. Will the products/services be available and at what cost?

3. What are the bottom-line effects of selling these products/services?

4. How can we maximize the value *received* by our property and the value *perceived* by our guests in the products/services that we offer for sale?

Only after answering these questions can management develop a list of products and services to be offered.

Value: An Essential Concern

Some hospitality managers may not understand the direct relationship between purchasing activities and the value received in products and services. These managers attempt to quantify every component of value. While some of the components can be expressed in quantitative or numerical terms, others are only qualitative judgments. Since these qualitative components cannot be expressed numerically, the concept of value cannot be measured solely in terms of dollars and cents.

The National Association of Purchasing Management (NAPM) has developed a concise definition of value. According to NAPM, "value is a systematic study of the function of an item or system for the purpose of identifying unnecessary cost, which can be eliminated without impairing the capacity of the item or system to perform as required."[1] NAPM's definition suggests that before value can be determined, the function of an item must be systematically researched. Costs must be understood and classified as essential or non-essential. The non-essential costs should be eliminated as long as they do not affect the performance of the item or system. It is management's responsibility to determine value.

Several food service and lodging industry professionals were asked to define value in relation to their hospitality businesses. Each professional had a slightly different definition of value based upon his or her position within the hospitality industry.

❝Value is related to five factors in procurement: quality, service, product availability, information, and price. The quality levels offered by a hospitality business depend on its target markets and the expectations of those markets. Service is affected by ordering procedures and delivery schedules. Product availability is influenced by the purchasing power of the supplier. Information and ideas are provided by the supplier's sales representatives. Some suppliers also schedule educational seminars for their customers. The price of a product is important in establishing the business relationship; however, it is less important in weekly dealings. The key to survival is the establishment of a partnership with your suppliers so value is maximized. **"**

—Richard Weil, MHS
Manager of Major Accounts
Kraft-Westman Food Service

"The definition of value is constantly evolving as the demands of consumers change. It is important to relate value to the basics. For example, when soliciting a price quotation from a supplier, you should know three things: what you want to buy, how much you want to buy, and where you need the item shipped. If this information can be maintained on a current and accurate basis, you will be ahead of the game. It is important to develop a reputation for yourself, your department, and your company as being an honest and fair business entity. Value is received when the person in charge of procurement displays impeccable integrity, keeps costs in line, and positively affects bottom-line profits at every opportunity. **"**

—Donna Lynes
President
Arcop, Inc.

"A food service operation buys, stores, prepares, and serves products in a manner that best satisfies those being served. The markets determine the value. You must be in tune with the needs and desires of your operation's target markets. The perceived value on the part of your customers is one of the most important factors to consider. Value is not what it *is*, but what it *does* based on the optimum benefit received for the money you spend. Both quality and value are a matter of personal judgment. **"**

—Robert Krump, MHS
Regional Sales Manager
L. J. Minor Corporation

"Value is the best buy based on the job you have to do. After you determine what it is that you want to buy, specifications and yield tests are used to establish and monitor the value received from your suppliers. Specifications and yields must be tied in to your initial determinations of what to buy. It is important to consider all factors that affect value for each product purchased. For example, consider the purchase of a piece of equipment. In addition to the purchase price, you must think about the life expectancy of the equipment, installation charges, and maintenance and repair costs. The determination of value is slightly different for each item you procure. **"**

—Robert L. Barker, Jr.
Vice President of Purchasing
Szabo Food Service, Inc.

❝The value received is related to quality, price, and service. Specifications help establish acceptable levels of quality. The process of procurement begins with a precise definition of what you want. Then you need to ensure that you buy exactly what you want. Price is based on the intended use of the product. The lowest price is not necessarily the best price. Once purchase specifications are established, it is important to price within those specifications. Service requirements vary from operation to operation. You must define acceptable service levels based on your needs. **❞**

—**James Ratliff**
Corporate Director of Procurement
Hilton Hotels Corporation

All of these industry professionals have defined value in ways that are unique to their organizations. However, two common threads emerge. First, value must be established and monitored based on the expectations of the target markets. The customers' perceptions of value are more important today than ever before. Second, value can be maximized only if management establishes systems to ensure optimal results.

The value received is a function of quality, service, and price, within the constraints of intended use. For purposes of illustration, this relationship can be expressed in the following manner:

$$V = \frac{(Q \times S)}{P}$$

where: V = Value
Q = Quality
S = Service
P = Price

As indicated by the formula, value has an inverse relationship with price; as price increases, value decreases (assuming no change in quality or service). By contrast, value varies directly with changes in quality and service; as quality and service improve, value increases (assuming price remains constant).

Consider the question of value in relation to the make-or-buy decision. The make-or-buy decision deals with the question of whether to make a product on-site or buy the product in a convenience (processed) form. Considerations of labor cost, ingredient cost, facilities and equipment, and quality are all involved in the make-or-buy decision.

The food and beverage manager may wish to purchase convenience foods as an alternative to food currently being produced on-site. Before the decision can be made, management usually considers three important factors: quality, service, and price.

Let's examine the options available for dinner rolls. The operation can (1) prepare freshly baked rolls from scratch using basic ingredients, (2) purchase fully baked, ready-to-serve dinner rolls from a local bakery, or (3) buy frozen dough and bake rolls fresh daily.

Value determination in the make-or-buy decision begins with an analysis of quality. The quality level available in convenience frozen doughs must be acceptable to the operation's guests. In the strictest terms, a convenience product should only be used if it is equal to or greater than the quality of similar products made on-site. Some guests may choose one operation over the competition because of its unique dinner rolls produced in its own kitchen.

Next, service must be considered. If an operation decides to rely on a commercial bakery for dinner rolls, the operation must be sure that the bakery will deliver the product on time and in the required quantity and quality.

Finally, the price must be calculated. It is important to realize that a simple comparison of the raw ingredient costs to the price of the finished product is not sufficient. In the "make" decision, you must also determine training and labor costs, available equipment and facilities, and energy costs. After all of these components are addressed, an objective make-or-buy decision can be made.

Goals of Purchasing Systems

How does management use a purchasing system to maximize value for an operation and its guests? While each hospitality company must develop its own specific statement of goals and objectives, some general concerns should be addressed as a purchasing system is designed and implemented:

- Product
- Price
- Quality
- Quantity
- Time
- Supplier

The aim of the purchasing system is to obtain the right *product* at the right *price*. In addition, the product should be of the proper *quality* and purchased in the correct *quantity*. The product should also be purchased at the right *time* from the best *supplier*.

While it is difficult to attain all of these goals consistently, each represents an integral element in the successful operation of a hospitality property. Systems must be planned, implemented, and evaluated to help ensure that these goals are met with regularity.

The Task of Purchasing

The purchasing function encompasses a full range of management activities, from listing supply needs to controlling inventory. Every activity influences the nature and effectiveness of the systems by which hospitality organizations purchase the products and services required to please the guest.

Procurement relates to a broad series of management activities that are designed to maximize value for the company and its guests. The terms "procurement" and "purchasing" are used interchangeably in the hospitality industry, so, in keeping with common industry practice, we will use the terms as if they have the same meaning. The reader should recognize, however, that our use of these terms relates to all functions involved in the management of products both before and after they are received by the operation. Let's examine the broad scope of functions that relate to purchasing by identifying some integral elements in the process:

- Requisitioning—the process by which staff members responsible for inventory notify those with purchasing responsibilities about the need to order additional quantities of products.

- Determining required product quality—setting quality levels through a careful assessment of the expectations of guests as well as economic concerns of the organization.

- Determining quantity needs—the estimation of purchase needs based on the amount of product in inventory and forecasted use.

- Selecting suppliers—evaluating the possible suppliers of a product in terms of prices, selection, and service.

- Negotiating prices—the tactics and strategies used to secure the lowest price without sacrificing product quality or service.

- Making the purchase decision—a careful analysis considering all available information as decisions are made regarding product, quality, quantity, and supplier.

- Arranging for payment—reaching agreement on financial terms of purchase between the hospitality organization and the supplier.

- Expediting orders—following up on orders to ensure that required products reach the facility at the right time.

- Maintaining proper supplier relations—fostering a professional relationship (rather than an adversarial one) between the hospitality organization and its suppliers, often with respect to legal and ethical concerns.

- Receiving products—the process by which products are brought into the operation, involving basic practices designed to check quality, quantity, and price.

- Storing products—the transfer of products to the proper facilities for storage after meeting acceptance in the receiving process.

- Inspecting products—an examination of products in inventory and at various phases of production to determine that the quality requirements demanded by the facility are attained.

- Controlling inventory—procedures for effective management of products in inventory, in order to maximize efficient handling of supplies, minimize loss in quality, and reduce the opportunity for theft.

- Dispensing with surplus equipment—selling, trading, or scrapping capital equipment items no longer needed by the operation.

- Maintaining necessary records—detailing information about such matters as previous orders, past experiences with suppliers, and orders in process, often with the aid of computerized recordkeeping.

- Researching markets and gathering information—investigating new products, changing market conditions, and other relevant matters in order to advise management staff within the organization.

As you can see, the task of purchasing comprises many individual steps, all related to managing available resources. Good purchasing management continually assesses needs and, when successful, satisfies those needs in a manner which maximizes value for both the operation and its guests.

The Role of Purchasing Personnel

The role of purchasing personnel and other staff may be best understood in the context of "line" and "staff" positions. Line positions are in the chain of command. For example, the general manager, resident manager, department heads, and supervisors are all line positions. In contrast, individuals in staff positions provide specialized advisory assistance to those in line positions. Typical examples of staff positions in hospitality organizations include individuals in the purchasing, accounting, and personnel departments. Because purchasing so directly affects daily operations in smaller properties, it is generally undertaken by managers within each operating department.

When a separate purchasing department is first organized, the purchasing manager may report to the financial officer. More often than not, this is a compromise in the interest of maintaining unity. Large operations and particularly those with multiple units will appoint purchasing managers to consolidate volumes with the goal of achieving cost reductions.

Examine the sample organization chart for a hotel shown in Exhibit 1 and note the chain of command represented by management staff at all organizational levels. Contrast this with the placement of the purchasing agent who advises decision-makers by providing help in matters pertaining to one specific area of expertise: purchasing.

Purchasing personnel have a great deal of specialized information that can be made available to the food and beverage manager and other line personnel. Speculation about price changes, suggestions about quality requirements, assistance in budgeting, and proposing ordering and inventory control systems are among possible contributions made by staff members in the purchasing department.

While the input of purchasing staff can be valuable, these personnel should not make unilateral decisions on such matters as the following:

- Purchasing products not dictated by menu or operational needs

- Determining the quantities of products to be carried in inventory

- Establishing quality requirements for products

- Determining whether products should be purchased or prepared on-site

The responsibilities for judgments on these matters rests with line decision-makers, who should receive advice (but not mandates) from purchasing officials.

Line managers can help purchasing personnel by defining job requirements in clear terms. To accomplish this aim, policies should be set, job descriptions developed, and performance standards established.

Exhibit 1   Sample Organization Chart for a Large Hotel

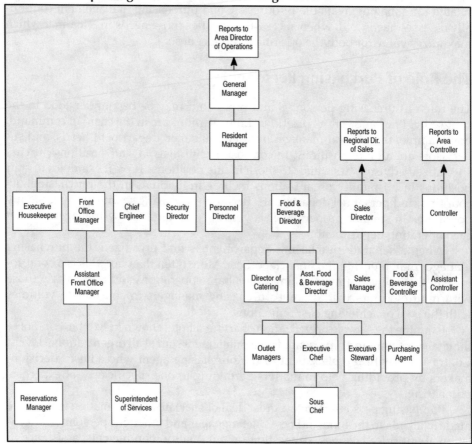

Set policies. These define responsibility and establish authority in broad terms; policies, once established, must be clearly communicated to all members of the organization.

Develop job descriptions. This reduces policies to specific job functions. Job descriptions should be reviewed annually. Exhibit 2 shows examples of tasks that may be considered part of a purchaser's job.

Establish standards of performance in purchasing. Such standards supplement job descriptions. Performance standards generally cover a precise time frame (typically a year), focus upon major areas, and suggest a definite plan for improvement. They usually set forth definite objectives to guide improvements.

The Need for Effective Purchasing Practices

To hospitality operations, purchasing systems may represent an opportunity for improved operation and greater success. Effective purchasing practices have beneficial results in several important areas.[2]

Exhibit 2   Typical Functions in Commercial Food Service

I. Purchasing/Procurement
   1. Issue purchasing orders for needed materials and services
   2. Recognize the importance of the buying process and its impact on the organization and suppliers
   3. Coordinate the procurement and distribution of food items with production operations
   4. Contribute to the organization's profits by effective purchasing policies and procedures
   5. Obtain the best value at the lowest price consistent with established quality standards and delivery schedules
   6. Maintain files of vendors' stock lists, catalogs, price sheets, and discounts
   7. Forecast market conditions, availability of materials, and economic conditions
   8. Keep informed of current laws, rules, and regulations affecting purchasing
   9. Monitor purchase orders to determine if deliveries are correct
  10. Check purchase orders for clarity and completeness
  11. Handle communications concerning overshipment, shortages, price changes, and related matters
  12. Determine the cost of deliveries and the best method of transportation

II. Specifications
   1. Develop specifications for materials and services in cooperation with personnel responsible for production
   2. Audit packaging specifications
   3. Authorize rejection of materials which fail to meet specifications
   4. Promote standardization of materials and services through specifications
   5. Maintain file of current specifications

III. Inventory/Warehouse Management
   1. Conduct periodic physical counts of stocks to verify records
   2. Minimize losses from pilferage, spoilage, or obsolescence
   3. Minimize operating costs for storage of food and supplies
   4. Determine necessary stock levels to provide adequate food and supplies and to minimize capital investment
   5. Inspect storage areas
   6. Monitor records of inventory, materials on-order, and potential demands for food and supplies
   7. Monitor maintenance and repair of storage facilities

IV. Vendor/Supplier Relations
   1. Select suppliers
   2. Negotiate reasonable terms with suppliers
   3. Act as liaison between suppliers and other departments in the organization
   4. Compare suppliers' product quality, services, dependability, and costs
   5. Create goodwill for the organization through effective trade relations
   6. Solve problems with vendors
   7. Establish a system for vendor rating and selection
   8. Work with sales representatives to identify new products, materials, and processes
   9. Oversee distribution of bids and receipt of quotations
  10. Investigate suppliers' facilities
  11. Interview salespersons

V. Contracts
   1. Negotiate contracts for food, supplies, and services

(continued)

Exhibit 2   *(continued)*

　　2.　Determine whether open market or contract purchasing is preferable for various materials and services

　　3.　Coordinate review of contracts by legal counsel and/or other appropriate personnel

　VI.　Personnel Management

　　1.　Develop job descriptions for purchasing and storeroom personnel

　　2.　Aid in training purchasing and storeroom personnel

　　3.　Manage purchasing and storeroom personnel

　　4.　Promote good relations between purchasing and other personnel in the organization

　　5.　Select qualified personnel for purchasing and storage functions

　　6.　Train buyers to follow established purchasing procedures

　　7.　Determine staffing needs for purchasing and storage functions

　　8.　Supervise clerical activities involved in purchasing

　VII.　General Management

　　1.　Monitor flow of materials through the system, from selection to production to service

　　2.　Serve on policy-making team of the organization

　　3.　Participate in "make-or-buy" decisions

　　4.　Maintain current knowledge of changing markets by reviewing trade literature, attending trade shows, and other means

　　5.　Establish priorities for meeting objectives

　　6.　Develop policies and procedures to guide performance and to reduce duplication of effort

　　7.　Support a program of data processing

　　8.　Meet with personnel in the organization to discuss problems with products, deliveries, or services

　　9.　Develop a budget for operation within the scope of responsibility

　　10.　Review financial statements to monitor expenditures in operational areas

　　11.　Coordinate efforts with quality control division

　　12.　Promote energy conservation in operations within the scope of responsibility

---

Adapted from Kimberly A. Loecker, Marian C. Spears, and Allene G. Vaden, "Purchasing Managers in Commercial Foodservice Organizations: Clarifying the Role," *Professional.* Spring 1983, pp. 9–16.

Control of Costs. The first phase of any cost-control system considers the prices paid for products and services. The foundation for a successful control program must begin with the purchasing process. A cost-control program cannot be successful without an efficient purchasing system.

Volume of Purchased Products/Services. Food and beverages are just two of the products purchased by hospitality operations. Linens, glassware, cleaning supplies, furniture, and capital equipment must also be purchased. Since more sales dollars are typically used for purchasing products, supplies, and services than are used for any other purpose, it is easy to defend the necessity for strong purchasing control.

Effect on Cash Flow. Even large high-profit hospitality operations can have cash flow problems. An important principle of financial management requires that cash be available to pay bills when they become due. The quantity of items purchased, price, and timing of deliveries ultimately affect the amount of money (cash) that will be required to satisfy payment. Only line managers should make decisions about deferring purchases (which increases the possibility of depleted stocks) and buying in small quantities (which reduces the possibility of volume discounts). Input from purchasing staff can be helpful as such decisions are made. These tactics, along with directives from line management, can help to prevent cash flow problems caused by ineffective purchasing practices.

Supply of Information. It is important in the fast-changing business world for managers to keep up with new technology. Purchasing personnel are in constant contact with numerous suppliers who, in turn, are in contact with manufacturers, other suppliers, and many hospitality operations. Purchasers can be a valuable source of information about new products and services. Purchasing staff should collect new ideas and information to pass on to user departments.

Continuity of Supply. A very important role played by the purchasing department is the provision of necessary items at the right time. The concept of continuous supply is critical to customer satisfaction. From the perspective of the food and beverage department, purchasing personnel are at fault when required products are not available. Purchasing staff must follow up on orders to help ensure that suppliers meet contractual requirements regarding such concerns as quality, quantity, and delivery dates. Effective purchasing is required to provide a continuous source of supply. Unavailability of a menu item due to stockouts (depleted inventory) produces dissatisfied guests and may discourage repeat business.

Purchasing Options

When purchasing products and services, operators usually have several options available. However, each option carries with it certain requirements and limitations. A great deal depends on the willingness of suppliers to enter into these purchasing arrangements. Similarly, a purchaser may be limited to specific options by the nature and volume of the business.

As a hospitality company grows, it often experiences cost advantages simply as a result of its size. Distribution charges may be lower due to consolidation of orders or suppliers may offer discounts based on greater purchase volume. These benefits, relating to the organization's larger size, are termed economies of scale.

We will discuss some common purchasing options here.

Ride the Market. The phrase "ride the market" simply means waiting until the goods are needed, then taking bids or negotiating with a single supplier to fulfill purchase needs.

This method is common among companies with a "maintenance" purchasing philosophy. In effect, these companies are permitting their cost decisions to be made by others in the market. Generally, these buyers receive prices at the top of the market's range. They have inadequate information to make the judgments and take the risks that lead to lower costs.

Cost-Plus. Using cost-plus, a contract is developed to price goods at a specified rate over the supplier's cost. To be successful, various aspects of costs are specified to be either included or excluded. The task then involves measuring and managing the supplier's costs.

This measurement is best done through use of independent price sources. Base cost may also be determined by reviewing actual invoices of the supplier. The purpose of cost-plus is to establish a lower level of pricing than would be achieved through maintenance buying.

Buy-and-Inventory. When a continuing supply of goods is required, a fixed quantity can be bought and stored in inventory. These buys may be made to guarantee supply of a critical item or to avoid anticipated price increases. In either case, all costs of storage, handling, inventory, and potential loss of value (through damage or obsolescence) must be calculated. An estimate of the product's future cost is necessary to calculate the economical consequences of the transaction.

Long-Term Contract. Long-term contracts may be based on fixed or accelerating prices. To be cost-effective, however, prices should be forecasted by the purchaser well before entering into such agreements. While similar in many respects to buy-and-inventory, long-term contracts make the supplier responsible for the physical management of products. In most cases, payment is made by the buyer upon receipt of the merchandise. Many of these contracts have clauses which authorize price accelerations to offset storage and carrying costs.

Hedging. For certain products, hedging (also called forward contracting) can be accomplished through the futures markets. Because these contracts are "on margin" or leveraged (that is, using credit to enhance speculative capacity), investment and carrying costs are less. However, the buyer is at risk for the total contract amount.

This option will only be utilized by companies with relatively large volumes and sophisticated purchasing systems. Information is readily available regarding future price levels and is of major importance to even small users. Such information reflects the market's estimate of future price levels and provides a negotiating tool for all buyers.

Endnotes

1. NAPM Ad Hoc Committee on Continuing Education, "The Continuing Education Program," in *Guide to Purchasing*, edited by J. R. Megliola (New York: National Association of Purchasing Management, 1973).

2. This section is adapted from Jack D. Ninemeier, *Purchasing, Receiving, and Storage: A Systems Manual for Restaurants, Hotels, and Clubs* (New York: Van Nostrand Reinhold Company, 1983), pp. 8–9.

REVIEW QUIZ

When you feel you have covered all of the material in this chapter, answer these questions. Choose the *best* answer. Check your answers with the correct ones found on the Review Quiz Answer Key at the end of this book.

True (T) or False (F)

T (F) 1. Choosing a supplier is a routine decision involving very little research. F

T (F) 2. The level of authority held by a purchaser should be undefined in order to create initiative and competition. F

T (F) 3. It is only important to control product costs before items reach the facility, since costs cannot be controlled after products reach the facility. F

(T) F 4. The main components of value are quality, service, and price. T

T (F) 5. All components of value may be expressed in monetary terms. F ?

T (F) 6. Purchasing personnel are in a line relationship with production personnel. F
staff

(T) F 7. The purchasing department should share information gained from suppliers with production department personnel. T

Multiple Choice

8. If an operation anticipates a shortage of a product it uses regularly and expects a sharp price increase, it may consider using the purchase option of:

   a. cost-plus.
   b. buy-and-inventory. ✓
   c. hedging.
   d. ride the market.

9. Which is *not* a function of the purchasing department?

   a. negotiating contracts with suppliers
   b. securing supply items requested by the production department
   c. providing valuable information to management
   d. determining which items to include on the menu

Chapter Outline

History of Distribution Systems
Profit Opportunities in Improved
    Distribution
Management of Products Through the
    Marketplace
    Source
    Manufacturer or Processor
    Broker
    Manufacturer's Representative
    Interpacker and Intermanufacturer
        Agent
    Distributor
    End-User
Distribution Restraints
Within-Company Distribution Channels
    Approved Local Sources
    Approved Regional/National Sources
    Contract for Goods with Leased
        Distribution
    Self-Provided Distribution
    Commissary Operations
Measuring Distribution Effectiveness
Typical Distribution Systems
    Four Examples

Learning Objectives

1. Describe food service distribution: its history and its present state.

2. Explain the key elements in the procurement channel of distribution.

3. Summarize the different types of value added as products move through procurement channels.

4. List factors that affect selection of a purchasing program and factors that affect distribution decisions.

5. Explain within-company distribution channels.

2

Distribution

DISTRIBUTION IS THE MEANS by which products are transferred in the marketplace, moving in turn through a series of intermediaries from the source (manufacturer, processor, or grower) to the hospitality operation. Distribution costs—transport, inventory investment, storage, advertising, labor—are great and continue to escalate at a faster pace than the actual cost of products at the processing plants.

History of Distribution Systems

Distribution systems for the hospitality industry grew out of those developed for retail food distribution. In the 1920s and 1930s, large retail food chains such as A & P (Great Atlantic and Pacific Tea Company) and Safeway began to emerge. To compete with these large companies, coalitions of independent grocery owners formed cooperatives. One of the first was IGA (Independent Grocers Association) and one of the largest today is Super Value Stores.

The chains and cooperatives, in direct competition with each other, were constantly searching for ways to buy, produce, and handle their products at a lower cost. Some chains and cooperatives used one or more of the following approaches: (1) they went further back into the processing chain to operate manufacturing or packing plants; (2) they entered into the private or controlled label business by contracting directly with a product packer or packing the product themselves, and thus bypassed the large producers who had built consumer franchises for their products; (3) they developed large retail outlets which were well-located and efficiently operated; and/or (4) they attempted to be more efficient in moving products from producers to their customers by transporting in large quantities, by using in-transit storage warehouses, by becoming better price negotiators, and by using automated, computerized warehouse and inventory management devices.

As the chains and cooperatives penetrated more markets, independent grocers, saddled with the higher cost of products, became non-competitive. Faced with the threat of closing, they either joined cooperatives or changed their product lines to market to a different customer base. Local wholesale distributors which served the independent grocers lost business; some were absorbed by the chains and cooperatives.

Fortunately, the trend toward "dining out" gained momentum during the late 1940s and many of these distributors looked toward the growing number of restaurants and hotels as new markets. At first, the majority of these distributors served both retail grocers and hospitality industry customers, but this approach required a double product line, which was costly and difficult to manage.

Restaurant companies such as Howard Johnson's, Elias Brothers, Stouffers, and Horn & Hardhart developed at a time when suppliers and distributors still lacked the capacity to produce and deliver some food items. As these companies grew into large multi-unit organizations, their needs were met by commissary systems. These combination production/distribution facilities made unique products at lower costs than those available from outside company sources. The need for quality control and reliable service also spurred their growth.

Two significant events occurred in the 1950s that further changed the face of food service distribution:

1. As a result of eroding profit margins, some distributors agreed to purchase products jointly. To purchase competitively with the major food manufacturers (which were oriented toward popular consumer brands), these independent distributors formed non-profit organizations. One of the first was National Institutional Food Distributor Associates (NIFDA), which began with seven distribution companies in 1957 and has over 165 today. NIFDA offers over 12,000 items, representing about one-third of their members' sales. Other examples of large buying groups include CODE (Continental Organization of Distributor Enterprises, Inc.), North American Food Services, Frosty Acres, and Nugget Distributors.

2. Fast-food chains emerged and, at first, their product needs were met by the distributor groups mentioned previously. But as these fast-food chains grew, their requirements became so immense that they were able to dictate policy—just as the retail chains had done in the preceding decades. Some of these fast-food chains developed their own distribution and/or manufacturing capabilities. Quantity requirements led these organizations to demand exclusive facilities or, if necessary, shared facilities with a few other companies. A new type of distribution facility evolved with goods priced on a cost-plus basis and the distributor's revenue based on return on investment.

Much of this chain growth was through franchising. At this time, the need arose for large quantities of similar types of equipment and furnishings. Many franchisors provided their franchisees with equipment packages, which ranged from individual pieces of equipment to entire "turnkey" proposals (systems which are built, supplied, and/or installed complete and ready to operate). To serve their franchises and other customers, some franchisors maintained supply facilities, providing necessary items on a cost pass-through basis or by means of a profit-making division (company).

Today, products are distributed throughout the hospitality industry in six basic ways:

1. Large national and/or regional organizations with broad product lines, serving a wide range of customers.

2. Large national and/or regional organizations with relatively narrow product lines, serving a specific customer or market segment.

3. Distribution companies which are owned or directed by large hospitality companies. In some cases, these firms sell to companies outside of their owner's organization.

4. Commissary systems which are used by many regional chain companies to distribute items ranging from basic commodities to ready-to-use products.

5. Local independent full-line distributors. These companies are rapidly being absorbed by the national companies.

6. Local specialized distributors that exceed in number and sales dollars all other categories combined.

Each of the above types of distributors typically supplements distribution with the manufacture of some products, usually ones for which each has developed a strong sales base.

The hospitality buyer will generally have a wide variety of distribution options available. Care must be exercised to select those that maximize the goals of quality, service, and price, which together equate to value.

Profit Opportunities in Improved Distribution

Steady improvements in distribution have contributed greatly to the success of hospitality operations in recent years. To take advantage of these opportunities, food service managers must first recognize several factors:

1. Competition is on the increase, creating a need to assess new methods of reducing costs.

2. Hospitality operators must become knowledgeable about distribution systems, which, if effectively designed, can increase profits.

3. Hospitality organizations often have widely dispersed units geographically, producing a special set of distribution problems.

4. The entrepreneurial spirit of many operators has discouraged cooperative purchasing and/or distribution, despite the possibility of raising profit levels.

5. Some segments of the food service industry operate on relatively short-term contracts.

6. Because distributors vary widely in their capabilities, those required to meet the operator's needs must be identified.

7. Rarely does a single distributor offer all required products; more typically, the hospitality operator uses multiple suppliers.

8. A general lack of distribution expertise has hampered hospitality management. The immediate needs of the operation take precedence over long-range distribution and supply issues.

9. Distribution programs allow management to improve quality control of products.

What does the future hold? The distribution industry will gradually evolve. Aggressive buyers will continue to find ways to maximize value to their company while working within the existing system of product distribution. Opportunities will be available to the operator who understands the distribution system. These

Exhibit 1   Key Elements in the Procurement Channel of Distribution

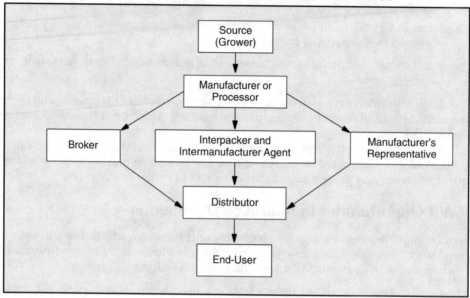

operators will realize the advantages of contracting for longer terms, will recognize what can reasonably be demanded and received, and will systematically identify suppliers who offer the best value.

Management of Products Through the Marketplace

The procurement channel of distribution is illustrated in Exhibit 1. Each individual in the channel plays a key role and adds value as products move through the marketplace from source to end-user.

Hospitality managers may actively communicate with any of the key elements in the procurement channel of distribution.

Source

The source adds value by transforming the raw materials into products usable by the processor. The source for most food products and many beverage items used by hospitality businesses is the grower. A grower may be a farmer or rancher who starts the procurement channel in motion. In all cases, the channel becomes geared up to produce a product of greater value than the starting materials.

Basic laws of supply and demand have a substantial effect at the source level. For example, consider the supply and demand of fresh seafood in the United States. The demand tends to be relatively constant; however, weather conditions may cause the supply for certain varieties of seafood to fluctuate widely. When supply levels decline because of reduced catches, prices rise. When the catch exceeds demand, increased supply results in a price decrease. These price fluctuations are passed on to the manufacturer/processor.

Manufacturer or Processor

Most food and beverage products are processed to some degree. Grain is harvested, milled, and converted into flour, which may be further processed into batter mixes, frozen doughs, or finished bakery products. Steers and heifers are transported from the ranch to the feedlot, fed a nutritious diet, slaughtered, and fabricated into wholesale and retail cuts. In all of these instances, processors add value to the products.

Manufacturers convert raw materials such as wood and metals into items like equipment, furniture, and fixtures used in hospitality operations. They transform the physical appearance of the raw materials and add form value. Some processors buy semi-prepared products from other manufacturers for further processing. For example, a processor may purchase frozen beef and manufacture canned stew and chili. The value added is translated into the price charged to a broker or manufacturer's representative.

Broker

Brokers are intermediaries in the procurement channel of distribution, providing time and place value (that is, getting the right product to the right place at the right time). They represent processors or manufacturers, but as independent contractors, not employees. Brokers do not take title to the products. Most receive a commission based upon the quantity of units sold to the distributor.

Buyers will primarily have contact with brokers who live and work near the buyer's operation. These brokers are generally assigned a sales territory by the firms they represent. These territories may be small or large geographically, depending in large measure on the sales potential of the area. Generally, brokers will not represent two principals (processors) with similar product lines but, instead, sell non-competing items to the hospitality operation.

In addition to time and place value, brokers also add informational value to food and beverage products. Most brokers work closely with the sales representatives of distributors who sell their products to end-users. Brokers provide information to educate the sales staff so they can provide this value to their customers. Some brokers work directly with end-users to promote their products being sold by distributors.

Buyers should be aware of "field brokers." These persons typically represent competing growers of fresh fruits and vegetables. They provide a pricing source in the growing area for large buyers (both distributors and end-users) located all over the country. Field brokers provide a consolidation and shipping service for growers and serve as intermediaries between grower and buyer. When field brokers are used, the processor may have no local broker representation.

Manufacturer's Representative

While the term "manufacturer's representative" applies primarily to the sale of non-food products, a manufacturer's representative is similar in some ways to a broker. A manufacturer's representative, like a broker, contributes time, place, and informational value to products as they move from the manufacturer to the distributor. The representative often works with the sales force of the distributor to introduce new product lines and to build sales of existing lines. Many manufacturer's representatives also contact end-users to explain the features and benefits of their products.

However, one major difference separates the functions of a broker from those of a manufacturer's representative. Unlike a broker, the representative is an employee of the processor or manufacturer and typically represents only one organization.

Interpacker and Intermanufacturer Agent

In some cases, a primary processor may arrange to function as an agent for another processor. Such agents will then sell, ship, bill, and collect for the products. They are usually paid a flat percentage by the processor.

The advantage for small original processors is that their products will be sold and distributed more extensively. Primary processors desire to fill out their product lines to reach more users. This plan also helps primary processors make the most of their sales resources. In some ways, this arrangement competes with the field broker system.

Distributor

Both the broker and the manufacturer's representative interact with the distributor. Distributors may also be called purveyors, suppliers, wholesalers, and vendors. Of all the key elements in the procurement channel of distribution, the distributor is perhaps the most important to the end-user. Also, hospitality managers generally have the most contact with this element of the distribution system.

Distributors buy, store, sell, and deliver products to be used by hospitality operations. Unlike brokers and manufacturer's representatives, distributors own the products; therefore, they can directly determine prices charged to end-users. For example, a price charged for a case of 24 heads of lettuce in Denver, Colorado, is determined by the supply of lettuce in the distributor's warehouse in Denver and by the demand for lettuce by the Denver market of end-users.

A distributor adds value as products flow through the warehouse facilities. Place value is added because a distributor buys products from manufacturers, brokers, and representatives who may be located around the country or throughout the world. Time value is added by the distributor when the products are delivered to the hospitality business when needed. Form value may be added if the distributor has the facilities and equipment to process certain food products. For example, a distributor may prepare cubed potatoes, tossed salads, shredded cabbage, and a variety of fresh, peeled vegetables; these forms more closely fit the needs of hospitality operations.

In addition to place, time, and form values, distributors also contribute informational value. This value should be a major consideration when selecting and evaluating a distributor. Many distributors keep their accounts informed of constantly changing market conditions. For example, a produce distributor may inform the end-user that the price of lettuce in the Midwest may increase substantially next week due to heavy rains this week in California.

Another form of informational value stems from the distributor's ideas on product preparation and presentation. A produce distributor may provide economical alternatives to high-priced lettuce (for instance, romaine and endive) for the end-user's salad bar. The distributor may furnish standard recipes as well as nutritional and promotional material for the operator of the salad bar.

Some distributors sponsor professional development seminars, thus offering their accounts the opportunity to earn continuing-education credits and to improve their operations. Distributors frequently offer volume discounts and new ideas at trade shows. Other distributors provide their accounts with timely information via a centralized computer system. This system may produce periodic summaries, called velocity reports, for use in inventory control. These reports detail the volume of products purchased from that distributor.

End-User

The end-user in the procurement channel of distribution is the hotel/motel, restaurant, or institution. The hospitality operator purchases products from distributors and adds incremental value. The incremental value varies with the product, the hospitality business, and the target market. Form value is added when a restaurant fabricates wholesale cuts of beef into portion-cut steaks, broils the steaks, and serves them to customers. Place value is attached when a hotel purchasing agent orders and receives fresh strawberries from Mexico to serve as a dessert at a special banquet. Form value is also added as the strawberries are cleaned, hulled, and served with a liqueur-based sauce.

Time value may be affixed to a product offered for sale by the end-user. For example, a hospital food service department may provide nutrient supplements at 3:00 P.M. for patients recovering from surgery. Time value is also added by the fast-food segment of the industry. Customers of fast-food restaurants wish to save time and money while receiving a fair value.

Like brokers, manufacturer's representatives, and distributors, end-users also furnish informational value. A menu is a marketing tool that provides information to potential customers. This information may be complemented by the merchandising and in-house selling techniques of the operation's service staff. The assumption is that a better informed customer will be able to make a more intelligent purchasing decision and receive a better value.

Today, end-users realize that purchasing techniques affect the bottom-line. They have a long-range view that focuses on the best combination of prices, service, and quality—consistent with the goals and objectives of the hospitality organization. Purchasing professionals recognize that distribution systems have a direct effect on profitability, cost containment, and value.

Distribution Restraints

Distribution systems vary greatly in response to individual differences in the markets that they serve. Several factors influence the point of contact in the marketplace where purchasing needs are met.

Purchase Volume (Number of Dollars Spent). A single operator spending one million dollars or less annually in one location might be well served to have cost-plus arrangements with local distributors and guarantee them constant business. By contrast, a 50-unit limited-menu fast-food chain with all operations within a 100-mile radius could probably justify a distribution center, operated either by the chain itself or by others.

Number of Items. Contrast a purchasing program for a fast-food company needing only 300 items and one for a worldwide chain of hotels (each hotel with a number of food and beverage outlets) requiring a greater variety of food items.

Types of Products Needed. Fresh food may be desirable, but it has a relatively limited shelf life and requires more service than many other types of food. Fresh food must be delivered more frequently and must be received in satisfactory condition. Distributors capable of providing this service may be limited in number and, as a result, the operator's options are reduced.

Geographic Spread. The distribution options for the 50-unit fast-food chain mentioned earlier are comparatively good. However, the options for a 50-unit hotel chain operating in 40 states are more limited. Both organizations may have the same dollar volume, but they may not receive the same markup from their distributors since their geographic spreads are different.

Variety of Hospitality Operations Served. A contract food service organization serving a variety of clients, such as hospitals, vending plants, colleges, and sports arenas, has restricted distribution options due to the large number of products that are required. If these units are spread geographically, options are limited further.

This type of firm will probably require a large number of distributors to supply all required products. By contrast, a single-unit restaurant with a limited menu could, if desired, work with only a few local distributors.

Quality and Other Control Factors. The distribution system is influenced by management's concern for quality, consistency, and availability. The commissary system grew out of this need by responding to a lack of distributor/supplier capability in this area.

Expertise. Companies with executives that have distribution and purchasing experience will develop good options. Those without this expertise may accept the status quo, which is influenced by the competence and candor of their distributors.

Capital and Financing. Proper facilities and working capital are required to provide distribution; trucks, buildings, and inventories require extensive capital commitments. The company may provide these services for itself if funding can be obtained and justified. In any event, these costs must be recovered in the cost of the product, whether self-financed or financed by distributors.

Within-Company Distribution Channels

Hospitality operations use a number of means to satisfy their internal distribution needs. In many single-unit properties, where costs of purchased goods can represent over 50% of sales dollars spent, owners solely manage the purchasing function. Distribution is a part of the delivered product cost, traditionally built into the selling price.

In other situations, the owner may retain purchase responsibility for high-cost items (meat and liquors, for example) while delegating responsibility for other purchases to the unit manager or bookkeeper. The owner can thus monitor product costs and keep menu prices current based upon this information. This system works best when the number of items is limited and operations, assuming more than one, are concentrated in a close geographical area.

Operators should be aware of the pitfalls encountered by some small owners. The single-unit operator primarily requires service, even if forced to pay the high end of market prices for those services. Many new or single-unit owners must also depend entirely upon suppliers for information regarding market conditions. Because of the need for credit, some operators in effect sacrifice low prices for extended payment terms.

What distribution alternatives are available to larger single-unit and multi-unit operators? Several systems should be assessed individually by reviewing the impact of the distribution restraints noted previously.

Approved Local Sources

Many hospitality operations identify local suppliers with acceptable products, take bids from them, and fix prices for a certain time period. For example, fresh produce, meat, and seafood could be bid and priced weekly, groceries once monthly, and bakery and dairy products for a longer time period.

The price level is typically established at the time of bid. An agreement is necessary to lock in any price changes to recognized indicators, for instance, regularly published market reports. Some distribution companies maintain list prices from which they offer discounts.

Non-food items are generally the last category to be managed (if at all). Markups of as much as 40% over costs may occur. A bid followed by some type of percentage-over-cost agreement is probably the best means by which a small organization can manage the costs of these items.

Approved Regional/National Sources

This source can be used by single or multi-unit operators. There are two basic systems which focus upon the degree of control exercised by management.

With one plan, firms may develop quality specifications for some of their high-cost/high-volume items and negotiate prices at the corporate level or similarly high level in the organization. Using this plan, factors such as seller's costs and quantities are agreed upon in advance; the manufacturer, processor, broker, or other organization that is party to the agreement arranges for a distributor or other supply source for all units. Each company-operated property is required to use products from the approved source; franchisees may also use these products if they desire. Product requirements beyond those negotiated at the corporation level are purchased by each unit locally.

In the second instance, firms may contract directly with processors/manufacturers for their major items as described previously. In addition, they may contract with local distributors for the remaining items that are needed. The items contracted from processors/manufacturers pass through the distributors at an agreed-upon markup price. The additional items that are required may be priced at the distributor's cost plus a fee or on some other basis to which the two parties have agreed.

Contract for Goods with Leased Distribution

This distribution alternative is used by multi-unit companies and is a further refinement to the system just described. Practically all of the goods are contracted directly with processors or manufacturers by the user. The goods then flow through pre-established distribution channels at contracted markups. Two examples of contract for goods with leased distribution are exclusive distribution and shared distribution.

Exclusive Distribution. In this system, the user company bids and contracts for the merchandise, usually FOB processing plants.* The distribution companies utilized are specialists serving only the user company. In fact, their facility is usually designed specifically for the customer's needs.

In effect, the user company negotiates a markup-over-cost with the distribution company. The goods are priced to the individual properties on a specified amount per purchase unit. Different categories of merchandise may carry a different charge or all goods may carry the same charge.

There are some occasions when the user actually finances and owns the products in the warehouse. In these cases, the company storing and delivering the product acts as a warehouse and provides storage and cartage services. Fees can be charged on either a weight, cubic foot, or per case basis. Accounting and other controls become more complicated as inventories must be maintained by the user company. Some companies have decided, however, that this system provides the control they desire.

Shared Distribution. In this system, the end-user contracts for the goods personally but has an insufficient concentration of outlets to command an exclusive facility. Generally, the distribution companies providing these services prefer to have no more than three customers in one facility.

Shared facilities produce difficulties in management of space, inventory turnovers, and investment, making these operations less efficient than one-customer centers. In addition to the physical issues, separate accounting must be maintained and, to the extent that markups are different, confidentiality is an issue. Still, these facilities can typically deliver products more efficiently than traditional full-line distributors.

Both exclusive and shared facilities are found most often serving limited-line fast-food organizations, but some airline companies have also applied this concept

---

*FOB means free on board; costs agreed upon are exclusive of freight, which must be borne by the purchaser.

in order to guarantee that their contract caterers use specified food products. Economic concerns have been less a factor here than quality control.

Self-Provided Distribution

A limited number of very large food service organizations provide distribution through company-owned facilities. The system is similar to that described in contract for goods with leased distribution. Some major companies operate their own distribution system where unit concentration is adequate, but use contract distribution in areas of lower density.

Self-distribution is a philosophical outgrowth of commissary operations. In general, companies with self-distribution are also involved in manufacturing. These manufacturing facilities may be started to support the needs of the company and may be added as companies are acquired.

Commissary Operations

These operations were first developed to provide required food service items at a time when supplier support was lacking. Commissaries filled the need for unique products, thus enabling the units to concentrate on customers rather than production. Distribution was required in order for the units to receive needed products. Labor costs were reduced, retail units could have quality products at less cost, and items could be priced below the competition.

Distribution of products produced by others has always been a part of the commissary system. Many companies that formerly operated commissaries to produce most of their products have reduced this manufacturing effort and have evolved into distribution. The manufactured items may be sold to either the hospitality or retail trade in addition to their own operations.

Some commissaries provide customer-ready items, usually made fresh daily. Soups, sauces, dressings, ground and fabricated meats (some precooked), bakery products, ice cream, prepared vegetables, and salads are among the products frequently prepared.

Growth in the commissary system slowed dramatically with the arrival of fast-food chains. Customers were lost to national companies who could deliver a satisfactory product at a lower cost. By its nature, a commissary requires a regional concentration of retail stores, all of which use similar menus. It became economically impractical to expand the commissary system nationally to compete with the cost-efficient distribution systems used by the fast-food chains.

Today, the major operators of commissaries are cafeterias, which offer customers a wide selection of items. The trend toward using fresh food has also renewed some interest in commissary-type manufacturing. Besides several large operations with multiple units, however, the overall use of commissary systems seems to be diminishing in the hospitality industry.

Measuring Distribution Effectiveness

Operators must select distribution systems based upon their needs and resources. To make the best choice, they need to measure value. Quality, service, and price are the measures of value. Quality and service are immediately apparent, while price measurement is more subjective.

Quality poses two major concerns for the operator: whether products meet specifications and whether products are received in satisfactory condition. Examples of the first instance include:

- Hamburger patties must have the specified fat to lean ratio.

- Printed forms must be manufactured so that they will be compatible with the front office equipment.

- Housekeeping carts must have the proper casters to permit easy movement and stability.

Quality also relates to condition. While this primarily has to do with perishable food, it also applies to damage (perhaps hidden) on cased products. Operators do not want to deal with distributors who cause frequent disputes over quality.

Service is quite easily measured. One simply has to ask the question, was the product delivered when required? Prior agreement as to the level of service required will diminish debate on this point.

Some method of measurement is required for each distribution alternative. Methods may range from simple bid comparisons to sophisticated cost-plus arrangements based on processor or manufacturer raw material cost.

Operators want to do business with distributors best equipped to satisfy their needs. This means that distributors (1) must have appropriate facilities, equipment, and personnel; (2) must carry adequate inventory of the proper quality level; and (3) must themselves be efficient buyers. Distributors must operate their facility effectively so as to offer competitive prices to the hospitality operation.

Operators should consider six cost elements in selecting distributors:

- Product cost: Is the distributor buying from the primary processor? Is the distributor buying at maximum discount levels?

- Transportation costs: Is the distributor ordering in the proper quantities to minimize freight costs?

- Storage: Does the distributor have an efficiently designed warehouse? Is there an adequate sales volume to turn the inventory frequently?

- Handling: Does the distributor have adequate, experienced labor? Are personnel fully utilized?

- Delivery Charges: Are the trucks full when they leave the warehouse? How far must they travel to complete deliveries?

- Management/Overhead: Is management actively involved in running the business? Are there other costs which ultimately will be passed on to the hospitality operator?

Buyers should know the pros and cons associated with two common methods of setting distribution rates. Costs of distribution may be based on either a percentage markup or flat fee per pound. In an inflationary environment, especially with volatile commodity prices, a percentage markup is undesirable. Distribution charges may increase greatly while the actual cost of distribution may have stayed constant. A fixed fee may be more equitable for buyers in this situation. (When prices fall, however, a percentage markup is advantageous to buyers since distribution charges decrease.)

Typical Distribution Systems

Each hospitality operation needs to select appropriate procedures to acquire and move products through the marketplace. Let's take a look at four typical distribution systems to assess factors at work in selecting procedures for distribution.

Example #1: A 200-Room Motel

The staff consists of a manager, rooms supervisor, front office supervisor, and engineer. Food service is leased out, so none of these staff members is directly responsible for purchasing items needed by the food service unit.

Selection of distributors is made primarily by each department supervisor with the manager becoming involved in major purchases, such as the annual renewal of the laundry contract. Once established, the same suppliers will be used unless some problem arises, at which point a search for new suppliers is instituted. Often these problems are self-induced as a result of not providing sufficient delivery lead time or by failing to use quality specifications to define the purchased products.

An operator of this type may have some affiliation with a national organization. Occasionally, national organizations offer some purchasing assistance by negotiating contracts on behalf of members. These contracts are generally for promotional materials, but various types of operating supplies could be included.

This system depends on the effectiveness of each supervisor to obtain the right product at the proper prices. Since cost of suppliers is not a major concern of room sales, purchasing often is not a high priority. However, cost savings will directly add to profit margins. Extra effort spent on the purchase of cleaning products, paper supplies, and other items will result in higher profits.

Example #2: A 750-Room Resort Hotel

The resort hotel is a large facility with three dining rooms, three bars, and banquet facilities. Its annual sales are as follows:

Rooms	$ 24 million
Food and Beverage	12 million
Banquet	4 million
Bar	5 million
Total	$ 45 million

Department heads for food and beverage, rooms, sales, finance, and engineering report to a general manager. The hotel has a purchasing staff consisting of a manager (purchasing agent) and four assistants; all report to the chief financial officer. This compromise was reached when the department was established and decentralized purchasing responsibility was withdrawn from specific departments.

Each department does have the authority to establish specifications for the products or services that are required. Department heads approve specifications and process item requisition forms which indicate quantity and delivery requirements. Purchasing staff then seek sources, take bids, award contracts, and expedite delivery. Much communication is required between purchasing and the user departments concerning quality requirements, alternative products which bidders may offer, reliability of suppliers, and performance and emergency needs.

Over time, user departments have grown to rely upon purchasing personnel and a predictable routine has been established. One of the purchasing manager's assistants has been assigned to each of the user departments (and, in the case of food and beverage, is actually located in that department). If a contract is in force, the function of these assistants is to call the supplier when a requisition is received and order the product based on the contract terms. This process is used for china, silver, and linen, all of which are contracted annually. When the item is not on contract, the assistant's function is to locate the best price source and obtain the goods.

However, exceptions do exist to this simple routine. For example, the food and beverage manager is well versed in wines and selects them monthly based on availability. On the other hand, engineering often requires products or equipment of a technical nature, frequently a one-time purchase. Purchasing generally does not become involved in these acquisitions.

It is the responsibility of the purchasing agent to negotiate long-term contracts and to search out additional opportunities. To do this, an annual contract calendar is usually established according to product class. Using that schedule, each product class is reviewed on its assigned date, the specification is reconfirmed with the user, prices are solicited, and contracts are awarded for an agreed-upon time. This information is then passed to the assistants who order based on the contract terms.

Example #3: A Food Service Company

This is a multi-division contract food service company that operates in-plant, hospital, and sports center food services and also provides for airline catering. The company operates nationally and does over $300 million in annual sales. This is a competitive business, with low profit margins. Because of this, the company has made a significant investment in purchasing and distribution to capture all economies of scale.

The vice president of purchasing reports directly to the company president. Purchasing directors for food, supplies, and equipment along with directors of product testing and distribution report to the vice president of purchasing. The company has four regional distribution offices located around the country.

The headquarters buying staff concentrates on high-volume items needed by all divisions. In most companies, 20% of the items constitute 80% of the volume; the headquarters staff spend their time on the purchase of these items. Their objective is to buy items of the required quality at the lowest cost. To accomplish this, they deal entirely with processors and manufacturers. (They want to buy as well as or better than small distributors do.)

The product testing director helps locate products that will meet specifications at the lowest cost. This job also involves obtaining agreements on product specifications across the operating division lines so that greater purchase volume can help yield lower prices.

The distribution director's function is to develop and supervise delivery systems that will provide the proper service and products to the many operating outlets. This official must arrange local distribution for products contracted by the headquarters buyers. Since this represents a big job, all four regional offices help with the details. Dairy, fresh produce, and fresh baked goods are some of the categories contracted locally by the regional offices. A system of price feedback is maintained which enables the distribution director to compare unit product costs across the entire country, in order to highlight trouble spots.

Example #4: A Brand-Oriented Hotel Chain

This company operates 46 company-owned and 15 franchise properties. Each property averages 450 rooms and typically has two restaurants, two bars, and banquet facilities. Annual sales are:

Rooms	$300 million
Food	150 million
Beverages	50 million
Total	$500 million

Food costs average 40%; beverage costs are 20%. Menus are developed locally by each property. They have developed certain generic specifications for high-ticket items (for example, shrimp and USDA Choice beef) and they have some brand specifications (for condiments and other tabletop items).

The company has limited headquarters staff: one buyer is located at headquarters. This staff member's function is to develop national programs, provide advice to operations, and perform on-location purchasing inspections.

The company has a fairly sophisticated information system. A record of all purchases is prepared by each operation and submitted to headquarters weekly. This information is fed into the headquarters computer and various reports are generated relating to inventories, turnover, food cost, and prices. The buyer reviews this information and contacts properties whose costs appear high. (One problem is that items listed are not always comparable, so incorrect conclusions may be drawn.) The current status of the purchasing and distribution program is as follows:

1. **Food**—All items are bought locally by the properties. Three hotels in the headquarters city buy meat and certain other items cooperatively. The buyer obtains these prices in addition to others (such as produce) and telexes them to the other units for their use.

2. **Supplies**—Contracts are in effect for certain items. Linens and soaps, for example, are contracted and drop-shipped from manufacturers directly to the properties on a regularly scheduled basis. The buyer bids and renews these contracts each year.

3. **Beverages**—A contract is in effect for imported French wines, while a controlled label wine from California is purchased according to house specifications. Distribution has been worked out through local distributors with the help of the bottlers. All alcoholic beverages are purchased locally by the properties.

Exhibit 2   Checklist for Evaluation of Hotel Purchasing

1. Are specifications on hand?
2. Are specifications given to suppliers?
3. Are quotations taken?
4. Is the lowest bidder chosen? If not, why?
5. Are regular order days used?
6. How many emergency orders were placed this week? What were the reasons?
7. Are weekly inventories taken? (Look at the latest one.)
8. Are there inventory sheets in the buyer's desk?
9. Is the par stock inventory system in effect?
10. How are order quantities developed?
11. Are purchase orders/purchase logs used?
12. Are these records accurately completed?
13. Are they used by receiving personnel?
14. Is incoming merchandise weighed and recorded?
15. Is incoming merchandise checked for quality?
16. How are discrepancies handled?
17. Have any credits been requested this week?
18. What is the condition of the storage areas?
19. Are stored items rotated regularly?
20. What is the current inventory value?
21. How does this compare to the standard inventory value?
22. How are receipts and issues recorded?
23. Is perpetual inventory used? If not, why?
24. If so, how do the counts of five selected items compare with the perpetual inventory record?

Note: This is a partial list. Each type of operation must tailor its checklist to its own business.

4. **Inspection**—The buyer visits each property twice annually and talks with the major suppliers, examines the merchandise on hand, and evaluates the effectiveness of that unit's purchasing. A written checklist is used (see Exhibit 2). The purchasing official completes and reviews it with both the individual doing the buying and the general manager. Discrepancies are followed up by the general manager.

5. **General**—The hotel general managers operate autonomously in this company; purchasing is an advisory staff position. The emphasis given to purchasing primarily depends on the general manager's interest. The headquarters staff attempts to motivate the general manager to pursue the cost-saving opportunities.

REVIEW QUIZ

When you feel you have covered all of the material in this chapter, answer these questions. Choose the *best* answer. Check your answers with the correct ones found on the Review Quiz Answer Key at the end of this book.

True (T) or False (F)

(T) F   1. Brokers do not take title to the goods that they sell.

T   (F)   2. The actual costs of products at the processing plants are escalating at a faster pace than the costs of distribution.

(T) F   3. In most cases, distributors own the products at their facilities and can directly determine prices charged to end-users. T

(T) F   4. Large hospitality operations handling their own distribution may sell manufactured items to firms outside their organization. T

(T) F   5. Intermanufacturer agents may represent other processors in addition to their primary processors. T

(T) F   6. In general, the overall use of commissary systems has been diminishing in the hospitality industry. T

T   (F)   7. The only consideration in selecting a distributor should be product cost.

(T) F   8. Approved local suppliers may be an excellent source for such items as fresh produce, meats, baked goods, and dairy products.

Multiple Choice

9. _____ work primarily with the sale of non-food items and are employees of the processor or manufacturer.

    a. Brokers
    b. Distributors
    c. Interpacker agents
    d. Manufacturer's representatives

10. If products are delivered to an organization when they are needed, _____ value has been added to the products.

    a. time
    b. form
    c. informational
    d. no appreciable

11. Food and beverage buyers for hotels, restaurants, and fast-food operations are classified as:

    a. jobbers/brokers.
    b. retail buyers.
    c. end-users.
    d. industrial suppliers.

Chapter Outline

Styles of Buying
     Informal Buying Methods
     Formal Buying Systems
Supply Concepts in Purchasing Systems
Procedures for Supplier Selection
     What Is a "Good" Supplier?
     Identification of Suppliers
     Considerations in Selecting Suppliers
     Dealing with New Suppliers
One-Stop Shopping Systems
Cooperative (Group) Purchasing

Learning Objectives

1. Describe the importance of supplier selection.

2. Compare the two styles of buying.

3. Explain the various approaches to suppliers.

4. Describe the purchasing philosophy that views the supplier as a partner.

5. Differentiate the ways of identifying supply sources.

6. Compare methods of evaluating current suppliers with those used for new suppliers.

7. Summarize the pros and cons of one-stop shopping.

8. List the advantages and disadvantages of cooperative/group purchasing.

3

Supplier Selection

THE OBJECTIVES of an effective purchasing system involve purchasing the right product of the right quality and quantity at the right time and price from the right supplier. In this chapter, we will examine factors to address as decisions are made regarding the selection of suppliers.

For some managers, supplier selection options are limited. Buyers in isolated areas, for example, may have only a few suppliers from whom purchases can be made. Even buyers in major metropolitan areas may be limited to one supplier when manufacturers grant exclusive territories to distributors (as may be the case with specialized equipment or branded items). These cases characterize a seller's market in which a manager's decision becomes one of accepting a product or revising the menu to exclude the need for the product in question.

More typically, however, today's manager is able to select from a number of suppliers offering products of similar quality. How is the supplier selection decision made in these instances?

Several buying methods and options influence the selection of suppliers. For example, suppliers with relatively small business volumes may have difficulty in meeting the quantity requirements of large-volume purchasers. By contrast, large supplier organizations may have less interest in meeting the specific purchase needs of small operations. Suppliers may or may not be interested in the cost-plus system, a long-term contract, hedging, and related buying options. Depending on the situation, the operator wishing to utilize these buying options may have a reduced number of suppliers interested in such non-traditional product pricing plans.

Today, the systems of one-stop shopping and cooperative (group) purchasing are becoming well-established. Again, an operator's interest in these alternatives will affect the decision regarding suppliers.

Styles of Buying

As you will note, many elements affect the supplier selection process. The professional purchaser must be aware of these elements so that the goal of purchasing from the right supplier will be realized. The mission is to move the purchasing system from routine order-placing to careful, considerate buying.

Informal Buying Methods

Hospitality operations of all sizes must incorporate basic management principles into their buying methods. Products are expensive and operating problems arise when products are purchased in incorrect quantities. Therefore, an organized

Exhibit 1   Purchase Record

Date Ordered	Item Description	Unit	Price	No. of Units	Total Cost	Invoice No.	Comments
		(supplier)					

method should be used by even a small operation to monitor purchasing agreements that may have been made.

Some purchasers may order regularly from the same supplier. Because they have complete trust in the supplier, they may use very informal buying methods. For example, they may call in an order and make a purchase agreement without inquiring about purchase price. Similarly, a supplier representative may visit their operation and write up an order without an in-house written record of products, quantities, or agreed-upon purchase price. These types of purchasing situations are usually ineffective and often lead to errors.

Hospitality managers are very busy; they cannot be expected to recall details about the purchase of the several hundred or more products that are ordered. In addition, the person who orders may not be the one who receives incoming products. Without an in-house record of purchases, managers have no way to confirm that incoming items match those ordered in terms of purchase price, quantity, and quality.

Exhibit 1 illustrates a simple form for recording basic information about product purchases. It can be completed by the purchaser whenever an order is placed. The form can then be used at the time of product receiving; information about incoming products can be recorded and problems (such as back orders or shortages at the time of receiving) can be noted. The purchase record can also serve as a source document to the accounting system. After products are received, the purchase record can be matched with the supplier's delivery invoice as bills are processed for payment.

If purchasing and receiving activities are handled by more than one individual, a copy of the purchase record should be provided to receiving personnel. They will then be alert to what products are expected and which suppliers will be delivering the required items. Such personnel will also have information helpful in product receiving.

Formal Buying Systems

The purchase record system just described is useful for small operations, which require simple and practical records of purchase agreements.* By contrast, larger operations may make use of a formalized purchase order system, particularly when more precise communication is advisable. Exhibit 2 illustrates a document that can be used. Some basic procedures found in many formal purchase order systems include:

- Quality requirements for products to be purchased are identified in a standard purchase specification.

- Eligible suppliers are provided with copies of applicable purchase specifications and are informed that prices to be quoted should be for products of that quality defined by the specifications.

- A wide range of legal/contractual concerns are defined by the operation. These may be included as part of the purchase order agreement, or they can be sent along with purchase specifications and made to apply to all orders placed by the hospitality operation.

- Suppliers are asked to respond to a request for price quotation (RFP). Frequently, the RFP form is designed so that it can be used as the purchase order when the supplier is given the order.

- When the purchase order is issued, one copy is given to the supplier and additional copies are distributed as necessary to applicable departments within the property. For example, food and beverage, receiving, accounting, and purchasing department staff may require copies.

When the purchase order system is combined with formal bidding, a number of other requirements can be established. For example, bids may need to be received by the operation within a specified time period, penalties for failure to deliver the required quantity and quality of products may be imposed, and procedures to formally ask questions about required products may be addressed in a legally binding document. A formal bidding system is, of course, used by only relatively large operations.

As suppliers are screened, it is important to ensure that they will participate in the buying method utilized by the operation. Selection of a supplier by the operation is often a result of the type of purchasing system used.

Supply Concepts in Purchasing Systems

We have noted that the value of products received by a hospitality operation is directly related to the purchasing system employed. Just as systems vary with the

---

*Informal buying is also widely used by large operations, including multi-unit ones, for certain classes of products. For example, most fresh food products are ordered for next day delivery by operators, both small and large. There is inadequate time to pass written documents. Records of the transaction are internal to both buyer and seller; it is critical to both that accurate records be maintained.

Exhibit 2 Purchase Order

Purchase Order Number: _____	Order Date: _____
	Payment Terms: _____
To: _____ (supplier)	From/ Ship to: _____ (name of food service operation)
_____	_____
_____ (address)	_____ (address)
	Delivery Date: _____

Please Ship:

Quantity Ordered	Description	✔	Units Shipped	Unit Cost	Total Cost

Total Cost _____

Important: This Purchase Order expressly limits acceptance to the terms and conditions stated above, noted on the reverse side hereof, and any additional terms and conditions affixed hereto or otherwise referenced. Any additional terms and conditions proposed by seller are objected to and rejected.

_____
Authorized Signature

nature and volume of the business, supply concepts may reflect a variety of individual approaches.

Short-Term vs. Long-Range. In some systems, suppliers simply function as a "warehouse." When a product is needed, the manager calls the sales representative, places the order, and has the product delivered. The supplier may "rescue" the manager when product needs are overlooked and orders neglected. A hospitality business tends to focus on the short term when it follows this system.

Using a different approach, management sets standards based upon historical records that quantify consumption and past price trends. Historical data are then modified based upon a knowledgeable appraisal of anticipated market conditions. Managers are expected to formalize goals and, as a result, planning becomes detailed and consistent.

Since bids solicited from suppliers may tend to run for fixed time periods, it may be more difficult to change suppliers if the time period has not expired. To some operators, a system based on the short term offers greater ease and flexibility than one linked to long-range commitments.

Number of Suppliers. Some operations, by their nature, require fewer suppliers than others. By consolidating buying efforts, ordering is simplified and the opportunity for volume discounts is improved. However, dependency on a single supplier is a risky proposition. Supply shortages may be felt more directly in terms of quality and price if additional sources are overlooked. Purchasing decisions should not be based solely upon loyalty to a supplier—the overall goal is to maximize value.

Source of Information. Many hospitality managers depend heavily upon the sales representative's knowledge and willingness to communicate product information and source. When managers deal with sales representatives, rather than top management or ownership of the supplier's firm, the possibility exists that timely and accurate information will be lacking, thus hampering the purchasing decision.

Some suppliers automatically provide formal, written market information each month. In certain instances, suppliers may telephone hospitality managers with market updates as conditions change. The relationship between management and the supplier is transformed from decisions based on personal factors to business decisions based on facts.

Some suppliers provide additional service in the form of computer data. Electronic data processing (EDP) systems are used to track invoice amounts and product purchasing trends. Many suppliers provide velocity reports, which segregate expenditures by product category. This service permits management to identify where control efforts must be focused. Along with velocity reports, suppliers may also furnish price reports on a regular basis.

Quality vs. Price. Some systems allow managers to function with a minimal knowledge of purchase specifications. Quality levels may be difficult to control when written specifications are lacking.

In other systems, quality is defined by management's standards. The increased emphasis on quality helps ensure that the operation is more likely to receive the products specified. In addition, the cost and quality control systems of the operation are strengthened, enhancing customer satisfaction.

Intended Use. By incorporating purchase specifications, the intended use of the product is accurately defined. Therefore, product yields on items such as beef roast are usually more consistent. If shortages develop in key products, the distributor may be authorized to deliver preauthorized substitutions.

Purchasing systems often place purchasing responsibility on the unit manager, who then "delegates" it to suppliers. This makes it more difficult to precisely assign accountability. It becomes easy to "blame" purchasing problems upon the suppliers rather than attempting to identify the true cause(s) of problems, which may be within the property's management system.

Value in the purchasing system is generally enhanced when management has more control. Managers should build into this system those checks and balances that address quality, service, and price at the unit level. On the other hand, value is reduced when the amount of time that management spends controlling the system outweighs the benefits received.

Procedures for Supplier Selection

A hospitality operation requires suppliers who meet product quality and price concerns while providing dependable service. The manager should build long-term relationships with those suppliers who consistently furnish useful information, meet quality standards, and offer the best prices. As the routine business of ordering, expediting, invoice processing, and payment is transacted, the hospitality operation needs to have a supplier who participates in a "partnership" rather than one who fosters an adversarial relationship.

What Is a "Good" Supplier?

A good supplier is one with whom the operator can have a long-term relationship. Performance characteristics of suppliers that form the basis for a long-term relationship include the following:

- The supplier must have the capability and commitment to perform well.

- The supplier must provide timely information regarding price changes, thus maintaining a competitive price level.

- The supplier must understand the market served by the operation and must have ideas about how to best meet this market's needs, including special services.

- The supplier must be able to consistently provide the proper quality and quantity of products.

- The supplier must inform buyers as to new or improved products which may be applicable to their operations.

- The supplier must have an ongoing interest in improving products and services provided to the hospitality operation.

- The supplier must be professional. It should be easy to follow up on problems, to resolve difficulties that arise, and to negotiate any concerns.

- The supplier must be concerned that facilities meet or exceed accepted levels of sanitation.

- The supplier must be financially capable of growing—with both the industry and its customers.

The interests of both managers and suppliers are served when a cooperative, working relationship exists. If either party tries to take advantage of the other by engaging in an "I win, you lose" strategy, then problems will be created.

Identification of Suppliers

How does one develop a list of potential suppliers? While one-stop shopping has its benefits, most operators will be required to deal with a large number of suppliers, most of them specialized. The objective is to have as few suppliers as possible, yet still obtain the desired levels of quality, service, and price.

The first step in the process is to identify the product categories that are required. Some might be:

1. Laundry service
2. External maintenance (lawn and garden service)
3. Linen
4. Meat
5. Produce
6. Dairy
7. Bakery
8. Paper goods
9. Janitorial supplies
10. Engineering supplies
11. Office supplies
12. China, glass, silverware, and smallwares

While some consolidation of categories is probable, most moderately sized lodging operations will have over 50 separate suppliers. After identifying the product categories and determining possible consolidations, the next step is to determine some sequence of review of suppliers. For new units, review and selection must be complete to coincide with opening for business. For existing units, the schedule will reflect either (1) a potential cost saving, (2) some deficiency with the current supplier, or (3) a new requirement.

The number of potential suppliers is, in part, a function of the demographics in the area in which the operation is located. Many will be found in urban areas where sales potential is high. On the other hand, some rural locations may have only one supplier for some product classes. The task is to locate these potential suppliers promptly, then decide if they can be deemed "eligible."

Experienced hospitality managers typically are aware of suppliers who carry the products required, but they may not be aware of the best sources of supply. Among the techniques to identify supply sources are the following:

- Previous experiences—What has been the operator's experience with suppliers? If previous experiences have been good, then this evidence suggests that the supplier should be eligible for future business. By contrast, poor experiences suggest the need to identify other sources of supply.

- Sales representatives—Knowledgeable salespeople will know who the best suppliers are within their territory. They will definitely know who the major competitors are on their own product lines. While their responses are naturally biased toward their companies, generally they are candid in the interest of developing trust in the relationship with the buyer.

- Written information—Many suppliers issue catalogs, descriptive brochures, and related information, which can help provide basic background information about their firm and the products carried.

- Trade publications—Suppliers often advertise in trade journals and newspapers. Reviewing these publications will identify potential suppliers, and responding to advertisements may yield even more specific information about products and services available from these suppliers.

- Trade exhibits and conventions—Suppliers typically staff exhibits at trade shows and conventions. Hospitality operators attending these meetings can visit with various suppliers, sample their products, and obtain further information helpful in selecting suppliers.

- Competitors—During visits with competitors at professional meetings, trade shows, and other occasions, operators can get answers to specific questions regarding sources of particular items.

- References—The supplier should be able to provide a list of reputable references.

The imaginative manager can discover much more information about supply sources. The "yellow pages" section of a telephone book offers listings of potential suppliers, often advertising specialties and services. Personnel in professional associations may be informative as to possible supply sources. Conversations with other hospitality employees may also yield facts regarding new suppliers.

Considerations in Selecting Suppliers

A large number of suppliers can be identified for every product need, but purchasers usually prefer to have as few suppliers as possible. One approach is to periodically evaluate the suppliers identified as eligible and to select several who will be contacted regularly about product availability, price, and related concerns important at the time purchase decisions are made.

Some purchasers may believe that price is the most important concern. In fact, a few "price-conscious" buyers will buy from the supplier offering the lowest price, regardless of quality. By contrast, other purchasers have little, if any, regard for price; such "quality-conscious" buyers are interested in securing the highest quality product regardless of its price. Most purchasers are "value-conscious," concerned about both quality and price and, therefore, seeking value in their purchases. These buyers look for the supplier who most consistently provides the best value.

Many additional factors can be addressed as the list of potential suppliers is narrowed to the relatively few who will be routinely contacted when orders are placed. Considerations include:

- Supplier's facility—Important concerns can be addressed as a visit is made to the supplier's operation. The hospitality operator can assess the supplier's capability in a number of areas. Does the supplier have adequate inventory and the correct brands? Are sufficient personnel and equipment available to service the volumes of business? Are conditions sanitary? Who is the supplier doing business with, both sources of supply and other customers?

- Technical capability of staff—The hospitality operator seeks pertinent information as purchase decisions are made. The competence of the supplier's representatives in providing this technical support is of vital importance.

- Business relationship—The ability to develop a professional relationship is necessary in order to conduct business. Both the buyer and seller must be able to relate to each other's interests in order to develop a mutual commitment for overall success and for pleasing customers. The supplier who is honest, fair, and reasonable in dealings with the hospitality operation will have a competitive edge over others without these traits.

Once selection decisions are made, evaluation is necessary to ensure that the decision has consistent benefits for the hospitality operation.

We can review factors important in selecting suppliers by studying special concerns. For example, it is generally not cost-beneficial for a purchaser to spend an extensive amount of time searching for a supplier of an item used relatively infrequently. If one or two suppliers are available who can provide products of the required quality, perhaps the search for suppliers should stop there.

The purchaser should also be concerned with exclusive sales territories. If a specific brand of food item, liquor, or equipment is desired, it may be necessary to purchase these items from one supplier. In these instances, specifying a brand is a limiting factor affecting the selection of suppliers.

Reciprocity can be another limiting factor of concern to buyers. For example, line managers may negotiate "trade out" agreements to purchase products from a specific supplier in return for the supplier spending entertainment dollars at the operation. In any case, decisions about reciprocal purchasing should be made by line operating managers—not by staff purchasing officials—and only after having consulted with legal counsel on the legality of specific reciprocal purchases.

The purchase of large quantities of items can also limit options. Some small suppliers may not be able to supply the needed items in large enough quantities. Discount levels for volume purchases may have an additional impact upon supplier selection.

Some hospitality operations, especially fast-food chains and other large companies, can bypass suppliers/distributors entirely and, instead, purchase directly from a manufacturer, processor, or grower. These operations reduce costs by eliminating the markups associated with the movement of products through normal distribution channels.

Dealing with New Suppliers

Purchasers should not be afraid to purchase from other than established suppliers. After all, new suppliers are going into business daily just as new hospitality operations open with great frequency. Many professional purchasers initiate trial or sample orders with a new supplier to help in evaluating their interest in a continuing relationship.

In order to reduce the possibility of "surprises" during initial orders, detailed agreements should be made between the buyer and seller about products, quality, quantity, time of delivery, and related concerns. In other words, the purchaser should practice the same basic principles of purchasing management that are needed each time an order is placed.

References should be requested of the new supplier and then contacted. Purchasers should be aware that suppliers may offer large discounts and provide exceptional service as their business is developing. What sets suppliers apart, however, is the long-term and ongoing concern for price, quality, and consistency of service.

One-Stop Shopping Systems

Traditionally, suppliers have specialized in specific product lines such as meat, fresh produce, canned goods and groceries, and specialty items. While this still remains the norm, today many suppliers have broadened their lines to carry a vast range of products. In fact, some suppliers carry or can obtain almost any product, supply item, or piece of equipment needed by a hospitality operation.

Should purchasers consider use of a one-stop shopping service if available? One-stop shopping obviously eliminates the potentially time-consuming process of selecting individual suppliers. Another advantage is reduced time necessary to negotiate with suppliers, process orders, and receive incoming goods. Also, dealing with one supplier tends to build the supplier's trust in the operation and provides purchasing leverage for the operation.

Possible disadvantages to using a one-stop shopping service include:

- Higher prices—Suppliers selling popular products at a competitive price typically sell other items at a higher markup. When all products are purchased from one supplier, prices paid for some items will likely be higher than those available elsewhere. (On the other hand, one-stop shopping may reflect volume efficiencies conferred by consolidated shipments from a single source, resulting in lower prices.)

- Lack of specialized information—With the increased number of product lines comes a decreased likelihood that a supplier representative can be an "expert" in each of the many items being offered.

- Decreased variety within a product line—Typical one-stop suppliers offer relatively few varieties of each item and, in many cases, only one.

Purchasers must consider the benefits of a one-stop shopping system as they relate to the specific needs of their own operation. This system may be able to satisfy all purchasing needs of small properties. While time can be saved, this time must be effectively utilized in order to be of cost-benefit to the operation. One-stop shopping does have its place in the food service industry and its use is increasing.

Cooperative (Group) Purchasing

In a cooperative (group) purchasing system, a number of individual organizations use a common source to conduct many of the required purchasing tasks.* The objective is to achieve a better, more efficient purchasing system, one that will generate lower prices for products and services while ensuring that the required quality is received.

This form of purchasing has increased in popularity in recent years due to the economic pressures placed on hospitality operators. Organizations have realized that combined buying power supports strict cost-consciousness. However, all group procurement programs should be reviewed by legal counsel for potential antitrust violations. For example, buyers may be liable for inducing sellers to give unjustified discounts.

Several advantages are associated with group purchasing. Standardized quality and lowered prices are the main benefits. By sharing evaluations of product quality and new items, cooperative members are able to spend less time with sales representatives and can devote more time to other management functions. Since service and delivery requirements are reduced, management is easier. The overall effect is to consolidate and centralize the purchasing system, allowing even small operators to gain the competitive edge of volume purchases typically reserved to large operations.

The group purchasing system has a number of disadvantages which some buyers may find unacceptable. The food service operator loses some autonomy in the determination of quality and is generally limited in the variety of products from which to choose. Committees, which form the basis of group purchasing decisions, can be slow, cumbersome, and time-consuming for members. In order to join the group, individual operators must be willing to put aside competitive urges and supplier loyalties.

Some legal questions arise when group purchasing techniques are used. For example, the Federal Trade Commission (FTC) may not permit some cooperative arrangements under the antitrust provisions of the Robinson-Patman Act. In addition, specific legal clauses may be required for the bid and contract, including terms for awarding contracts and conditions under which supply contracts may be terminated. The group may also limit its liability for any losses as a result of inaccurate forecasts by members, who may be expected to order the amount agreed upon by an earlier forecast.

---

*Cooperative purchasing generally refers to non-profit organizations (e.g., hospitals), while group purchasing generally describes free enterprise organizations (e.g., franchisees) with a profit motive. For our purposes, we will use the terms interchangeably.

Despite the drawbacks, group purchasing will likely become more popular in the future. Its growth will largely be a result of the economies of scale obtained by group members with local distributors. In addition, many distributors find this purchasing option to their advantage as a means of sharing information with a larger group of buyers.

REVIEW QUIZ

When you feel you have covered all of the material in this chapter, answer these questions. Choose the *best* answer. Check your answers with the correct ones found on the Review Quiz Answer Key at the end of this book.

True (T) or False (F)

T (F) 1. The purchasing systems used by large operations are identical to those used by small operations.

(T) F 2. An on-site inspection of a supplier's operation is useful in determining its size and technical capabilities.

T (F) 3. Changing suppliers is more difficult with a short-term approach to purchasing than with a long-term commitment.

(T) F 4. The opportunity for volume discounts is improved by consolidating buying efforts.

T (F) 5. Sales representatives should not be considered useful sources of information because they are always biased.

T (F) 6. Geographic location has no effect on the number of suppliers available to a hospitality operation.

(T) F 7. Trial or sample orders may help in evaluating new suppliers.

(T) F 8. In order to avoid potential antitrust violations, legal counsel should review group purchasing programs.

Multiple Choice

9. Selection of suppliers is based on all of the following *except*:

    a. ability to meet specifications.
    b. performance in service.
    c. reputation for quality.
    (d.) pre-negotiation promises.

Chapter Outline

Ethical and Professional Standards
    Need for Ethical Conduct
    Obligations to the Company
    Obligations to Suppliers
    The Policy Statement
    Conflict of Interest
The Negotiating Process
    Preparations for Negotiation
    The Negotiation Plan
    Techniques for Negotiating
    Topics of Negotiation
    The Close of Negotiations
Legal Aspects of Purchasing
    Law of Agency
    Contracts and Bids
    Warranties
    Remedies for Contract Breach
    Sales Law
    Antitrust Laws
    Relations with Suppliers

Learning Objectives

1. Define common terms relating to ethical standards.

2. Describe ways in which buyers are obligated to suppliers.

3. List important points in the negotiation process.

4. Cite some topics of negotiation.

5. Explain some major areas of law which affect purchasing.

6. Summarize antitrust laws.

4

Buyer-Supplier Relations

W<small>HILE SELECTING THE BEST SUPPLIER</small> signals the completion of one goal of purchasing, it represents the beginning of an entirely new series of interactions between buyer and supplier. The resulting relationship will in large part determine the outcome of such goals as price and quality.

As an integral function of their position, purchasers need to be able to negotiate with suppliers. In addition, they must know the law as it affects purchasing activities and adhere to professional and ethical standards. The skill and expertise with which these activities are handled can significantly influence the success of purchasing management.

Ethical and Professional Standards

Ethical concerns deal with the concepts of good and bad, right and wrong, moral duty, professional obligation, proper values, and personal conduct. The hospitality operation must have policies and procedures reflecting ethical and professional standards.

Purchasers have obligations to the company, to colleagues, to suppliers, and to themselves. Many factors affect the working relationships between purchaser and supplier. The appropriateness of any action will vary according to the individual viewpoints and specific situations. An organizational code of ethics and professional standards can assist the hospitality operation in promoting a positive image throughout the industry.

Need for Ethical Conduct

The maintenance of ethical relationships with suppliers is critical for several reasons. First, fairness is in the long-range best interest of the hospitality operation in dealings with all of its external publics, including suppliers. Second, since staff members performing purchasing functions represent their employer, they must be consistent in their interactions with suppliers. Third, the operation can suffer if the purchaser places personal interests before those of the organization.

Ethical standards, established at the time of purchasing, permeate the organization, benefiting every department. These policies can help ensure that maximum value is received for purchasing dollars expended, improving the operation's competitive edge.

Obligations to the Company

The purchaser's relationship with suppliers and other external publics should always reinforce and strengthen the company's image and reputation. Commitment

Exhibit 1   Code of Ethics

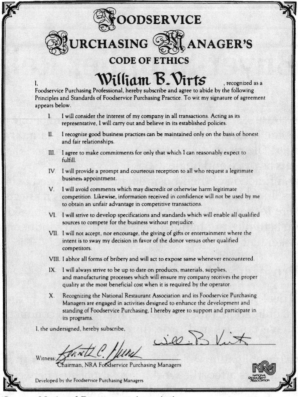

FOODSERVICE PURCHASING MANAGER'S CODE OF ETHICS

I, **William B. Virts**, recognized as a Foodservice Purchasing Professional, hereby subscribe and agree to abide by the following Principles and Standards of Foodservice Purchasing Practice. To wit my signature of agreement appears below.

I.   I will consider the interest of my company in all transactions. Acting as its representative, I will carry out and believe in its established policies.

II.   I recognize good business practices can be maintained only on the basis of honest and fair relationships.

III. I agree to make commitments for only that which I can reasonably expect to fulfill.

IV.   I will provide a prompt and courteous reception to all who request a legitimate business appointment.

V.   I will avoid comments which may discredit or otherwise harm legitimate competition. Likewise, information received in confidence will not be used by me to obtain an unfair advantage in competitive transactions.

VI.   I will strive to develop specifications and standards which will enable all qualified sources to compete for the business without prejudice.

VII. I will not accept, nor encourage, the giving of gifts or entertainment where the intent is to sway my decision in favor of the donor versus other qualified competitors.

VIII. I abhor all forms of bribery and will act to expose same whenever encountered.

IX.   I will always strive to be up to date on products, materials, supplies, and manufacturing processes which will ensure my company receives the proper quality at the most beneficial cost when it is required by the operator.

X.   Recognizing the National Restaurant Association and its Foodservice Purchasing Managers are engaged in activities designed to enhance the development and standing of Foodservice Purchasing, I hereby agree to support and participate in its programs.

I, the undersigned, hereby subscribe,

Witness: _____
Chairman, NRA Foodservice Purchasing Managers

Developed by the Foodservice Purchasing Managers

Source: National Restaurant Association.

to fairness, consistency, and quality should be the common goals. Toward these ends, the purchaser should:

- Adhere to all company policies and procedures in order to maximize goals and objectives.
- Seek optimal value for purchasing dollars spent.
- Protect the legal rights of the company.
- Ensure that the company enjoys a reputation for fair and honest dealings with suppliers.

These and related obligations are listed in the code of ethics for purchasing managers (Exhibit 1). Professional purchasers recognize and adhere to the practices outlined in this code.

Obligations to Suppliers

Study of Exhibit 1 suggests that purchasers also have obligations to suppliers. Nurturing an "ethical" relationship between purchaser and supplier strengthens the

Exhibit 2   Sample Letter

Mr. _____, President
Acme Company

_____

Dear Sir:

We, here at _____ Co., value the relationship with our suppliers. It is our practice to annually reaffirm the business principles of our Company and we have attached a copy for you. As it pertains to our purchasing functions, the intent is to avoid placing our suppliers and employees in any situation which might be construed as a conflict of interest. This normally arises over the "Gift" issue and we request that our policy of "Nominal Value Only" be followed.

We are sure that you understand our position on this and look forward to a continuing good relationship.

---

reputation of the operation, clarifies policies and procedures, and encourages consistent performance from other staff members.

Long-term relationships between supplier and purchaser are enhanced when operating guidelines are also provided. These guidelines should provide the supplier with the following information:

- Potential volume of product (or level of service needed) and reasonable estimates of use

- Preferred appointment and delivery times, allowing ample lead time to develop price quotations

- Prompt notification of bids accepted or rejected

- Changes or modifications in purchase specifications

- "Rush" or emergency orders, with consideration given to extenuating circumstances

Purchasers must recognize that suppliers should be treated with courtesy, professionalism, and personal concern. Under no circumstances should purchasers divulge the supplier's price or trade secrets. Suppliers should be able to trust that the purchaser's operation has a history of honoring commitments and avoiding legal loopholes.

The Policy Statement

A policy statement outlines the basic philosophy of the hospitality operation. By setting forth policies in clear, unambiguous terms, the operation lays the foundation for good buyer-supplier relations. Exhibit 2 is a sample letter sent to suppliers outlining company policies.

Most policy statements relating to ethical concerns simply state that the operation and its employees intend to maintain legal and professional standards in conducting business. The operation assures suppliers that all transactions will be carefully documented and promises that its employees will avoid any possible conflict of interest.

Exhibit 3   Sample Conflict of Interest Statement

> I have read and am familiar with the Company's policies relating to supplier relations and conflict of interest.
>
> I have no interest which conflicts with these policies.
>
> The following may be in conflict and I request that they be examined by counsel.
>
> 1. _____
>
> 2. _____
>
> 3. _____   _____
>
>   Signature

Such statements usually encourage competition by supporting the consideration of all qualified and reputable suppliers. Policies should dictate that contracts are awarded to the lowest responsible bidder meeting specifications, with any exceptions justified by the appropriate authority. The statement should also express an interest in developing supplier loyalty.

Written policy statements are not all-inclusive documents. A purchaser may have a situation that "feels" wrong and may be uncertain as to what action to take. In this case, the purchaser could seek advice and counsel from another source, always preserving that invaluable commodity: personal integrity.

Conflict of Interest

High standards of professionalism are required of purchasers as they interact with suppliers. Conflicts of interest often result in personal and financial gains at the expense of the hospitality operation and, ultimately, its guests. Exhibit 3 is a sample of a "conflict of interest" statement for internal use by the purchaser.

To maintain an honest reputation, purchasers should avoid personal use of company property, personal purchases for non-business purposes, and any financial interest in a supplier's company. The hospitality company should formulate specific policies regarding solicitations for charitable or political donations, travel and related expenses incurred in visiting a supplier's location, and personal concessions from suppliers.

Sometimes, individuals responsible for purchasing are prone to the temptation of accepting gifts, loans, and cash in return for favors bestowed upon a supplier's company. While some companies place upper limits as to the value of gifts which can be accepted, the best policy is to reject any gift, no matter how small its value. A professional purchaser considers company interest, not personal benefit.

The Negotiating Process

Negotiation is the use of persuasion and information to influence behavior. As purchaser and supplier transact business, whether placing an order or securing a price quotation, they negotiate an understanding. The negotiating process enables the purchaser and supplier, through give and take, to reach a mutually beneficial agreement. Successful negotiators develop clear goals, understand the facts, and use timing to their advantage.

Preparations for Negotiation

An effective negotiation plan requires preparation and evaluation. By collecting preliminary data at this time, a skilled negotiator assesses the needs, strengths, and weaknesses of both parties. This information should provide answers to crucial questions, enabling the purchaser to make intelligent buying decisions. These questions basically fall into three categories:

1. User-related

    a. What does the purchaser need?
    b. How much time can be invested in fact-finding, planning, and negotiation activities?
    c. How quickly is the product/service needed (what are the deadlines)?

2. Supplier-related

    a. What does the seller need and how urgent is this need?
    b. How quickly can the product/service be delivered?
    c. What has been the seller's product delivery and service performance history?
    d. Have changes within the supplier's company affected performance?

3. Negotiation-related

    a. What are the limits to the concessions that can be made?
    b. Who has the authority to make concessions? What are the limitations of authority?
    c. What has been the supplier's negotiating method in the past (collaborative or competitive)?

These and similar questions are considered so as to focus the negotiation and determine the approach most likely to produce satisfactory results. Solid preparation of the type just outlined leads the way toward a formalized negotiation plan.

The Negotiation Plan

The negotiation plan identifies the resources of the hospitality operation (e.g., personnel and inventory), the buyer's negotiation method, and the resources at the supplier's disposal (e.g., personnel, inventory, and equipment). The purchaser will hold the advantage during negotiations if he/she can organize this information into a plan of action, but the purchaser must have the appropriate authority to implement this plan.

In negotiations, authority is power. The amount of power that one is perceived to have greatly influences the negotiation process. The purchaser's power is derived from several sources:

- Position or status within the company
- Supplier's perception of purchaser's authority
- Knowledge of the hospitality industry
- Awareness of the supplier's competition

- Commitment to meeting obligations
- Willingness to establish long-term relationships
- Reputation for fairness and promptness in paying bills
- Economic factors (for instance, purchase volume)

The purchaser's authority depends on management's commitment to the purchaser and how well the purchaser adheres to company goals and objectives. The purchaser is more effective during negotiations if this power is used strategically.

With this power and a collection of pertinent facts and figures, the purchaser, as negotiator, develops the "game plan." The planning process determines who will do the negotiating. In some cases, a team approach is preferred; one person conducts the actual negotiations while a backup team provides information (facts, options).

The purchaser usually begins the negotiation process and in so doing establishes the "style" or method. There are two methods: collaborative and competitive.

Collaborative negotiations are based upon two assumptions: that compromise is preferable to conflict and that a give-and-take exchange is better than no settlement at all. This method addresses the needs of both parties and facilitates a commitment to that end.

Competitive negotiations can be varied. Sometimes they are inflexible, rigid sessions, beginning with tough and usually unreasonable demands. Conflict continues unresolved throughout the entire process, creating an imbalance between negotiators as they grudgingly grant concessions and ignore deadlines.

The risk in using the competitive method is an abrupt break in communications, causing one or both parties to terminate negotiations altogether. However, competitive negotiations can be productive in some situations; details will be discussed later in this chapter.

Negotiations can also be classified as "win-win" or "win-lose" according to the outcome. A "win-win" outcome results in the mutual satisfaction of both parties, who come out of the process feeling they have gained something. It in no way implies that the buyer is easy, pliable, or weak.

In a "win-lose" outcome, one party gains a sense of satisfaction while the other party feels frustrated. When negotiations break down into this situation, the purchaser may initially win the advantage, but may eventually receive unsatisfactory performance from the supplier. Impatience and insecurity contribute to the "win-lose" situation.

Techniques for Negotiating

The negotiation plan prepares the foundation for the next phase of the process—the strategy. Through the use of location, timing, negotiating method, communication (telephone or face-to-face), and authority, the purchaser gains the advantage of control.

The purchaser should choose the location for the negotiations. The site chosen, in this case, may be the hospitality operation. However, it may be to the purchaser's advantage to visit the supplier's facilities in order to obtain additional information, meet other members of that organization, and evaluate quality control, production, shipping, and sanitary measures.

The purchaser should realize the importance of timing. For instance, the purchaser's initial advantage of placing the order diminishes as the deadline approaches. The original goals and objectives of management need to be firmly fixed in the negotiator's mind, along with an awareness of the supplier's own set of needs (differences in deadlines, prices, and volume). These pre-established goals should be attained before the final session. Conflict should only occur on minor points during the final stages.

The purchaser's negotiating method or "style" should be flexible. Beginning with a collaborative approach, the purchaser may then switch to a more competitive strategy (such as providing fewer options as the supplier invests more time). At this point, the purchaser could list potential benefits to the supplier as a result of conducting business with the hospitality operation. Termination of the negotiation process is less likely to occur as the supplier invests more time and expectation levels are raised.

Communication is a central factor in formulating strategy. The purchaser should evaluate the suitability of negotiations conducted over the telephone or in person. Pros and cons can be found in either approach depending on the situation.

For example, the telephone forfeits visual feedback and preparation (the caller is usually better prepared than the recipient). Whenever transactions occur over the telephone, the purchaser should submit to the supplier a written summary (memorandum) of all the issues discussed and the resulting agreements made. The supplier is less likely to retract or take issue with the transaction later.

Face-to-face communication carries disadvantages also. There is no way of "returning the call" when it's more convenient and when more time is needed to assemble necessary information. The supplier expects immediate feedback. While face-to-face communication generally reduces the risk of misinterpretation, it can create problems since the communication is spoken rather than written.

The ability to listen is the cornerstone of effective communication. Knowing how to listen (letting the supplier provide the bulk of information) and when to speak judiciously can significantly influence the negotiation's outcome. Listening also improves the level of feedback to the supplier's proposals.

Productive communication and interaction can be marred, however, by personality conflicts and ego differences. By identifying problems in the early stages of negotiation, more compatible personality types can be substituted, decreasing the threat of a "win-lose" outcome.

Dealing with persons in proper authority can work to the purchaser's advantage during negotiations. The decision-maker within the supplier's organization, not the intermediate representative, holds the power. Lost time and misunderstandings can be avoided if the purchaser deals directly with the appropriate person.

Sometimes, the purchaser may suggest to the supplier that a third party must be brought into the process, because the purchaser lacks the appropriate authority to negotiate. To avoid the inclusion of a third party, the supplier may concede additional demands. (Note: In this case, the purchaser is switching from a collaborative to competitive method.) The purchaser should observe the supplier's reaction to this strategy and be prepared to seek alternative solutions.

Topics of Negotiation

A buyer desires to give up as little as possible during the negotiation and hopes to gain as great a value as possible from the supplier. In the process, concessions are inevitably made by both parties. Some suggestions for managing concessions during negotiations are:

- Attempt to have the other side make the first concession. Don't accept the first offer made on a significant point.

- Set negotiating goals very high. Don't give up something without receiving something in return.

- Avoid responding to a high demand with a counteroffer (first, request that the demand be reduced).

- Be aware of the economic and strategic consequences of concessions, which may also significantly affect your abilities and aspirations.

- Ensure that each concession received brings you closer to your negotiating goal.

- Recognize that all concessions should be tentative until you decide to make them final.

Base price is, of course, a major topic for negotiation. The best negotiating approach is typically to agree upon a base price and then negotiate adjustments to the base price for concessions made by the buyer.

However, other topics contribute to pricing as well. For instance, the purchaser may save by taking advantage of rebate agreements and discounts for volume purchases. However, legal counsel should be consulted on these procedures. Payment terms can also be devised to reduce purchase costs if the purchaser pays cash or agrees to a short billing period.

Specific clauses can be used to limit rising prices. Some restrictive clauses limit price increases to a maximum percentage or specify dates by which increases must be scheduled. Escalator or de-escalator clauses adjust costs by using price indicators, including private/government indexes and the expenses of raw material and labor.

The Close of Negotiations

When negotiations are closed (that is, when goals have been met and conflicts resolved) all relevant information discussed thus far should be contractually agreed upon—sometimes orally but preferably in writing. Written contracts specify the precise commitments and responsibilities of both purchaser and supplier. Some purchasers write the contract on their own letterhead.

In all negotiations, the purchaser should strive to make the transaction profitable. The purchaser should learn to predict, not expect, and combine those predictions with experience to gain a sense of the probable. Finally, the purchaser has to know when to conclude negotiations and move on to other concerns. Understanding human nature is of great help in accomplishing this final task.

Legal Aspects of Purchasing

Purchasers should not undertake the task of interpreting laws, but it is helpful to have some general knowledge of law in order to recognize and avoid some of the legal problems that they and their companies may face. (Note: Since laws vary among states and since many concepts are not included in the general discussion which follows, it is always critical to obtain information from a licensed attorney as specific legal problems are encountered.)

Law of Agency

Sometimes, especially in smaller hospitality operations, the owner is the purchaser. As the size of the property increases, someone else usually assumes the purchasing responsibilities, thus representing the owner. Frequently, an owner hires a manager, who then employs a purchaser. According to the law of agency, however, the buyer may be acting on behalf of the owner—not the manager. In the role of agent, the purchaser may have the power to obligate the operation within the limits of the discretion which has been delegated.

The laws generally recognize that a purchaser may act as agent for the hospitality operation and has the authority to legally obligate it. This is the case when the purchaser is formally told to represent the operation and/or has been permitted to act as if performance is on its behalf.

By contrast, a sales representative, whose job it is to generate business, may in fact not be able to establish prices and make "binding" agreements beyond broad parameters established by the company. As noted earlier in this chapter, an important principle of negotiation requires that one negotiate with a person in appropriate authority. Therefore, the purchaser must typically negotiate with the sales manager, not with a sales representative.

In serving as an agent for the owner, a purchaser may often perform the following duties:

- Represent the best interest of the employer.

- Keep secret information confidential.

- Follow instructions that are within the law.

- Keep within the limits of expressed or implied authority.

A purchaser may obligate the company by his/her decisions and commitments. In other instances, it may be the purchasers themselves who are liable; this is the case, for example, when a purchaser (1) contracts without the proper authority to do so, (2) agrees to be personally responsible, (3) receives money which is due to the operation, and (4) receives money which is due to the supplier.

Guard Against the "Lowball"

The lowball is a seller who, in an effort to secure business, bids low on prices initially but expects to increase these prices at a later date. In an effort to guard against these practices, some buyers include a protection clause within each contract stating that the buyer may purchase elsewhere anything that the seller fails to supply at the available price. If the seller fails to meet the contract terms, the buyer may purchase the goods or services from other sources and hold the contracted seller responsible for paying the difference in excess of the agreed upon price.

Contracts and Bids

A contract is a binding agreement between two or more persons that specifies the obligations of each individual. A contract consists of an offer by one person and acceptance by another. Generally, a bid is an offer that is made before the acceptance that creates the contract.

In food service purchasing, a bid is usually an informal, sometimes oral, and often short-term offer. Once a seller agrees to sell products or services at a certain price and after the buyer accepts the offer, the seller can be held to the contract regardless of changes in market conditions. Buyers have responsibility to fulfill their obligations, including timely payment.

In any contract, consideration must be present. Consideration, in most contracts, consists of payment by the purchaser for the products and services that are delivered by the seller. However, consideration may be in the form of a promise to deliver or make payment on delivery.

Generally, an offer may be withdrawn before it is accepted by another. However, after acceptance, the contract becomes binding. The acceptance has to conform to the terms of the offer. For example, if the seller calls a buyer and offers a specified meat product, USDA Choice #168 inside rounds for $2.00 per pound, and the buyer responds with an order for 400 pounds, the contract is in force.

However, if in the preceding example the buyer asks the seller to lower the price to $1.90 per pound, no agreement or contract has been made. This is a counteroffer which requires acceptance by the seller. An offer must be accepted within a reasonable time if no deadline is specified. Usually, the length of time is determined by the commercial practice prevalent in trading that specific commodity or commodity group.

A contract is invalid if it is illegal or somehow induced by misrepresentation or fraud. A contract is also invalid if a mistake was made and one party had prior knowledge of the error and did not inform the other party.

A contract contains the essential elements of an agreement, which usually include the parties to the agreement, price, specifications, quantity, required delivery date, payment terms, delivery method, and any other material and essential details. A written contract is often easier to enforce than an oral agreement. Moreover, the Uniform Commercial Code §2-201 generally provides that a contract for the sale of goods for a price of $500 or more is only enforceable if in writing. An oral contract, however, is commonplace within the food industry. Buyers must be familiar with the commercial practices surrounding the classes of merchandise. Again, the purchaser should review state laws and the customary practice prevailing for that class of commodities.

The buyer must make sure that the products and services received are those that were requested. Close inspection of an incoming order is always a crucial step in the receiving process.

Warranties

There are two basic kinds of warranties: express warranties and implied warranties.[1] Express warranties are oral or written representations made by the seller to the buyer relating to the goods which become part of the basis for the sale. Implied warranties are those imposed by law on the sale unless the seller negates or limits them to the extent permitted by the law, that is, the Uniform Commercial Code (UCC).* Generally speaking, if the seller is a merchant with respect to the kind of goods being sold, a warranty that the goods shall be merchantable is implied in a contract for sale. No particular language or action is necessary to evidence those implied warranties that arise in a sale pursuant to law.

The Uniform Commercial Code sets forth in Article 2 the law of warranties as applied to transactions for the sale of "goods."**

Express Warranties. The Code describes the requirements of express warranties as follows:

> (§2-313) Express Warranties by Affirmation, Promise, Description, Sample
>
> (1) Express warranties by the seller are created as follows:
>
>   (a) Any affirmation of fact or promise made by the seller to the buyer which relates to the goods and becomes part of the basis of the bargain creates an express warranty that the goods shall conform to the affirmation or promise.
>
>   (b) Any description of the goods which is made part of the basis of the bargain creates an express warranty that the goods shall conform to the description.
>
>   (c) Any sample or model which is made part of the basis of the bargain creates an express warranty that the whole of the goods shall conform to the sample or model.
>
> (2) It is not necessary to the creation of an express warranty that the seller use formal words such as "warrant" or "guarantee" or that he have a specific intention to make a warranty, but an affirmation merely of the value of the

---

*The Uniform Commercial Code as adopted and modified in each state would govern (except in Louisiana which has not adopted this Code).

**The code defines goods as:
> all things (including specially manufactured goods) which are movable at the time of identification to the contract for sale other than the money in which the price is to be paid, investment securities (Article 8) and things in action. "Goods" also includes the unborn young of animals and growing crops and other identified things attached to realty as described in the section on goods to be severed from realty (Section 2-107).

goods or a statement purporting to be merely the seller's opinion or commendation of the goods does not create a warranty.

The whole purpose of the law of warranties is to determine what the seller has in essence agreed to sell. As Official Comment No. 3 to §2-313 of the Code states:

No specific intention to make a warranty is necessary if any of these factors is made part of the basis of the bargain. In actual practice, affirmations of fact made by the seller about the goods during a bargain are regarded as part of the description of those goods; hence no particular reliance on such statements need be shown in order to weave them into the fabric of the agreement. Rather, any fact which is to take such affirmations, once made, out of the agreement requires clear affirmative proof. The issue normally is one of fact.

Implied Warranties. As mentioned earlier, implied warranties are those that are automatically imposed by operation of law on the sale, unless the seller *expressly* negates or limits them to the extent permitted under the Uniform Commercial Code, as adopted and perhaps modified by each state (except Louisiana). There are two basic kinds of implied warranties under the Code: that the goods are merchantable and that they are fit for a particular purpose.

Implied warranty of merchantability. Section 2-314 of the Code states (in part):

§2-314. Implied Warranty: Merchantability; Usage of Trade.
(1) Unless excluded or modified (Section 2-316), a warranty that the goods shall be merchantable is implied in a contract for their sale if the seller is a merchant with respect to goods of that kind. Under this section, the serving for value of food or drink to be consumed either on the premises or elsewhere is a sale.
(2) Goods to be merchantable must be at least such as
    (a) pass without objection in the trade under the contract description; and
    (b) in the case of fungible goods, are of fair average quality within the description; and
    (c) are fit for the ordinary purposes for which such goods are used; and
    (d) run, within the variations permitted by the agreement, of even kind, quality and quantity within each unit and among all units involved; and
    (e) are adequately contained, packaged, and labeled as the agreement may require; and
    (f) conform to the promises or affirmations of fact made on the container or label if any.

Official Comment No. 13 to §2-314 states:

In an action based on breach of warranty, it is of course necessary to show not only the existence of the warranty but the fact that the warranty was broken and that the breach of the warranty was the proximate cause of the loss sustained. In such an action an affirmative showing by the seller that the loss resulted from some action or event following his own delivery of the goods can operate as a defense. Equally, evidence indicating that the seller exercised care in the manufacture, processing or selection of the goods is relevant to the issue of whether the warranty was in fact broken. Action by the buyer following an examination of the goods which ought to have indicated the defect complained of can be shown as matter bearing on whether the breach itself was the cause of the injury.

Implied warranty of fitness for a particular purpose. Another type of implied warranty that may benefit hotels as purchasers of goods from a seller with knowledge of the particular use to which the goods will be used is the implied warranty of fitness for a particular purpose. Section 2-315 states the rule with respect to this implied warranty.

§2-315. Implied Warranty: Fitness for Particular Purpose.

Where the seller at the time of contracting has reason to know any particular purpose for which the goods are required and that the buyer is relying on the seller's skill or judgment to select or furnish suitable goods, there is unless excluded or modified under the next section an implied warranty that the goods shall be fit for such purpose.

Seller's Disclaimers of Express and Implied Warranties. In many contracts the seller attempts to disclaim the existence of any express or implied warranties with respect to the goods sold. Section 2-316 of the Code deals with disclaimers of both kinds of warranties. The general purpose of §2-316 is explained by Official Comment No. 1 as follows:

1. This section is designed principally to deal with those frequent clauses in sales contracts which seek to exclude "all warranties, express or implied." It seeks to protect a buyer from unexpected and unbargained language of disclaimer by denying effect to such language when inconsistent with language of express warranty and permitting the exclusion of implied warranties only by conspicuous language or other circumstances which protect the buyer from surprise.

2. The seller is protected under this Article against false allegations of oral warranties by its provisions on parol and extrinsic evidence and against unauthorized representations by the customary "lack of authority" clauses.

As §2-316(2) makes clear, there must be rather specific language to disclaim the *implied* warranties of fitness for a particular purpose and of merchantability. Subsection 3 points out, however, that certain language, such as expressions that the goods are purchased "as is" or "with all faults," will negate any implied warranties. However, one court has held that while an "as is" clause may negate implied warranties, express warranties made by the seller continue to provide a remedy if the sold item or goods did not live up to the express warranty.[2]

As §2-316 states:

Unlike the implied warranty of merchantability, implied warranties of fitness for a particular purpose may be excluded by general language, but only if it is in writing and conspicuous.

In the Official Comments No. 8 to §2-316, Paragraph B of Subsection 3 regarding examination reads:

Application of the doctrine of "caveat emptor" in all cases where the buyer examines the goods regardless of statements made by the seller is, however,

---

Product Indemnification Insurance

What is the hotel's responsibility if a guest consumes food containing foreign substances when brought into the property? What happens if improper sanitation practices spoil food en route to the hotel and the unwholesome food is unknowingly received?

Buyers should include product indemnification insurance in their contracts. Then, if a guest incurs some personal injury through use of the product, the seller's company may be sued. The seller is obviously "out of specification," since it is reasonable to assume that all foods purchased should be fit for human consumption. The buyer has remedy through contract breach, but it is much better, if possible, to have the seller's company handle these actions directly.

---

rejected by this Article. Thus, if the offer of examination is accompanied by words as to their merchantability or specific attributes and the buyer indicates clearly that he is relying on those words rather than on his examination, they give rise to an "express" warranty. In such cases the question is one of fact as to whether a warranty of merchantability has been expressly incorporated in the agreement. Disclaimer of such an express warranty is governed by subsection (1) of the present section.

The particular buyer's skill and the normal method of examining goods in the circumstances determine what defects are excluded by the examination. A failure to notice defects which are obvious cannot excuse the buyer. However, an examination under circumstances which do not permit chemical or other testing of the goods would not exclude defects which could be ascertained only by such testing. Nor can latent defects be excluded by a simple examination. A professional buyer examining a product in his field will be held to have assumed the risk as to all defects which a professional in the field ought to observe, while a nonprofessional buyer will be held to have assumed the risk only for such defects as a layman might be expected to observe.

Questions about whether or not a hotel as buyer has a warranty should be referred to a lawyer. Often there are remedies under the law of warranties if the buyer is willing to pursue his/her rights and if the pursuit is worth the projected legal expense under the circumstances.

Remedies for Contract Breach

What should the purchaser do if the supplier fails to abide by a binding contract? From the buyer's perspective, this usually occurs if the product fails to meet specifications or when the price differs from the contract.

Disputes about whether products are "in or out" of specification start with the terms of the contract. Interpretation of a written contract will usually rest only on what is in that contract. Oral deletions or oral addenda may not be considered to modify a written contract; whenever possible, purchasers should commit agreement terms to writing.

Standard alternative remedies for contract breach are: (1) to require specific performance, (2) to rescind the agreement and seek restitution, or (3) to obtain damages. Damages are usually assessed on the basis of actual loss incurred. The buyer's actual loss is the determining factor and a major effort goes toward establishing the figure which represents compensatory damages.

Sales Law

Sales law is addressed by the Uniform Commercial Code. One specific area of sales law which buyers should understand is transportation and title. The place of delivery and method of shipment should be specified in the contract. In the absence of agreement on this point, the place of delivery is generally the seller's place of business. Selection of the transportation mode and selection of carrier influence when title passes and are, therefore, extremely important.

"FOB" (free on board) and "CIF" (cash, insurance, freight) are terms which help determine when title passes and when responsibility is assumed for the shipment. For example, "FOB Shipping Point" means that the buyer assumes title when the seller puts goods in the hands of a carrier. "FOB Destination" means that the buyer assumes title when the goods are delivered to the buyer's specified delivery point in the specified condition.

These occurrences, while traditional, can be altered by specific contract agreements. For example, the buyer can agree to an FOB shipping point price, but specify in the contract that it is the seller's responsibility to have the goods delivered at a specified time and in a specified condition. If this is a condition of the contract, the seller is responsible to file any necessary claims against the carrier.

The law of agency has an impact upon transportation responsibility. Assume that the goods are contracted FOB destination and that the buyer reserves the right to select the carrier. If the buyer then asks the seller to "ship the best way," the buyer has asked the seller to act as his/her agent. Under certain conditions, title then can pass FOB the seller's dock. The best solution is to have the terms spelled out in the contract and to perform under those terms. Exhibit 4 reviews some alternatives for FOB shipments.

CIF means that the buyer assumes title when the goods reach the buyer's dock. This is the common procedure for import/export shipments. Where these shipments require customs clearance or FDA inspection, the buyer normally takes title upon the completion of those procedures. Depending on the contract, the buyer can specify that the goods clear dock procedures and be placed into a bonded warehouse where title will pass.

The preceding factors affect title considerations. This is important since responsibility for theft, damage, loss, and spoilage usually rests with the party who has title at the time that loss occurs.

Antitrust Laws

No hospitality operator can afford to be unaware of the federal and state antitrust laws. Their reach is too broad, their enforcement too strict, and their penalties too severe to be ignored. Moreover, a hotel or motel operator can violate the antitrust laws and be subject to their penalties *without meaning to do so.*

Exhibit 4   Transportation Terms of Sale

Transportation	Point of Title Passage	Responsibility for Freight
FOB buyer's plant Freight collect Freight allowed	Buyer's plant	Seller initially, eventually buyer
FOB buyer's plant Freight collect	Buyer's plant	Buyer
FOB buyer's plant Freight prepaid	Buyer's plant	Seller
FOB seller's plant Freight prepaid	Seller's plant	Seller
FOB seller's plant Freight prepaid and charged back	Buyer's plant	Buyer
FOB seller's plant Freight collect	Seller's plant	Buyer

The general aim of the antitrust laws is simple: the regulation of business conduct to preserve competition and to prevent economic coercion. Antitrust laws are primarily concerned with limiting collusive conduct between competitors ("horizontal" agreements) and with regulating certain forms of activity between businesses that do not compete but are in a vertical relationship, as, for example, a hotel operator and its customers or suppliers.

The antitrust laws are based upon the simple assumption that vigorous but fair competition results in the most efficient allocation of economic resources and the best terms of sale to consumers.

Major Antitrust Statutes. Three major statutes comprise the bulk of federal antitrust laws: the Sherman Act of 1890,[3] the Clayton Act of 1914 and its amendments,[4] and the Federal Trade Commission Act of 1914.[5] The statutory framework of the antitrust laws is broad. In addition, many states have enacted their own antitrust laws governing activities conducted exclusively within the state and not in "interstate or foreign commerce."* Some state statutes, in fact, expand the scope of prohibited activity beyond that of the federal antitrust laws on conduct occurring within the state. Furthermore, each state has its own case law interpreting its own antitrust statutes.

Sherman Act. Section 1 of the Sherman Act is the cornerstone of our antitrust laws. It states in pertinent part:

---

*The term "interstate commerce" is a term of art in the law. Loosely speaking, "commerce" means business activity, and "interstate commerce" means business activity which moves between two or more states. However, the meaning of "interstate commerce" has, in fact, become quite broad and encompasses most business activity in the United States today. The federal antitrust laws apply to interstate commerce (and also foreign commerce, that is, commerce that moves between the United States and foreign countries).

> Every contract, combination in the form of trust or otherwise, or conspiracy, in restraint of trade or commerce among the several States, or with foreign nations, is declared to be illegal.

According to the U.S. Supreme Court, this broad statutory mandate prohibits every contract, combination, or conspiracy that constitutes an *unreasonable* restraint of trade.[6] The courts have interpreted the word "contract" broadly to mean any form of understanding. A duly executed, written agreement is not required. A wink or a nod, or even silence in the face of statements by others, may be enough for a jury to infer that an agreement in violation of antitrust laws has been reached.

In determining what restraints of trade are unreasonable, the courts apply two general types of standards: the standard of the *per se* rule and the standard of the rule of reason. Some types of restraints are deemed to be so inherently anticompetitive that they are conclusively presumed to be unreasonable. Such restraints are called *per se** violations of the antitrust laws and are absolutely forbidden regardless of the alleged justifications for, or the competitive benefits from, the particular activity.

Among the business practices that the courts have held to be *per se* violations of §1 of the Sherman Act are:

1. Horizontal or vertical agreements fixing or "tampering with" prices (for example, two or more hotel operators agreeing on the room rates they will charge their customers).

2. Horizontal agreements allocating geographic areas, customers, or products or services (for example, two hotel operators agreeing as to which conventions each hotel will bid upon while the other refrains from bidding).

3. Horizontal or vertical agreements boycotting third parties (for example, the members of a hotel association agreeing that they will establish unreasonable terms for any future memberships to block some of their competitors from joining and thereby to prevent them from gaining the competitive benefits of association membership services).

4. In certain circumstances, conditioning the purchase of one product or service on the purchase of another product or service (for example, a hotel operator saying to a customer that the customer cannot rent the grand ballroom unless he/she uses the hotel's florist to decorate it).

If a particular activity is not classified as illegal *per se*, then the second standard, a so-called *rule of reason* standard, is applied to determine whether the activity violates §1 of the Sherman Act. Under this standard, proof that the party engaged in a particular activity is not itself proof of a violation of the antitrust laws. Rather, the court examines the various facts and circumstances surrounding the

---

*The term *per se* is derived from the Latin meaning "by itself" and denotes that proof of the alleged conduct alone proves the violation—no defense of the reasonableness or propriety of the conduct under the circumstances will be considered by the courts in determining whether a violation of law has occurred. *Northern Pacific Ry. Co. v. United States*, 356 U.S. 1, 5 (1958).

party's actions and decides whether the party *intended* to restrain trade unreasonably or whether, regardless of intent, its conduct had the *effect* of unreasonably restraining trade.

An agreement not to compete following the sale of a business is an example of the types of business arrangements commonly judged by the rule of reason standard. However, any agreement with a competitor or customer that affects the production, distribution, or sale of a product or service and which is not governed by the *per se* standard is potentially subject to examination under the rule of reason standard.

In summary, it can be said as an immutable principle that agreements with competitors to fix or tamper with prices or other terms of sale, or to allocate territories or customers, or to refuse to deal with others are unlawful. Other agreements among two or more hotels that affect the furnishing or sale of a service may be found unlawful under the circumstances. Therefore, before any action is taken to enter into or to implement such an agreement, the plan should first be submitted for analysis by legal counsel.

Clayton Act. The present Clayton Act contains the original Clayton Act and several amendments to the original Act, including the Robinson-Patman Act of 1936 and the Celler-Kefauver Amendment of 1950. The Clayton Act more precisely describes certain types of prohibited business activity than does the Sherman Act. However, it is still necessary to examine the case law in order to determine whether certain conduct falls within the Clayton Act's statutory proscriptions.

Federal Trade Commission Act. Section 5 of the Federal Trade Commission Act empowers the Federal Trade Commission (FTC) to enjoin "[u]nfair methods of competition ... and unfair or deceptive acts or practices...."[7] Under this statutory mandate, the FTC is empowered to attack anticompetitive practices that violate the Sherman and Clayton Acts and to attack practices that, while not Sherman or Clayton Act violations, nonetheless constitute unfair methods of competition. Under §5, the FTC also has a consumer protection mandate from the U.S. Congress. Under this mandate, the FTC has attacked misrepresentations in advertising and other sales or marketing practices that it judged to be deceptive to the consumer.

Relations with Suppliers

Hotel and motel operators and their purchasing staffs should not collectively determine whether or not they will deal with certain suppliers or customers. Following are several types of agreements which a hotel or motel operation, even though it acts individually and not after consultation with a competitor, should not enter into with its suppliers or customers. A hotel or motel operation generally has the right to select its suppliers and customers and to decline to deal with anyone that it does not want as a supplier or customer. However, such decisions should never be based on the willingness of the supplier or customer to enter into certain arrangements. For example:

- A hotel or motel operator should not restrict a supplier's right to determine individually the prices of its products to others.

- A hotel or motel operator should not require a supplier or customer to deal exclusively with it generally or within a certain geographical area unless the arrangement has been submitted for prior review by legal counsel and has met with counsel's approval after a full analysis of the circumstances.

The Robinson-Patman Act is of primary concern to purchasers. This Act makes it unlawful to sell the same products to competing customers at different prices if their requirements are essentially the same. On the other side, a purchaser may not induce a lower price than that offered to like buyers. While the buyer is not expected to know the competitor's prices (that raises other legal issues) if he/she knowingly induces and accepts a lower price, the purchaser is equally at risk with the seller.

Advertising allowances and brokerage are particularly scrutinized by antitrust law since they have been frequently abused. It is unlawful to use either as a basis for price discrimination. Advertising allowances must be offered portionally to equal buyers.

Endnotes

1. The sections on warranties and antitrust laws are adapted from: Jack P. Jefferies, *Understanding Hospitality Law*, 3d ed. (East Lansing, Mich.: Educational Institute of the American Hotel and Motel Association, 1995).

2. *Limited Flying Club, Inc.* v. *Wood*, 632 F. 2d 51 (8th Cir. 1980).

3. 15 U.S.C. §§1–7 (1976).

4. 15 U.S.C. §§12–27 (1976). The several amendments to the Clayton Act include the Robinson-Patman Act of 1936, 15 U.S.C. §§13, 13a, 13b, 21a, the Celler-Kefauver Amendment of 1950 (§7 of the Clayton Act), 15 U.S.C. §18, the Antitrust Procedures and Penalties Act of 1974, 15 U.S.C. §16(b)–(h), and the Antitrust Improvements Act of 1976. 15 U.S.C. §§15(c)–(h), 18(a)66.

5. 15 U.S.C. §§41–58.

6. *Standard Oil Co.* v. *United States*, 221 U.S. 1 (1911). The distinction between "reasonable" and "unreasonable" restraints of trade has great practical importance. Otherwise, any business contract by which one party agrees to do something for another could be found to be a "contract in restraint of trade" since it may keep the participants from agreeing to do the same thing or something else with some other party.

7. U.S.C. §45(a)(1976).

REVIEW QUIZ

When you feel you have covered all of the material in this chapter, answer these questions. Choose the *best* answer. Check your answers with the correct ones found on the Review Quiz Answer Key at the end of this book.

True (T) or False (F)

(T) F   1. While a hospitality company may place an upper limit on the value of gifts which can be accepted, the best policy for a purchasing agent is to reject any gift, no matter how small its value.

(T) F   2. In order to maintain control and give as little as possible during negotiations, the purchaser should attempt to have the supplier make the first concession.

(T) F   3. Suppliers should be promptly notified upon acceptance or rejection of bids.

T   (F)   4. According to general principles of contract law, an offer may be withdrawn by a seller after it has been accepted by the purchaser.

(T) F   5. CIF (cash, insurance, freight) means the buyer assumes title when goods reach the buyer's dock.

T   (F)   6. A contract for goods over $500 is generally enforceable under the Uniform Commercial Code even if it isn't in writing.

(T) F   7. A hospitality operation may be affected by state antitrust laws as well as federal ones.

Multiple Choice

8. From a buyer's perspective, a supplier fails to abide by a binding contract when:

   a. the delivered price differs from the contract.
   b. the supplier rescinds an offer before acceptance.
   c. products fail to meet specifications.
   (d.) a and c.

9. Which of the following is most clearly associated with antitrust laws?

   a. The Uniform Commercial Code
   b. Law of Agency
   (c.) The Robinson-Patman Act
   d. Breach of Contract

10. An _____ warranty is automatically imposed by operation of law on the sale unless the seller expressly negates or limits it in advance.

    a. express
    b. unlimited
    c. oral
    (d.) implied

11.   FOB shipping point means that the buyer assumes title when:

    a.   the seller puts the goods in the hands of the carrier.
    b.   the goods reach the seller's dock.
    c.   the goods reach the buyer's dock.
    d.   the goods are delivered to the buyer's specified delivery point.

Chapter Outline

Learning Objectives

1. Explain how purchasing needs are determined.

2. Describe the relationship between quality and value.

3. List some ways in which quality may be measured.

4. Describe specifications, focusing on their development.

5. Summarize the disadvantages of ordering the wrong quantity.

6. Explain the ordering systems used for perishable and non-perishable items.

5

Quality and Quantity Concerns

FOR ORGANIZATIONAL SUCCESS and guest satisfaction, the hospitality purchaser strives to obtain required products of the right quality and in the correct quantity. In this case, "right" refers to specific quality requirements set forth for every item purchased, usually dictated by the menu and intended use. Buying in the correct quantity can have far-reaching effects in terms of product costs, operational profits, shelf life, and storage capacity. The strong influence that quality and quantity concerns exert on purchasing decisions will be explored throughout this chapter.

Determining Purchasing Needs

Responsibility for determining the specific items and quantities to be purchased rests with the operating department which uses the product. Within a hotel, the departments typically include rooms, engineering, sales, finance, and food and beverage.

The menu primarily determines what items must be purchased by the food and beverage department (see Exhibit 1). Standard recipes should be developed to yield menu items which meet the quality requirements set by the hospitality property. While the menu forms the basis of purchasing needs, several other factors should also be considered: (1) current inventory in the storeroom; (2) level of preparation required; and (3) coordination of efforts between departments.

When menus change, items once needed to fulfill menu demands may be left in storage indefinitely. Perhaps sales for a particular item are lower than anticipated, resulting in excess stock and less storage space for other needs. Efficiency in menu planning requires anticipation of the property's quantity reserves as well as its current requirements. Effective use of reserve supplies should not be overlooked when menus change.

The use of fully or partially prepared foods is another factor in menu planning. The hospitality property decides to what extent menu items are prepared on-site or are purchased in convenience form. If items are prepared on-site, standard recipes indicating all necessary ingredients are required. Practically all ingredients are supplied when purchasing convenience foods, which require fewer items in storage and pose a different set of storage needs. Some hospitality operators use convenience food recipes in combination with additional seasonings, garnishes, sauces, or other items in order to make them unique to their property.

Exhibit 1   Factors Determining Required Products

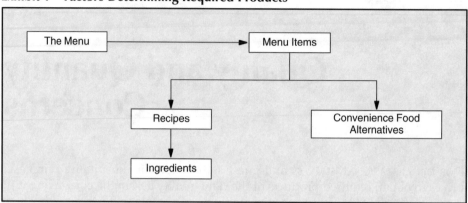

Coordination between departments is necessary for efficient menu planning. Sometimes, the best purchasing procedures are undermined by inadequate receiving practices. Since storage activities can affect product quality, interaction with storeroom employees is a must. Good coordination and communication skills significantly influence the menu-planning process.

The food and beverage manager and staff need to solicit information and opinions from other departments as a menu-planning activity. For example, the marketing/sales department can offer valuable comments about the needs and desires of the target markets. The food and beverage department maintains historical records reflecting past preferences of guests. Another source of feedback, whenever appropriate, comes from surveying the guests.

In determining menu requirements, coordination between purchasing and the food and beverage department is beneficial for several reasons. Alternative products can be discussed among personnel in these two departments. Samples and trial orders can be arranged and evaluated for suitability. Tentative specifications can be developed, critiqued, and improved before use. Suppliers can then be apprised of final versions of specifications and other pertinent information.

As you can see, the hospitality purchaser must have a thorough awareness of menu requirements in order to effectively determine purchasing needs for the property. Menus determine the products' intended uses and proper functions.

Purchasing the "Right" Quality

Guests define quality in terms of their personal sensory responses of sight, taste, smell, and feel. Operators further refine that definition by adding in such factors as portion size, menu requirements, and yield. Quality then can be considered in terms of a product's suitability in fulfilling its function or intended purpose.

A product of the appropriate quality serves its intended purpose better than any other product available. For instance, if chicken is intended for breading and deep-frying, skin tears may be quite acceptable. However, if the chicken is to be

Use the "A B C" Approach

Food service operations may use hundreds of food and beverage products. Therefore, it may not be practical to develop specifications for each of these items. Where should the purchaser concerned about developing specifications start? The concept of "A B C analysis" suggests that most of a property's purchase dollars are used to purchase a relatively small number of the total items needed. Therefore, a priority should be given to the development of purchase specifications for those few "A" items which represent the most significant cost to the operator. Other items for specification development include those which are purchased in large volumes, those which appear to be available in inconsistent qualities, those which are used for signature ("specialty") items prepared by the property, and those for which the food service operation has experienced other purchasing problems.

A time schedule for development of purchase specifications is important. To do it "when time permits" or "when one gets around to it" is not satisfactory. Rather, a time limit is required such as one specification per week, all "A" specifications to be developed within six months, etc.

oven-roasted for presentation without a sauce, a higher quality of chicken may be required. In another example, if the intended product is tomato purée, canned tomatoes are probably more cost-effective than purchasing whole tomatoes with perfect color, consistent shape, and premium size.

Quality assurance literature offers additional dimensions to the concept of quality. In this context, quality refers to "the consistent delivery of products and services according to expected standards."[1] It is up to each property to establish its own individual standards according to the types of guests (guest profiles) attracted to the property as well as the services provided. Standards make quality determinations possible by defining and measuring the level of performance required by the hospitality operation.

Value

Simply stated, value refers to the relationship between quality and price. Hospitality guests expect a consistent level of quality that meets their personal expectations of value. Initial and subsequent visits to the property are based upon the guest's perception of value. If the total experience (including food service, accommodations, and cleanliness) is judged to be worth what was spent, the guest has received a good value.

Professional buyers recognize that more than just a physical product is purchased from suppliers. Other important factors contributing to product price are quality of the goods received and level of service (timely delivery and prompt response). Information and technical ability represent two additional considerations. These factors all influence the purchaser as he/she considers whether value was received for the purchase dollars expended.

Some purchasers are concerned about quality as a standard of excellence. They purchase products of the highest quality regardless of cost. Typically, high-check average properties require high quality products whose costs are passed to guests in the form of increased charges. By contrast, cost-conscious buyers are more concerned with low cost than quality. Ideally, most buyers are value-conscious. They consider product quality relative to price.

As quality and price relationships change, perceived value also changes. For example, if product quality remains constant as the price increases, value from the buyer's perspective diminishes; if quality improves as the price remains constant, value increases. The reverse of each case is also true.

As purchase decisions are made, professional buyers focus on value as well as quality. They recognize that high quality at a low cost (excluding supplier services, technical ability and knowledge, and credit arrangements) may not necessarily be a "good deal."

Measuring Quality

Quality is measured in any number of ways, many unique to the commodity they pertain to. The typical means of describing quality are by brands, grades/standards, and fully developed specifications. In some cases, a brand or standard may itself constitute the specification.

Brands. One common method of describing quality involves the use of a brand or trade name. For example, if a purchaser requests a particular brand of canned food or grocery item, the quality is represented by that brand. Branded items have stood the test of consumer acceptance, while affording the hospitality operator a high level of consistency and reliability.

One disadvantage of this method, however, is that brand name purchases can limit the number of suppliers and distributors available to the buyer. The advantage of competitive prices between suppliers may be lost since many manufacturers assign exclusive territories to distributors in designated areas. If branded products are desired, the best option may be to select several brands of comparable quality to offer for competitive bids.

Grades and Standards. Industry and/or federal grades and standards are another way to describe the quality of certain products. Unfortunately, they are not available for every product and may be incomplete in specific details.

A purchaser requesting "#136 ground beef" has indicated specific requirements for that beef product according to USDA Institutional Meat Purchase Specification (IMPS) #136. This description presents a detailed quality standard which is well-known and understood throughout the industry, covering raw material source, grinding procedure, and fat content. It does not include statements on minimum bacterial counts, product state (fresh or frozen), packaging, and other user requirements.

In another case, an IMPS #180 strip loin describes a boneless short loin with certain trim requirements, but does not specify federal grade (USDA Prime, USDA Choice, etc.). The purchaser must specify grade and any other requirements, such as special trim, age, and packaging.

Purchase Specifications and Standardization

Use of purchase specifications helps to standardize purchasing, production, and service systems. This is good for the hospitality operation, its employees, and the guests it serves. Use of a purchase specification provides a standard quality definition for products purchased. It represents the products required for standard recipes and which are perceived to provide optimal value for the guests being served. Use of specifications, then, helps to ensure consistent product quality regardless of the source of purchases. Both the property and the guests desire consistent quality. Properly developed and utilized purchase specifications help to ensure that there are no surprises. Everyone benefits from their use.

Industry and/or federal grades and standards should always be used when available, even though additions or modifications will probably be required. When these standards are coupled with brand products, the average hospitality operator can adequately describe the quality desired in terms of a specification. On occasion, it becomes necessary to develop specifications independently of these two sources.

Specifications. The process of developing purchase specifications often begins with prevailing industry practices. Specifications generally apply to imported or manufactured products. For example, sizing and packaging is fairly consistent for imported lobster tails, but the operator may prefer the product from one country over another. In this case, the quality specification may be the country of origin.

Specifications offer several distinct advantages:

- In developing purchase specifications, hospitality personnel gain a better understanding of requirements and quality standards.

- Receiving personnel can check incoming products against the quality requirements noted in the property's specifications.

- Specifications may reduce the variety of products purchased and managed. The research involved in developing specifications may suggest additional ways to use the same product in different menu items.

- Specifications can lower purchase costs, since the operation will not be paying extra for a product of higher quality than needed.

- Generic purchase specifications enable several suppliers to quote competitive prices, thus increasing the level of competition.

In addition to the advantages just listed, specifications have several drawbacks as well. Their development involves time and effort, thus increasing the duties of purchasing staff and operating personnel. They also require updating as the needs of the property change.

Special formulas may be specified, but quantity requirements demanded by manufacturers put this option beyond the reach of most operators. At a minimum, operators should develop purchase specifications for the 20% of items that represent

80% of dollar costs. In most cases, all three sources described will be used, often in combination.

A Closer Look at Purchase Specifications

Exhibit 2 gives a possible format for purchase specifications, which indicates the categories of information often included. Of particular importance is product use and test procedures.

Regardless of the product for which quality standards are being developed, several minimum requirements must be addressed in every specification. These requirements dictate that:

- An accurate quality description of the product should focus on easily observable, testable features.

- A quality description should be realistic. When specifications allow little or no deviation or allowance for slight differences between desired and acceptable products, the likely result will be higher prices. Overly strict specifications limit the number of suppliers who can provide items and may even make it impossible to purchase necessary items. For example, when a 6-ounce strip steak is specified with no tare allowance (range of acceptable weight), few suppliers will be interested and the cost per pound will be significantly greater than if a small allowance (perhaps $1/2$ ounce) is permitted.

- Descriptions should be clear and simple. Excessive detail is neither practical nor helpful for the majority of purchasers and/or suppliers.

- Specifications should permit purchase of readily available products in most instances. Costs rise dramatically and minimum purchase volumes are significant when products must be prefabricated for the specific organization.

- Supply from more than one vendor should be possible. Costs are reduced when several suppliers are able to provide product needs.

- There should be flexibility for both the buyer and the seller. The key here relates to practicality and reasonableness. Specifications which are too tight or inflexible will defeat their intended purpose.

Some general information is required for all orders placed with suppliers, but should *not* be included in purchase specifications. Examples include: general delivery instructions, personnel authorized to purchase/receive products, quantity needed, agreed-upon purchase price, and purchase unit size. The purchaser's concern is minimizing the need to modify purchase specifications; quantity and purchase price often change from order to order.

Suppliers should understand the intended use of the product. As experts in their own product lines, they may suggest product alternatives which are more suited to the property. The purchaser should also check the qualifications of eligible suppliers in order to judge their expertise in a given area.

When product test procedures are indicated, quality requirements can clearly be verified. Test information makes it possible to identify substandard products.

Exhibit 2   Purchase Specification Format

(name of food and beverage operation)

1. Product name: _____

2. Product used for:

> Clearly indicate product use (such as olive garnish for beverage, hamburger patty for grill frying for sandwich, etc.)

3. Product general description:

> Provide general quality information about desired product. For example, "iceberg lettuce; heads to be green, firm without spoilage, excessive dirt or damage. No more than 10 outer leaves; packed 24 heads per case."

4. Detailed description:

> Purchaser should state other factors which help to clearly identify desired product. Examples of specific factors, which vary by product being described, may include:
>
> - Geographic origin
> - Variety
> - Type
> - Style
> - Grade
> - Product size
> - Portion size
> - Brand name
> - Density
> - Medium of pack
> - Specific gravity
> - Container size
> - Edible yield, trim

5. Product test procedures:

> Test procedures occur at time product is received and as/after product is prepared/used. Thus, for example, products to be at a refrigerated temperature upon delivery can be tested with a thermometer. Portion-cut meat patties can be randomly weighed. Lettuce packed 24 heads per case can be counted.

6. Special instructions and requirements:

> Any additional information needed to clearly indicate quality expectations can be included here. Examples include bidding procedures, if applicable, labeling and/or packaging requirements and special delivery and service requirements.

Test procedures will also notify suppliers about the objective (measurable) procedures being used.

Note the extensive detail in the purchase specification shown in Exhibit 3. This federal government specification, while containing requirements not easily verified

Exhibit 3   Sample Specification

Item No. 136—Ground Beef, Regular

Material

Regular ground beef may be prepared from any beef (graded or ungraded) including trimmings. Meat from the head, tongue, heart, or esophagus, or straight (added) fat is not acceptable. Meat with dark discoloration, all bones, cartilage, backstrap, exposed large blood vessels, heavy connective tissue, and the prescapular, popliteal, and prefemoral lymph glands shall be removed. The thick tendinous ends of shanks shall be removed by cutting back until a cross-sectional cut shows at least 75 percent lean.

Processing

After being prepared as described above, the boneless meat shall be ground at least once through a plate having holes no larger than $3/4$ inch in diameter (or it may be otherwise reduced in size provided the texture and appearance of the product after final grinding is typical of ground beef prepared by grinding only). Final grinding shall be through a plate having holes $1/8$ inch in diameter.

The meat shall be thoroughly blended prior to and subsequent to each reduction in size except that the ground beef shall not be mixed after the final grinding.

The boneless meat shall not exceed 50°F during grinding and packaging. The ground beef shall be packaged in the amount specified by the purchaser and packed immediately upon completion of grinding.

Fat Content

The visual fat content of the boneless meat, determined prior to grinding, shall not exceed 25 percent.

However, if specified, for product to be delivered frozen, the fat content of the finished product shall be determined by chemical analysis. In such cases, compliance shall be based on the analyses of 4 samples of finished product from a lot. (A lot shall be not more than the amount of product produced in a single workshift.) Analyses shall be performed in an AMS laboratory in accordance with the Official Methods of Analyses of the Association of Official Analytical Chemists. Product shall be rejected (1) if the fat content analysis of one or more of the individual 4 sample units is more than 30.0 percent and/or (2) if the arithmetic average of the fat content analyses of the 4 individual sample units exceeds 25.00 percent. When chemical analysis is specified, the ground beef shall be produced a sufficient number of days prior to shipping to permit receipt of the fat content analysis results.

Withdrawing Samples for Chemical Analysis

The grader shall randomly select four filled shipping containers from each lot. From each container he shall select (1) either one unit of bulk ground beef from which he shall cut three adjacent approximately 1-pound samples, or (2) 12 adjacent patties which shall be divided into 3 samples of 4 adjacent patties each. Each of the three samples shall be placed in an individual container that will prevent loss or gain of moisture or contamination. The three samples from each individual unit shall be assigned the same identification number and one sample from each individual unit shall be submitted to an AMS laboratory for fat content analysis; one sample from each unit shall be solidly frozen and retained by the grader as a reserve sample; the remaining sample from each unit shall be offered to the contractor. The reserve samples shall be used for analysis (1) when the original is lost, or (2) if requested by the purchaser or the contractor. When reserve samples are analyzed, all four samples shall be analyzed. Unused reserve samples shall be returned to the contractor after final acceptance or rejection of the involved product.

After withdrawal of samples, the contractor shall make correct fills of the boxes sampled by adding the necessary ground beef produced from the same lot.

Source: U.S. Department of Agriculture, Agricultural Marketing Service, *Institutional Meat Purchase Specifications for Fresh Beef Approved by USDA* (Washington, D.C.: U.S. Government Printing Office, January, 1975), pp. 6–7.

by a unit purchaser, outlines the requirements to be considered by an inspector during preparation and processing of an item. An operator is able to communicate requirements for raw material, grinding, and fat content merely by specifying USDA #136 ground beef. In addition to this basic specification, the operator must specify bacterial count limits, packaging, and any other unique features.

Developing Purchase Specifications

Purchase specifications are developed through the efforts of several departments, staff, and other individuals. Let's consider three groups in particular: food and beverage personnel; purchasing staff; and suppliers.

Food and Beverage Personnel. The food and beverage department must make the final decisions regarding purchase specifications for the products the department uses. The responsibility of menu planning rests with this department; specifically, with the food service manager. Since the menu determines required items as well as intended use, specifications need only be developed for those designated items.

This department may suggest suppliers. Staff members have a wealth of information from trade journals, trade shows, and contacts in other properties. Their feedback can suggest suppliers who can then provide appropriate information for developing specifications.

Food and beverage personnel also evaluate and test items received under tentative purchase specifications. The expertise of the food service staff is invaluable in measuring the adequacy of specifications, from the perspective of both operations and guest satisfaction.

Purchasing Staff. The responsibility of the purchasing staff is to obtain information and provide assistance—not to make the final decisions. For example, purchasers question suppliers, study applicable product data, conduct make-or-buy analyses, and research topics suggested by the food service manager.

Purchasing staff arrange for sample/trial orders. Through use of tentative specifications, they obtain sample products for analysis and selection by food and beverage personnel. Purchasers can evaluate initial shipments of these samples and check to see that incoming products meet specifications. Exhibit 4 provides a data sheet which may be used to evaluate food samples.

Purchasers also provide advice about specifications. Their experience in developing specifications, working with eligible suppliers, and evaluating product samples is of invaluable assistance to line managers.

Suppliers. Suppliers are not directly responsible for developing specifications. They do, however, provide information and assist the hospitality operation in this process. In general, suppliers may:

- Inform properties about available products.
- Offer advice on activities and attitudes of other properties toward various products.
- Counsel buyers regarding new products about to be introduced. Supplier representatives often learn about new products before operators and purchasers do.

Exhibit 4   Food Sample Data Sheet

1. Product: _____

2. Brand Name: _____

3. Presented By: _____   Date: _____

4. Varieties Available: _____

5. Shelf Life: (Frozen) _____ (Thawed, Refrigerated, Dry) _____

6. Preparation and Sanitation Considerations: _____

   _____

   _____

   _____

7. Menu Suggestions: _____

8. Merchandising Aids Available (Poster, Table Tents, etc.): _____

9. Case Size (Number of Portions): _____

10. Portion Size: _____

11. Distributed By: _____

12. Minimum Order: _____

13. Any Additional Ordering Information: _____

    _____

14. Lead Time: _____

15. Approximate Price Per Serving: _____

NOTE: Were the following information sheets received with products?

    a. Nutritional and Ingredient Analysis: Yes _____   No _____

    b. Specification Sheet: Yes _____   No _____

- Review and critique proposed specifications. Suppliers may evaluate whether a product defined by the specification is useful. Whenever practical, specifications should apply to products offered from more than one supplier.

Specifications for Current Products

When a product is in current use, the food service manager and purchaser are probably both familiar with it and are able to judge its suitability. They recognize the required characteristics and are able to identify which product meets minimum quality standards. Exhibit 5 shows the basic steps required to develop specifications for current products.

Exhibit 5   Developing a Specification for a Current Product

Step 1	Select a sample judged to be of proper quality
Step 2	Ask the supplier providing the product to describe it (size, grade, etc.)
Step 3	Write a specification using information described in this chapter
Step 4	Ask other eligible suppliers to criticize the tentative specification:
	• Does it describe the correct quality?
	• Is it available from several sources?
Step 5	Modify the written description as necessary
Step 6	*Use* the specification

Exhibit 6   Developing a Specification for a New Product

Step 1	Give a verbal description of product need to reputable suppliers; *stress* its use
Step 2	Analyze samples which are provided
Step 3	Select product of correct quality
Step 4	Ask supplier providing the product to describe it
Step 5	Write a specification using information described in this chapter
Step 6	Ask other suppliers to criticize the specification
Step 7	Modify the specification as necessary
Step 8	*Use* the specification

After the specification is developed, purchasers should submit copies to eligible suppliers, indicating that price quotations should be based on the quality descriptions defined by the specification. Contracts should state the possible remedies available to the property upon receiving substandard products or performance.

Specifications for New Products

Exhibit 6 outlines the process which can be used to establish specifications for new products. Many governmental and trade references can also provide assistance. Based upon this information, several suppliers should be able to provide samples which may accommodate the purchaser's needs.

Specifications in Cooperative Purchasing Systems

The incidence of centralized (pool, group, or cooperative) purchasing systems is increasing in many segments of the hospitality industry. By combining orders from many properties, buyers can take advantage of volume purchase discounts. Such a system, however, should be established and operated under the guidance of legal counsel to ensure that the federal and state antitrust laws are not violated.

Participating purchasers must agree on minimum quality requirements for items to be purchased. Frequently, developing specifications acceptable to all concerned parties is one of the most time-consuming aspects to implementing a

---

Specifications for Small Properties

Are purchase specifications practical for small properties in which the manager must perform a wide variety of tasks in addition to purchasing? Yes, with slight modification of the development process, they can be just as helpful for the small property as they are for the large organization.

Many of the techniques suggested throughout this chapter are relevant to the small organization. For example, it is possible to write brief statements to describe the most important quality factors. Soliciting help from suppliers can also be time-efficient and beneficial. Likewise, placing a priority on the relatively few "A" items will help ensure that attention is given to the most important products being purchased. As this is done, time is made available for managing the many other concerns which confront operators of small food service organizations.

---

centralized purchasing system. In fact, if standardized specifications cannot be agreed upon, it is difficult to continue with the planning necessary to develop a centralized system.

A committee approach is frequently used in developing specifications. Wide differences in specifications must generally be minimized in order to take advantage of volume discounts. This usually entails some compromise on specifications by individual members of the buying cooperative.

Participation in centralized purchasing is typically not an either/or decision. It is possible to purchase some items through the cooperative system and purchase others on an independent basis, though cost advantages to centralized purchasing are decreased when this mixed approach is used.

Specifications for Specific Products

We have indicated some general factors to consider in developing specifications. Exhibit 7 reviews specific concerns addressed in the development of purchase specifications for various products required by hospitality operations. As a specification is developed, this information might best be used by considering whether each factor is both necessary and important. If so, the purchaser should incorporate information addressing that concern in the specification.

Purchasing the "Right" Quantity

The quantity of items purchased is just as important as proper quality specifications. Problems occur when too much of a product is ordered. Money is unnecessarily tied up in inventory which may result in cash flow problems. Over-purchasing increases storage costs, including interest, insurance, and rented storage space. Products can deteriorate in quality with time and are more likely to be damaged by overcrowding. The chance of theft and pilferage increases when extra quantities are stocked.

Exhibit 7 Purchase Specification Factors: Specific Products

Meats

- Inspection (mandatory)
- Grading (if desired)
- IMPS/Meat Buyers Guide descriptions
- Weight/thickness limitations
- Fat limitations
- Aging of product (when needed)
- State of refrigeration
- Miscellaneous (packaging, etc.)

Seafoods

- Type (finfish or shellfish)
- Market form (finfish—whole, eviscerated, etc.; shellfish—alive, whole, shucked, etc.)
- Condition (describe flesh, eyes, skin, gills, etc.)
- Grade (if desired and available)
- Inspection (if available)
- Place of origin (if necessary)
- State of refrigeration
- Miscellaneous (count, sizing, packaging)

Poultry

- Kind (chicken, turkey, duck, goose)
- Class (broiler, hen)

- Grading (if desired)
- Inspection (mandatory)
- Style (whole, breasts, breasts w/ribs, etc.)
- Size (weight limitations)
- State of refrigeration
- Miscellaneous (packaging, etc.)

Fresh Fruits and Vegetables

- Grade (if desired)
- Variety
- Size
- Type of container
- Weight per container
- Count per container
- Growing area

Processed Fruits and Vegetables

- Grade (if desired)
- Variety
- Drained weight or count per case
- Weight per case
- Packing medium
- Can/package size
- Variety and/or style
- Growing area (only if necessary)

Purchasing insufficient quantities also has disadvantages. The possibility always exists for stockouts and dissatisfied customers. Production scheduling and other operating problems may result from last-minute changes. Emergency and rush orders are frequently expensive and time-consuming. Small quantity purchasing reduces the opportunity for discounts from volume purchases.

Purchasing the proper quantity of products depends upon several factors. As sales of menu items increase, additional quantities of required ingredients are needed. Higher product costs caused by changes in market conditions may result in increased selling prices which, in turn, may lead to decreased sales levels to guests. In this case, the need for continued purchase of the product should be evaluated. (Obviously, a steak house must buy steak, even as costs increase; by contrast, other properties may discontinue or de-emphasize steak, which influences the quantity needs and cost trends.)

Management may also make judgments based on future prices. When prices are expected to change, managers may respond by buying more or less of a product.

This type of speculative purchasing is based upon information provided by the purchaser, but is the responsibility of management.

Maintaining a safety or minimum level of product on hand may require buying a quantity above that actually needed. The purpose of overstocking is to allow for delivery delays, increased popularity (runs) of items, or other unexpected developments. On the other hand, if large amounts of products are already in storage, the quantities purchased can be reduced. Available space may also limit quantities purchased.

Suppliers may specify minimum dollar and/or poundage requirements for delivery. Some suppliers will not break cases, bags, or other packing containers to meet smaller purchase quantities. Buyers may need to purchase less than optimal quantities when standard unit packaging affects quantity decisions.

In order to obtain a contract, some suppliers may make concessions and ship "less than minimum" quantities. In addition, they may agree to restock if the volume of merchandise purchased is great. These are both negotiating considerations.

Purchasing Perishable and Non-Perishable Items

Products may be purchased for immediate use and for use over an extended time period. Extremely perishable items such as fresh produce, baked goods, and dairy products must be used immediately. Examples of products which may be stored in inventory for longer periods include frozen products, canned goods, and liquor.

Perishable Products

Perishable products are normally ordered several times weekly according to the following formula:

$$\frac{\text{Purchase}}{\text{Quantity}} = \frac{\text{Quantity}}{\text{Needed}} - \frac{\text{Quantity}}{\text{Available}}$$

A system for determining the quantity of perishable products to purchase can include the following steps:

1. Determine normal usage rates. For example, in a normal two-day purchasing period, the operation typically purchases a specific amount of selected items: pounds of fresh meat, fresh poultry fryers, cases of lettuce, and other perishable products.

2. Consider whether additional quantities are needed for special catered events.

3. Determine the amount of each item currently in inventory.

4. Deduct that amount from the normal usage rate to calculate the quantity to purchase.

5. Make adjustments as necessary for holidays, special events, or other factors unique to the order period.

When purchasing items for immediate use, it is helpful to use a form such as the one illustrated in Exhibit 8:

Exhibit 8 Perishable Product Quotation/Call Sheet

Item	Amount			Supplier		
	Needed	On Hand	Order	A & B Co.	Green Produce	Local Supplier
1	2	3	4	5	6	7
Spinach	6 cs	2 1/2 cs	4 cs	22^{00}/cs = $88.00	14^{85}/cs = $59.40	21^{70}/cs = $86.80
Ice. Lettuce	8 cs	1 cs	7 cs	17^{00}/cs = $119.00	16^{75}/cs = $117.25	18^{10}/cs = $126.70
Carrots	3-20#	20#	2-20#	14^{70}/bag = $29.40	13^{90}/bag = $27.80	13^{80}/bag = $27.60
Tomatoes	2 lugs	1/2 lug	2 lugs	18^{60}/lug = $37.20	18^{00}/lug = $36.00	18^{10}/lug = $36.20
			Totals	$861.40	$799.25	$842.15

- Perishable items are listed in column 1.
- The quantity of each item needed for the time covered by the order is recorded in column 2.
- The inventory amount noted in column 3 is determined by an actual physical count of the quantity available.
- Subtracting the quantity on hand (column 3) from the amount needed (column 2) yields the amount to order (column 4). In the first example, only $3 1/2$ cases of spinach are needed (6 cases $-$ $2 1/2$ cases $=$ $3 1/2$ cases), but four cases should be purchased if suppliers will not break cases or if the increased price for breaking a case is excessive.
- Examples of prices quoted by eligible suppliers are listed in columns 5 through 7. In this example, each supplier has copies of the quality specifications developed by the hospitality operation on which to base prices for each item. The buyer can either select the supplier with the lowest total price for every product required or can use several suppliers depending on who has the lowest price item by item. (Minimum delivery requirements and costs to receive, process, and write checks for separate purchases may limit this option.)

Minimum/Maximum Ordering System

In order to determine the quantity of non-perishable products to purchase, a minimum/maximum system of inventory management can be used. This system is based on the fact that only a few of all products purchased represent high-cost items or ones with a high frequency of use. For example, 80% of an operation's purchase dollars may be spent on only 20% of all the products it buys. The development of a minimum/maximum ordering system should give first priority to these high-cost items.

Basically, the minimum/maximum inventory system helps managers determine when products must be purchased and how much of each product to order. The minimum level is the safety level—the number of purchase units that must always remain in inventory. The maximum level is the greatest number of purchase units permitted in storage.

The most important factor for determining when more purchase units should be ordered is the rate at which they are used by the operation. The usage rate is the number of purchase units used per order period. For example, if ten cases (60 cans) of green peas are normally used between deliveries, this quantity represents the usage rate for green peas.

In addition to usage rates, managers must also determine a lead time quantity for each purchase item. This is the number of purchase units typically withdrawn from inventory between the time the order is placed and when it is delivered. Again, quantities are counted in terms of normal size shipping containers. For example, if two cases of green peas are used between ordering and receiving, the lead time is two cases. This lead time quantity is distinct from the safety (minimum) level of purchase units kept in inventory. The safety level must allow for such things as late deliveries and greater than normal usage.

The order point is the number of purchase units in stock when an order is placed. The order point is reached when the number of purchase units in inventory equals the lead time quantity plus the minimum safety level. Additional quantities of a product are ordered when the quantity available reaches the order point.

$$\begin{array}{c}\text{Purchase units} \\ \text{at order point}\end{array} = \begin{array}{c}\text{Purchase units in} \\ \text{lead time}\end{array} + \begin{array}{c}\text{Purchase units in} \\ \text{safety level}\end{array}$$

The above formula means that if products are ordered at the order point, the quantity in inventory will be reduced to the safety (minimum) level by the time products are received. When the order arrives, the inventory levels for the product will again be brought back to the maximum level. The maximum number of purchase units permitted in storage will be the usage rate plus the safety (minimum) level.

Purchasers recognize both advantages and disadvantages of the minimum/maximum system. Advantages include:

- Excessive quantities of inventory are less likely to occupy valuable storage space.

- There is a reduced chance of stockouts and associated problems.

- The system is easy to use and develop for a specific property's needs.

- Minimum/maximum systems may make it possible to measure actual performance against expected performance.

- Such systems may reduce quantities of products stored without reducing the likelihood of stockouts.

Potential disadvantages of the minimum/maximum inventory system include the following:

- The information generated is not optimal. More sophisticated computer-assisted inventory management systems are available. However, small properties may have difficulty in justifying the cost of computerization.

- Lead, safety, and order point levels incorporate a wide range of assumptions. To the extent that these assumptions are incorrect, problems can arise.

- Time is required to develop minimum/maximum inventory levels to manage specific products.

- Sales promotions by suppliers can make all data invalid and render the exercise worthless.

Typically, the advantages to using this system outweigh its disadvantages. Implementing the system can help buyers to attain an important purchasing objective: to order the "right" quantity of required items.

Endnotes

1. Quality information is taken from: *Quality Assurance Workshop* (East Lansing, Mich.: Educational Institute of the American Hotel & Motel Association, 1985).

REVIEW QUIZ

When you feel you have covered all of the material in this chapter, answer these questions. Choose the *best* answer. Check your answers with the correct ones found on the Review Quiz Answer Key at the end of this book.

True (T) or False (F)

T F   1. Specifications define a detailed list of requirements in a particular commodity.

T F   2. Preparing a set of specifications requires very little research or modification.

T F   3. Price is the first and foremost element to consider as products are compared.

T F   4. IMPS numbers tend to make meat purchasing more difficult and confusing.

T F   5. Lead time is required in order to predict how many units of a particular product are used between ordering and delivery.

T F   6. The best purchasing procedures may be undermined by inadequate receiving practices.

T F   7. The minimum/maximum ordering system is used in determining when to order quantities of perishable goods.

T F   8. The quality of a product needed is dictated by its intended use and menu requirements.

T F   9. Value relates to price and quality: as the price rises and quality remains the same, value (to the operation and its guests) increases.

T F   10. Purchasing staff and suppliers can help food and beverage personnel develop specifications.

T F   11. Purchase quantity is not particularly important as long as the right quality is purchased.

T F   12. Perishable products are normally purchased several times weekly.

T F   13. A committee approach is often used in developing specifications for cooperative purchasing systems.

Multiple Choice

14.   All of the following statements describe likely advantages of using purchase specifications *except*:

   a.   Receiving personnel can use specifications to check incoming orders.
   b.   Specifications can lead to consolidation of different varieties of the same product.
   c.   Specifications can lower purchase costs by precisely defining quality.
   d.   Increased duties of purchasing staff and operating personnel are necessary to develop specifications.

15.   Any of the following may be found in a specification *except*:

   a.   brand name.
   b.   grade of product.
   c.   delivery instructions.
   d.   type of processing.

16.   Product needs are dictated by:

   a.   menus.
   b.   recipes.
   c.   convenience food alternatives.
   d.   all of the above.

Chapter Outline

The Flow of Source Documents
Document Flow Prior to Purchasing
    Requisition
        Storeroom Accounting Controls
        Purchase Requisition
Purchasing Documents
    Purchase Order
    Purchase Record
Receiving Procedures
Post-Receiving Activities
    Close Look at the Billing Process
    Processing Credit Memos
    Processing Checks for Payment
The Accounting Department and Capital
    Purchases
The Importance of Cooperation

Learning Objectives

1. Explain the importance of source documents to the accounting function.

2. Differentiate between a requisition and a purchase requisition.

3. Explain the perpetual inventory system of storeroom control.

4. Compare methods of recording purchases.

5. Explain the basic steps involved in receiving products.

6. Describe the two methods by which bills may be paid.

7. Summarize how credit memos are used to adjust for delivery problems.

6

The Audit Trail

THE ACTIVITIES that compose the purchasing function are numerous and diverse. A hospitality operation depends on the orderly flow of information, records, and documents to control and monitor each of these required tasks.

Hospitality purchasing is best controlled through the establishment of an audit trail which creates an organized and rational flow for source documents and written records. Managers use these control tools to determine if the system is working properly and, if not, to identify action(s) which may correct any problems. The audit trail also helps evaluate the effectiveness of purchasing decisions.

Experienced purchasers are aware of the need for close, cooperative interaction with other departments and staff members. Smooth interdepartmental communications directly influence the effectiveness of the overall purchasing system. This chapter addresses the relationship between the purchasing department and the accounting department.

The Flow of Source Documents

How exactly do purchasing and accounting functions relate to each other? The most obvious connection is the payment of supplier bills (invoices) by the accounting department. Accurate records of products received and supporting documentation must be generated and maintained in order to control this function.

Source documents are original points of entry for financial information into the accounting system and include such forms as purchase requisitions, purchase orders, purchase records, receiving reports, invoices, and disbursement (payment) vouchers. Exhibit 1 illustrates the movement of source documents within the hospitality operation and between the operation and its suppliers. We will use Exhibit 1 as a guide to review source document flow in the entire purchasing process.

Document Flow Prior to Purchasing

Documentation is required at each stage in the purchasing process. The accounting department must process this "paperwork" at the time bills are paid. However, before bills are paid, products must be purchased and received. Storage and issuing practices influence consumption and, therefore, purchase requirements.

Requisition

The requisition is used to communicate information from the requesting department (for instance, kitchen or lounge) to applicable storeroom personnel. This form identifies the type and quantity of product to be removed from inventory.

Exhibit 1   The Purchasing Cycle: An Audit Trail

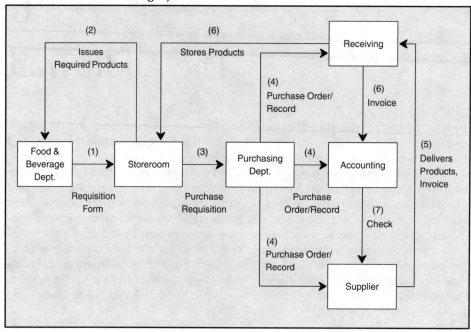

Exhibit 2 illustrates a requisition form. This example includes printed names of required items to simplify the requisition process.

Based upon the authorized requisition, items are then transferred (issued) from storage to the requesting "user" department. The term "user" refers to the line operating department requiring the items to be issued.

Small hospitality operations may choose not to use the requisition. For instance, staff members may simply remove items directly from storage. This practice may be a practical way of reducing paperwork but it is a poor method of controlling inventory. This method lacks the written audit trail which is so vital to controlling the flow of assets. Some managers of small properties compromise by locking up expensive and theft-prone items and keeping a running balance of quantity-on-hand. All other items are withdrawn as needed.

Storeroom Accounting Controls

Food in storage represents a substantial investment to the typical food and beverage operation, which expends approximately 30 to 50% of all income dollars on food purchases. Inventory controls are clearly important if one considers storage areas as bank vaults and products within these areas as assets to be protected.

The management of storage activities by accounting personnel, rather than the user department, is one example of inventory control. Through the separation of duties and responsibilities, the accounting department discourages theft and pilferage by being closely involved with storage activities.

Exhibit 2 Requisition Form

GNAC CORPORATION FOOD REQUISITION No 07131

OUTLET: MAIN KITCHEN
Time Ordered ....
Date ....
Time Delivered ....

Quan.	ITEM	Quan. Ord.	Quan. Iss.	Unit Cost	Ext. Cost	✓		Quan.	ITEM	Quan. Ord.	Quan. Iss.	Unit Cost	Ext. Cost	✓
	101 Hash Brown								Elbow Macaroni					
	L. I. Duck								Noodles					
	Diced Chicken								Spaghetti					
	Bay Scallops								Vermicelli					
	Breaded Scallops								Rigatoni					
	Cod Cheeks								Barley Pearl					
	Sea Legs								Kidney Beans					
	IQF Flounder								Navy Beans					
	Plain Omelette								Lentils					
	Cuisine D. Ramanoff								Green Split Peas					
	Cheese Blintz								Rice					
	Chicken Cordon Bleu								Honey					
	Crepe Nancy								Molasses					
	Pieces Chicken - 4 Pcs								Worcestershire - Gal.					
	Stuffed Pepper								Open Pit BBQ					
	Stuffed Cabbage								Teriyaki Sauce					
	Lasagna								Mustard					
	Stuffed Shells								White Vinegar					
	Chicken and Dumplings								White Milk					
	Ravioli								Sweet Butter					
	Frozen Scrambled Eggs								Butter Blens					
	Bay Shrimps								Aromat					
									Caraway Ground					
									Celery Salt					
									Salt					
	Tomato Catsup								Garlic Powder					
	Tomato Paste								Marjoram Leaves					
	Tomato Puree								Onion Salt					
	Chili Sauce								Oregano Whole					
	Diced Tomato								Paprika Hungarian					
	All Purpose Tomato								Black Pepper					
	White Whole Potatoes, small								White Pepper					
	Instant Potatoes								Cornstarch					
	Corned Beef Hash								Flour					
	Chopped Clams								Lemon Juice					
	Clam Juice								Great Garlic Jars					
	Sliced Mushroom								Half & Half - Qts.					
	Chicken Base								Baked Potatoes (Wrapped)					
	Beef Base								Brown Sugar					
	Double Beef Consomme								Pineapple Juice					
	Minor Ham Base								Cabbage					
	Minor Clam Base													
	Lobster Base													
	Cottonseed Oil													
	Fry Max													
	Vegetable Spray													

WHITE: Food & Beverage Control   CANARY: Storeroom

ORDERED BY ....   RECEIVED BY ....   ISSUED BY ....

REV. 5/84

Source: Golden Nugget.

Exhibit 3   Perpetual Inventory Form

Perpetual Inventory							
Product Name: _P.D.Q. Shrimp_				**Purchase Unit Size:** _5 lb bag_			
Date	**In** **Carried Forward**	**Out**	**Balance** 15	**Date**	**In** **Carried Forward**	**Out**	**Balance**
1	2	3	4	1	2	3	4
5/16		3	12				
5/17		3	9				
5/18	6		15				
5/19		2	13				

One of the most important accounting control tools is the perpetual inventory system. As items enter storage, the quantity is recorded on the perpetual inventory record (see Exhibit 3) to show an increase in inventory. As items are removed by using the requisition form, the quantity depleted is also recorded. This running balance enables the controller (a member of the accounting department), through physical observation and count, to match how much product *is* available to how much product *should* be available. Differences between these figures give a measure of the effectiveness of inventory control methods.

Controls of this type assist the purchasing function in at least three ways:

- As theft/pilferage is curtailed, quantities of product required in inventory are reduced and, as a result, the total dollar amount committed to inventory is decreased.

- Since a perpetual inventory system logs item quantity, such records provide usage rates and other input useful in making purchase decisions.

- A perpetual inventory system reduces stockouts caused by inaccurate record-keeping.

Prevention of losses not only represents a real savings to the operation, but also contributes to the maintenance of inventory levels. While perpetual inventory recordkeeping may not be necessary for every item, it is advised for the relatively few items that represent the largest portion of food costs.

Purchase Requisition

Another accounting tool, the purchase requisition, is illustrated in Exhibit 4. Storeroom personnel send this form to the purchasing department when product

Exhibit 4   Purchase Requisition

GNOC CORP.

12914

PURCHASE REQUISITION

Date Submitted _____

Suggested
VENDOR(S)
and
Ordering
Information
_____
_____
_____
_____

Date Required _____
Dept. of Orig. _____
Requested by _____
Dept. Head _____

QUANTITY	DISTRIBUTION		PLEASE ORDER ITEM(S) LISTED BELOW	EST. UNIT PRICE	EST. TOTAL
	DEPT.	A/C			

FOR PURCHASING USE ONLY

JUSTIFICATION: All variations in excess of Budget must be noted below:

P.O. #	
SHIP VIA	
DELIVER TO	
F.O.B.	
ORDERED BY	

PRICE/COST INFO REQ. BY DEPT. OF ORIGINATION? ☐ Yes ☐ No

GNOC PR1 REV. 9/83

ACCOUNTING

Source: Golden Nugget.

quantity levels reach a pre-established minimum level. Purchase requisitions indicate what items are required, when to order, and how much of each item is needed to maintain par levels.

Some properties route this form directly to the user department, instead of to the purchasing department. The department head who is familiar with usage levels (volume of purchases) and product requirements can confirm that purchase requisitions are appropriate.

Purchasing Documents

Requests for products eventually reach the purchasing department. Provided these documents are authorized and legitimate, the specific function of purchasing begins at this point.

When receiving a purchase requisition from the storeroom, the purchasing department is made aware that additional quantities of the specified items must be

Exhibit 5   Purchase Order

GOLDEN NUGGET HOTEL CASINO GNOC, CORP P.O. BOX 1737 Atlantic City, NJ 08404 Telephone: (609) 347-7111	PURCHASE ORDER
	THIS PURCHASE ORDER NO. MUST APPEAR ON ALL INVOICES, PACKING SLIPS, CASES, BILLS OF LADING, ETC.

V E N D O R   PURCHASE ORDER   S H I P   T O

READ ALL INSTRUCTIONS, TERMS, CONDITIONS HEREIN AND ATTACHMENTS HERETO. ONLY SUCH INSTRUCTIONS, TERMS, CONDITIONS AND ATTACHMENTS SHALL CONSTITUTE THE AGREEMENT BETWEEN THE PARTIES.

PLEASE ENTER OUR PURCHASE ORDER OF THE ABOVE NUMBER, SUBJECT TO ALL INSTRUCTIONS, TERMS AND CONDITIONS HEREOF.

DATE ORDERED	DATE REQUIRED	SHIP VIA	F.O.B.	TERMS	AS PER YOUR QUOTATION

ITEM	UNIT	Quantity Ordered	Quantity Received	COST	ITEM	UNIT	Quantity Ordered	Quantity Received	COST

GNOC, CORP.

Order Received by: _____   By: _____ PURCHASING AGENT

Date: _____   _____ AUTHORIZED SIGNATURE

White Copy: RECEIVING/ACCOUNTING Canary Copy: FOOD & BEVERAGE STOREROOM Pink Copy: NUMERICAL

(2/86-2M) Marine Printing Co., Inc.

Source: Golden Nugget.

purchased. The professional purchasing department develops and circulates purchase specifications to all eligible suppliers. When purchase requisitions are received from the storeroom, the purchasing task is simplified; the minimum quality of product required is defined in the purchase specifications and several eligible suppliers of the items are already identified.

Purchasing staff can use many different methods to solicit prices. Telephone calls or visits from suppliers can provide this information. Some large-volume properties use a special purchase order form to solicit requests for price quotations (see Exhibit 5). The supplier who is awarded the purchase then receives a confirming order on the original purchase order. Some properties tie prices to market indicators and simply order from the approved supplier, assuring the property that the price will be at a predetermined level above the current market price.

Purchase Order

After selecting the supplier, the purchaser issues a purchase order (especially in the case of a large property) or makes an oral non-written agreement with the supplier. Documentation is submitted to the receiving department, which needs details regarding items, quantities, and prices for each incoming order. This documentation may be a copy of the purchase order, if one is issued, or an in-house record of the purchase agreement.

A copy of the purchase order is also sent to the accounting department so that a later audit can be performed as part of invoice processing. In large operations, an additional copy of the purchase order might be forwarded to the storeroom, confirming the receipt of the purchase requisition, indicating the order of additional products, and noting the quantity of incoming items and date of delivery.

Purchase Record

As an alternative to issuing a purchase order, small-volume properties may instead use an in-house purchase record. This saves time for the department head or other managers, who may be too busy to handle the necessary paperwork. The supplier is not provided with a copy, since orders have been placed by informal means (phone or personal visit). Receiving personnel should be furnished with a copy of the purchase record so that they can be prepared to properly receive the products when delivered and thus avoid last-minute surprises. Staff members with receiving responsibility need to check incoming items against the purchase record, which indicates products ordered, quantity, and price.

Receiving Procedures

Proper receiving demands a thorough knowledge of quality specifications and careful attention to details regarding price and quantity. Unfortunately, many hospitality operations regard receiving as little more than signing an invoice and placing items in storage. Follow-up procedures are often lacking, making it impossible to confirm that the "right" products are being received.

Very large operations may have personnel with full-time receiving duties. More typically, however, properties overlap receiving and storeroom duties. The chef, food and beverage manager, or other employee may perform these tasks for incoming items. Delivery personnel may notify the security guard at the employee entrance about an incoming shipment; a representative from housekeeping may then go to the designated area to perform receiving duties.

Regardless of size, the same basic procedures should be followed as products are received. Basic steps in product receiving include:

Step 1: Check incoming products against the purchase order or in-house purchase record.

Step 2:   Check incoming products against specifications. At this point, someone with specialized training is needed to recognize the quality characteristics required in every item purchased by the various departments. Testing procedures outlined in purchase specifications should be undertaken by receiving personnel or other staff members to confirm that the quality of items purchased (upon which costs are based) equals the quality of items actually received.

   In the case of items with a high cost per unit, it is also necessary to check product temperature, weight, trim, grade, and refrigeration state (for instance, whether the product has been thawed and refrozen).

Step 3:   Check the delivery invoice. (See Exhibit 6 for an example.) After product quality and quantity are verified, the invoice can be signed. The invoice becomes a source document required for further processing of bills.

Step 4:   Complete receiving documents to make sure all information is provided. Exhibit 7 shows a daily receiving report. Information from the delivery invoice can be abstracted on this report.

Step 5:   Check to see that products are promptly moved to proper storage areas.

Delivery personnel should only have access to "back-of-house" areas. While the offer of assistance may be helpful to the receiving staff, suppliers or representatives should not be involved with storage activities.

   Receiving involves time-consuming but important tasks. To accommodate the schedules of responsible staff, delivery times can be limited. Non-acceptance of deliveries is common at certain times, for example, from 11:30 A.M. to 1:30 P.M. in the food and beverage department, when staff is busy preparing and cooking for the lunch rush period.

   As can be noted in Exhibit 1, the purchase order (or purchase record), delivery invoice, and receiving report must be assembled. The three documents are routed, sometimes through the purchasing department, and eventually reach the accounting department for final processing and bill paying.

   In some operations, receiving staff are responsible for an initial verification of invoice extensions. Extensions involve checking to ensure that the number of units purchased, when multiplied by the agreed-upon purchase price, equals the supplier's charge. Even if receiving employees verify charges, the accounting department should check over all arithmetic on invoices as an integral part of the payment process.

   Properties with a specialized receiving department may direct documents to the user department before forwarding to the purchasing department; this helps confirm that types and quantities of products received fit the requirements dictated by levels of product sales.

Post-Receiving Activities

Purchasing department staff should compare the purchase order (or purchase record), delivery invoice, and other receiving records routed from the receiving

Exhibit 6   Delivery Invoice

GRACE	INVOICE	INVENTORY CONTROL

GRACE
Restaurant Services, Inc.
344 No. Cliffwood Park
Brea, California 92621
(714) 990-8553

INVOICE

INVENTORY CONTROL

OUTSIDE CALIFORNIA
(800) 233-6300 – EXT. 8553

FOR DELIVERY SHORTAGES CALL
FWS   (714) 863-6348
ET   (714) 863-8874
        (714) 863-8876
        (714) 863-8878

SOLD
TO

SHIP
TO

STORE NO.	ORDER RECEIVED BY	ORDERED BY	ENTRY DATE	INVOICE NUMBER	INVOICE DATE

SPECIAL INFORMATION	ROUTE NAME	ROUTE NO.

QUANTITY			PRODUCT CODE	DESCRIPTION	WEIGHT	PRICE/PER	AMOUNT
ORDER	SHIPPED	B/O					

VOID

		TOTAL WEIGHT OF INVOICE	FREIGHT AMOUNT	TOTAL AMOUNT

Source: Grace Restaurant Services, Inc.

department with their own copy of the purchasing documents. They will be interested in determining the following:

- Whether any discrepancies exist between qualities, quantities, and prices agreed upon at time of purchase and those actually received.

- Whether any products are back ordered or out of stock.

- Whether results of expediting were effective.

- Whether any problems require invoice adjustments. (Credit memos will be discussed later in this chapter.)

Exhibit 7   Daily Receiving Report

GNAC CORP.
DAILY FOOD and BEVERAGE RECEIVING REPORT

Date _____

	VENDOR NAME	INVOICE NO.	# of Invoice	TIME	P.O. NUMBER	FOOD AMOUNT	BEVERAGE AMOUNT	SUNDRIES
1.								
2.								
3.								
4.								
5.								
6.								
7.								
8.								
9.								
10.								
11.								
12.								
13.								
14.								
15.								
40.								
41.								
42.								
43.								

TOTALS

	TODAY	M.T.D.	Y.T.D.
FOOD			
BEVERAGE			
SUNDRIES			
TOTALS			

SIGNATURES:

_____
(Receiving Manager)

_____
(Accounts Payable Clerk)

Distribution:
WHITE: F&B Control
CANARY: Receiving Manager
PINK: Accounts Payable

PAGE _____ of _____ PAGES   GNAC FBC-110 2/82

Source: Golden Nugget.

As you can see, the role of the purchasing department extends far beyond the actual purchasing of items. Purchasing goals involving price, quality, quantity, supplier, and time are more consistently met by screening source documents as they move throughout the various departments. This provides the necessary audit trail and system of checks and balances for accounting.

Close Look at the Billing Process

Even before supplier bills are ready for processing, the accounting department has a role to play in the procurement process. It has, for example, received a copy of the purchase order or purchase record. Its first active task in the billing process, however, occurs when the delivery invoice and, if applicable, the receiving records are routed from the purchasing department.

An initial step in the bill-paying process occurs as the invoice extensions are checked (ideally, for the second time). The importance of this verification cannot be overstated. The invoice is used as the basis for establishing amounts owed to the supplier and, therefore, serves as the basic input to various expense categories on the property's income statement.

There are two basic ways to process supplier bills for payment: by invoice or by statement. When bills are paid by statement, the purchaser reaches an agreement with the supplier that a statement covering all applicable delivery invoices will be sent to the property on a regular schedule. Invoices which have been filed on a "by-supplier" basis are retrieved when the statement is received. Applicable invoices are matched with invoice number, date, amount owed, and other information noted on the statement. The total of all invoices is verified to confirm that the amount requested on the statement is correct. One check is then written to cover all invoices. The invoices should be attached to the statement and information about payment date, check number, and check amount should be recorded. Rubber stamps can be used to quickly and consistently indicate needed information.

When bills are paid by invoice, the same basic information should be recorded on each invoice. The difference is that no statement is sent from the supplier or, at least, a statement is not used as the basis for payment. After extensions are confirmed, invoices are filed by payment date. For example, if an invoice must be paid by the 20th of the month, it may be filed for processing on the 15th of the month. This will allow time for that activity and for mailing the supplier's payment.

In either case, the source documents (statement with attached invoices or invoices alone) should be filed by supplier name after payment. Some properties also attach copies of the receiving record and/or purchase order (purchase record) for a complete documentation of the transaction.

Processing Credit Memos

Problems that may arise at the time of receiving include delivery of incorrect quantities of items and delivery of items that are of the wrong quality or brand. In some operations, these problems are handled simply by a notation made on the delivery invoice before it is signed. While this is often the practice, such notations may go unnoticed or may give rise to questions. Even worse is the common situation in which a verbal agreement is made with the delivery person: "Just sign the invoice this time and we'll bring the items on the next trip without putting them on the invoice."

The best solution to these problems involves using a credit memo system. A credit memo is prepared by supplier personnel and does just what its name implies: it provides a written record of adjustments made to the invoice. This form helps accounting personnel limit payments to those items which were actually received and accepted. Exhibit 8 provides an example of a credit memo.

Suppliers provide credit memos for their driver's use, but they are sometimes forgotten or simply lacking. When credit memos are not immediately available, the

Exhibit 8   Credit Memo

	CUSTOMER ADJUSTMENT MEMO **69558**

GRACE Restaurant Services
1672 REYNOLDS • P.O. BOX 19561 • IRVINE, CALIFORNIA 92714
CALIFORNIA (714) 863-6348
OUTSIDE CALIFORNIA (714) 863-0122 OR (800) 233-6300 EXT. 6348

☐ CREDIT   ☐ ADD-ON

☐ DRIVER PICK UP   ☐ WILL CALL

☐ SHORTAGE DEL.   ☐ SHIPPED BY

☐ CREDIT BILLING ADJUSTMENT

☐ DEBIT BILLING ADJUSTMENT

SHOP NUMBER   NAME

ADDRESS

CITY   STATE   ZIP   OPENING ORDER ☐

CONTACT   DATE   INVOICE NUMBER

NOT FOR ADD-ON USE

ORIGINAL INVOICE NO.	ORDER DATE	SHIP DATE	ITEM DESCRIPTION	ITEM NUMBER	QUAN-TITY	SELL UNIT PRICE	EXTENDED AMOUNT	ADJ. CODE
			Void					

EXPLANATION:

ORIGINATED BY

APPROVED BY

ALL TRANSACTIONS SUBJECT TO FUTURE BILLING PROCESS

CUSTOMER ACKNOWLEDGMENT

CUSTOMER

Source: Grace Restaurant Services, Inc.

hospitality property should use a simple form requesting that the supplier issue a credit memo. The request for credit memo is sent to the accounting and purchasing departments as well as the supplier. The supplier then issues a credit memo or simply credits the property's account.

A proper procedure for processing credit memos may include the following steps:

1. A problem is noted and brought to the driver's attention when items are received. The driver agrees that there is a difference between the incoming shipment and the order included on the original delivery invoice.

2. Applicable information is recorded on the credit memo, including the number of the delivery invoice.

3. The driver signs the credit memo after all required information is noted.

4. The receiving employee signs the delivery invoice and notes the credit memo number on the delivery invoice.

5. The receiving staff member retains a copy of the credit memo, generally the original. This should be attached to the applicable invoice.

6. The delivery invoice with attached credit memo and, as applicable, the purchase order (purchase record) and receiving report is routed through the purchasing department to the accounting department. A purchasing staff member should verify any concerns or problems regarding the credit memo with the receiving employee or appropriate departmental representative. Frequent notation of credit memo problems provides useful input to the ongoing supplier evaluation process.

7. As soon as the credit memo and invoice are received by accounting, an arithmetic check of all extensions is undertaken.

8. Some properties require that the supplier be called to confirm that the supplier's copy of the credit memo was received and is being processed.

Before a check is signed, the amount of the original invoice should be reduced by the amount recorded on the credit memo either on the invoice itself (if this is used as the basis for payment), or on the statement provided by the supplier. The entire amount of the invoice is stated and the amount of the credit memo is noted separately. Information about the invoice and credit memo should be noted on the check.

Credit memos should be treated exactly like money, because that is really what they represent. If, for example, credit memos are lost or improperly processed, the hospitality operator stands to lose the deductions; costs will be higher than they should be. The staff member with receiving responsibility has a most significant role to play in managing quality and costs. The credit memo can be an effective tool to help an operation "get its money's worth" as items are received.

Processing Checks for Payment

Except when petty cash expenses are involved, payments should always be made by check. For auditing purposes, funds to pay bills should never be taken out of daily income before bank deposits are made. Unless the owner or manager performs both activities, invoice/statement processing and check signing should be done by two different employees. For similar reasons, persons who process income records, funds, or prepared deposits should not be involved in check-writing procedures.

The invoice/statement with supporting records—purchase order (or purchase record), invoice, and receiving reports—should be given, along with the check, to a management official to sign. Many properties require more than one signature on large checks. A specific person or supplier organization should be designated on the check, rather than "cash" or "bearer." Top-level management should routinely examine the list of checks written to keep current with new suppliers and transactions. Lists of payees should be circulated to the purchasing staff to prevent checks from being written for fraudulent purposes (for example, payment to fictitious companies).

The Accounting Department and Capital Purchases

Accounting personnel may not be aware of routine purchases until after items are received and purchasing documents routed to the accounting department. However, when expensive capital equipment is purchased, this process may be modified. The term "capital equipment" generally refers to an item which has a useful life greater than one year and whose cost is above a given dollar amount, depending on the individual operation's definition.

Many properties use a separate capital budget for this. The approval process for capital purchases involves two steps:

- Management approval for the purchase of the item itself. For example, management may approve the purchase of new lobby furniture.

- Allocation of funds used to purchase the capital equipment item. Approval of the equipment may not signal its purchase, since funds must be separately allocated for purchase. In addition, loan or leasing agreements may need to be negotiated before a purchase can be made.

After approval has been granted for capital equipment, the purchasing staff will research information to facilitate a final decision by the user department. Once the decision is made and a purchase order has been filled out, a copy should be forwarded to the accounting department so that funds can be set aside as necessary. The purchasing staff will need to confirm the availability of funds with accounting personnel.

Capital equipment can be purchased by cash payment, financing, or leasing. Because of cash flow and tax implications concerning these alternatives, accounting personnel must be involved in the evaluation of options.

The Importance of Cooperation

Teamwork and communication between purchasing and accounting department staff has been represented throughout this chapter. Sometimes, large properties have staff accounting specialists with responsibilities for each of the activities discussed. By contrast, smaller properties may not have a full-time accountant; the manager/owner may perform many of the tasks with external assistance from a professional accountant. Other properties may use a "bookkeeper" for invoice processing, check writing, and a myriad of other duties. Regardless of the organizational plan, however, the "experts" in purchasing must work closely with the "experts" in accounting to design systems for the appropriation of limited funds at the property's disposal.

REVIEW QUIZ

When you feel you have covered all of the material in this chapter, answer these questions. Choose the *best* answer. Check your answers with the correct ones found on the Review Quiz Answer Key at the end of this book.

True (T) or False (F)

(T) F 1. Purchase requisitions indicate when to order and how much of each item is needed to maintain par levels. *True* *Pg 95*

T (F) 2. A perpetual inventory should be kept for all items in stock. *False*

(T) F 3. Receiving personnel should receive a copy of the purchase record or purchase order to ensure proper receiving procedures. *T*

T (F) 4. Suppliers should be expected to assist with storage activities. *False*

(T) F 5. Purchasing staff should compare receiving records with purchase records to check for discrepancies in quality, quantity, and price. *T*

(T) F 6. Supplier bills may be processed for payment by invoice or by statement. *T*

T (F) 7. A credit memo is unnecessary if the delivery person orally agrees to supply the missing merchandise with the next delivery. *False*

T (F) 8. Funds with which to pay bills may be removed from daily income before bank deposits are made. *False*

Multiple Choice

9. Which of the following is *not* a source document for accounting purposes?

    a. purchase order   *specification*
    b. invoice
    c. disbursement voucher
    (d.) specification

10. Which of the following is an internal document which authorizes and identifies the type and quantity of product to be transferred from stock to a user department?

    a. purchase order
    b. purchase record   *requisition from*
    (c.) requisition form
    d. receiving report

11. According to accepted practices, checks to suppliers should be written to:

    a. the bearer.
    b. cash.
    (c.) the specific person or organization. ✓
    d. any of the above.

Chapter Outline

The Need for Evaluation
Evaluation Principles
Roles in Purchasing Evaluation
    Top-Level Management
    Purchasing Staff
    Line Management
    Outside Consultants
The Evaluation Process
    Identifying Goals
    Assessing Performance
    Improving the Purchasing System
    Guide to Purchasing Evaluation
Focus on Supplier Evaluation
    Measurement of Costs
    Use of Pricing Information
    Cost Components of Distribution
    Measurement of Supplier Efficiency

Learning Objectives

1. Assess the need for evaluation of the purchasing function.

2. Describe the roles of management, purchasing staff, and outside consultants in the evaluation process.

3. Explain the first step of the evaluation process: identifying goals.

4. Explain the second step of the evaluation process: assessing performance.

5. Explain the third step of the evaluation process: improving the purchasing system.

6. Explain how suppliers are evaluated.

7

Evaluation of Purchasing Systems

Those with purchasing responsibilities are very busy indeed. Much effort is required to properly perform the wide range of duties which are integral to the purchasing function. Perhaps the most challenging task facing those with purchasing responsibilities is that of evaluating the purchasing system.

How well is the purchasing system working? How can it be improved? How should priorities for improvements be established? These and related questions can only be answered through the process of evaluation. Managers should not postpone evaluation "until there is time" or "until they get around to it." Rather, evaluation activities must be part of an ongoing process, conducted according to basic management principles.

The Need for Evaluation

The evaluation of a purchasing system has two primary objectives: (1) to measure the extent to which current purchasing goals are being met, and (2) to improve the system in order to more effectively achieve future purchasing goals. These objectives can best be attained by means of a critical analysis that measures, monitors, and improves the productivity of the purchasing system.

Evaluation of the purchasing process helps provide the information and financial control essential to good management. Hospitality operations typically work within low profit margins. If an operation is to succeed, it is essential to minimize purchasing costs, which constitute a very significant percentage of the property's total income. At the same time, the operation must maintain its required quality levels. How much the property spends for purchases is relatively easy to measure (the income statement recaps this information for each fiscal period). However, it may be more difficult to discover whether each purchase dollar represents a necessary and reasonable cost.

Besides contributing to cost-effectiveness, an evaluation of the purchasing system can lead to other benefits. An evaluation may reveal ways in which to improve the overall effectiveness of the purchasing process. While change for the sake of change should be discouraged, purposeful change is desirable. Analysis of current purchasing procedures may generate new ideas regarding work practices which can aid line managers, purchasing staff, and the operation as a whole. Since guests will be affected by actions of the purchasing department, the constant need to evaluate the effectiveness of the purchaser becomes even more apparent.

Exhibit 1   The Management Loop

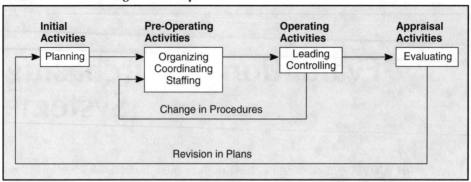

A hospitality operation comprises a number of closely related sub-systems. Many departments depend heavily on the purchasing function. They should, therefore, provide feedback on issues such as product yields, quality, delivery time, and shortages.

Changes in the purchasing system may produce spin-off effects leading to changes in other departments. For example, procedural improvements for conducting make-or-buy analyses may suggest that convenience food products should be purchased. Several changes may then occur within the production department: fewer personnel hours may be involved in the food production task and more time may be available to accomplish other activities.

Evaluation Principles

We have noted that an operator needs to assign a high priority to the evaluation process. We have also indicated reasons why the task of evaluation is vital to proper purchasing. It is useful to review a number of basic principles that are directly related to this task.

To be most effective, evaluations must be done in an objective manner, on a timely basis, and with input from purchasing staff and others outside the department.

Exhibit 1 outlines the basic management process and shows how the management functions relate to one another. In the context of purchasing, for example, measurable goals must be developed. Based upon these goals, purchasing tasks must be organized, coordinated, and communicated to ensure that resources allocated to the purchasing function are used efficiently.

Purchasing staff must be hired, trained, supervised, and evaluated. In small hospitality operations, purchasing tasks may be spread among various personnel or handled by a single person. In this situation, specific tasks should be included in the job descriptions for those designated staff members.

Purchasing activities must also be controlled. Expected performance must be compared with actual performance, and corrective action taken as necessary. Evaluation is part of this control process.

Where Can the Most Money Be Saved?

More than many other aspects of the food and beverage operation, improved purchasing can increase bottom-line profits.

For example, if purchasing costs can be reduced by $100 through more effective purchasing, the entire $100 savings will "drop" to the bottom line; profits will increase by $100. By contrast, if sales are increased by $100 because of marketing efforts and the property is operating at a profit level of, say, 10% of sales, the impact on the bottom line will likely be only $10.

Increased profits are one of the most important reasons purchasing activities should be evaluated. Formal analysis typically reveals how money can be saved. A simple way to evaluate cost savings is to compare actual savings with projected savings. A well-defined plan for a certain property may call for a 10% cost savings over past purchases of a particular item. After a bid or negotiation is complete, the purchaser carries out the following calculations:

$$\text{Previous Expenditure} = \text{Old Cost} \times \text{Use}$$
$$\text{Upcoming Expenditure} = \text{New Cost} \times \text{Use}$$
$$\text{Cost Savings} = \text{Previous Expenditure} - \text{Upcoming Expenditure}$$

Assuming use level to be equal, the difference between these two figures, converted to a percentage, will allow the purchaser to determine whether that property's projected goal of 10% cost savings was met or exceeded.

Roles in Purchasing Evaluation

Who should be responsible for the evaluation of the purchasing system? Typically, the evaluation is conducted by line department managers, who additionally may be responsible for preparing job descriptions, creating financial controls, setting dollar purchase limits, and qualifying suppliers.

Top-Level Management

Top-level management will be concerned about aspects of purchasing relating to quality and economics. How much money is being spent? How can expenses be reduced without sacrificing quality? Top-level management, however, is seldom involved in the actual evaluation process. Its role generally is to establish policies identifying what the organization expects from the purchasing function (for example: to purchase required goods and services at the lowest possible price consistent with quality and service standards established by the operations department).

Managers often review the effectiveness of the purchasing system by studying income statements. However, purchasing practices may not be the cause of higher (or lower) purchasing costs. For example, market prices may have changed unexpectedly. Also, excessive purchasing costs may be traced to problems in receiving, storing, issuing, production, or service—all of which are typically beyond the control of the purchasing staff. These examples illustrate the need to establish definable and measurable goals for the purchasing activity. The purchasing department can be given direct responsibility for these goals and allowed control over areas which may affect the department's ability to achieve them.

Purchasing Staff

Purchasing department staff should participate in the evaluation process. They should know, for example, whether policies, plans, budgets, and other financial goals are followed consistently. They should also be made aware if certain activities or situations exist which are creating purchasing problems which do not turn up on the financial statements. For instance, the purchaser should examine relations with suppliers, encourage feedback from the production staff, and analyze the frequent need to expedite orders.

A basic management rule states that persons responsible for a task cannot be solely responsible for evaluating its completion. This certainly applies to the purchasing staff. However, input from the purchasing staff should be solicited as the evaluation process develops. Staff members are knowledgeable about the purchasing system and may have suggestions for its improvement.

Line Management

Line operating personnel should also be involved in evaluation. They may suggest ways to improve equipment, products, services, and the purchasing system itself. This type of feedback enhances the communication process. For example, a manager may find that a specific product is undesirable in quality. An evaluation may reveal, however, that the purchasing department is using an outdated specification. Management may have changed the specific need for an item without notifying the purchasing department of the updated quality requirements. Communication between management and purchasing staff may uncover problems like this as the evaluation process unfolds.

Outside Consultants

When an operation undertakes an internal evaluation, several advantages are apparent. An internal evaluation saves time and expenses associated with hiring an external organization for evaluation. Internal evaluation can also be an effective tool to help resolve subtle problems which may go unnoticed in the course of day-to-day operations. Also, operational goals are more likely to be achieved when all concerned individuals become familiar with the company's systems and procedures, which make actual results measurable.

However, there are some potential disadvantages to an internal evaluation process. The evaluation process may receive too low a priority within the organization, or may be ignored altogether. Also, currently employed staff may lack the expertise and broad-based experience required to define or resolve problems. Concerns about discipline or job loss, reduced level of self-esteem, or fraudulent work practices may discourage purchasing staff from objectively evaluating current practices.

These disadvantages may be countered by supplementing an internal evaluation with the use of outside consultants who can offer a fresh and objective evaluation of the purchasing system. Consultants are sometimes employed to analyze and resolve problems that may include the purchasing system. For instance, when consultants are hired to investigate excessive costs of operations, the purchasing system may also be scrutinized. Findings of the consultants may then be integrated within the internal evaluation report.

The Evaluation Process

The process of evaluation resembles an internal control audit and addresses such questions as: Do proper policies and procedures exist? Are they accurately used in business transactions? What level of performance is achieved as measured against pre-established standards?

Evaluating purchasing activities involves three basic steps. The first step identifies the goals of purchasing. These goals should reflect established company practices and be clearly written and communicated to all purchasing personnel. The second step assesses performance by comparing the actual results of purchasing activities against the goals set forth in step one. The final step in the evaluation process improves the purchasing system by implementing the necessary corrective actions to resolve any problems revealed in step two.

Identifying Goals

Basic purchasing goals involve concerns about product, quality, price, quantity, supplier, and timing. Purchasing goals must be reasonable and within the control of purchasing department staff members. Once general goals pertaining to each of these broad areas have been identified, they may be further defined in terms of specific actions which will help to achieve them. This can best be done by keeping a simple question in mind: "What do we want to accomplish and how will we measure whether we are successful?" Each hospitality operation must establish goals and action plans appropriate for its own particular situation. The following set of goals and action plans is offered only as an illustration of the kind of specificity and measurability that is necessary in the first step of the evaluation process.[1]

Goal—To purchase the right products.
Action plans may include:

1. Items will be rejected and price adjustments will be made no more than five times this year because of quality problems.

2. Instances where items accepted from a supplier are found to be inferior in quality will not occur more than once this year.

3. Suppliers will be asked to provide suggestions about quality requirements at least twice this year.

Goal—To purchase at the right price.
Action plans may include:

1. Total cost of purchased goods will increase or decrease in direct proportion to sales. Since the ratio of sales revenue to gross purchasing cost was four to one last year, this year the ratio should also be four to one.

2. Per unit costs of expensive and large-volume products will increase or decrease in direct proportion to the Consumer Price Index (CPI).

Goal—To purchase in the right quantity.
Action plans may include:

1. There will be no more than ten stockouts for all items this year.

2. Items in inventory will be controlled so that the maximum limit is not exceeded more than ten times during the year.

3. Not more than a specified value of perishable items will need to be discarded annually.

Goal—To purchase from the right supplier.
Action plans may include:

1. Samples and prices will be obtained this year for all major products with the goal of identifying eligible suppliers.

2. There will be no more than ten complaints of any kind against any supplier within the coming year.

3. There will be no cases of back-door selling by a supplier this year. (Back-door selling occurs when the salesperson bypasses the designated purchaser in order to persuade another employee to exert influence on the purchasing decision.)

Goal—To purchase at the right time.
Action plans may include:

1. There will be no more than ten rush orders this year.

2. A supplier will not deliver later than an agreed-upon date more than eight times this year.

3. Suppliers will *never* deliver more than one week early.

A wide range of additional goals and actions can also be established. For example, action plans may call for a specific number of make-or-buy analyses, purchase specifications, and equipment purchase studies to be developed during a specific fiscal period. Personnel in the purchasing department may be required to take part in professional development seminars and other training activities. Budgetary goals, development of policy handbooks, and computerization all lend themselves to quantification and objective measurement.

Assessing Performance

How does one actually determine whether goals are met? Obviously, procedures for assessment must be determined when goals are first established. This is the reason for extending goals to include specific, measurable purchasing actions. Comparing actual performance with expected performance (outlined in the goal-setting action plan) is the central element in the evaluation activity.

Evaluation Extends Beyond Product and Supplier Concerns

The purchaser is most concerned with ensuring that the six basic purchasing goals are met. Much of the evaluation process focuses on these goals. However, there is typically a wide range of other factors in the purchasing management system which lend themselves to objective evaluation. Consider the following questions:

- Is the purchasing department properly organized?
- Are all purchasing positions cost-effective?
- Is there a coordinated flow of communication between purchasing and other departments?
- Are purchasing policies reasonable from the perspective of both company and supplier personnel?
- Do reports and records circulated among departments provide adequate and timely information?
- Is the importance of effective purchasing recognized throughout the organization?
- Are all purchasing procedures written and consistently followed?
- Are purchasing activities centralized within the hospitality organization?
- Are all purchasing staff qualified for the work they do?
- What procedures are used to select the "best" suppliers?
- Does the purchasing department always function in a staff (advisory) role rather than a line (management) role?

How often should the comparison process take place? The answer to this question depends upon the goals. If goals relate to activities covering a period of 6 or 12 months, evaluation must take place at the end of that period. Some formal evaluation of the purchasing system is in order as preparation for the evaluation of purchasing staff begins.

If the comparison suggests that goals have not been attained, it will be necessary to implement a decision-making process to discover the reason(s) for failure and to plan corrective action strategies. By contrast, if comparison indicates that goals have been achieved, new priorities can be established and further techniques for improving the purchasing management system can be implemented. Without making comparisons between expected performance and actual results, it is much more difficult to develop effective plans and strategies for improving the purchasing system.

Some variance between expected and actual performance is permitted before corrective action must be taken. If the plan is to develop 20 purchase specifications during a particular period, a questioning process to uncover problems may only be necessary if less than 18 are actually developed. A variance of 10%, for example, may be acceptable to certain properties in this instance. Regardless of the variance limit, purchasing problems become of greater concern as the frequency of occurrence increases; as the incidence of problems increases, the priority for their resolution also becomes greater.

The goal-setting and action plan method of assessing performance may be supplemented by a variety of other techniques. For example, requests for price quotation sheets and actual delivery invoices can be used to determine current prices and can be compared with similar documents from previous periods. These assessments can review both per unit cost and charges for total volumes of purchases—if volumes were similar to quantities purchased during previous periods.

Various inventory tools can be used to help evaluate purchasing procedures related to quantity. Perpetual inventory forms can help the operator keep a running account of stock levels of critical items. Other forms can be used to calculate quantities and values of stock on hand during calculations of physical inventory. Another useful gauge is to measure rates of average inventory turnover.

Choice of suppliers is another goal worth assessing. Rating sheets which evaluate suppliers, credit memos indicating a poor delivery record, and relevant correspondence between accounting and supplier personnel can help in evaluating whether the right supplier has been used.

Diaries are in-house records related to operational activities. Critical incidents logs can be maintained to record delivery and/or storage problems which relate to purchasing. Work logs can be used to indicate stockouts and times when maximum inventory levels were overridden.

Improving the Purchasing System

Let's assume that the assessment of performance indicates a problem: the incidence of stockouts is unacceptable, with approximately 25% more stockouts than planned. A traditional decision-making approach might be used to resolve the problem. This begins with problem definition and expands to consideration and analysis of alternatives. It concludes with testing of possible resolution strategies and implementation of revised procedures.

Corrective action is then required to resolve the problem. After procedures to reduce problems have been undertaken, it becomes necessary to evaluate their worth. The purpose of this evaluation is twofold: (1) to ensure that the problem (excessive variance between planned and actual goal attainment) is resolved, and (2) to make certain that no other problems are created.

During this evaluation, it is necessary to observe the extent to which the problem is reduced. Input from top-level managers, purchasing staff, and production department employees may prove valuable. Suggestions about further improvements can be solicited from this group. Time will be needed to gather enough objective information to evaluate the appropriateness of the corrective action.

The list of supplemental factors to be evaluated can become extensive. However, the point to remember is that the most important concerns must be addressed first in an evaluation program. Over time, other elements can be considered, as the process of improvement is a continuous one.

Guide to Purchasing Evaluation

Exhibit 2 shows a sample form used to note factors worth considering as evaluation activities are undertaken. While a unique list needs to be developed for each property, the form does suggest a practical process for evaluation. After selecting each

Exhibit 2   Purchasing Evaluation Guide

Date _____   Completed by
                       staff member in: ☐ Purchasing Dept.
                                            ☐ Food/Bev. Dept.
                                            ☐ Management
Instructions: For each of the following activities consider whether improve-   ☐ Accounting Dept.
                   ments can be made that will make purchasing more effective.
                   Specific ideas/suggestions will be very helpful.

Activity	Yes	No	Comments
1. Organization of purchasing dept.			
2. Relations with user dept.			
3. Purchasing controls.			
4. Receiving controls.			
5. Storage controls.			
6. Make/buy analysis.			
7. Writing purchase specifications.			
8. Locating/working with suppliers.			
9. Personnel cooperation.			
10. Employee training.			
11. Document processing for payment.			
12. Policies.			
13. Standard operating procedures.			
14. "Paperwork."			
15. Product quality determination.			
16. Product quantity determination.			
17. Expediting/follow-up.			
18. Delivery timing.			
19. Other activities (list).			

Source: Jack D. Ninemeier, *Purchasing, Receiving, and Storage: A Systems Manual for Restaurants, Hotels, and Clubs* (New York: Van Nostrand Reinhold Company, 1983), p. 315.

activity to be considered, the evaluator can indicate (by marking either "Yes" or "No") whether improvements are needed. Specific comments can indicate examples of problems and propose corrective action strategies which might be helpful.

Ideally, the purchasing evaluation guide can be completed by personnel in several departments. Over time, it should be possible to track improvements and eliminate the repetition of similar problems. If several activities require improvements, problems of the highest priority should be selected for immediate attention; other activities can be addressed after the more important problems are resolved. Once problems have been identified, a time frame for resolving them should be established. This element of timing is an integral part of purchasing evaluation.

As a supplement to internal evaluation, it may be beneficial to request that suppliers evaluate an operation's purchasing practices. The list of questions must be framed differently and some responses may be discarded, but excellent suggestions are often received. Experienced suppliers know that it is always less costly for them to retain customers than to obtain new ones, so they may be helpful in the evaluation process.

Focus on Supplier Evaluation

Procedures to evaluate whether products are being purchased from the right source were noted earlier in this chapter. However, since the supplier is such an integral element in the success or failure of the purchasing department, much attention should be focused on evaluating supplier effectiveness.

Measurement of Costs

Hospitality operators are obviously concerned with operating costs. Suppliers should be able to deliver products of the quality specified when they are needed and at the lowest possible cost.

Situations often arise when a low-cost supplier does not perform satisfactorily in terms of service or quality. Operators do not want to eliminate a potentially cost-effective supplier. Steps should be taken to determine if supplier performance can be improved:

- The purchaser should meet with the supplier to establish and discuss the basic problems.

- The supplier should be asked to determine the nature and cause of the problem. Often, the problem relates to the hospitality operation itself—for instance, its ordering system.

- The purchaser should visit the supplier's facility to assess its capability. The purchaser should check for adequate inventory levels, sanitary storage areas, proper storeroom temperatures, and well-trained and efficient personnel.

If at all possible, it is better to help a current supplier improve below-standard performance rather than replace the supplier with one who may have higher prices. However, if poor performance continues, obviously the supplier must be eliminated from eligibility.

More often, the purchaser already has a number of suppliers who provide satisfactory quality and service. In this case, the purchaser concentrates on finding ways to reduce costs. To be successful, the purchaser must seek competitive prices or find some other means to measure the supplier's price performance.

Use of Pricing Information

There are many market price sources. For example, the major California fruit packers publish competitive price lists with an FOB price base. One can compare these lists with prices charged by local distributors. Reports for meat, fish, poultry, and dairy products provide benchmarks for measuring prices of these items. This kind of data is available to single-unit operators and can be used as a base for improvement of purchasing techniques.

Exhibit 3   Example of Product List with Prices Based on Assumed Costs

Item	Amount		Distributor Charge per Unit to Operator		Total Purchase Price	Market Price Per Unit	Estimated Cost at Processor*	Estimated Distribution Cost ** $	%
Peaches	50 cases	×	$25.00	=	$1,250	$16.00	$800	$450	56
Tomatoes	20 cases	×	15.00	=	300	10.00	200	100	50
Catsup	30 cases	×	20.00	=	600	14.00	420	180	43
Flour	20 bags	×	22.00	=	440	17.00	340	100	29
Sugar	10 bags	×	25.00	=	250	22.00	220	30	14
Shrimp	2000 lb	×	7.50	=	15,000	6.00	12,000	3,000	25
Ribs (#109)	2000 lb	×	2.55	=	5,100	2.05	4,100	1,000	24
					$22,940		$18,080	$4,860	27

* Estimated cost at processor = number of units × market price per unit
** Estimated distribution cost ($) = total purchase price − estimated cost at processor

$$\text{Estimated distribution cost (\%)} = \frac{\text{estimated distribution cost (\$)}}{\text{estimated cost at processor}} \times 100\%$$

Consider a small hospitality operation using a specified list of products each month, shown in Exhibit 3 with certain cost and price assumptions. The average spread between the market price and the distributor's charge to the hospitality operator for these products is 27%. This spread could probably be reduced with some management attention to the purchasing task. For the small operator, simply taking bids from other distributors might suffice. Larger operators and distributors need to examine the dynamics of the business for each commodity.

Cost Components of Distribution

Six components affect distribution costs: product cost, transportation, storage, handling, delivery charges, and management/overhead. Each of these components requires time and effort, resulting in added costs. Whenever a product changes hands in the distribution channel, costs are usually added to the price of the product. These costs tend to be cumulative, affecting each link in the chain of product transfer.

Each company, whatever its size, should calculate the cost effectiveness of the extra work required to reduce purchasing costs. Purchasing in large quantity carries with it a unique set of concerns.

Measurement of Supplier Efficiency

Evaluation of a supplier's performance was discussed previously with an example of a low-cost supplier who was deficient in the service and quality areas. A visit to the supplier's facility was suggested as a means to determine if the supplier had the capability to perform. Areas suggested for checking were inventory level, quality of personnel, and cleanliness.

While the focus of a supplier visit will vary depending on the issues involved, the value of such a visit should not be underestimated. Exhibit 4 is a checklist that might be used by a large hospitality operation in evaluating a distributor organization.

Exhibit 4   Measuring Supplier Efficiency

1.	**Customer Service**
_____	Number of complaints or adjustments in dollars and units relative to product volume distributed
_____	Number of emergency orders
_____	Order backlog and average time to ship ("turnaround time")
_____	Employee error rates
_____	Number of back orders
_____	Percentage of invoices filled, by line item and dollar
_____	Percentage of units shipped relative to goals and previous year's volume
_____	Number of units delivered per order compared to goals of the previous year
_____	Percentage of goods returned versus previous year
2.	**Inventory Control**
_____	Total inventory dollars and line items
_____	Inventory turns (total and by product class)
_____	Stockouts as a percentage of daily issue costs
_____	Number of items in inventory compared to previous year
_____	Physical inventory frequency and magnitude of adjustments
_____	Type of system used (manual or computerized) and its accuracy
3.	**Employee Productivity**
	(Each function is to be measured, including receiving, warehousing, loading, transportation, clerical, and maintenance)
_____	Cases per labor hour
_____	Weight or volume per labor hour
_____	Cases per truck
_____	Cases per delivery
_____	Dollars per order and delivery
_____	Time required for delivery
_____	Trucks loaded per labor hour
4.	**Cost Effectiveness**
_____	Inbound freight cost by unit
_____	Outbound freight cost by unit
_____	Vehicle cost per mile
_____	Costs per case for all warehousing functions
_____	Sales per labor hour and/or employee
_____	Cost percentage to sales compared to previous year
_____	Sales per vehicle mile
5.	**Facility Utilization**
_____	Storage locations used, expressed as a percent of locations available
_____	Inventory value per square or cubic foot compared to previous year's value
_____	Cost to maintain inventory per square foot compared to previous year

Endnotes

1. The remainder of this section is adapted from Jack D. Ninemeier, *Purchasing, Receiving, and Storage: A Systems Manual for Restaurants, Hotels, and Clubs* (New York: Van Nostrand Reinhold Company, 1983), pp. 191–192.

REVIEW QUIZ

When you feel you have covered all of the material in this chapter, answer these questions. Choose the *best* answer. Check your answers with the correct ones found on the Review Quiz Answer Key at the end of this book.

True (T) or False (F)

T   F   1. Measurable goals must be developed to effectively evaluate the purchasing system.   T

T   F   2. Purchasing staff should be solely responsible for evaluating whether purchasing tasks were successfully completed.   F

T   F   3. High purchase costs may be not the fault of purchasing practices, but rather beyond the control of the purchasing staff.   T

T   F   4. Goals associated with purchasing evaluation should not be confined to any specific time period.   F

T   F   5. Some variance between expected and actual performance is permitted before corrective action must be taken.   T

T   F   6. After implementing corrective actions, no further evaluation is necessary.   F

T   F   7. Each additional product transfer in the distribution system adds to product costs.   T

Multiple Choice

8. Which is *not* a basic step in the evaluation of purchasing activities?

   a. identifying goals of purchasing
   b. assessing performance by comparing actual results with goals
   c. taking corrective action to resolve problems
   d. comparing all products within a single category

9. An evaluation of supplier efficiency should be based on:

   a. customer service.
   b. inventory control.
   c. cost effectiveness.
   d. all of the above.

Part II
The Commodities

Buying techniques are as diverse as the different industries which market goods. Purchasers must be familiar with traditional marketing practices prevailing in each industry in order to make intelligent buying decisions. Buyers must also realize that federal and state governments are active participants in many areas of the food industry. This book will inform buyers of what they need to know so that government *helps* rather than *hinders* the purchasing process.

For many hospitality operations, meat and meat products represent the largest single category of expenses. Accordingly, we devote considerable attention to this area of purchases. The topic has been divided into two chapters. Chapter 8 provides an overview of the meat industry with special consideration given to beef. Chapter 9 focuses on yield and pricing issues and extends the discussion to characteristics unique to the purchase of pork, veal, and lamb.

Rates of per capita consumption for both fish and poultry have been on the rise in recent years. Chapter 10 presents the fishing industry as a worldwide enterprise. Many commercially important varieties of fish and shellfish are highlighted; concern for quality is at the forefront of our discussion. Chapter 11 shifts the spotlight to poultry and eggs. Distribution patterns and pricing examples will help the reader develop a clear understanding of poultry and egg marketing.

The dairy industry is subject to a highly restrictive system of production and marketing. Chapter 12 clarifies the major aspects of this complex industry to illustrate how these items move through distribution channels. It also gives quality checks for milk, cream, processed dairy products, frozen desserts, cheese, and butter.

Due to the perishability of fresh fruits and vegetables, yield on the plate is as important a factor in selecting these products as cost itself. In Chapter 13, you will learn how to follow the costs of fresh produce from the various seasonal shipping areas, through local distribution systems, to the hospitality operation.

Baked goods and miscellaneous food items together form the core of Chapter 14. Distribution options for baked goods are analyzed in terms of recent trends. The chapter also discusses purchase factors for a wide range of groceries—including grains, sugar products, spices, and field products. Another broad category of hospitality purchases is convenience foods. Chapter 15 views this critical topic from a management standpoint.

Beverages are among the highest profit items served in food service operations. Chapter 16 examines the choice between recognized beverage brands and private labels in light of costs and guest preferences. Chapter 17 rounds out the discussion with a look at equipment, services, and supplies, often neglected but nonetheless important areas of expenses.

Chapter Outline

Background
    Changing Geography of Meat
        Production
    Meat Consumption and Production
        Cycles
    Supplier Distribution Systems
The Government's Role in Regulating Meat
    Commerce
    Quality Grading Service
Meat Specifications
Information for Meat Purchasers
Forecasting Meat Prices
    Short-Term Planning
    Long-Term Planning
Meat-Buying Systems
    Ride the Market
    Cost-Plus
    Buy-and-Inventory
    Long-Term Contracts
    Cross-Hedging
    Vertical Integration

Learning Objectives

1. Describe the economic factors that influence the production, supply, and pricing of meat.

2. Explain the major legislation affecting the meat industry.

3. Explain the grading services available for meat.

4. Explain the criteria and content of meat specifications.

5. List the sources of information available to assist in purchase decisions.

6. Explain the factors involved in price forecasting.

7. List and explain the six major systems for buying meat.

8

Meat Products: An Overview

MEAT PRODUCTS are "big ticket" items for most hospitality operations, representing a substantial portion of total food costs. This chapter serves as an overview of information regarding imports/exports, production areas and cycles, governmental role, grades and standards, and marketing and distribution, as well as detailed criteria for meat specifications.

Background

The United States leads the world in meat production. High-quality meat produced in the United States is exported primarily to Japan and Middle Eastern nations. In most meat-producing nations, cattle are used both for meat and milk. The meat from these animals is typically of a lower quality grade than grain-fed beef. In the United States, grain is used extensively to produce meat that is flavorful and well-marbled (flecked with fat). No other nation uses grain supplies to this extent as a means to raise beef. Many countries (notably Argentina, Australia, and New Zealand) produce meat stock animals, but they are grass-fed.

Though a leader in meat production, the United States still imports more meat than it exports. Imported lamb (good quality, ready-to-use form) and frozen beef come from Australia, New Zealand, and Central America. Imported beef is further processed into such products as ground beef, sausage, and luncheon meats. While some specialty beef (top round, boneless strip loin, and tenderloin) is imported, the only pork product imported in any quantity is canned ham from Europe. Quotas are established annually by Congress to regulate meat import volumes. Countries exporting to the United States must use disease-free animals and follow U.S. sanitation standards. Cooked meat products may be imported into the United States if certain bacteriological standards and sanitary regulations are followed by the processing plant and importer.

Changing Geography of Meat Production

The economy of the midwestern United States historically was based upon small self-contained farms. Animals were shipped to major metropolitan areas for slaughter and distribution. As refrigeration and transportation techniques improved, production facilities concentrated in major transportation hubs such as Chicago and Kansas City. As the meat industry was evolving in middle America, a separate meat industry grew on the West Coast. Its independence was due primarily to distribution problems caused by its remoteness and inadequate modes of transportation.

During World War II, sanitation became important as it became necessary to hold meat for longer periods of time. Transportation methods improved as did

---

Federal Government Influences Meat Prices

The federal government has considerable impact on grain prices. Farm production is influenced through the use of subsidies, loans, and support prices. Grain export activity is regulated in attempts to satisfy political considerations, both international and domestic in nature. These factors help determine the price of feed grain which, in turn, affects meat prices.

---

packaging, and meat products were successfully frozen. Although these developments improved product quality and permitted better distribution, they also added costs. In an effort to hold down these costs, production facilities moved closer to the animal supply centers. New organizations and cooperatives in Iowa, Nebraska, Missouri, Kansas, and western Illinois began to process animals for shipment to large cities.

Today, beef production is moving toward the South, with large plants in southern Missouri, western Texas, and Oklahoma. Primary reasons for this move south include the availability of improved grain supplies, a climate permitting better weight gains, and low-cost non-unionized labor. The future will probably see production plants along the Gulf Coast as well.

In the United States, pork production is decentralized and largely dependent upon local farmers for animals. The best known brand names are manufactured by pork processing plants located in the upper Midwest. However, manufacturers of private label pork products are concentrating in the South for the same reasons as the beef industry.

Meat Consumption and Production Cycles

The per capita consumption of beef, pork, and poultry products varies in relation to their prices. Meat prices are largely determined by supply levels, which may vary depending on any number of influences. For example, consumer health and fitness concerns, import volumes from foreign countries, and governmental regulation of the industry all affect meat availability.

The meat production industry is cyclical: overproduction increases supply levels and lowers prices to such an extent that animal herds are eventually reduced to lower supply levels and increase prices. In the effort to benefit from the higher prices, the industry increases supply levels and soon overproduction once again creates conditions for lower prices, and the cycle repeats itself. However, meat production is not determined solely by market prices. For instance, the slaughter of cows (mature female bovines once used for milk production) adds significantly to the U.S. meat supply.* The number of cows available for meat production not only

---

*Cow meat is primarily used for manufacturing ground meat and other processed products and does not directly compete with "fat" cattle (heifers and steers raised for meat production).

depends on market prices for meat, but also on milk prices, animal age, and the availability and price of feed.

Supplier Distribution Systems

Today, the meat processing (packing) industry is consolidated, with large national companies controlling most of the supply. Imports are handled by a relatively small number of companies located in the major port cities. Few animals are raised and processed near the areas where they are consumed, so transportation costs represent a large percentage of consumer prices. A response to lower transportation costs has been the change in packaging from traditional hanging cuts to boxed beef. Most of the fresh meat used by hospitality operators is shipped by the processor in boxed form.

Just as the meat processing industry has evolved, so have local urban area distribution systems. Large retail chains may buy direct from processors and provide their own distribution and further processing if required. Large hospitality chains may buy direct from processors; they may provide their own distribution or contract with local purveyors for this service, as well as further processing. Regional chains or cooperatives may buy certain items direct or may delegate this function to local purveyors, who then provide distribution and any further processing that is required. Local operators usually depend on local purveyors to obtain, further process, and distribute needed products.

As just noted, local purveyors offer a variety of different services to local hospitality operators. In addition to the standard cut and ground products, they produce value-added items such as beef kabobs and chicken patties. Distribution channels may also include specialized distributors.

Meat processors, distributors, and chains tend to stick with their sources of supply, since a constant product volume is needed. Price may be negotiated and/or based on one of the market news services which report prices. Purchasers usually have at least two processor sources and vary business between them depending upon price. Also, effective purchasing techniques include:

- Buying under a measurable agreement negotiated when supplies are abundant.

- Insisting on compliance by the seller during periods of shortage.

- Resisting those "bargains" that do not actually save money or improve inventory.

The Government's Role in Regulating Meat Commerce

The Federal Meat Inspection Act of 1906 gave the federal government responsibility for ensuring that all red meat and meat products moving through interstate and foreign commerce are wholesome, processed under sanitary conditions, and accurately labeled.[1] Since meat products shipped within a state were not covered by the 1906 act, states had to develop programs to accommodate that need. The Wholesome Meat Act of 1967 strengthened the enforcement of standards at plants exporting to this country and also established federal-state cooperative inspection

Exhibit 1   Sample USDA Wholesomeness Inspection Stamps

Sample Stamp	Use
38 U.S. INSP'D & P'S'D	Carcass (Hanging Meat)
U.S. INSPECTED AND PASSED BY DEPARTMENT OF AGRICULTURE EST. 38	Prepackaged/Processed Meat Products

programs and required state programs to be at least equal to federal inspection requirements and standards. Products inspected solely under state inspection programs can be distributed only within that state.

Meat Inspection and Labeling. Animal inspection occurs before and during slaughter. After slaughter, the carcass and organs are examined for disease or contamination. If the carcass is wholesome, it receives a stamp by an on-line inspector from the United States Department of Agriculture (USDA). Veterinarians oversee this inspection process and regularly visit slaughtering plants.

After slaughter, a great deal of meat is processed into consumer products such as frankfurters. Since the original inspection stamp is obliterated during processing, an additional inspection is required. The USDA may authorize a plant meeting certain standards to perform this inspection itself, through the company's quality control department. USDA personnel visit plants using this program to determine if the plant is in compliance. The official label is issued on the authority of the Food Safety and Quality Service (FSQS) agency of the USDA.

Inspection Stamps. A USDA inspection stamp appears on all meat products, both hanging (carcass) and boxed (processed), if federally inspected for wholesomeness or fitness for human consumption. Exhibit 1 displays inspection stamps for carcass and processed meat products. Inspection stamp numbers refer to the establishment number of the processing plant. States may have their own inspection stamps.

Exhibit 2 displays a side of beef showing wholesomeness inspection stamps. Note that a number of stamps are located on different parts of the carcass so that the identity will be retained when the animal is broken into primal (wholesale) cuts. All beef moving in interstate commerce must carry such inspection stamps on the primal cuts.

Exhibit 2   Carcass Displaying USDA Inspection Stamps

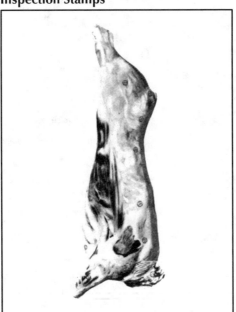

Quality Grading Service

Beef, veal, and lamb may be graded for quality. Pork grades incorporate some quality aspects, but are primarily based on yield. Quality grading programs have become the basis for most commercial transactions in the meat industry. To be eligible for quality grading, the carcass must first pass the inspection for wholesomeness. Quality grading, unlike inspection for wholesomeness, is a federal government service to meat packers and must be paid for. A grade shield is applied by a USDA inspector as carcasses move along the production line. Inspectors grade on the basis of the amount of marbling (flecks of fat in the main muscle tissue), the condition of the lean, the color of the fat, and the color of the bones of the carcass.

If the packer does not use the USDA grading service, products can be marketed in either of the following ways: (1) the packer can use a private label identifying the packer's personal quality levels, or (2) the product can be sold as a "no-roll" (which means that it has not been quality graded).

USDA Grades. USDA Prime and USDA Choice are synonymous with quality, representing the two top grades of beef. Exhibit 3 summarizes the grades for which the USDA has issued official standards. The various kinds of meat are distinguished by class, which is essentially determined by species, age, and sex of the animal. As a practical matter, little grain-fed beef below the level of Choice is quality graded.

Marbling and animal maturity have historically been required to classify an item as either USDA Prime or USDA Choice. The amount of marbling influences flavor; more marbling is associated with more flavor. However, changes were

Exhibit 3   USDA Classification and Grading Schedule for Carcass Meats

Animal	Grade Designations*
Beef	
Quality grades	
• steer, heifer, cow**	prime, choice, good, standard, commercial, utility, cutter, and canner
• bull and stag	choice, good, commercial, utility, cutter, and canner
Yield grades (cutability)	1, 2, 3, 4, 5
Calf	prime, choice, good, standard, utility, cull
Veal	prime, choice, good, standard, utility, cull
Lamb, Yearling Mutton, and Mutton	
Quality grades for lamb and yearling mutton	prime, choice, good, utility, cull
Quality grades for mutton	choice, good, utility, cull
Yield grades (cutability)	1, 2, 3, 4, 5
Pork Carcasses	
Quality grades	
• barrows and gilts	U.S. No. 1, 2, 3, 4, utility
• sows	U.S. No. 1, 2, 3, medium, cull

*In descending order
**Cows are not eligible for prime grade.

made in traditional grading standards in 1976. The net result was to permit some animals which previously would have been graded as USDA Good to be classified as USDA Choice and those previously in the top portion of the USDA Choice grade to be classified as USDA Prime.

Buyers should understand that there are really two non-official quality levels within the Choice grade: top half and lower half. The buyer who wants the highest quality within the grade should designate the top half of the range (for example, top choice). Frequently, packers accept this request and, for a fee, retain an employee on the production line to select the highest quality products from among those graded. Most products in the lower half of the range regularly appear in retail grocery stores.

Yield Grades. Yield grades for beef, lamb, and mutton carcasses are designed to identify carcasses for differences in cutability or yield of boneless, closely trimmed cuts from the round, loin, chuck, and rib. Yield grades help the buyer indicate the amount of usable meat relative to the amount of waste that is trimmed and removed. The primary considerations used in yield grading are:

Beef
Thickness of fat over ribeye muscle
Percentage of kidney, pelvic, and
   heart fat
Area of the ribeye muscle
Carcass weight

Lamb/Mutton
Amount of external fat
Amount of kidney and pelvic fat
Conformation grade of the leg

Exhibit 4   USDA Yield Grade Stamps

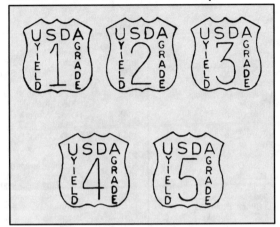

Exhibit 4 illustrates yield grade marks. Yield grades range from 1 through 5 within each quality grade. Carcasses in yield grade 1 have the highest degree of cutability; those in yield grade 5 have the lowest. The most important factor in determining the yield grade of beef and lamb is the amount of external fat measured over the area of the 12th rib. Yield grade 1 provides more usable meat than yield grade 5, which has excessive fat cover and a small ribeye muscle. Most beef from feedlots receives a yield grade of 3 or 4.[2]

Meat Specifications

Since most meat is sold sight unseen, standard purchase specifications are required. Fortunately, well-established standards form the basis for meat commerce. The USDA established specifications in the early part of this century. These specifications have been amended many times, often with industry input, and are referred to as Institutional Meat Purchase Specifications (IMPS).

For easy reference, IMPS numbers have been assigned to specifications for a variety of meat products. For example, IMPS numbers in the 100 series refer to fresh beef: item #100 is carcass; item #101 is side; item #103 is rib, primal; and so on. By telling the supplier that a #109 roast-ready rib is desired, the guesswork regarding trim and cutting is eliminated. Exhibit 5 illustrates the wide range of beef products which have established IMPS designations.

In addition to IMPS number, the buyer must provide other specifics for products desired. For example, in the case of roasts and portion items, buyers should specify grade, age of the animal, packaging, unit weight and tolerance, and any modification in trim compared to the standard item. In the case of ground portions, buyers should indicate raw material components, fat percentages, permitted bacterial count, packaging, condition (frozen or fresh), and unit weights.

No standard specifications exist for products such as precooked rounds, corned beef, and hot dogs. In the case of hot dogs, grades and type of meat can be

Exhibit 5   Index of Beef Products Covered by IMPS

Item No.	Product	Item No.	Product
100	Carcass	163	Round, Shank Off, 3-Way, Boneless
101	Side	164	Round, Rump & Shank Off
102	Forequarter	165	Round, Rump & Shank Off, Boneless
102A	Forequarter, Boneless	165A	Round, Rump & Shank Off, Boneless, Special
103	Rib, Primal		
107	Rib, Oven-Prepared	165B	Round, Rump & Shank Off, Boneless, Tied, Special
109	Rib, Roast-Ready		
109A	Rib, Roast-Ready, Special	166	Round, Rump & Shank Off, Boneless, Tied
109B	Blade Meat		
110	Rib, Roast-Ready, Boneless, Tied	166A	Round, Rump Partially Removed, Shank Off
111	Spencer Roll		
112	Ribeye Roll	167	Knuckle
112A	Ribeye Roll, Lip-On	167A	Knuckle, Trimmed
113	Square-Cut Chuck	168	Top (Inside) Round
114	Shoulder Clod	170	Bottom (Gooseneck) Round
114A	Shoulder Clod Roast	170A	Bottom (Gooseneck) Round, Heel Out
115	Square-Cut Chuck, Boneless	171	Bottom (Gooseneck) Round, Untrimmed
116	Square-Cut Chuck, Boneless, Clod Out	171A	Bottom (Gooseneck) Round, Untrimmed, Heel Out
116A	Chuck Roll		
117	Foreshank	171B	Outside Round
118	Brisket	171C	Eye of Round
119	Brisket, Boneless, Deckle On	172	Full Loin, Trimmed
120	Brisket, Boneless, Deckle Off	173	Short Loin
121	Short Plate	174	Short Loin, Short Cut
121A	Short Plate, Boneless	175	Strip Loin
122	Full Plate	176	Strip Loin, Boneless
122A	Full Plate, Boneless	177	Strip Loin, Intermediate
123	Short Ribs	178	Strip Loin, Intermediate, Boneless
123A	Short Ribs, Short Plate	179	Strip Loin, Short Cut
123B	Short Ribs, Special	180	Strip Loin, Short Cut, Boneless
125	Armbone Chuck	181	Sirloin
126	Armbone Chuck, Boneless, Clod Out	182	Sirloin Butt, Boneless
127	Cross-Cut Chuck	183	Sirloin Butt, Trimmed
128	Cross-Cut Chuck, Boneless	184	Top Sirloin Butt
132	Triangle	185	Bottom Sirloin Butt
133	Triangle, Boneless	185A	Bottom Sirloin, Flap
134	Beef Bones	185B	Bottom Sirloin, Ball Tip
135	Diced Beef	185C	Bottom Sirloin, Triangle
135A	Beef for Stewing	185D	Bottom Sirloin Butt, Trimmed
136	Ground Beef, Regular	186	Bottom Sirloin Butt, Triangle
136A	Ground Beef, Regular, TVP Added	189	Full Tenderloin
137	Ground Beef, Special	189A	Full Tenderloin, Defatted
155	Hindquarter	190	Full Tenderloin, Special
155A	Hindquarter, Boneless	190A	Full Tenderloin, Skinned
158	Round, Primal	191	Butt Tenderloin
159	Round, Boneless	192	Short Tenderloin
160	Round, Shank Off, Partially Boneless	193	Flank Steak
161	Round, Shank Off, Boneless		

Source: USDA, *Institutional Meat Purchase Specifications for Fresh Beef* (Washington, D.C.: U.S. Government Printing Office, 1975).

specified, but are impossible to verify after the product is processed. USDA regulations for labeling can help in this instance. Hot dogs must be labeled for content depending on the raw material used (beef, all meat, chicken). Labels also help in purchasing boxed meats. If USDA Choice cooked top rounds are purchased, the box should be labeled USDA Choice. If not so labeled, the buyer has no way to confirm the grade. In the case of ham, the label must state "water added" if the cure process included this step.

Good procedures for establishing and evaluating specifications for processed items include:

- Conducting comparative evaluations of two or more competitive products, which include such factors as palatability (flavor, tenderness, and juiciness), appearance, packaging, yields, and shelf life.

- Developing specifics for required products. For example, a specification for cooked top rounds should indicate USDA grade, fat, seasoning level, degree of doneness, free liquid in the bag, and packaging requirements.

Specifications should be stated in commonly understood terminology. For red meat, common terms are based on the USDA/IMPS number system. For processed items, industry practices may be modified to meet the organization's specific needs.

Information for Meat Purchasers

The buying system used by the purchasing agent depends on the size of the organization and its facilities. Many of the techniques used by large-volume buyers can be used by buyers at smaller properties who deal with local purveyors, but buyers must make adjustments depending on local conditions. Purchasing performance can be improved by taking advantage of common practices used throughout the industry to ascertain meat prices. Knowledgeable buyers must know sources of price information.

Meat prices are determined by buyer-seller interactions in the marketing channels, which allow transfer of products from ranchers to end-users through such intermediaries as feedlots, packers, and purveyors. Buyers must be in the marketplace interacting with sellers. In addition to information from sellers, outside sources provide price information. While the USDA publishes price data, two competing publications are more widely used: *The Yellow Sheet* and *The Meat Sheet*. Both publish weekly reports and provide market data and opinions regarding prices on a wide range of meat products.[3] Data used to form price opinions are obtained by telephone contact with buyers and sellers.

Excerpts from a typical report of *The Yellow Sheet* (published by the National Provisioner) are found in Exhibit 6, which illustrates the type of information helpful in making buying decisions. The prices shown are primarily identified as carload, less than carload (LCL), and job lot. While some purveyors buy in carloads (approximately 36,000 pounds), most buy in LCL or job lot quantities.

FOB points are identified in both publications. Freight costs to destinations must be added when making local item comparisons; these costs vary with distance and shipment size. The buyer should allow one week lag time for the packer prices shown in these publications to affect local purveyors, since meat requires approximately one week to reach purveyors.

The National Provisioner also publishes *Hotel, Restaurant, Institution Meat Price Report* (often called "The Green Sheet") as shown in Exhibit 7. This report provides an opinion of prices paid to wholesalers and purveyors by commercial feeders (hospitality operators). Data from Exhibits 6 and 7 are used throughout this chapter.

Exhibit 6 Sample Issue of *The Yellow Sheet*, Thursday, April 24, 1986

PRICES REPRESENT F.O.B. MIDWEST RIVER AREA AT END OF TRADING DAY ON STANDARD PRODUCT, CARLOT BASIS LOOSE, IMMEDIATE SHIPMENT, UNLESS OTHERWISE STATED.

KEY: b-bid; ax-asked; n-nominal (approximate value in absence of trading); f.f.a.-fresh freezer accumulation; @-to; f.c. full carcass; c.t.-cellar trim; p.t.-private terms; l.c.l.-less than carlot; l.t.l.-less than truck load; t.i.s.-transfer in store; f.o.b. price does not incl. freight; c.a.f.-cost includes freight; f.a.s.-export sale price includes freight to shipside; c.i.f.-cost insurance, freight to export destination; unq-unquoted; inactive; inconsistent.

FRESH PORK CUTS

FROZEN F.O.B. MIDWEST RIVER AREA		F.F.A. OR FRESH F.O.B. MIDWEST RIVER AREA
unq	Skd. Hams 14/dn	unq
unq	Skd. Hams 14/17	57@58
unq	Skd. Hams 17/20	53@54
unq	Skd. Hams 20/26	53@54
unq	Skd. Hams 26/32	52
unq	Skd. Hams 32/up, 2's in	52
	Picnics 4/8	38@39
	Picnics 8/up, 2's in	35
	(Square Cut Seedless)	
	Bellies 10/12	40½
	Bellies 12/14	48½
	Bellies 14/16	48½
	Bellies 16/18	45
	Bellies 18/20	41
	Bellies 20/25	39

JOB LOT FRESH CHGO. BASIS	(PACKED)	CAR LOT FRESH F.O.B. MIDWEST RIVER AREA
95	Reg. Loins 14/dn	91
95	Reg. Loins 14/18	90@91
96	Reg. Loins 18/22	91@92
92	Reg. Loins 22/up	88
67	Bst. Btts, 4/8 (Dom)	63
67	Bst. Btts, 8/up (Dom)	63
57½	Skd. Shoulders 16/dn	53½
55	Skd. Shoulders 16/up	51
		FROZEN
200@210	Canadian Backs 5/9	unq
235@245	Tenderloins 10's	unq
135	Bnls. Butts, C.T. 1½/3	120
135	Bnls. Butts, C.T. 3/4½	120
135	Bnls. Butts, C.T. 4½/6	120
130	Spareribs 3½/dn	125@126
100	Spareribs 3½/5½	96
65	Spareribs 5½/up	61

FRESH PORK CUTS

JOB LOT FRESH CHGO. BASIS	(PACKED)	CAR LOT FROZEN F.O.B. MIDWEST RIVER AREA
150@160	Bk. Loin Ribs 1¾/dn	unq
15½	Neckbones	11@11½
34	Tails	30
19	Feet Front, Toes On	15
	Skins (Selected) Dom	8½
	Skins Gelatin (Dom.)	5
	Skins Gelatin (Export)	unq

SAUSAGE MATERIALS

JOB LOT FRESH CHGO. BASIS	(PACKED)	CAR LOT F.O.B. MIDWEST RIVER AREA FRESH	FROZEN
41	50% Lean Trg. *(42%)	31	unq
70	80% Lean Trg. *(72%)	58	59
70½	Bnls. Picnics *(72%)	58½	61
105	Blade Meat	unq	75
37½	Skinned Jowls	27½	25

*CHEMICAL

PORK VARIETY MEAT

JOB LOT CHGO. BASIS FRESH OR FROZEN	(PACKED)	CAR LOT F.O.B. MIDWEST RIVER AREA FROZEN
26½	Chitterlings, 10's	23½
65	Cheek Meat, Trimmed	62
18	Ears	15
21½	Hearts	18½
16½	Kidneys (Domestic) Lge. Bxs.	13½
unq	Salivary Glands	14
17½	Livers (Domestic) Lge. Bxs.	14½
unq	Livers (Export) Boxes	14½
14	Melts	11
unq	Head Meat	40
19	Snouts, Lean in.	16
unq	Tongues, Bnls. Scld. & Scrpd.	49
unq	Tongues Bnls. (Green)	47
17½	Stomachs, Scalded 30/35's	14½
17½	Stomachs, Scalded 80's	14½

D.R. TANKAGE (UNGROUND)

F.O.B. MIDWEST RIVER AREA		F.O.B. ILL. IND.-WIS.-MICH.
2.20	Lo. Test	2.20
2.10	Md. Test	2.10
2.00	Hi. Test	2.00

DRIED BLOOD

F.O.B. MIDWEST RIVER AREA		F.O.B. ILL. IND.-WIS.-MICH.
275	Ring Dry	275
132½	50% Mt & Bomeal	135@137½
	Feather Meal, South	110

CALF SKINS (N.Y. PACKER TRIM)

(CURED-SELECTED)	CARLOT
5/7 lb.	12.75
7/9 lb.	14.25
9/12 lb.	17.50
12/17 lb.	21.00
17/25 lb.	22.50
17/25 lb. H&W	25.00

HIDES MIDWEST SMALL PACKER

AVG. (PLUMP & MEDIUM)	NATIVE
60/62 (all wts.)	51
50/52 (all wts.)	54
50/60 (56 avg.)	55
30/50 (45 avg.)	60

LARD & EDIBLE TALLOW

TANK TRUCKS & TANK CARS
C.A.F. CHICAGO BASIS

P.S. and/or C.P.	
Loose Lard	11
Edible Tallow	11@11½

CRUDE VEGETABLE OILS

Corn Oil, Mill	18½
Soybean Oil, Decatur	17¼
Peanut Oil, S.E.	unq
Coconut Oil, Pac. Coast	12
Cottonseed Oil, Valley	17½
Cottonseed Oil, Texas	17½
Palm Oil, West Coast)	13¼

PROCESSOR HIDES

	F.O.B. MIDWEST RIVER AREA	PACKER
65	Strs. Lt. Nat.	67
unq	Strs. Hvy. Nat.	65@66
unq	Strs. Colo.	60½
unq	Strs. Butt Brd.	62½
unq	Heifers Brd.	61½
56	Cows Lt. Nat.	58
unq	Cows Hvy. Nat.	53
45@48	Cows Brd.	50@51
unq	Bulls Nat.	39

TALLOWS AND GREASES-INEDIBLE

TANK TRUCKS & TANK CARS
C.A.F. CHICAGO BASIS

TALLOWS:	TITRE MIN.	F.F.A. MAX.	F.A.C. MAX. UNBLEACHED	
Fan. Blch.	41.5	4	1.5RB	10¾@11
Prime Tal.	40.6	6	13 or 11B	10½
Special	40.5	10	19 (11C)	9¼
No. 1	40.5	15	33	9n
No. 2	40	35	NO COL.	7
GREASES:				
Choice White (All Hog)	37	2/4	11	10
B-White	36	10	19	9¼
Yellow	36	15	37	8¾
House	37.5	20	39	7n

F.O.B. MIDWEST RIVER AREA

Fan. Blch.	41.5	4	1.5RB	9¼
Choice White	37	2/4	11	9⅛
Yellow	36	15	37	8

C.A.F. GULF PORTS

Fan. Blch.	41.5	4	1.5RB	11@11½
Choice White	37	2/4	11	11¼ax

THE NATIONAL PROVISIONER DAILY MARKET SERVICE
Thurs., Apr. 24, 1986--Series BL No. 78

PRICES REPRESENT F.O.B. MIDWEST RIVER AREA AT END OF TRADING DAY ON STANDARD PRODUCT, CARLOT BASIS LOOSE, IMMEDIATE SHIPMENT, UNLESS OTHERWISE STATED.

U.S. GRADE CARCASSES

F.O.B. MIDWEST RIVER AREA

HOLSTEIN	CARLOT	NATIVE
unq	Gd. Hfrs. 4/5	69
unq	Gd. Hfrs. 5/550	69
unq	Gd. Hfrs. 550/7	76
72	Gd. Strs. 6/7	80
72	Gd. Strs. 7/8	80
72	Gd. Strs. 8/9	80
75	Ch. Strs. 5/8	
YIELD 4		YIELD 3
unq	Ch. Hfrs. 4/5	78
68@69	Ch. Hfrs. 5/550	79
68@69	Ch. Hfrs. 550/7	82ax
unq	Ch. Strs. 5/6	unq
68@69	Ch. Strs. 6/7	83
68@69	Ch. Strs. 7/8	83
68@69	Ch. Strs. 8/9	83
HEIFERS	CHOICE YIELD 3	STEERS
64ax	Fores, 5/7	64ax
64ax	Fores, 7/8	64ax
102@103	Hinds, 5/7	unq
unq	Hinds, 7/8	unq

CHOICE PRIMAL CUTS YIELD 3

F.O.B. MIDWEST RIVER AREA
4,000 lb. LOTS/UP

Ribs, 25/30	110
Ribs, 30/35	112
No. 1 Briskets, 12/up	unq
No. 1 Navels	39
No. 1 Rough Flanks	30@33

CARCASS COWS AND BULLS

SOUTH	F.O.B. MIDWEST RIVER AREA	NORTH
68½@69	C.C. 350/up	70
63@64	Bng. Utl. 4/up	65@66
unq	Brk. Utl. 5/up	unq
	Bolo Bulls 5/up.	81½

BNLS. PROCESSING BEEF

CARLOT FRESH	F.O.B. MIDWEST RIVER AREA	CARLOT FROZEN
32	Trmgs. 50/Ln Chm.	35
57ax.	Trmgs. 65/Ln Chm.	unq
75½	Trmgs. 75/Ln Chm.	71
89	Trmgs. 85/Ln Chm.	unq
98	Trmgs. 90/Ln Chm.	unq

L.C.L. FRESH		CARLOT FROZEN
106	Carc. Bolo Bullmt.	unq

UTIL. BONELESS BEEF

L.C.L. FRESH	F.O.B. MIDWEST RIVER AREA	CARLOT FROZEN
103@106	Bls. Chucks	unq
103@106	Shldr. Clods	unq
132@236	Insides	128ax
130@134	Outsides	unq
122@124	Knuckles	unq

CHOICE LAMBS

F.O.B. MIDWEST RIVER AREA

Lambs, 35/45	150
Lambs, 45/50	150
Lambs, 50/55	150
Lambs, 55/65	145
Lambs, 65/75	140

AUST. N.Z.FROZ.IMPORTED MEATS

F.O.B. PORT OF ENTRY-USUAL TERMS

SPOT	CHEM. LEAN		7 TO 45 DAYS
94½@95	Blend Cow	90%	unq
unq	Separate	85%	92½ax
86@87	CFM Fore	85%	83@85
90	Chucks	85%	unq
100	Bull	90%	93@96
96	Shank	85%	93ax
116	GAQ Inside		109@112
unq	GAQ Outside		unq
unq	GAQ Knuckle		110@111
84	MX. Trim.	85%	unq
69½	MX. Trim.	75%	67@68
57ax	MX. Trim.	65%	52@54

BEEF VARIETY MEATS

F.O.B. MIDWEST RIVER AREA

BOXED CARLOT	FROZEN
Sel. Oxtails (Sm. Boxes)	44
Oxtails (Cow)	40@43
No. 1 Tongues, 8 to box	unq
No. 2 Tongues	unq
Trimmed Cheek Meat	51
Head Meat	46
Hearts, Bone Removed	unq
Kidneys (Sm. Boxes)	14½
Livers, Sel. 2/box, Dom.	17ax
Livers, Sel. 2/box, Exp.	19ax
Livers, Reg. 2/box, Dom.	14ax
Livers, Reg. 2/box, Exp.	15ax
Sel. Oxlips, Unscalded	31ax
Oxlips, (Cow) Unscalded	27ax
Melts	8ax
Salivary Glands	10ax
Tripe, Scalded	11ax

CHOICE FABRICATED BEEF CUTS-VACUUM PACKED/BOXED F.O.B. MIDWEST RIVER AREA

	WTS.	CARS	L.C.L.
...	3x4 Rib 18/30	149@154	150@156
109	Rib Roast 20/dn	unq	174@180
109	Rib Roast 20/up	unq	187@190
112A	Rib Eye Lip On 8/14	unq	299@300
113A	2Pc. Chuck 70/110	66@68	72
...	2Pc. Bnls. Chuck 60/100	85	84@88
...	3Pc. Chuck 70/110	71@72	unq
114	Shoulder Clod 13/25	90@91	90@98
116A	Chuck Roll 12/20	95@98	101
120	Brisket 7/15	75½@81	79@81
126	Bnls Arm Chuck 60/110	76	77@80
160	Round 45/75	106½@111	105@113
161	Bnls. Round 40/70	120@122	116@120
167	Knuckles 8/12	unq	130
168	Insides 15/25	136@137	132@139
170	Goosenecks 20/30	103	106@108
...	8" Diamond Loin 40/55	185@194	181@192
174	Short Loin 20/up	unq	233@238
175	Strip Loin 15/up	185	195
180	Bnls. Strip Loin 8/10	unq	unq
180	Bnls. Strip Loin 10/14	unq	275@277
184	Top Sirloin Butt 8/10	unq	200@203
184	Top Sirloin Butt 10/14	190	200@203
185	Bott Sirloin Butt 7/dn	unq	unq
185	Bott Sirloin Butt 7/up	71@79	73
189	Tenderloin 5/7	unq	320@332
189	Tenderloin 7/9	unq	343@348
189A	Tenderloin Defat 5/dn	unq	421@431
189A	Tenderloin Defat 5/up	unq	444@450
193	Flank Steak	unq	215@225
...	73% Ln. Coarse Ground	69@71	74@80
...	80% Ln. Coarse Ground	84	84@90

GOOD OR NO-ROLL EQUIVALENT FABRICATED BEEF CUTS-VACUUM PACKED/BOXED F.O.B. MIDWEST RIVER AREA

	WTS.	CARS	L.C.L.
...	3x4 Rib 18/30	144	unq
109	Rib Roast 20/dn	unq	173@177
109	Rib Roast 20/up	unq	173@177
112A	Rib Eye Lip On 8/14	unq	281@289
113A	2Pc. Chuck 70/110	67@68	67
...	2Pc. Bnls. Chuck 60/100	86	88
...	3Pc. Chuck 70/110	unq	unq
114	Shoulder Clod 13/25	95@96	99
116A	Chuck Roll 12/20	98	99
120	Brisket 7/15	77	77@80
126	Bnls Arm Chuck 60/110	78½	83
160	Round 45/75	106	109
161	Bnls Round 40/70	121	118@124
167	Knuckles 8/12	124	130
168	Insides 15/25	131	128@132
170	Goosenecks 20/30	101	100@103
...	8" Diamond Loin 40/55	182	unq
174	Short Loin 20/up	unq	228
175	Strip Loin 15/up	unq	186@194
180	Bnls. Strip Loin 8/10	unq	248@254
180	Bnls. Strip Loin 10/14	248	248@254
184	Top Sir Butt 8/10	unq	177@188
184	Top Sir Butt 10/14	177	177@188
185	Bott. Sir Butt 7/dn	unq	unq
185	Bott. Sir Butt 7/up	unq	unq
189	Tenderloin 5/7	unq	314@329
189	Tenderloin 7/9	unq	320@329
193	Flank Steak	unq	227

THE NATIONAL PROVISIONER DAILY MARKET SERVICE
Thurs., Apr. 24, 1986--Series BL No. 78

Source: The National Provisioner, Inc., Chicago, Ill.

Exhibit 7   Sample Issue of *Hotel, Restaurant, Institution Meat Price Report*, Thursday, April 24, 1986

HOTEL   •   RESTAURANT   •   INSTITUTION

MEAT PRICE REPORT

A GUIDE TO CURRENT MEAT PRICES BEING PAID TO WHOLESALERS AND PURVEYORS BY COMMERCIAL FEEDERS

PUBLISHED BY NATIONAL PROVISIONER, INC. • *"SINCE 1891"* • 15 W. HURON ST. • CHICAGO, IL 60610 • 312/944-3380
PUBLISHED THURSDAYS • SUBSCRIPTION RATES: ANNUAL $125.00–SEMI-ANNUAL $75.00

IMPS	BEEF PORTION CUT	IMPS	PRIME	CHOICE	UTILITY
193	Flank Steak, Skinned	193	—	290@300 –	210@215 –
—	Skirts—Outside	—	—	275@285	—
—	Skirts—Outside Peeled	—	—	405@415	—
—	Skirts—Inside	—	—	280@290	—
1100	Cubed Steaks	1100	—	230@240	—
1101	Cubed Steaks, Special	1101	—	260@270	—
1102	Braising Steak, Swiss	1102	—	275@285	—
1103A	Rib Steaks, Boneless	1103A	—	400@410	—
1112	Ribeye Roll Steaks	1112	640@650 –	560@570	380@390
1112A	Ribeye Roll, Lip-On Steaks	1112A	560@570 –	480@490	—
1173	Porterhouse Steaks	1173	—	520@530	—
1174	T-Bone Steaks	1174	760@770 +	510@520	—
1179	Strip Loin Steaks, Bone-In Short Cut	1179	770@780 +	510@520	—
1180	Strip Loin Steaks, Bnls., Short Cut, Regular	1180	950@960	590@600 +	—
1180	Strip Loin Steaks, Bnls., Short Cut, Center Cut	1180	1055@1065	660@670 +	—
1184	Top Sirloin Butt Steaks	1184	500@510 +	430@440 +	—
1184A	Top Sirloin Butt Steaks, Semi-Center Cut	1184A	590@600 +	465@475 +	—
1184B	Top Sirloin Butt Steaks, Center Cut	1184B	640@650 +	555@565 +	—
1189	Tenderloin Steaks, Side Muscle On	1189	720@730 +	630@640 +	—
1189A	Tenderloin Steaks, Defatted, Side Muscle On	1189A	785@795 +	740@750 +	—
1190	Tenderloin Steaks, Spec'l, Side Muscle Off "Skin" On	1190	880@890 +	825@835 +	—
1190A	Tenderloin Steaks, Completely Skinned	1190A	970@980 +	950@960 +	530@540

Source: The National Provisioner, Inc., Chicago, Ill.

Forecasting Meat Prices

A price forecast is a plan which depends on gathering data, examining past history, assessing current and expected events, and converting all these factors into a price. Buyers need both short-term and long-term plans.

Short-Term Planning

Short-term planning should extend for several ordering cycles. If inventories are replenished weekly, one month is considered short term. The purpose is to predict events so that price increases are avoided. An example of this involves planning around holidays. Several predictable things happen during holiday seasons:

- Processing plants take the day off, so the week has one less day for meat production.

- More people eat out, so higher quantities will be consumed than during regular periods.

- Purveyors do not work on the holiday, but the workload for preceding days is heavier. Therefore, purveyors are more likely to run out of products.

Other events covered by a short-term plan are seasonal business and promotions. Strikes also require special attention and, if possible, their duration should be estimated. Predicting these events permits the buyer to maintain an orderly flow of product delivery.

Long-Term Planning

Long-term planning enables the hospitality company to generate financial budgets and to undertake market forecasting. Price forecasting is the result of a series of calculations and assumptions directed toward predicting and managing future events.

Today, meat price forecasting begins with the USDA. The USDA maintains historical data on price and production levels, consumption and spending habits, and other factors of interest to buyers. It also publishes data estimating number of animals on a specified date, number marketed since the last report, and age or market condition of animals in inventory. Figures for daily slaughter rates and farmers' intended herd replenishment are also available. These figures are relatively accurate and used by economists to generate price forecasts.

The USDA also publishes general price information which can be helpful in forecasting prices. Independent companies use these figures to develop forecasts which are offered to subscribers for a fee. Most of the major economic planning companies have agricultural departments which issue price forecasts. Trading companies, such as Merrill Lynch, issue advice to encourage trading on futures exchanges.

If the USDA report, *Cattle on Feed*, shows either more or fewer animals than anticipated, price swings can be dramatic. A significant world event, such as a trade embargo, the threat of war, or political upheaval, can also influence prices. The meat buyer should follow the Chicago Board of Trade (CBT) contracts for the feed grain complex and the Chicago Mercantile Exchange (CME) contracts for feeder cattle, slaughter cattle, hogs, and pork bellies. As already noted, a great many factors influence the accuracy of price forecasting. Still, the wise buyer understands and uses price information in an effort to determine the appropriate time to purchase.

Meat-Buying Systems

The rest of this chapter reviews six major systems for buying meats. These systems include: ride the market (bid and buy weekly), cost-plus system, buy-and-inventory, long-term contracts, hedging (using futures markets), and vertical integration (providing various services for one's own company which are normally performed by purveyors, packers, feedlot operators, and/or ranchers).

Various combinations of these systems can be used by buyers. The actual system used will vary based on economics and company philosophy, but three steps are common to all systems:

1. Write standard specifications beginning with industry standards (IMPS) and modify them as necessary.

2. Select the purveyor who is best equipped to satisfy the operation's demands. The purveyor should routinely carry an adequate inventory of items matching required specifications.

3. Implement receiving practices to ensure that incoming products meet purchase specification standards.

Buyers should also visit the prospective supplier's facility, inspect raw material inventory, observe sanitation practices, read labels (when applicable), and examine the processing operation. Buyers should learn the delivery schedule in their areas, and determine if it is fixed (same days each week) or variable (shipped as loads are accumulated). Some of the prospective supplier's customers should be called to check on reliability and consistency. When the buyer is satisfied, a trial order may be placed.

Let's take a closer look at each of the six systems for buying meat.

Ride the Market

All companies "ride the market" at one time or another. This system involves soliciting price quotations from competing suppliers, who then quote prices based upon specifications each has received from the buyer. Bidding suppliers should also know the approximate quantities required and the order should be consistent with those estimated quantities. Delivery frequencies and points of delivery should be part of the bid.

Knowing the specific day of the week on which bids are taken is important, since mid-week prices tend to be more stable. Many meat purveyors place their own orders for the following week's delivery on Wednesday. If the purveyor has an unusually large order, orders may be placed on Tuesday so the packer is able to accumulate the merchandise. If the local purveyor buys on Wednesday for the following week, so should the buyer who purchases regularly each week. With this plan, the price will best reflect the current market price.

A simple system may be used to measure the validity of quotations: compare the difference between raw material quoted in one of the information sheets (Exhibit 6) and purveyors' quotations for the finished product. Let's consider IMPS #1180A strip steaks which are made from #180 boneless strip loins. Assume IMPS #180 strips are reported at $2.95 in *The Yellow Sheet* and #1180 steaks made from those loins are quoted by the purveyor at $4.97. The difference is $2.02. A purchaser who buys steaks weekly on a bid basis but lacks data regarding yield and cost can record the difference between steak prices and the #180 strips. For example:

Date	#180 Strips	#1180 Steaks	Difference
4/30	$2.95	$4.97	$2.02
5/7	$3.05	$5.15	$2.10
5/14	$3.20	$5.38	$2.18
5/20	$3.10	$5.24	$2.14
5/27	$3.20	$5.39	$2.19

Some buyers negotiate a price based on the differences. In the previous example, the buyer would like the agreed price spread to be $2.02, but the purveyor would prefer $2.19. The values of by-products (usable portion remaining after making the desired cut), variations in payment practices, size of order, and level of service all affect the size of the spread. Buyers who are consistent in these areas can develop spreads that are accurate in predicting purveyor quotes. Such information can be used to measure performance for any item whose raw material source is quoted in one of the information sheets.

If the buyer requires aged meat, the purveyor must carry additional inventory and an agreement on price must be reached. Agreement must be reached as to whether price will be based on current market cost, actual purchase cost, or some other source. It is easier for the buyer to use current prices, since they can be verified by the week's national prices. Most purveyors prefer purchase cost because this lowers their risk.

Cost-Plus

A cost-plus system based solely on the purveyor's figures is generally not preferred by meat purchasers. When combined with some mutually agreed-upon measurement, however, it can be beneficial. It enables the supplier to plan purchasing, production, and deliveries. The buyer may find an aggressive supplier who is willing to perform extra services, guarantee delivery of products when needed, and provide a standard pricing arrangement. However, the system is difficult for a buyer who feels "out of control" when it comes to purchasing.

A properly negotiated agreement can reduce problems involved with the cost-plus buying system. As an example, assume a company has ten restaurants and uses five meat items. Three approved suppliers submit cost-plus proposals on two types of transactions:

- A price based on a specified amount (cents per pound) over cost for merchandise purchased and re-delivered by the supplier without alteration.

- A price for manufactured items based on a defined formula to be verified by tests.

A sample bid proposal is shown in Exhibit 8. When bids are received and the supplier is tentatively selected, yield tests are performed with the buyer present. Once yield percentages have been agreed upon, they should be consistently followed. Each week, the buyer and seller must agree upon two areas: (1) the price paid by the purveyor for raw material, and (2) the value of the by-products remaining after processing of required products.

Exhibit 9 shows how this information could be furnished to the buyer. If the supplier wishes to change the yield percentages, the tests must be redone. The buyer can verify the reasonableness of the purveyor's costs by using the market information sheets. A buyer may also inspect the purveyor's invoices if that is part of the agreement.

A cost-plus system works best for multi-unit operations, although many single-unit properties use this approach without realizing it. Single-unit operators usually select purveyors and stay with them as long as performance is satisfactory; the calculations are made and costs are established, but the purveyor does not share them with the buyer.

Exhibit 8   Sample Bid Proposal and Conditions

BID PROPOSAL

_____ Company submits the following proposal: To supply meat products to the _____ Company located in _____.

1. All meat products which require no further processing, such as boxed beef, lamb, pork, veal, etc., will be priced at _____ per pound over cost.
2. Further processed items will be priced on a formulation:
   a. Delivered cost of the sub-primal or primal less:
      1. by-product credits, divided by:
      2. yield of primary products, plus:
      3. labor costs, plus:
      4. packaging cost, plus:
      5. mark-up of _____ per pound, which includes overhead, distribution costs, and profit.
3. Yield, labor costs, and packaging will be established on the basis of actual experience and will conform to accepted industry standards.
4. By-product values will be negotiated based on industry market value.
5. Pricing will be established each week based on inventory replacement costs.
6. The prices for the following week's delivery will be quoted each Wednesday.

Signatures: _____   _____
                  Name   Date   Name   Date

                  Title   Title

                  Vendor   Buyer

BID CONDITIONS

1. Submit one cents-over-cost figure for all boxed products: #109 ribs, #165 rounds, and so forth.
2. Submit cutting test for strip steaks and tenderloin steaks and grinding formula for patties. These will be reviewed with the winning bidder.
3. Deliveries—twice per week to each unit, orders will be received 24 hours prior to delivery.
4. All pricing information is confidential.
5. Payment terms, net 15 days.
6. Product liability insurance required in the amount of $_____ with the company named as co-insured.
7. Copies of price lists furnished weekly to each unit and the buyer. In addition, to the buyer only:
   a. previous week's cutting yields
   b. previous week's sales in pounds to the company
8. The company will inspect the purveyor's facilities and invoices relating to the company.
9. This agreement can be terminated by either party without cause with 60 days written notice. It may be terminated earlier with cause.

Direct bids to the buyer's attention.

In multi-unit chains, the buyer may have similar contracts with one or more suppliers around the country and may manage them quite easily. If the chain operates its own processing operation in one part of the country and contracts cost-plus arrangements in other areas, it will be more familiar with costs, having been in the market buying raw materials and performing other functions. Ironically, purveyors can often perform more efficiently than self-provided services. Some large

Exhibit 9   Sample Weekly Price Computation

Weekly Price Computation

Date: _____

Sample Item #1	Cost		Credits		Yield		Overage		Sell Price
#180 striploin	(2.95	−	.502)	÷	56%	+	.60	=	$4.97

Credits:	Yield		Price		Total
Vein steaks	12%	×	2.95	=	.354
Stew meat	2%	×	1.75	=	.035
Fat	11%	×	.08	=	.009
Trim	18%	×	.58	=	.104
Shrink	1%	×	—	=	—
Total credit	44%				.502

Sample Item #2	Cost		Credits		Yield		Overage		Sell Price
#189 tenderloin	(3.25	−	.296)	÷	62%	+	.60	=	$5.36

Credits:	Yield		Price		Total
Brochette	6%	×	2.60	=	.156
Stew meat	2.5%	×	1.75	=	.044
Fat	17%	×	.08	=	.014
Trim-lean	4%	×	1.10	=	.044
Trim-fat	6.5%	×	.58	=	.038
Shrink	2%	×	—	=	—
Total credit	38%				.296

Sample Item #3	Raw Material	Blend Formula		Cost		Blend Cost	Overage		Sell Price
Ground beef	85% lean meat	85%	×	1.13	=	.961			
patties,	50% lean meat	15%	×	.58	=	+.087			
80% lean						$1.048	+	.20	=	$1.25

companies contract directly for raw materials, then furnish them to their local purveyors to use in further processing.

Buy-and-Inventory

With this system, the buyer either wants to beat market advances or ensure supply
through an anticipated shortage. While buying and storing can be profitable, risk
becomes part of the buyer's responsibility. Historical trends, current USDA and industry data, past experience, futures markets, and supplier information become
critical indicators.

Buyers must calculate the return for buy-and-inventory transactions, making
sure to cover all costs and adding a factor for unanticipated price changes. Consider the purchase of IMPS #109 ribs with a current market price of $2.05 per
pound. Suppose the best estimate is that their price will reach $2.55 per pound
within six months, rising steadily over that period of time, before falling back. The
buyer's charts and historical records show that ribs have a seasonal pattern with a
low point in January. Assume the supplier needs cash and is willing to sell a
six-month supply of 30,000 pounds for $1.75 per pound delivered. Does this trans-
action constitute a good deal?

Exhibit 10   Example of a Buy-and-Inventory Calculation

Ride the Market	
Market today: #109 ribs	$2.05/lb
Market prediction (6 months)	2.55/lb
Market average	$2.30/lb
Cost for six months (30,000 lb @ $2.30)	$69,000
Buy-and-Inventory	
Product purchased (30,000 lb @ $1.75)	$52,500
Storage costs ($.02/lb per month)	1,800 (1)
Interest costs (20% annualized)	2,625 (2)
Total cost if deal is accepted	$56,925
Cost Difference	
Ride the Market	$69,000
Buy-and-Inventory	−56,926
Savings if deal is accepted	$12,075

(1) Storage costs computed as follows:
   15,000 lb (average inventory level = 30,000 lb/2) × $.12/lb
   (6 months @ $.02 per month) = $1,800
(2) Interest costs computed as follows:
   $26,250 (average investment = $52,500/2) @ 10% (annual
   rate of 20% for six-month period = 10%) = $2,625

First, the purchaser must consider several questions. Are frozen ribs acceptable? Can the restaurants store them? Is the quality up to the property's standards? Will there be more cooking shrinkage? If these and related factors suggest no problems, the arithmetic should be performed. Exhibit 10 shows an example of a buy-and-inventory calculation.

The cost is locked in at $1.90 per pound ($56,925 ÷ 30,000 lb) and it will be simple to measure the results each week. The key, as always, is in the price forecast. Will the $2.55 per pound cost materialize? With large orders of this size, other concessions in the form of freight allowances, first month's storage free, and extended payment terms could be available and should be brought into the negotiations. The cash position of the company must be such that payment can be made comfortably.

Long-Term Contracts

Buyers may occasionally have the opportunity to make a purchase commitment or fix the price without taking possession or paying in advance. Products involved are usually processed items, such as hams or hot dogs, and may be available because the processor has fixed costs. Look for these items around major holidays. Use the price forecast techniques to determine when and if these products should be purchased.

Cross-Hedging

Cross-hedging involves translating price forecasts into a purchase by using sophisticated meat pricing techniques. The premise is that as the price of individual meat cuts fluctuates, futures prices for live cattle will move in a similar direction. The practice requires the purchaser to:

- Examine live cattle futures prices for the anticipated month of delivery.
- Study seasonal trends, current predictions, and existing factors judged to influence prices.
- Track current cattle prices.
- Estimate the price for the delivery month by using data from previous years.

Cross-hedging is done by following the futures markets and is only applicable to large-volume buyers. The uncertainty and associated risks require that this buying system be attempted by experienced buyers only.

Vertical Integration

The meat industry is constantly changing. Trends seem to be toward large companies merging with other large companies also in the processing business. As the industry becomes concentrated in a few giant companies, competition will gradually diminish.

The retail and hospitality industries have historically marketed products on a cost pass-through basis. This is becoming increasingly difficult as competition continues to intensify. Some type of internal control or ownership of meat supply operations will likely continue to increase in several forms: (1) long-term commitments with processors or growers who concentrate on large-volume customers, or (2) sole or joint ownership of processing and/or grower facilities.

Whatever structure evolves for ownership of meat processing operations, the emphasis on gaining a competitive edge will remain. Hospitality buyers and their managers must be alert to events which influence pricing systems. Large hospitality companies may be able to make their own decisions. Smaller properties have even more reason to be innovative in their planning and forecasting. Since they seldom have the volume to exert a great deal of influence over purchases, these properties must find ways to combine their needs and interests with others while maintaining their integrity at the point of sale.

Endnotes

1. For more information on this subject, see Ronald F. Cichy, *Quality Sanitation Management* (East Lansing, Mich.: Educational Institute of the American Hotel & Motel Association, 1994), Chapter 2 ("Regulatory and Professional Organizations").

2. *The Meat Evaluation Handbook*, published by The National Live Stock and Meat Board, is an excellent reference for quality and grading standards and procedures.

3. *The Yellow Sheet* is published by the National Provisioner, Inc., Chicago, Ill. *The Meat Sheet* is published by Meat Sheet, Inc., Elmhurst, Ill.

REVIEW QUIZ

When you feel you have covered all of the material in this chapter, answer these questions. Choose the *best* answer. Check your answers with the correct ones found on the Review Quiz Answer Key at the end of this book.

True (T) or False (F)

T F 1. In many meat-producing nations, cattle are used for both meat and milk. T

T F 2. The United States is one of the few nations to use grain extensively to T
feed animals raised for meat.

T F 3. Pork production is completely restricted to the southern part of the F
United States.

T F 4. Rates of per capita consumption for beef, pork, and poultry vary in rela- T
tion to their prices.

T F 5. The supply of beef in the United States is controlled by a few large com- T
panies.

T F 6. Transportation costs do not represent a large percentage of consumer F
prices for meat.

T F 7. Most of the fresh meat used by hospitality operators is shipped by the T
processor in boxed form.

T F 8. An inspection stamp is the same as a quality stamp. F

T F 9. A quality grade always indicates the corresponding yield grade. F

T F 10. Packers in some instances may use their own grading system. T

T F 11. In meat grading, there are two unofficial grades within the official grade T
of Choice.

T F 12. Midweek is usually considered a good time to take bids as the prices tend T
to be more stable.

T F 13. The USDA offers very little data useful in forecasting for the long term. F

T F 14. Standard specifications exist for processed products such as corned beef F
and hot dogs. NO!

Multiple Choice

15. Meat prices are primarily determined by:

a. supply levels. ✓
b. consumer health concerns.
c. import quotas.
d. the federal government.

16. The _____ gave the federal government responsibility for ensuring that meat products shipped in interstate and foreign commerce were wholesome, processed under sanitary conditions, and accurately labeled.

    a. Agricultural Marketing Services Act
    b. Wholesome Meat Act of 1967
    c. Federal Meat Act of 1906 ✓
    d. Truth-in-Advertising Act

17. Which is *not* a factor in quality grading of beef?

    a. marbling
    b. conformation of the animal ✓
    c. condition of the lean
    d. maturity of the animal

18. The trade publications *The Meat Sheet* and *The Yellow Sheet* report market data and prices paid by processors on a _____ basis.

    a. daily
    b. weekly ✓
    c. monthly
    d. yearly

19. A _____ system is based on the premise that as prices of individual meat cuts fluctuate, futures prices for live cattle will move in a similar direction.

    a. cost-plus
    b. ride the market
    c. buy-and-inventory
    d. cross-hedging ✓

Chapter Outline

Processing of Beef Carcasses
Cuts of Beef
      Chuck
      Rib
      Loin
      Round
      Ground Beef
Pork Products
      Hams
      Pork Loins
      Bacon
      Sausages
      Buying Patterns for Pork
Veal and Lamb
      Traits
      Specifications
      Production

Learning Objectives

1. Describe the basic factors involved in processing beef carcasses.

2. Identify the major cuts of beef and the main traits of each.

3. Explain characteristics, sources, and pricing of ground beef.

4. List the popular cuts of pork and identify related quality factors.

5. Describe buying patterns for pork.

6. Explain basic characteristics of veal and factors that affect its production.

7. Explain basic characteristics of lamb and factors that affect its production.

9

Meat Products: Yields and Pricing

Meat products represent the largest single category of commodity purchases in many hospitality operations. Buyers who understand how these products are processed and priced can use this information to negotiate with meat purveyors and to generate cost savings for their organizations. Many of the techniques used by large-volume purchasers are cost-effective for those in smaller hospitality organizations as well.

In this chapter, we will focus on many popular meat products. Cattle, swine (hogs), and sheep are the three primary species. First, let's look at how beef carcasses are processed.

Processing of Beef Carcasses

In order to make informed pricing decisions, purchasers should understand basic information regarding the processing of beef carcasses. Let's assume that a yearling steer (neutered male bovine) goes into a feedlot at 700 pounds, is slaughtered at 1,176 pounds, and yields a 700-pound carcass.* A typical percentage breakdown of that carcass is shown in Exhibit 1.

Packers must process the carcass and sell the components in order to recover costs and make a profit. The typical value of a dressed carcass may be calculated as in the following example:

$$
\begin{array}{ll}
\text{1,176-lb animal, live—} & \\
\quad \text{approximately \$.53/lb} \;=\; & \$623.00 \\
\quad \text{Credit for by-products} & \underline{-\,50.00} \\
& \\
\text{700-lb dressed carcass—} & \\
\quad \text{approximately \$.82/lb} \;=\; & \underline{\underline{\$573.00}}
\end{array}
$$

Exhibit 2 shows a price of \$.83 per pound for 7 to 8 weight, yield grade 3, dressed steers. However, most beef is sold in boxes rather than by full carcasses. Exhibit 3 shows how a 700-pound carcass could be separated, and places values on the cuts given in Exhibit 2. The total return is \$621.54 or approximately \$.89 per pound for the 700-pound dressed carcass. Thus, the \$.53 per pound live animal translates to \$.89 per pound boxed, FOB Midwest. The cost per pound boxed is

---

*The Drovers Journal, a weekly business publication of the cattle industry, reports that dressed yield is 59 to 60% from live animals.

Exhibit 1   Typical Beef Carcass Breakdown

	Bone-In Primal Cuts		**Typical Restaurant Cuts**			
IMPS#		% of Carcass (1)	IMPS#	% of Carcass	Fat/Bone	Trim and Other Cuts
Forequarter						
#125–arm chuck including shank		29.4%	#126–arm chuck bnls (2), clod in	23.4%	5.1%	0.9%
#118–brisket		4.9%	#120–bnls brisket deckle off	2.9%	1.8%	0.2%
#103–primal rib		9.4%	#109–roast-ready rib	5.7%	1.4%	2.3%
#121–short plate/other		8.3%	#123A–short rib	1.1%	1.1%	6.1%
Total Forequarter		52.0%		33.1%	9.4%	9.5%
Hindquarter						
#172–loin		14.9%	#180–bnls short loin	3.4%		
			#184–bnls top butt	2.5%	3.9% (3)	1.4% (3)
			#185–bnls bottom butt	1.7%		
			#189–bnls tenderloin	2.0%		
#158–round		23.7%	#161–bnls round	17.8%	4.0%	1.9%
#193–flank/other		9.4%	#193–flank steak	0.9%	5.6%	2.9%
Total Hindquarter		48.0%		28.3%	13.5%	6.2%
TOTAL CARCASS		100.00%		61.4%	22.9%	15.7%

(1) Percentages will vary due to animal conformation and extent of trimming.
(2) Bnls is the abbreviation for boneless.
(3) These figures represent totals for cuts #180, #184, #185, and #189.

called the "cut out value" and is a widely used measure of profitability in the beef packing industry. Cut out values are reported weekly in *The Drovers Journal*. The individual values, which make up the $.89 per pound composite, reflect actual buy-sell transactions as found in reports published by the National Provisioner. Purchasers can expect a time lag of approximately one week for these values to reach the local purveyor.

Cuts of Beef

As shown in Exhibit 4, beef carcasses are butchered into many different cuts. Brief information about each is presented in this section. Chuck and rib are forequarter cuts, while loin and round are from the hindquarter.

Chuck

Chuck is the least expensive of the primal cuts and composes approximately 30% of the carcass. The IMPS #114 shoulder clod is sometimes used by institutional buyers for roast beef. It is flavorful and solid, but may not slice or yield as well as round cuts. The approximate weight range is 80 to 94 pounds.

Rib

The IMPS #103 primal rib makes up approximately 9% of the carcass. It is second to the loin in value per pound. The approximate weight range is 28 to 35 pounds.

Exhibit 2   Sample Issue of *The Yellow Sheet*, Thursday, April 24, 1986

Exhibit 3   Portion Cuts

**Oven-Ready Yields and Values
(700-lb. Carcass)**

Item	Weight		Price FOB Midwest		Total Value
#126–arm chuck clod-in	164.0 lb	×	$ .80	=	$131.20
#109–roast-ready rib	39.6 lb	×	1.90	=	75.24
Blade meat, defatted	6.0 lb	×	2.60	=	15.60
#120–bnls brisket	20.0 lb	×	.81	=	16.20
Deckle	1.0 lb	×	2.60	=	2.60
#123A–short rib	8.0 lb	×	1.50	=	12.00
#161–bnls round	124.6 lb	×	1.20	=	149.52
#180–bnls striploin	24.0 lb	×	2.77	=	66.48
#184–bnls top butt	18.0 lb	×	2.03	=	36.54
#185–bnls bottom butt	12.0 lb	×	.73	=	8.76
#189–tenderloin	14.0 lb	×	3.48	=	48.72
#193–bnls flank	6.0 lb	×	2.25	=	13.50
50/50 trim	103.2 lb	×	.33	=	34.06
Fat	79.0 lb	×	.10	=	7.90
Bone	80.6 lb	×	.04	=	3.22
TOTAL	700.0 lb		.89*		$621.54

* Total price/lb is calculated by dividing total value ($621.54) by total weight (700 pounds), and rounding off to the nearest cent.

Knowledge about rib structure helps the buyer make informed purchases. There are 13 ribs in a beef side, counted from the front to the rear; Exhibit 5 shows the first 12 ribs. The chuck contains 5 ribs (1–5), the rib has 7 rib bones (6–12), and the hindquarter contains the 13th rib. Sometimes, the packer includes 8 rib bones in the primal rib, taking the 5th (chuck) rib. However, this is contrary to IMPS specifications.

IMPS #103 through #112 detail different processed forms of rib roast. Differences relate to the amount of trim and bone removed. Exhibit 6 demonstrates how this processing affects the yields on three rib roasts. Note that removing the 2-inch lip reduces the primary yield from 34% to 28%.

Increased trimming improves the primary product but also makes it necessary for the processor to generate revenue from the pieces and parts removed. Calculating these by-product values is critical in the pricing process; their value, like everything else, depends on demand. In the short run, little change occurs in by-product prices. However, when primal meat prices fluctuate to a higher or lower level, prices for portion cuts tend to move in the same direction.

The #109 rib is a popular roast used by many fine restaurants. It weighs approximately 16 to 19 pounds and is made from an IMPS #103 primal cut. Cutting test information is shown in Exhibit 7.

Using certain assumptions, Exhibit 7 shows how the cost for the IMPS #109 rib may be established. To determine the final delivered cost, however, purveyor profits and distribution costs must be added in. These two costs depend on such factors

Exhibit 4   Food Service Cuts of Beef

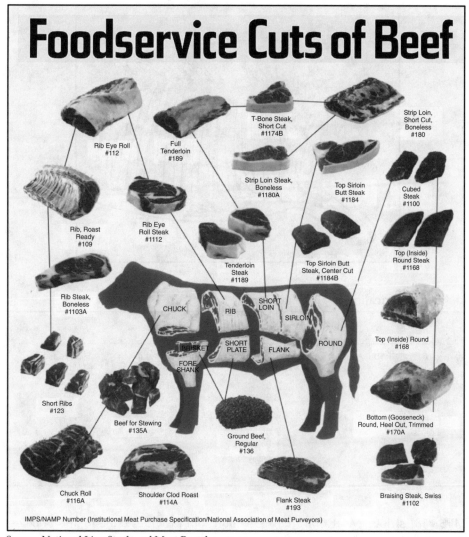

Foodservice Cuts of Beef

Rib Eye Roll #112

Full Tenderloin #189

T-Bone Steak, Short Cut #1174B

Strip Loin, Short Cut, Boneless #180

Strip Loin Steak, Boneless #1180A

Top Sirloin Butt Steak #1184

Cubed Steak #1100

Rib, Roast Ready #109

Rib Eye Roll Steak #1112

Tenderloin Steak #1189

Top Sirloin Butt Steak, Center Cut #1184B

Top (Inside) Round Steak #1168

Rib Steak, Boneless #1103A

CHUCK   RIB   SHORT LOIN   SIRLOIN

Top (Inside) Round #168

BRISKET   SHORT PLATE   FLANK   ROUND

FORE SHANK

Short Ribs #123

Beef for Stewing #135A

Ground Beef, Regular #136

Bottom (Gooseneck) Round, Heel Out, Trimmed #170A

Chuck Roll #116A

Shoulder Clod Roast #114A

Flank Steak #193

Braising Steak, Swiss #1102

IMPS/NAMP Number (Institutional Meat Purchase Specification/National Association of Meat Purveyors)

Source: National Live Stock and Meat Board.

as volume, payment practices, level of service required, and administration and overhead. Buyers often negotiate this fee with their purveyors as a fixed cents-per-pound over the purveyor's cost.

Loin

The IMPS #172 full beef loin makes up approximately 15% of the carcass and is the most expensive cut on a per pound basis. The full loin, after separation from the round, is frequently processed into two sub-primal cuts: IMPS #173 short loin and

Exhibit 5   Counting Ribs in a Beef Forequarter

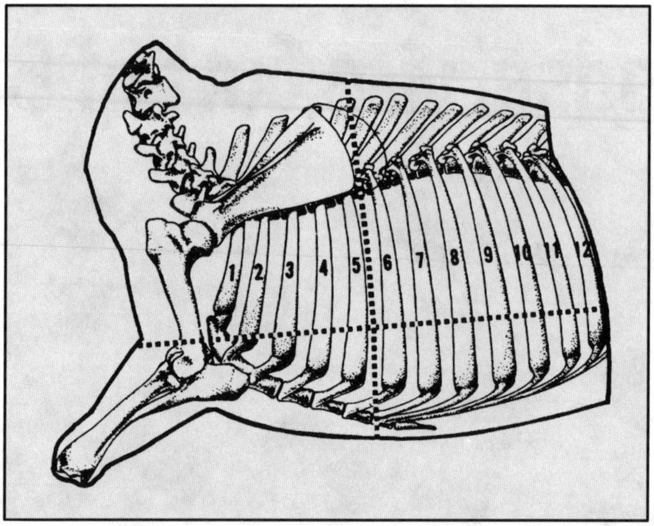

Exhibit 6   Fabrication of Three Rib Roasts

	Basis: #103 Primal, 100%		
Fabricate to:	Roast-Ready Rib #109—60.0%	Ribeye Roll, Lip On #112A—34.0%	Ribeye Roll #112—28.0%
Cap meat	9.5%	9.5%	9.5%
Short ribs	8.0%	8.0%	8.0%
Trim	7.0%	12.5%	17.0%
Fat	7.5%	20.5%	22.0%
Bones	7.0%	14.5%	14.5%
Shrink	1.0%	1.0%	1.0%
	100.0%	100.0%	100.0%

IMPS #181 sirloin. Meat from the #173 short loin provides bone-in and boneless steaks of the highest quality. They are known by many names including T-bone, porterhouse, strips, New York strips, and Kansas City strips. On T-bone and porterhouse steaks, the tenderloin is attached to the bone. To produce bone-in strip steaks, the tenderloin is removed (to be sold as a separate item).

Exhibit 4 illustrates the short loin and several popular portion cuts that it yields. For food service, the packer generally removes the bones from the loin, providing three major items: #180 strip loin, #189 tenderloin, and #184 top butt. The most important measurement on the #180 is from the loin eye (meaty interior section with minimal amount of fat) to the edge of the flank, shown in IMPS specifications as 3 inches on rib end and 2 inches on the loin end. When strip steaks are cut, this part of the loin is identified as "tail." The amount of tail in inches is part of the

Pricing Relates to Retail Supply

Food service operations primarily use rib and loin meat and ground beef. When large retail grocery chains run sales on chucks, rounds, and other items, prices for these items are usually driven up as demand is created. Some food service cuts are then in oversupply; prices may be lowered to balance product movement. By contrast, when the chain stores are inactive in the market, food service cuts are generally higher in price. Meat pricing is to a large extent dictated by the grocery store chains. Food service buyers may be wise in establishing a rapport with their counterparts in grocery operations so that they can formulate their own purchase plans.

Exhibit 7   Results of Cutting Test #1

Cutting Test: #103 Primal to #109 Oven-Ready Rib
(Yield Grade 3)

Description	Yield		Price/lb FOB Midwest		Total FOB Midwest
Start with:					
#103–primal rib	100.0 lb	×	$1.12	=	$112.00
Add:					
Labor, packaging, and overhead			.30		30.00
Cost to be recovered			$1.42		$142.00
By-product return:					
Cap meat (deckle)	9.5 lb	×	$1.25	=	$11.88
Short ribs	8.0 lb	×	1.50	=	12.00
Grinding meat (50% lean)	7.5 lb	×	.33	=	2.48
Fat	7.5 lb	×	.10	=	.75
Bones/shrink	7.5 lb	×	.04	=	.30
TOTAL	40.0 lb		.685*		$27.41
Primary product return:					
#109–fabricated rib	60.0 lb	×	$1.91	=	$114.60
Recovered costs:	40.0 lb				$ 27.41
	+ 60.0 lb				114.60
	100.0 lb		$1.42		$142.01

* Total price/lb for by-products ($.685/lb) is calculatd by totaling by-product prices ($27.40), dividing by total weight of by-products (40.0 lb), and rounding off to the nearest cent.

specification. Measurement should be made from the natural eye of the loin. The loin should be clean where bone is removed; cover or surface fat should be trimmed evenly with no tears or scars. Packers have no obligation to trim this cover fat to a certain distance from the eye. This is one reason yield grade information is so helpful. Yield grades of 3 and lower provide more usable meat than

Exhibit 8   Strip Steaks

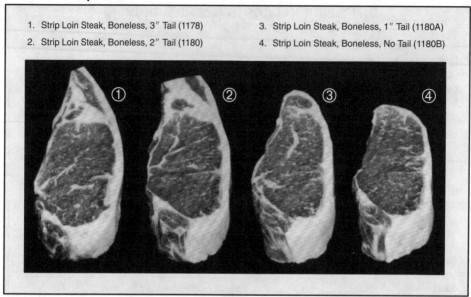

1. Strip Loin Steak, Boneless, 3″ Tail (1178)
2. Strip Loin Steak, Boneless, 2″ Tail (1180)
3. Strip Loin Steak, Boneless, 1″ Tail (1180A)
4. Strip Loin Steak, Boneless, No Tail (1180B)

Source: National Live Stock and Meat Board, *Merchandising Beef Loins,* 1977, p. 14.

higher yield grades. When buying primal cuts of any type, buyers should specify the yield grade and require the supplier to leave a USDA grade and yield shield on the fat cover. If this cannot be done, the depth of fat cover should be specified.

Yield grades are also of importance when purchasing steaks. Loins of yield grade 4 and up generally do not have the muscle depth to make strip steaks of 10 ounces and larger. The eye muscle narrows toward the round end so the steak must be cut thicker to maintain weight. The result is a long, narrow steak which does not give good plate coverage, cooks poorly, and is less appealing. However, if steaks of 8 ounces or smaller are required, loins of yield grade 4 are acceptable and costs per pound should be lower than for standard size steaks of 11 to 14 ounces, assuming trim specifications are equal.

Exhibit 8 displays four strip loin steaks. All have surface or cover fat trimmed to within 1/2 inch of the natural eye. The tail, however, varies from 3 inches to none. Center cut strip steaks are the most desirable. Vein or end steaks come from the round end of an IMPS #180 strip and are less desirable. These steaks have a line of cartilage (a hard, inedible semi-bone structure commonly called the vein) running through the eye muscle. Vein or end steaks extend into the loin making up 11 to 14% of the total boneless #180 weight. To be classified as center cut steaks, no vein should show on either side.

Let's examine costs of two center cut boneless steaks with an average 1/2 inch of surface or cover fat, one with a 3-inch tail and one with a 1-inch tail. All other trim is identical. The #180 strip cost is taken from *The Yellow Sheet* shown in Exhibit 2. Cutting test results are shown in Exhibits 9 and 10.

Exhibit 9   Results of Cutting Test #2

Cutting Test: #180 Strip to #1178 Steak w/3″ tail				
Description	Yield		Price/lb FOB Midwest	Total FOB Midwest
Start with:				
#180–boneless loin	100.0 lb	×	$2.77 =	$277.00
By-product return:				
Vein steaks (1)	14.0 lb	×	2.77 =	38.78
Stew meat	3.0 lb	×	1.75 =	5.25
Trim = 50%	10.0 lb	×	.33 =	3.30
Fat	9.0 lb	×	.10 =	.90
Cutting shrink	4.0 lb	×	.00 =	.00
TOTAL	40.0 lb		1.21 (2)	$48.23
Primary product return:				
Center cut strip steaks w/3″ tail	60.0 lb		3.81 (3)	$228.77
Add:				
Labor, supplies, distribution, and profit (4)			+ 1.25	
Price delivered to end-user			$5.06	

(1) By-products are estimated purveyor sales price. (Buyers must negotiate these.)
(2) Total price/lb for by-products ($1.21/lb) is calculated by totaling by-product prices ($48.23), dividing by total weight of by-products (40.0 lb), and rounding off to the nearest cent.
(3) Total primary product price/lb ($3.81/lb) is calculated by dividing total primary product price ($228.77) by total primary product weight (60.0 lb), and rounding off to the nearest cent.
(4) Negotiate figures for labor, supplies, etc.

Closer trim provides a better product to serve guests, but it is more expensive. Note that per pound costs are $5.06 for center cut boneless steak with a 3-inch tail (Exhibit 9) and $5.45 for one with a 1-inch tail (Exhibit 10). The buyer must determine which specification is required by the hospitality operation based upon the needs of its guests.

Two sizes of IMPS #189 tenderloins are listed in Exhibit 2: 5 to 7 pounds and 7 to 9 pounds. Both sizes are from young animals (steers or heifers), but the larger (7 to 9 pound) tenderloins are from more mature animals and generally have better appearance and flavor. They also have a more desirable yield for most applications which require steaks weighing 8 to 10 ounces and therefore command a premium price. A meat purveyor whose customers require different sizes of tenderloin has a distinct advantage over purveyors whose customers only require one or two sizes. This purveyor can utilize a greater percentage of the tenderloin in primary steaks and a lower percentage in by-products, thus spreading out initial raw material costs and overhead. This also enables the purveyor to cut more uniform steaks.

Cow tenderloins are also used for steaks. They are smaller, darker in color, and less expensive than those from steers, but are perfectly satisfactory for some uses. When in the frozen state, it is sometimes difficult to distinguish them from steer tenderloins. Unscrupulous vendors may substitute cow for steer items if buyers

Exhibit 10   Results of Cutting Test #3

Cutting Test: #180 Strip to #1180A Steak w/1″ tail				
Description	Yield		Price/lb FOB Midwest	Total FOB Midwest
Start with:				
#180–boneless loin	100.0 lb	×	$2.77 =	$277.00
By-product return:				
Vein steaks	14.0 lb	×	2.77 =	38.78
Stew meat	3.0 lb	×	1.75 =	5.25
Trim = 50%	15.0 lb	×	.33 =	4.95
Fat	10.0 lb	×	.10 =	1.00
Cutting shrink	4.0 lb	×	.00 =	.00
	46.0 lb		$1.09 (1)	$49.98
Primary product return:				
Center cut strip steaks w/1″ tail	54.0 lb		4.20 (2)	$227.02
Add:				
Labor, supplies, distribution, and profit (3)			+1.25	
Price delivered to end-user			$5.45	

(1) Total price/lb for by-products ($1.09/lb) is calculated by totaling by-product prices ($49.98), dividing by total weight of by-products (46.0 lb), and rounding off to the nearest cent.

(2) Total primary product price/lb ($4.20/lb) is calculated by dividing total primary product price ($227.02) by total primary product weight (54.0 lb), and rounding off to the nearest cent.
By-product values are similar to #1178, but primary product price is up $.39 per pound because yield is less.

(3) Negotiate figures for labor, supplies, etc.

are not alert. Lack of marbling, darker color, and a spongy, mushy texture are characteristic of cow tenderloins. The cost difference between steaks from cow and steer tenderloins may be well over a dollar per pound.

Round

The round is popular for hospitality and retail uses because of its good flavor, high yield of red meat, and low cost (compared to loins or ribs). These muscles are more developed than the inside muscles and are larger and somewhat tougher. Beef rounds make up approximately one quarter of carcass weight.

Traditional carcass separation merely divides the hindquarter into #172 loin and #158 round (also known as Chicago or Western round). No bone is removed from these cuts and little trimming is done. Increased use of boxed beef has practically eliminated this cut as a meat source for hospitality operations.

The IMPS description tells how the #158 round is separated into its main subprimal muscles. Meat processors follow this specification and pack like components together. For example, three #168 rounds weighing approximately 20 pounds each may be packed in a master carton weighing 60 pounds. The individual #168 rounds are generally encased in plastic wrap from which the air has been expelled. Hospitality buyers may select and buy the round component that best fits

Exhibit 11   Sample Issue of *Hotel, Restaurant, Institution Meat Price Report*, Thursday, April 24, 1986

HOTEL · RESTAURANT · INSTITUTION
MEAT PRICE REPORT
A GUIDE TO CURRENT MEAT PRICES BEING PAID TO WHOLESALERS AND PURVEYORS BY COMMERCIAL FEEDERS

PUBLISHED BY NATIONAL PROVISIONER, INC. • *"SINCE 1891"* • 15 W. HURON ST. • CHICAGO, IL 60610 • 312/944-3380
PUBLISHED THURSDAYS • SUBSCRIPTION RATES: ANNUAL $125.00–SEMI-ANNUAL $75.00

IMPS	BEEF PORTION CUT	IMPS	PRIME	CHOICE	UTILITY
193	Flank Steak, Skinned	193	.... —	.. 290@300 –	.210@215 –
—	Skirts—Outside	—	.... —	.. 275@285	.... —
—	Skirts—Outside Peeled	—	.... —	.. 405@415	.... —
—	Skirts—Inside	—	.... —	.. 280@290	.... —
1100	Cubed Steaks	1100	.... —	.. 230@240	.... —
1101	Cubed Steaks, Special	1101	.... —	.. 260@270	.... —
1102	Braising Steak, Swiss	1102	.... —	.. 275@285	.... —
1103A	Rib Steaks, Boneless	1103A	.... —	.. 400@410	.... —
1112	Ribeye Roll Steaks	1112	.. 640@650 –	.. 560@570	. 380@390
1112A	Ribeye Roll, Lip-On Steaks	1112A	.. 560@570 –	.. 480@490	.... —
1173	Porterhouse Steaks	1173	.... —	.. 520@530	.... —
1174	T-Bone Steaks	1174	.. 760@770 +	.. 510@520	.... —
1179	Strip Loin Steaks, Bone-In Short Cut	1179	.. 770@780 +	.. 510@520	.... —
1180	Strip Loin Steaks, Bnls., Short Cut, Regular	1180	.. 950@960	.. 590@600 +	.... —
1180	Strip Loin Steaks, Bnls., Short Cut, Center Cut	1180	1055@1065	.. 660@670 +	.... —
1184	Top Sirloin Butt Steaks	1184	.. 500@510 +	.. 430@440 +	.... —
1184A	Top Sirloin Butt Steaks, Semi-Center Cut	1184A	.. 590@600 +	.. 465@475 +	.... —
1184B	Top Sirloin Butt Steaks, Center Cut	1184B	.. 640@650 +	.. 555@565 +	.... —
1189	Tenderloin Steaks, Side Muscle On	1189	.. 720@730 +	.. 630@640 +	.... —
1189A	Tenderloin Steaks, Defatted, Side Muscle On	1189A	.. 785@795 +	.. 740@750 +	.... —
1190	Tenderloin Steaks, Spec'l, Side Muscle Off "Skin" On	1190	.. 880@890 +	.. 825@835 +	.... —
1190A	Tenderloin Steaks, Completely Skinned	1190A	.. 970@980 +	.. 950@960 +	.. 530@540

Source: The National Provisioner, Inc., Chicago, Ill.

their menu. Some of these standard products are described below. Prices for these cuts are shown in Exhibits 2 and 11.

Bone-In Round or Steamship Bone-In Round (IMPS #160). All bone is removed except the primary or round bone which runs through the center of the cut. This round can be roasted and sliced intact. Watch the trim to ensure that the shank and all outer fat is removed.

Boneless Steamship Round (IMPS #161). This round has the main or round bone removed. It is easier to carve and is generally preferred to the bone-in cut.

Knuckle (IMPS #167). The knuckle (tip) is the portion of the round which is beneath the round bone. This is the least desirable piece since it has less solid meat than other pieces.

Top or Inside Round (IMPS #168). This is the largest solid piece of meat in the round and it weighs approximately 20 pounds. The inside round may also be purchased as a cooked item processed to various degrees of doneness. Shrinkage during processing is often better controlled than when done on-site in individual restaurants. Buyers must confirm that they receive what they ordered since a cooked item loses its grading identity. The buyer can assume that the box will be marked "USDA Choice" if that grade was used. If no grade marking shows on the box, the buyer has know no way of knowing if Choice was actually used.

Gooseneck or Bottom Round (IMPS #170). This is the remaining muscle after removal of the knuckle, top round, and shank meat. The heel and rump are still attached, but are usually separated and sold in retail stores.

Eye Round and "the Flat." These remaining muscles are used by some operators. The two pieces are separated at the natural seam and cooked independently, as the meat grain on one is at a 90° angle to the other. The remainder of the round is used for stew or grinding meat.

Ground Beef

Ground beef is the most popular meat item consumed in the United States. USDA specifications include IMPS #136 ground beef (regular) and IMPS #137 ground beef (special). Two others, IMPS #136A and IMPS #137A, allow a specified percentage of textured vegetable protein or "TVP" (usually soybean meal) to be included in the product.

IMPS #136 ground beef (regular) may be made from any beef, graded or ungraded, including trimmings. The visual fat content of meat before grinding should not exceed 25%. Shanks or any trim meat with heavy tendon concentrations are to be removed. IMPS #137 ground beef (special) is identical to IMPS #136 except that at least 50% of the meat must be from graded primal solid muscles.

Specifications are very important for ground beef purchases. Packaging specifications are critical to protecting the product. With fresh products, air must be excluded in order to maintain quality. Some processors introduce CO_2 prior to sealing cases, which, in effect, replaces the oxygen. Other processors vacuum-seal the product. Freezing is the best way to preserve the meat, with quick freezing preferred to slow freezing. If the product is in patty form, buyers should require that the patties be IQF (individually quick frozen). In bulk form, there should be no more than 5 pounds in a package or bag, preferably flat (approximately 2-inch depth, maximum). Products should be blast frozen (frozen in a forced air chamber) at less than -20°F (-29°C) for less than one-half hour.

IMPS specifications do not serve the buyer as well for ground or further processed items as they do for solid muscle products. Each buyer must develop specific quality requirements by using *The Meat Buyers Guide* and *The NAMP Guide to Quality Assurance* as references and by being aware of current industry practices.

The following examples illustrate some typical ground beef specifications.

Example 1: Fresh ground beef patties (4 patties/lb)

- Round $3\frac{3}{4}''$ diameter; $\frac{3}{4}''$ deep; paper placed between patties

- Raw material to be solid muscle meat with no more than 40% fresh trimmings and to conform to IMPS #136 specifications

- 25% average fat; tolerance (+ or −) 1%

- Medium grind (buyers may include the final grind plate size)

- 12 lb carton; 48 patties per carton
- Bacterial level to be no more than 500,000 total count (population); 2,000 coliform (coliform bacteria are intestinal organisms—an indicator of contamination)
- Cartons to be 200-pound test; product sealed in CO_2-flushed bags
- Receiving temperature not to exceed 35°F (2°C)

This specification provides for fat tolerances which all processors need and states an *average* which all can meet.

Damage is often caused to fresh patties by improper handling. Each patty should rest on a piece of hard-finish, moisture-resistant paper; paper should separate each layer of patties. The top patty in each stack should also be covered by paper. Molded plastic trays (for one-time use) may be used to protect the patties and can be formed into a series of pockets for stacks of patties. For years, this packaging has been used for higher-cost steaks. As prices accelerated, these trays became cost-efficient for meat patties as well.

Packaging is a variable that must be calculated based on shelf life needs, degree of handling required, and distance shipped. When the product is frozen, many of these concerns become less important.

Example 2: Frozen ground beef patties (4 patties/lb)

- Round 3 3/4" diameter; 3/4" deep; paper placed between patties
- Raw material to be solid muscle meat with no more than 40% fresh trimmings
- 25% average fat; tolerance (+ or −) 1%
- Medium grind
- Product to be formed on Formax*
- 24 lb carton; 96 patties per carton
- Bacterial level to be no more than 500,000 total count; 2,000 coliform
- Cartons to be 200-pound test; product sealed in plastic bags to prevent freezer burn
- Product to be blast frozen in on-line tunnel freezer at –20°F (–29°C); product to be IQF
- Receiving temperature of external patties to be no higher than –10°F (–23°C)

The specification requires IQF patties and an on-line tunnel freezer. This means that the conveyor belt upon which the formed patties are placed carries these patties through a –20°F (–29°C) tunnel freezer where they are frozen from both sides. They are loosely packed by weight when they emerge from the tunnel.

A potential problem can be the length of time between forming and total freezing. Patties should not be packed in cartons and then placed in a –20°F (–29°C) blast

---

*The machine on which the patties are formed is specified as Formax in Example #2. This is a high-speed machine that has gained wide acceptance by fast-food chains. It provides some compression tolerance to permit more loosely formed patties to be made.

Exhibit 12 Calculating Lean Equivalent Price

Description	Price FOB Midwest		Lean (%)		Lean Equivalent Price
Boneless cow trimmings	$.89	÷	85%	=	$1.05
Boneless cow trimmings	.98	÷	90%	=	1.09
Fresh trimmings, beef	.32	÷	50%	=	.64
Fresh IMPS #126 choice chuck	.79	÷	70%	=	1.13
Frozen imported cow meat	.87	÷	85%	=	1.02
Lean coarse ground	.77	÷	73%	=	1.05

freezer. Patties frozen in this fashion are hard to separate, and generally have to be thawed before cooking.

Generally, less care is taken with frozen products than with fresh ones—at all levels of distribution. While frozen products can take more abuse, they can also deteriorate. A good rule to follow is to handle frozen products with as much care as fresh products.

Sources and Pricing of Lean Meat. Lean meat is the major cost ingredient in ground beef. Lean meat may come from a variety of cuts and sources (IMPS #137 states that ground beef must be at least 50% muscle meat from graded carcasses; IMPS #136 permits use of all trimmings). The largest source of muscle meat for grinding is the dairy industry. Animals retired from milk production are used for this purpose after the middle meat (ribs and loins) is removed. Sometimes, certain round and chuck cuts are also removed.

Steer trim and steer chucks are also used for grinding. This occurs most frequently when there is a shortage of dairy animals, for instance, when milk prices are high or when cows are held back for breeding and herd replenishment. Steer chuck then gains a competitive edge and is more likely to be used. Imported boneless meat, primarily from Australia, is also an important source of raw material.

For years, there have been attempts to breed special animals exclusively for ground meat. Most of these attempts have failed since adequate supplies from traditional sources have kept prices down. The successful efforts have used dairy animals taken off grass and put on feed for about 60 days prior to slaughter. The middle meat and certain chuck and round cuts enter the market as solid muscle meat.

After specifications are developed, prices can be verified or established through simple formulas. *The Yellow Sheet* publishes raw material component prices.

Let's assume that prices for alternative products are as reported in Exhibit 12. To compute the lean equivalent price, it is necessary to divide the price by the lean percentage. For example, note boneless cow trimmings in Exhibit 12:

$$\text{Lean Equivalent Price} = \frac{\text{Price}}{\text{Lean Percentage}}$$

$$\text{Lean Equivalent Price} = \frac{\$.89}{.85}$$

$$\text{Lean Equivalent Price} = \$1.05$$

Exhibit 13   Midwest Cost for Ground Beef Patties (25% Fat)

Description	Pounds	Lean (%)	Price/lb	Total
Formula:				
Boneless cow trimmings	72	85%	$.89	$64.08
Fresh beef trimmings	28	50%	.32	8.96
Mix cost (1)	100	75%	$.73	$73.04
Added costs:				
Mix cost			$.73	$73.04
Paper, packaging (2)			.10	10.00
Labor, overhead (2)			.10	10.00
Profit, distribution (2)			.10	+10.00
Cost at Midwest plants				$103.04

(1) Lean percentage is a weighted average calculated as follows:

$$\frac{(72 \text{ lb} \times 85\%) + (28 \text{ lb} \times 50\%)}{100 \text{ lb}} = 75.2\% \text{ rounded off to } 75\%$$

Mix cost price/lb ($.73/lb) is calculated by dividing total price ($73.04) by total weight (100 lb), and rounding off to the nearest cent.

(2) Negotiated figures; freight must be added for delivery to other parts of the country.

Exhibit 14   Midwest Cost for Ground Beef Patties (20% Fat)

Description	Pounds	Lean (%)	Price/lb	Total
Formula:				
Boneless cow trimmings	85	85%	$.89	$75.65
Fresh beef trimmings	15	50%	.32	4.80
Mix cost (1)	100	80%	$.80	$80.45
Added costs:				
Mix cost			$.80	$80.45
Paper, packaging (2)			.10	10.00
Labor, overhead (2)			.10	10.00
Profit, distribution (2)			.10	+10.00
Cost at Midwest plants				$110.45

(1) Lean percentage is a weighted average calculated as follows:

$$\frac{(85 \text{ lb} \times 85\%) + (15 \text{ lb} \times 50\%)}{100 \text{ lb}} = 79.75\% \text{ rounded off to } 80\%$$

Mix cost price/lb ($.80/lb) is calculated by dividing total price ($80.45) by total weight (100 lb), and rounding off to the nearest cent.

(2) Negotiated figures; freight must be added for delivery to other parts of the country.

With an awareness of prices (FOB Midwest), the buyer can estimate delivered cost as summarized in Exhibit 13 for ground beef with 25% fat content. Exhibit 14 summarizes estimated costs for ground beef with a 20% fat content. Note that a 5%

decrease in fat raised the per pound cost by 7.41¢, or about 1.48¢ per pound for each percentage point.

The patty processor must formulate on a least-cost basis and still satisfy customer requirements. The buyer must establish specifications, negotiate the price with knowledge of processor costs, and receive the proper product. Many companies negotiate a price formula, establish a day of the week, and calculate prices based on figures from *The Yellow Sheet* for that day. Others take bids weekly; some may buy and inventory. Regardless of the system employed, use of the foregoing information results in better prices.

Other Beef Cuts. Diced (or cubed) beef is covered by IMPS #135 and #135A. Specifications for these products relate to fat content, uniformity, and raw material source. Quality grades and modifications are added by the buyer. Buyers should specify that the product comes from steers and does not contain aged trim.

Diced beef is generally prepared by a machine. IMPS #135 requires that at least 75% of the cubes be between $3/4$ inch and $1\,1/2$ inch with a maximum of 25% visual fat. Tighter specifications require more hand labor and increase product costs. Diced beef is usually a by-product and brings whatever price the market will bear. Pricing formulas are not as useful for purchasing this item as they are for other products.

Cube and Swiss steaks are popular items. IMPS #1100 cube steak can be made from any part of the carcass. IMPS #1101 cube steak must come from the round, loin, rib, or chuck. IMPS #1102 Swiss steak must be made from select parts of these four prime cuts.

Like diced beef, cube steaks are usually made from sub-primal by-products. For example, deckle (the layer between the ribeye and the exterior cover fat) is a by-product of IMPS #109 rib production. Deckle, also called lifter meat or cap meat by some processors, makes excellent cube steaks when properly trimmed. Labor is required to remove fat from the product, which is then tenderized and shaped by machine.

Cube and Swiss steaks are generally made by local purveyors who buy the raw material from major primal processors. If cost information can be obtained from a major processor, the buyer has a better idea of raw material values and can develop a price formula. For example, assume deckle meat is credited at $1.25 per pound when fabricating a #109 roast-ready rib. If deckle meat yields 75% of IMPS #1101 steaks and labor profit is $.60, a price formula might be as follows:

$$\text{Finished Product Cost} = \frac{\text{Price}}{\text{Yield}} \quad + \quad \text{Labor Profit}$$

$$\text{Finished Product Cost} = \frac{\$1.25}{.75} \quad + \quad .60$$

$$\text{Finished Product Cost} = \$1.67 \quad + \quad .60$$

$$\text{Finished Product Cost} = \$2.27 \text{ per lb}$$

If purchase quantities are adequate, the purveyor may perform a cutting test and make this calculation at the buyer's request. Examples of prices for cube steaks are shown in Exhibit 11.

The full plate (IMPS #122) is what remains of the forequarter after the rib and chuck are removed. It is separated between the 5th and 6th ribs into the brisket (IMPS #119) and the short plate boneless (IMPS #121).

Short rib (IMPS #123) can be made from the plate as well as the rib by cutting across the plate parallel to the cut that was made separating the rib and plate. The balance of the plate is generally used for grinding.

The brisket (IMPS #118) can make an excellent roast if it is slowly cooked. Prices from *The Yellow Sheet* (see Exhibit 2) refer to #1 briskets which are 12 pounds or more. The amount of trim is a primary costing factor. The brisket is often used for corned beef cured in brine, since the fat absorbs the flavor of the curing solution. Cooked, corned briskets are often offered as well. Since cooked products are more expensive, the buyer must make a value determination.

The flank is located below the full loin. It is a flat oval muscle and is obtained by removing the muscle from the thick membrane in which it is encased. IMPS #193 flank steak is a completely skinned and trimmed piece. The term "#1 rough flanks" designates the flank before trimming. The buyer generally has no difficulty if #193 flanks are specified.

Liver, oxtails, tongue, kidneys, and other edible by-products may be purchased in different forms. Trim and labor input determine the cost while demand determines the price. An alert buyer uses figures from *The Yellow Sheet* to help gauge price changes.

Many processed products are also available. Most are consumer-oriented products promoted by national companies. Their brands are differentiated by type of seasonings used and cooking procedures. The IMPS series 800 establishes some minimum standards relating to fat and formula. The average hospitality buyer does not have the volume to warrant unique specifications and must depend on brand identification. However, formulas may change based upon raw material costs. For example, all meat frankfurters may contain beef and pork in any combination, as well as a percentage of chicken. All-beef franks and chicken franks are made exclusively from those raw materials. Trimmings are used extensively in the production of frankfurters and bologna-type products.

In purchasing processed products, it is generally best to have two acceptable products that can be competitively bid. Orders can then be allocated on the basis of price. Another technique is to measure price changes on the basis of raw material costs. While the buyer may not know exact product formulas, trimming prices provide some indication of costs. *The Yellow Sheet* reports costs for beef and pork trimmings. Exhibit 2 shows 73% lean coarse ground beef at $.77 per pound and 72% lean pork trimmings at $.70 per pound. If competitive bidding produced a frankfurter price of $1.25 per pound, buyers might negotiate with the supplier to maintain a spread over one of these raw materials. Using the pork trim price of $.70 per pound produces a $.55 per pound spread ($1.25 − $.70 = $.55). Frankfurter prices would advance or decline based on pork trim. Agreement must be reached on the timing of price changes and on the raw material cost base.

Pork Products

Fresh pork is used in the form of roast pork (usually hams), pork chops, ribs, pork BBQ, and fresh sausage. The IMPS series 400 provides specifications for fresh pork products. The most popular pork products are cured items such as hams, bacon, sausage, and Canadian bacon. As a basis for developing specifications, buyers can use the IMPS series 500 standards for cured products. (See Exhibit 15 for products covered by USDA specifications.) The National Live Stock and Meat Board has developed pictorial data displaying carcass yields, grades, and preparation techniques. Likewise, NAMP publishes *The Meat Buyers Guide*, which provides valuable information to purchasers.

Pork products are more consumer-oriented than beef. Brand recognition is strong, particularly at the retail level, and pork production is primarily aimed at this level. This handicaps the hospitality purchaser to some extent, but there are techniques similar to those for beef that can help the buyer judge if quotes are reasonable. Exhibit 16 gives a breakdown of pork carcass parts, priced from *The Yellow Sheet*. These percentages and value assignments serve only as examples, and will vary according to the packer's system of butchering and marketing, the type of hogs processed, and date of purchase.

Hams

Hams are sold bone-in, boneless, fresh, dry cure, water-added cure, and canned. The quality of cured hams relates to the amount of trim, flavor imparted by the cure, and yield in usable portions. These factors, in turn, depend on the size and type of hog, and the techniques used in manufacturing the ham.

There are two types of cured hams: dry cure and water added. Water may be used in curing hams (a process called pumping); however, dry hams must not exceed their original weight when curing is complete. A ham labeled "water added" may be up to 110% of its precooked (or pre-cured) weight. For example, if a boned, trimmed ham weighs 10 pounds before cure, it may weigh up to 11 pounds after adding water. There are significant price differences between dry cure and water-added hams.

Ham is available in a wide variety of trims. The basic trim, skinned ham (IMPS #402), provides the most accurate reference point for ham prices. Exhibit 17 gives cutting test information which enables the buyer to develop finished ham prices and evaluate vendors' bids. The example described is for a boneless ham (IMPS #402B) with a common type of trim: $^1/_2$ inch of fat except on the butt where 1 inch is permitted. It is boneless and tied with defatted shank meat tucked into the cavity; on menus, it is often identified as roast ham. Finished weight is between 10 and 13 pounds.

Imported canned hams from Europe have found acceptance in the United States. Traditionally, they are better trimmed and have less gelatin than domestic products. They are also more expensive, so a cost benefit analysis must be made. Some imported hams, if served unheated, can yield as high as 95% in usable portions; by comparison, domestic hams may have yields as low as 80%. Buyers should calculate yields for several brands at least annually, select several acceptable

Exhibit 15   Index of Pork Products Covered by IMPS

Item No.	Product	Item No.	Product
400	Carcass	515	Shoulder (Cured)
401	Ham, Regular	516	Shoulder (Cured and Smoked)
401A	Ham, Regular, Short Shank	517	Shoulder, Skinned (Cured)
402	Ham, Skinned	518	Shoulder, Skinned (Cured and Smoked)
402A	Ham, Skinned, Short Shank	525	Shoulder, Picnic (Cured)
402B	Ham, Boned and Tied	526	Shoulder, Picnic (Cured and Smoked)
403	Shoulder	527	Shoulder, Picnic (Cured and Smoked),
404	Shoulder, Skinned		Boneless, Skinless, Rolled and Tied
405	Shoulder, Picnic	530	Shoulder Butt, Boneless (Cured and
406	Boston Butt		Smoked)
406A	Boston Butt, Boned and Tied	535	Belly, Skin-On (Cured)
407	Shoulder Butt, Boneless	536	Bacon, Slab (Cured and Smoked),
408	Belly		Skin-On
409	Belly, Skinless	537	Bacon, Slab (Cured and Smoked),
410	Loin		Skinless, Formed
411	Loin, Bladeless	539	Bacon, Sliced (Cured and Smoked),
412	Loin, Center Cut		Skinless
413	Loin, Boneless	541	Bacon, Sliced (Cured and Smoked),
413A	Loin, Boned and Tied		Ends and Pieces
414	Canadian Back	545	Loin (Cured and Smoked)
415	Tenderloin	546	Loin, Bladeless (Cured and Smoked)
416	Spareribs	550	Canadian Back (Cured and Smoked),
416A	Spareribs, Breast Off		Unsliced
417	Shoulder Hock	551	Canadian Style Bacon (Cured and
418	Trimmings (90% Lean)		Smoked), Sliced
419	Trimmings (80% Lean)	555	Jowl Butts, Cellar Trim (Cured)
420	Front Feet	556	Jowl Squares (Cured and Smoked)
421	Neck Bones	558	Spareribs (Cured)
422	Back Ribs	559	Spareribs (Cured and Smoked)
423	Country Style Ribs	560	Hocks, Shoulder (Cured)
500	Ham, Short Shank (Cured)	561	Hocks, Shoulder (Cured and Smoked)
501	Ham, Short Shank (Cured and Smoked)	562	Fatback (Cured)
502	Ham, Skinned (Cured)	563	Feet, Front (Cured)
503	Ham, Skinned (Cured and Smoked)	1400	Fillets
504	Ham, Skinless (Cured and Smoked),	1406	Boston Butt Steaks, Bone-In
	Partially Boned	1407	Shoulder Butt Steaks, Boneless
505	Ham, Skinless (Cured and Smoked),	1410	Chops, Regular
	Completely Boneless	1410A	Chops, with Pocket
505A	Ham, Skinless, Boned, Rolled, and Tied	1410B	Rib Chops, with Pocket
	(Cured and Smoked)	1411	Chops, Bladeless
506	Ham, Skinned (Cured and Smoked),	1412	Chops, Center Cut
	Fully-Cooked, Dry Heat	1412A	Chops, Center Cut, Special
507	Ham, Boneless, Skinless (Cured and	1412B	Chops, Center Cut, Boneless
	Smoked), Fully-Cooked, Dry Heat	1413	Chops, Boneless
508	Ham, Boneless, Skinless (Cured),	1495	Pork for Chop Suey
	Pressed, Fully-Cooked, Moist Heat	1496	Ground Pork
509	Ham, Boneless, Skinless (Cured and	1496A	Ground Pork Patties
	Smoked), Pressed, Fully-Cooked,		
	Moist Heat		

Source: USDA, *Institutional Meat Purchase Specifications for Fresh Pork—Series 400* and *Institutional Meat Purchase Specifications for Cured, Cured and Smoked, and Fully-Cooked Pork Products—Series 500* (Washington, D.C.: U.S. Government Printing Office, 1975).

products, then buy based on the best usable meat cost. The buyer must, of course, periodically verify recorded yields.

It is important for the buyer to know that value comprises quality and price; the bottom line is the cost as served on the plate. Knowledge of usable meat costs is required to accurately measure the food cost performance of menu items. Exhibit

Exhibit 16   Pork Carcass Breakdown

Description	Percentage	Pounds		Price FOB Midwest		Value FOB Midwest
Fresh skinned ham	18.5%	40.7	×	$.58	=	$23.61
Loin–blade on	15.0%	33.0	×	.91	=	30.03
Boston butt	6.5%	14.3	×	.63	=	9.01
Regular picnic	8.5%	18.7	×	.39	=	7.29
Square cut bacon	17.5%	38.5	×	.485	=	18.67
Spare ribs	3.0%	6.6	×	1.26	=	8.32
Trimmed jowls	3.0%	6.6	×	.275	=	1.82
Tail, neck, bones	5.0%	11.0	×	.15	=	1.65
Fat and fat trim	18.0%	39.6	×	.31	=	12.28
Sausage trim	5.0%	11.0	×	.58	=	6.38
	100.0%	220.0		$.54*		$119.06

* Total price/lb ($.54/lb) is calculated by dividing total value ($119.06) by total pounds (220.0 lb), and rounding off to the nearest cent.

Exhibit 17   Results of Cutting Test #4

Cutting Test: Skinned Ham to Boneless (IMPS #402B)

Description	Yield		Price/lb FOB Midwest		Total FOB Midwest
Start with:					
Skinned ham	100 lb	×	$.58	=	$58.00
By-product return:					
Less fat, bone, skin, shrink (estimated)	−35 lb	×	.15	=	−5.25
Primary product return:					
#402B boneless ham	65 lb		$.81 (1)		$52.75
Add:					
Labor, overhead, profit (estimated)			+.50		+32.50
Value (FOB plant)			$1.31 (2)		$85.25

(1) Price/lb for boneless ham ($.81/lb) is calculated by dividing its total price ($52.75) by the resulting yield (65 lb), and rounding off to the nearest cent.
(2) Freight and local distribution costs must be added to this.

18 assumes certain costs for four ham items and examines the effects of shrinkage and portion yield on actual costs.

There are seasonal patterns for ham prices. Cured ham prices may show wide fluctuations due to holiday demand. Buyers should anticipate this and work with the supplier to protect prices.

Pork Loins

Pork loins yield chops, Canadian bacon, and roast pork. IMPS #410 loin is the item identified as "regular loin" in *The Yellow Sheet* (see Exhibit 2). For example, a

Exhibit 18   Effects of Shrinkage and Portion Yield on Usable Meat Cost

Item	Purchase Cost ($/lb)	Cooking Shrinkage	Net ($/lb)	Portion Yield	Usable Meat Cost
#402B—fresh ham	1.60	25%	2.13	90%	2.37
#509—cured ham	2.30	8%	2.50	96%	2.60
Cured ham (no water)	1.65	18%	2.01	90%	2.23
Canned ham (domestic)	2.00	—	2.00	80%	2.50
Canned ham (imported)	2.25	—	2.25	95%	2.37

Net price is calculated as follows:

$$\text{Net price} = \frac{\text{Purchase Cost}}{100\% - \text{Cooking Shrinkage}}$$

Usable meat cost is calculated as follows:

$$\text{Usable Meat Cost} = \frac{\text{Net Price}}{\text{Portion Yield}}$$

14-pound IMPS #410 loin yields approximately 6 pounds of center cut chops *or* 8 pounds of boneless meat and a $^3/4$ pound tenderloin. There are many other trim possibilities depending on the buyer's needs and applicable considerations of cost and pricing.

Bacon

Bacon is processed from the pork belly—the boneless underside of the pork carcass remaining after the loin and spareribs are removed. Processing includes curing, smoking, blocking, and, if required, slicing. Slice packaging is usually in 15-pound boxes, either shingle-pack or laid flat. Shingle-pack slices are similar to retail bacon. When bacon is laid flat, each slice is individually placed on parchment paper and separated into layers. While more expensive, this enables the cook to place 20 slices of bacon on the griddle at one time and also cuts down on broken pieces.

Bacon quality is determined by flavor, appearance, amount of lean and yield, and the presence of uniform, usable slices. The best lean bellies come from lighter, leaner hogs which produce bellies weighing 12 to 14 pounds. Prices vary dramatically based on trim styles and consumer acceptance. Bacon is a highly promoted cured pork item with significant consumer brand allegiance.

A typical specification might appear as follows: Bacon should conform to IMPS #539, should come from 12 to 16 pound bellies, and should be processed at 16 to 18 slices per pound. Slice width should be between 1 and 2 inches and length between 9 and 10 inches. The package should contain no scrap pieces and the product should be free of mold. Bacon should be well flecked with lean and cured to the same standard as a specified brand. Bacon is to be packed 15 pounds to the poly-lined box (containing between 240 and 270 slices) in laid-flat style with paper separating each layer, and should be shipped within 7 days of manufacture.

Sausages

Sausage links and patties are major breakfast items for food service operations. Portion control or count per pound are important since sausage is bought by the pound and sold by the portion. Raw materials vary: all trimmings may be used, but many products are specifically advertised as "whole hog" or "tenderloins included." Fat generally runs between 30% and 40%, but may exceed 40% by USDA definition.

Few hospitality operations use sufficient volumes of sausage to have their own specifications. The normal procedure is to test various products, identify acceptable choices from among these products, and then purchase using the most effective buying plan. Sausage prices, unlike bacon prices, can be checked using data from *The Yellow Sheet*.

Exhibit 2 has prices for the materials that are used in manufacturing these sausages. Buyers could follow prices for 72% lean trimming under "sausage materials," which are reported at $.70 per pound Chicago. A spread could then be developed, similar to that described for frankfurters. For example, competitive quotes may produce a patty price of $1.20 per pound. The spread then is $.50 per pound ($1.20 − .70 = $.50). This spread should then be maintained by the supplier.

Buying Patterns for Pork

Sellers of "brand" merchandise operate from price lists which are revised weekly. These lists reflect price differences based on pounds per delivery and distance from the processing plant. Large volume (truckload) warehouse deliveries carry another price. All reflect the cost of servicing a specific order. A small user benefits by receiving as many pounds at a time as possible. Buyers should try to combine many items with one vendor and take fewer deliveries (one per week) to move total pounds into a lower price bracket. The small user should:

- Evaluate competitive products on their quality, yield, and price.

- Select acceptable products from two vendors: a primary and an alternate.

- Order once a week with as many products as possible from the primary vendor.

- Compare the primary and alternate vendors' prices weekly.

- Compare quotations to reported prices each week to see if price changes are reasonable, using formulas whenever possible.

- Check quality and weight received to ensure that specifications are met.

Vendors provide services to assist steady customers in merchandising and product presentation. They may provide advance information on price changes, thus enabling the buyer to plan for the future.

Veal and Lamb

Relatively little veal or lamb is produced and consumed in the United States. The primary reason is lack of supply, which results in high prices. Surplus calves, which once were used to produce veal, are now marketed as mature animals. This is a result of grading standard changes made in 1976 that lowered the level of quality required to meet standards for the Choice grade of beef. Sheep populations diminished as wool began to be replaced by synthetic materials. Economic incentives are not sufficient to support production of sheep for meat only.

Traits

Veal has comparatively little flavor, so it is usually enhanced with seasonings or sauces. Its primary attribute is tenderness. Lamb has a very distinctive flavor which increases as the animal matures. In contrast to pork, the majority of veal and lamb is purchased by food service operations.

Veal and lamb quality relates to age. With lamb, fat is also a factor. Veal comes from young animals (up to 12 months). The meat grain is fine rather than mushy and light grayish pink in color. Bones are porous and red. The small amount of fat present is firm and white. Veal from light animals (100 to 150 pounds) has these characteristics. However, animals up to 350 pounds may classify as veal and, as the animal matures, the traditional "veal" characteristics disappear.

Specifications

Buyers needing large quantities can specify the primal cut from which the item is made. For example, assume the buyer desires veal cutlets (solid meat, with no knitting or cubing). The buyer can specify "produce from bone-in single leg, 22 to 28 pounds." Many fine restaurants buy primal cuts and prepare finished products. This enables them to know the size of the raw material and the age of the animals (bone-in legs that weigh 22 to 28 pounds come from carcasses under 150 pounds).

Small-volume buyers must write good specifications and carefully inspect veal and lamb products upon arrival. They can use the USDA grading system. While classifications such as USDA Prime and USDA Choice are the same for veal as for beef, the standards are somewhat different. Veal has no yield grades.

IMPS series 300 (see Exhibit 19) establishes trim specifications for veal primal cuts. IMPS series 1300 sets standards for portion cuts. Both are shown in *The Meat Buyers Guide* from NAMP and can be used to establish basic specifications. For example, IMPS #1336 for veal cutlets requires the item to be: (1) from the IMPS #336 leg, (2) solid muscle meat with no pieces knitted together, (3) free of fat and membrane, and (4) within 1/4-ounce weight tolerance per cutlet. The buyer adds grade (USDA Choice), primal cut size (22 to 28 pounds), and portion size (4 ounces) to the basic specification.

Lamb flesh darkens as the animal ages. In young lambs (5 to 6 months), the flesh is light to medium pink and is finely textured; fat is white. As the animal approaches the yearling class (10 to 12 months), it still qualifies as lamb but the flesh is darker (medium pink to light red). Above 14 months of age, an animal is classified as mutton. In USDA grade standards, this determination is made by examining the ankle bone area after removing the foot. If bone has replaced the cartilage, the animal is classified as mutton. USDA quality grades of interest to purchasers of lamb and mutton are USDA Prime, USDA Choice, and USDA Good. IMPS series 200 sets out trim specifications for primals and series 1200 specifies portion cut items (see Exhibit 20). Both are shown in *The Meat Buyers Guide*, which can be used to establish basic specifications with modifications in trim and quality as required.

Exhibit 19   Veal Products Covered by IMPS

Item No.	Product	Item No.	Product
300	Carcass	313	Breast
303	Side	330	Hindsaddle, 2 Ribs
303A	Side, 2 Rib Hindquarter	330A	Hindsaddle, 1 Rib
303B	Side, 1 Rib Hindquarter	331	Loin, 2 Ribs (Double)
303C	Side, Boneless	331A	Loin, 1 Rib (Double)
304	Foresaddle, 11 Ribs	332	Loin, 2 Ribs, Trimmed (Double)
304A	Foresaddle, 12 Ribs	332A	Loin, 1 Rib, Trimmed (Double)
305	Bracelet, 7 Ribs (Double)	333	Full Loin, Trimmed
306	Hotel Rack, 7 Ribs (Double)	334	Legs (Double)
308	Chucks, 4 Ribs (Double)	335	Leg, Oven-Prepared, Boneless
308A	Chucks, 5 Ribs (Double)	336	Leg, Shank Off, Oven-Prepared,
309	Square Cut Chucks, 4 Ribs (Double)		Boneless
309A	Square Cut Chucks, 5 Ribs (Double)	337	Hindshank
309B	Square Cut Chuck, 4 Ribs, Boneless	339	Leg, Short Cut
309C	Square Cut Chuck, 5 Ribs, Boneless	340	Back, 9 Ribs
309D	Square Cut Chuck, Neck Off, 4 Ribs,	340A	Back, 8 Ribs
	Boneless & Tied	341	Back, 9 Ribs, Trimmed
309E	Square Cut Chuck, Neck Off, 5 Ribs,	341A	Back, 8 Ribs, Trimmed
	Boneless & Tied	342	Hindsaddle, 9 Ribs, Long Cut
310	Shoulder Clod	342A	Hindsaddle, 8 Ribs, Long Cut
310A	Shoulder Clod, Special	343	Hindsaddle, 9 Ribs, Long Cut, Trimmed
310B	Shoulder Clod Roast	343A	Hindsaddle, 8 Ribs, Long Cut, Trimmed
311	Square Cut Chuck, 4 Ribs, Clod Out,	1300	Cubed Steaks
	Boneless	1301	Cubed Steaks, Special
311A	Square Cut Chuck, 5 Ribs, Clod Out,	1306	Rib Chops
	Boneless	1309	Shoulder Chops
311B	Square Cut Chuck, 4 Ribs, Clod Out,	1332	Loin Chops
	Boneless & Tied	1336	Cutlets
311C	Square Cut Chuck, 5 Ribs, Clod Out,	1395	Veal for Stewing
	Boneless & Tied	1396	Ground Veal
312	Foreshank	1396A	Ground Veal Patties

Source: USDA, *Institutional Meat Purchase Specifications for Fresh Veal and Calf—Series 300* (Washington, D.C.: U.S. Government Printing Office, 1975).

Exhibit 20   Lamb Products Covered by IMPS

Item No.	Product	Item No.	Product
200	Carcass	233C	Leg, Shank Off (Single)
202	Foresaddle	233D	Leg, Shank Off, Boneless
203	Bracelet (Double)	233E	Hindshank, Heel Attached
204	Rib Rack (Double)	234	Leg, Oven-Prepared
205	Chucks and Plates (Double)	234A	Leg, Oven-Prepared, Boneless, & Tied
206	Chucks (Double)	235	Back
207	Square-Cut Shoulders (Double)	236	Back, Trimmed
208	Square-Cut Shoulder, Boneless	237	Hindsaddle, Long Cut
209	Breast, Flank On	238	Hindsaddle, Long Cut, Trimmed
209A	Breast, Flank Off	1204	Rib Chops
210	Foreshank	1204A	Rib Chops, Frenched
230	Hindsaddle	1207	Shoulder Chops
231	Loin (Double)	1232	Loin Chops
232	Loin, Trimmed (Double)	1295	Lamb for Stewing
233	Leg (Double)	1296	Ground Lamb
233A	Leg, Lower Shank Off (Single)	1296A	Ground Lamb Patties
233B	Leg, Lower Shank Off, Boneless		

Source: USDA, *Institutional Meat Purchase Specifications for Fresh Lamb and Mutton—Series 200* (Washington, D.C.: U.S. Government Printing Office, 1975).

Production

Veal production is specialized and is associated with the dairy industry. Depending on the price of milk, some female calves are kept for dairy production. Many male animals, which were historically used for veal, now go to feedlot programs for production as roasts, steaks, or ground beef. Most large producers are located in states with dairy surpluses. These include Minnesota, Wisconsin, Illinois, New York, Texas, and California.

Lamb is part of the sheep system which includes wool production from mature animals. Domestic lamb production is centered in the western United States, supplemented by imports from New Zealand and Australia. Distribution is good and products are available in any major city. Interestingly, there is no national brand recognition for lamb products and most portion cuts are still produced by local purveyors.

Because the national production volume is small, there is little interaction between buyers and sellers at the carcass or primal cut level. Limited sources are available for price information; standard specifications and bid procedures are the best way to secure fair prices.

REVIEW QUIZ

When you feel you have covered all of the material in this chapter, answer these questions. Choose the *best* answer. Check your answers with the correct ones found on the Review Quiz Answer Key at the end of this book.

True (T) or False (F)

T ⊘(F) 1. Costs of meat are not particularly influenced by type of cut. F

(T) F 2. "Cut out value" refers to cost per pound of boxed beef. T

(T) F 3. Chuck and rib are the two primal cuts composing the majority of the fore-quarter. T

T (F) 4. Yield grades of 3 and lower provide less usable meat than higher yield grades. 1,2,3 usedble. F
          More

T (F) 5. Yield grades do not apply to primal cuts of meat. F.

T (F) 6. There is no discernible difference between cow tenderloins and steer tenderloins except price. F

(T) F 7. The top (inside) round is a popular cut often purchased precooked. T

T (F) 8. The most popular meat item consumed in the United States is round steak. GRound Beef F

T (F) 9. All ground beef must be made from graded primal solid muscles. F No any beef

(T) F 10. For ease of handling, frozen hamburger patties should be IQF. T

T (F) 11. Pork production is aimed primarily at the food service market. F

T (F) 12. Water-added hams may not exceed their pre-cured weight. T

T (F) 13. Veal may come from animals up to 14 months of age. F

T (F) 14. The color of lamb/mutton meat lightens with maturity. F-

Multiple Choice

15. The least expensive of the primal cuts is the:

C

   a. round.
   b. rib.
   c. chuck. ✓
   d. loin.

16. T-bone and porterhouse steaks come from the _____ section.

A

   a. loin ✓
   b. rib
   c. round
   d. flank

17.   Shingle pack is a term used in reference to:

B

    a.   sausage.   ✓
    b.) bacon.   ✓
    c.   hot dogs.
    d.   fresh hams.

18.   Veal is:

D

    a.   strongly flavored.
    b.   purchased primarily by food service operations.
    c.   associated with the dairy industry.   ✓
    d.) both b and c.   ✓

19.   Lamb is:

D

    a.   produced primarily in the western United States.
    b.   imported from New Zealand and Australia.
    c.   18 months of age or less.
    d.) both a and b.

Chapter Outline

Fishing: A World Industry
Popular Fish and Shellfish
    Shellfish
    Fish
Regulation of the Fishing Industry
    The National Marine Fisheries Service
    The Fishery Conservation and
        Management Act of 1976
    The Fishery Products Inspection
        Service
Fish and Shellfish Specifications
    Quality Factors
    Typical Specifications
Processing, Marketing, and Distribution
Pricing and Yields
Buying Systems in Review

Learning Objectives

1. Describe the fishing industry as a worldwide enterprise.

2. Describe factors affecting future fish populations.

3. Summarize the major categories of commercially important shellfish.

4. Summarize the major categories of commercially important fish.

5. Summarize regulations and agencies affecting the fishing industry.

6. Explain how a buyer can help ensure fish and shellfish quality.

7. Describe the quality characteristics of fresh, frozen, and processed forms of fish and shellfish.

8. Cite distribution and marketing channels for fish and shellfish.

9. Explain factors relating to pricing and yields of fish and shellfish.

10. Describe the basic buying systems for fish and shellfish.

10

Fish and Shellfish

THE SEA HAS ALWAYS supported those who live near it. Japan, for example, has the highest per capita fish consumption in the world. While Americans are not major fish consumers, certain areas—for instance, New England—have a relatively high per capita consumption. As a result of flavor preferences, Americans traditionally underutilized fish and shellfish as a food source. Unmarketable catches are discarded by boat captains at sea and many edible varieties are converted into fish meal and oil.

The development of superior fishing equipment by foreign nations contributed to deterioration in the American fishing industry. By the late 1960s and early 1970s, the New England fishing industry was essentially reduced to providing fresh fish and processing fish caught by other countries (much of it off American shores). All of this changed when the U.S. Congress passed the Fishery Conservation and Management Act of 1976 (FCMA). The United States took control of the fish populations to the end of the continental shelf (the so-called 200-mile limit) as well as migratory species that spawn in U.S. waters (West Coast and Alaskan salmon, for example).

The FCMA has helped create a dramatic rebound by the U.S. fishing industry. Catch quotas are set and American fishing interests receive a priority on these quotas. Problems remain with quotas, and the U.S. industry has not yet developed the capacity to harvest or process all the available fish. However, attrition in the fish population has been halted and the fishing industry is improving as a result of this important law.

Fishing: A World Industry

The annual world fish catch is approximately 160 billion pounds on a live weight basis. At approximately a 50% yield rate, this provides about 80 billion pounds of ready-to-use fish. Per capita consumption varies drastically from country to country.

The world's fish catch is utilized as follows:

Fresh	30.5%
Frozen	17.1%
Cured	11.1%
Canned	13.3%
Meal & Oil	26.6%
Miscellaneous	1.4%
	100.0%

Major exporters are Norway, Canada, Korea, Japan, Iceland, and the United States. Major importers are Japan, the United States, France, Germany, and the United Kingdom. On a ready-to-use basis, the United States imports approximately 2.4 billion pounds each year. Much of the fish imported to the United States is further processed in this country. For example, most of the breaded fish portions served here are imported in frozen block form.

There are more than 20,000 known fish species worldwide. New species are discovered regularly and some experts estimate there may actually be over 40,000 varieties. Only a small portion of these varieties is used commercially.

While fish inhabit all of the oceans, the vast majority are shelf dwellers. Those nations with extensive continental shelves have, therefore, the greatest variety of fish. Most species do not migrate over vast distances, but live out their life cycle within the same waters. Many fish spawn or lay their eggs in protected areas adjacent to shore.

Recently, conservation efforts have sought to preserve these spawning regions, which are usually marshy, tidal areas. The vast Chesapeake Bay no longer supports commercial fishing of migratory species such as sea bass (locally called rockfish), primarily because of pesticide contamination. Coastal areas in the northern Gulf of Mexico (offshore from Louisiana, Mississippi, and Texas) are under heavy pressure as a result of energy production activity. Offshore areas such as the Atlantic barrier reef system (which extends from Maryland to South Carolina) seem to be faring better, as are the Northwest coastal zones. The Potomac River system today shows some signs of recovery after years of neglect.

Fortunately, many of the cold-water varieties of fish inhabit inhospitable areas where population pressures seem unlikely to occur. Species inhabiting warm waters (such as shrimp) and the relatively immobile, shallow-water dwellers (such as lobsters, clams, crabs, and oysters) seem destined for trouble due to overdevelopment in spawning areas and pollution problems. A concentrated effort will be required to maintain these priceless assets.

Popular Fish and Shellfish

Exhibit 1 identifies the major species of importance to food service buyers and provides some summary data regarding pack sizes, seasons, countries of origin, and general information. One problem for the buyer and the general public is lack of information about fish and shellfish. Zoologically, fish are grouped according to body structure. For example, coho salmon is in the trout family and Eastern pollack is in the cod family, even though the flesh color and flavor of these varieties are quite different from their respective families.

While Americans are familiar with cod, haddock, and flounder, they are typically unaware that cusk or Pacific sand dab have the same general characteristics in terms of taste. Many underutilized species, such as orange roughy and New Zealand hoki, can be purchased at a lower cost; the smart buyer searches out these opportunities. The National Marine Fisheries Service has developed an edibility profile which is intended to help bridge this information gap and to encourage people to try more varieties (see Exhibit 2).

Exhibit 1 Popular Fish and Shellfish

Species/Variety	Pack Size	Season	Countries of Origin	Comments
Shellfish				
Clams *East Coast* Littlenecks Cherrystone Steamers Ipswich Surf (Skimmer) Razor *West Coast* Littlenecks Cherrystone Butter Pismo Surf Razor	Sold by bushel or bag. Counts vary by geographical area. Also sold shucked.	Year-round depending on weather.	Both U.S. coasts.	Only New England (or soft shell) are true clams. All hard shell also known as quahogs. Large sizes used for chowder. Littlenecks and cherrystones are both small quahogs.
Crabs & Crabmeat King Blue Snow Stone Dungeness	Live crabs sold by count in each market area. Cooked frozen meat from king and snow available, also legs and claws. Blue crabmeat usually sold fresh or pasteurized.	Warm months in producing areas. King and snow harvest is fall through spring.	King—Alaska through Aleutians Blue—Chesapeake to Gulf Snow—Alaska through Aleutians Stone—Gulf of Mexico Dungeness—Oregon and Washington	King crabmeat best for freezing. Most live crabs utilized near catch area. Blue crab caught as hard and soft shell. Leg or lump meat desired over body.
Lobsters • True or American	Sold live by the pound: • Jumbo = over 3 lb • Large = 1 1/2 to 2 1/2 lb • Quarters = 1 1/4 to 1 1/2 lb • Chicken = 3/4 to 1 lb	Year-round with some restrictions.	N.E. coastline of North America. Approximately 30% come from Canada.	North American lobster normally has two large claws. Culls are lobsters with one claw or a deformed/broken claw.
• Spiny Lobster	Varies with country of origin. • Brazil = 10-lb boxes • Australia = 20-lb & 25-lb boxes • U.S. = 20-lb boxes	Usually Nov. through March for New Zealand & Australia. Year-round in some areas of Gulf and Caribbean.	Brazil, New Zealand, Australia, U.S., Central America.	Also known as rock lobster and crayfish. It is best to specify size (oz) per tail and count per carton.
Oysters	Sold by the count in cartons. Medium = 200 per ctn. Also sold shucked by the gallon.	Year-round with best quality in fall and winter.	Practically worldwide.	Oysters from colder water are considered superior.
• Eastern or Atlantic (Bluepoint, Long Island, Chincoteague, etc.)	• X-Large = 160 per gal Large or X-Selects = 160/200 per gal Medium or Selects = 200/300 per gal Standards = 300/400 per gal		New England, Middle and South Atlantic, Gulf of Mexico.	
• Pacific (Westcott Bay, Olympia, European)	• Large = under 65 per gal Medium = 65/96 per gal Small = 97/144 per gal X-Small = over 144 per gal		Pacific Coast, Japan, Korea.	

(continued)

Exhibit 1 *(continued)*

Species/Variety	Pack Size	Season	Countries of Origin	Comments
Prawns	Same as shrimp, shell-on under 7 count/5-lb box, under 10 count/5-lb box, under 12 count/5-lb box, under 15 count/5-lb box	Caught during shrimping season.	Practically worldwide.	May be called scampi or Spanish reds. Larger sizes of shrimp.
Scallops Bay Sea Callico	Cut to the following counts per lb: Jumbo = 10/15; Large = 18/22; also counts of 30/40, 50/70, 70/90, 80/100, etc.	Year-round in some producing areas. For North Atlantic, generally from July through Dec.	N.E. North America, Nova Scotia, New England, England, Argentina, Australia, Iceland.	Packed differently by various countries of origin. Available individually quick frozen (IQF), block frozen, breaded. Bay scallops considered superior to sea variety.
Shrimp White Pink Brown	Sold shell-on (green), peeled and deveined (P&D), breaded and cooked. Sizing under 15 per lb, 16/20, 21/25, 26/30, 31/40, 41/50, etc. Generally packed in 5-lb boxes.	Year-round in some producing areas. For North America, generally July through Dec.	Gulf, Central & South America, Persian Gulf, China Sea.	Generally uniform count identification worldwide. Certain countries of origin may be less particular on sizing. White, pink, and brown shrimp considered desirable, in that order. P&D counts relate to shell-on counts. 16/20 P&D shrimp are from 21/25 shell-on shrimp.
Fish				
Canned Fish • Salmon	Generally 1-lb cans.	Aug. to Nov.	Northwestern U.S., North America.	For varieties see frozen section.
• Tuna	Generally 60-oz cans.	Year-round.	Japan, Taiwan, U.S., South Atlantic, Puerto Rico, South Pacific, San Diego.	Primarily albacore, yellowfin, skipjack varieties. Albacore is labeled white meat; other varieties light meat. Bluefin popular for raw oriental products.
Cod	Whole, fillets, blocks, or portions; cello wrap, layer pack, and IQF; skin-on or skinless.	Year-round, primarily July to Dec., age 6 to 9 yrs. when caught.	Canada, Iceland, Scotland, Norway, Japan, both U.S. coasts, England, Denmark.	A mild, white moist fish —good for breading. Size variations from some packers. Freezes well. Scrod is a form of cod weighing 1 1/2 lb or less.
Flounder Southern Winter Summer Yellowtail	Whole or fillets; cello wrap, layer pack, and IQF; skin-on or skinless.	July to Dec., with some year-round fishing.	Canada, Iceland, England, Scotland, both U.S. coasts, Denmark.	A flatfish normally sold whole or as fillets. Low in fat. Often confused with sole. Usually sized within a 2-oz tolerance.
Haddock	Whole, fillets, or portions; cello wrap, layer pack, and IQF; skin-on or skinless.	Year-round, primarily July to Dec.	Canada, Iceland, Scotland, Norway, New England, both U.S. coasts, Denmark.	A member of the cod family. Flesh is whiter. The catch is much less than cod. Commands a price premium over cod.
Halibut	Whole, fillets, or portioned (steaks). Whole halibut, under 10 lb—chickens; also 10/20 lb, 20/40 lb, 40/60 lb, 60/80 lb.	July, Aug., Sept. Catch controlled by Joint Commission of Fishing Nations.	U.S. (North Pacific and Alaska), Japan, Russia.	Moist, white flesh, mild flavor, good for broiling or baking.

Exhibit 1   *(continued)*

Species/Variety	Pack Size	Season	Countries of Origin	Comments
Mackerel Jack (Atlantic) Spanish King Pacific	Whole or fillets—sizing of fillets usually within 2-oz tolerance, i.e., 4/6 oz, 6/8 oz, etc.	• Jack—July to Oct. • Spanish & King—Dec. to March. • Pacific—July to Oct.	• Jack—North Atlantic (U.S.) • Spanish—Gulf ports (U.S.) and Mexico • King—South Atlantic, Gulf, Pacific Coast • Pacific—North Pacific	King usually exported to Caribbean nations. Spanish and king are flavorful fish, high in fat.
Perch, Ocean ("Redfish" or "Rosefish")	Skinless or skin-on; generally filleted; cello wrap, layer pack, and IQF. Fillets portioned as follows: 12/16 per lb, 4/6 per lb, 8/12 per lb, 2/4 per lb, 6/9 per lb.	July to Dec., with some year-round fishing	Canada, Iceland, Norway, Germany, Japan, both U.S. coasts.	Sizing is generally much less precise on this item than on haddock, cod, and flounder.
Pollack	Whole or fillets; cello wrap, layer pack, and IQF; skin-on or skinless; 11–18 lb at age of 6 yrs. 20″ to 30″ length.	Year-round, primarily July to Dec.	Canada, Iceland, Scotland, Norway, Japan, North Atlantic (U.S.) and Alaska.	Considered a member of the cod family. The flesh, however, is darker and less desirable. Has more fat and sells for less than cod.
Rainbow Trout	4, 6, 8, 10, 12 oz fillets. Available breaded also.	Year-round, freshwater.	U.S. (Idaho), Japan, Denmark.	"Farmed" fish. Expensive, Japanese somewhat less expensive.
Red Snapper Mangrove Yellowtail Vermillion	Generally filleted 6/8, 8/10, 10/12, 12/14, 14/16; can be bought whole head on, dressed 3/4, 4/6, 6/8, 8/10 lb each.	Year-round.	Gulf, Taiwan, Ecuador, Mexico, Brazil.	Gulf has only true snapper w/red tinge. Far East tends to be gray and less flavorful.
Salmon Chinook or King Pink or humpback Silver or coho Red or sockeye Chum, dog, or fall	15/25 lb each, round 5/7 lb each, round 7/12 lb each, round 5/16 lb each, round 8/14 lb each, round Whole, steaked, or canned.	Aug. to Nov.	N.W. Pacific, Oregon to Bering Sea. Some North Atlantic, Nova Scotia.	Chinook—bright salmon color Pink—light pink, canning variety Silver—reddish orange Red—reddish-dark, strong flavor Chum—light to pinkish red, strongest flavor, migratory fish
Sea Trout	Generally filleted 4/5, 5/6, 6/8, 8/10; IQF and cello pack.	Year-round.	Eastern seaboard of U.S., some Gulf, Central, and South American ports.	Fish run 1 to 4 lb round. Supply medium.
Sole Winter Lemon Dover English	Skin-on or skinless, generally filleted, all configurations from 1 oz to 10 oz each; IQF and cello pack; also dressed, whole head on.	July to Dec., with some year-round fishing.	North Atlantic predominantly, also Canada, Iceland, Scotland, Germany, Holland, Norway.	Member of flounder family. Price will vary dramatically with varieties.
Turbot, Greenland	Sized fillets and dressed with head on.	July to Nov.	Greenland, Norway, Iceland, Newfoundland.	Also known as blue halibut, gray halibut, or mock halibut, now Greenland turbot. Denmark turbot is different.
Whiting (or Silver Hake)	Generally sold skin-on. H&G (headed and gutted), whole is in 8/16 oz range. Available filleted in 4/8 oz range.	Year-round.	Maine, Canada, South Africa, Argentina, Brazil.	Inexpensive fish.

Exhibit 2   Fish Characteristics

White meat, very light, delicate flavor

    Cod, Pacific sand dab, cusk, haddock, lake whitefish, southern flounder, Dover sole, Rex sole, summer flounder, yellowtail flounder, Pacific halibut.

White meat, light to moderate flavor

    Snook, whiting, sea trout, butterfish, red snapper, catfish, American plaice, lingcod, winter flounder, mahi mahi, cobia, wolf fish, English sole, sauger.

Light meat, very light, delicate flavor

    Shovelnose sturgeon, smelt, pollack, ocean perch (Pacific), walleye, brook trout, white sea bass, grouper, bluegill, white crappie, rainbow trout, tautog.

Light meat, light to moderate flavor

    Atlantic salmon, pink salmon, lake sturgeon, monkfish, sculpin, ocean perch (Atlantic), scup, northern pike, rockfish, Eastern pollack, carp, swordfish, blackdrum, Greenland turbot, spot, sheepshead, Buffalo fish, croaker, chum salmon, pompano, striped bass, sand shark, perch, lake trout, mullet, coho salmon, eel.

Light meat, more pronounced flavor

    Atlantic mackerel, king mackerel, Spanish mackerel, redeye mullet, blue runner.

Darker meat, light to moderate flavor

    Black sea bass, ocean trout, chinook salmon, red (sockeye) salmon, bluefish.

Health-conscious consumers recognize the value of fish and shellfish as sources of high-quality protein. Many varieties are low in potentially dangerous fatty acids, high in vitamins and minerals, and relatively free of the indigestible materials associated with meats.

Shellfish

The term "shellfish" generally refers to organisms with visible shells which dwell in the ocean. There are two broad subcategories of shellfish: mollusks (true shellfish) and crustaceans. Mollusks include clams, oysters, snails, scallops, abalone, and squid. Lobsters, crab, crayfish, and shrimp are crustaceans.

    Shellfish are available in a variety of market forms. Lobsters, clams, oysters, and crab can be purchased live in the shell. Some species (crab and lobster) can be cooked in the shell and then chilled or frozen; in addition, the meat of shrimp, crab, and lobster is available cooked without the shell. Some mollusks (clams, oysters, and scallops) come in a shucked form, in which the meat is removed from the shell. Shrimp and spiny lobster tail can be obtained in a headless form, in which only the tail remains.

Shrimp. Three varieties of shrimp are of principal commercial importance—brown shrimp, white shrimp, and pink shrimp. Other common types include red, California rock, blue, and northern. Color relates to color before cooking; shrimp are virtually indistinguishable after cooking.

    The three principal varieties are all found in southern waters, ranging from the Carolinas south to Brazil on the east and from Mexico south to Peru on the west. Mexico fishes the entire length of both its coasts with a primary area located off the Yucatan Peninsula in the Bay of Campeche. The Gulf of California furnishes excellent quality white shrimp to Mexico, while the Gulf of Mexico provides most of the U.S. harvest. The Gulf of Mexico harvests primarily brown shrimp, which some consider inferior to whites and pinks. (Actually, quality is more a matter of the shrimp's feeding habits and handling after catch than variety differences.)

Major domestic fisheries are located off the South Carolina coast and the entire Gulf area from the Tortugas to New Orleans to Brownsville. Fishing is conducted offshore from all Central and northern South American countries, with Panama, Ecuador, and Brazil among the primary shippers. Large fisheries in the Indian Ocean and Persian Gulf regions export to the United States; the largest shippers are India and Thailand. Northern Pacific shrimp (primarily caught off Oregon, Washington, and Alaska) constitute less than 4% of total U.S. consumption. Small shrimp come from cold waters; larger sizes come from warm areas. Some larger species of shrimp (under 15 count per pound) are called prawns.

Lobster. The American (true) lobster fishing grounds extend from Virginia to the Canadian maritime provinces. However, practically all lobsters of this variety come from Canada, Maine, and northern Massachusetts. The harvest is regulated, with an estimated 90% of the legal population taken each year. Culls (lobsters with a missing, broken, or deformed claw) may be of any size and are sold at discounted prices. Lobsters sized as chickens (under $3/4$ to 1 pound) and selects or large ($1 1/2$ to $2 1/2$ pounds) are sold "in the shell."

During the summer, lobsters replace their shells, a process called molting. Fishing is not conducted during this season for conservation reasons. To maintain a steady supply of lobsters for market, holding ponds have been constructed in the Northeast, primarily in Maine. The lobsters are held live and brought into Boston for shipment as orders are received.

Spiny (spider or rock) lobster is really a form of ocean crayfish without the large claws of the true lobster. The tail is the only part used from these animals, which are caught worldwide. U.S. production is small and comes from the Bahamian flats (between Florida and the Bahamas) and the Gulf of Mexico. More than 40 million pounds are imported each year, about equally divided between two major harvest areas: Central/South America (warm water) and Australia/New Zealand (cold water).

Crab, Clams, Oysters, and Scallops. Crab production is dominated by Alaska, which is home to both the king and snow varieties. Next in importance is the East Coast blue crab, which is found from Maryland to Florida, with probably the best quality found in Chesapeake Bay. Another important variety, the Dungeness crab, is caught in the Pacific Ocean from northern California to Washington.

Clams and oysters are caught off the shores of both coasts of the United States. The variation between small, sweet cherrystone clams and the mature quahog is significant; clams take on a bitter flavor as they mature.

Scallops are available in both bay and sea varieties. The sea scallop is larger and somewhat less flavorful. Both varieties should have a sweetish odor.

Fish and Shellfish Farming

Fish farming has been practiced for thousands of years. Trout, which can be confined in pens and harvested when the fish reach marketable weight, have often been farmed. There has never been an apparent economic advantage to hatching and raising fry (young fish) and then releasing them into the ocean, since the mature fish may be harvested by anyone.

Salmon, however, return to spawn in the streams in which they were hatched. Since 1970, an effort has been underway in Alaska to hatch and release salmon fry and then recover them when they return as adults. The salmon industry has experienced substantial improvement in catch quantities, a trend which promises to continue. The catches must be managed carefully, though, so that an adequate supply of breeding fish is maintained. This natural balance makes agreements with foreign nations regarding high-seas harvest especially important.

Shrimp farming has been practiced for some years. Volatile price swings have made it financially troublesome, but sustained high prices over the last few years have brought more people into the business. Aggressive efforts have been made by Ecuador, where the climate and extensive salty flatlands of the coastal provinces combine to provide a hospitable habitat. Adult shrimp are captured at sea and confined to pens where they spawn. When the eggs hatch, the adolescent shrimp are transferred to saltwater ponds, where they are fed and grown to maturity. Some South and Central American countries, the Philippines, and Japan are also farming shrimp. Similar efforts are underway in California, Hawaii, Puerto Rico, and Florida. These programs promise to add significantly to shrimp production in the years ahead.

A successful oyster seeding and production facility exists on Long Island. Similar efforts have been made in other areas, including the Gulf of Mexico. Other bivalves, such as clams, mussels, and scallops, could also be candidates for seeding operations.

Fish

The category of fish may be further divided into freshwater and marine varieties. The major share of the world's fish catch is obtained from the oceans. With the exception of locally distributed catches, most freshwater fish are now farm-raised.

Codfishes. Codfishes, which include cod, haddock, pollack, and whiting (silver hake), are among the leading edible varieties of marine fish. Haddock belongs to the cod family, but is marketed as a separate variety. The term "scrod" is a size category under which cod, haddock, and pollack may be marketed. Haddock averages 3 to 7 pounds, but may reach 16 pounds. Cod usually weighs between 3 and 20 pounds. Pollack ranges from 1 1/2 to 12 pounds. Whiting weighs 1 1/2 to 4 pounds. Codfish are considered lean fish.

Flatfishes. Flatfishes include a number of characteristic species that usually live on the bottom of coastal shelves. Flounder, halibut, sole, and turbot are the major varieties. Flounder, halibut, and sole are found in both the Atlantic and Pacific oceans. Flounder and sole range from 3/4 to 4 pounds, but fluke or summer flounder can reach up to 12 pounds. Halibut weighs between 5 to 75 pounds. Turbot runs from 30 to 40 pounds in the round (whole) form.

Mackerel. Mackerels are found in temperate waters in both the Atlantic and Pacific oceans. Mackerel is a fat fish with a slightly strong flavor. Common varieties include jack mackerel, Spanish mackerel, king mackerel, and Pacific mackerel. Mackerels average about a pound or less in size, but king mackerel may weigh over 12 pounds.

Perch. Ocean perch (also called rosefish) come from the New England area as well as Iceland, Germany, England, Norway, and Canada. Their weight ranges from $1/2$ to 2 pounds. Although they are available all year, the best months to buy are May through September.

Other varieties of perch (white and yellow perch) are found in fresh water, including the Great Lakes. They normally range in size from $1/3$ to $3/4$ pound. Both ocean and freshwater varieties are lean fish.

Red Snapper. Red snapper is a highly prized fish which is available year-round. Grouper, sometimes substituted for snapper, is an excellent fish, but should not be confused with true snapper. True snapper has creamy pinkish-white flesh and is caught in Florida and Gulf waters.

Salmon. The salmon fishery runs from northern California to Alaska and the Bering Sea; Canada has a salmon fishery off Newfoundland. Salmon are migratory fish that return to spawn in the same stream in which they hatched. Salmon swim and feed together by class, for instance, chinooks or cohos. Therefore, the point and time of their return from migration as well as the route are fairly predictable. The FCMA attempted to prevent complete destruction of the salmon population by controlling the interception and harvest of salmon at sea—before they reach spawning grounds.

Trout. There are two major categories of trout: sea trout and freshwater trout. Rainbow trout and lake trout are the primary freshwater varieties. Rainbow trout, especially well-suited to aquaculture production (fish farming), generally weigh from $1/3$ to 2 pounds. Most lake trout come from the Great Lakes and weigh from $1 1/2$ to 10 pounds.

While freshwater trout are considered fat fish, sea trout are lean fish. Sea trout, also called weakfish, are fished in the Middle and South Atlantic. They generally weigh between 1 and 10 pounds.

Tuna. Tuna is a migratory fish, primarily caught in warm, tropical waters. It is fished worldwide and imports come from most of the fishing nations. The United States obtains domestic supplies off the coasts of western Mexico, Central and South America, and in the waters surrounding Puerto Rico.

Regulation of the Fishing Industry

Fishing rights have been disputed between nations since people first sailed the oceans. The economic benefits of fishing have created constant conflict between nations, states, and even communities. Territorial rights have been misinterpreted,

---

Fishery Market News Report

Fishery Market News Report is published by the National Marine Fisheries Service and issued from Boston, New York, New Orleans, Terminal Island, and Seattle. These reports show daily landings, market receipts, cold-storage holdings, daily vessel prices, weekly wholesale prices of fresh and frozen products, foreign-trade data, and other information relating to fish commerce. They are critical for fish buyers because they constitute the only national source of price data. Each report concentrates on the products landed in its particular area, but a summary of national events is regularly published. Buyers can subscribe to those reporting areas that best suit their needs and still receive some national information. Reports are published Monday, Wednesday, and Friday. A summary of the week's events is published in Friday's issue, which can be purchased separately if desired.

---

violated, and fought over continually. The right to manage and harvest fish populations remains a major source of irritation among nations to this day.

Through the years, various international commissions have unsuccessfully tried to cope with fishing rights and conservation issues. Recently, however, regulatory agencies as well as federal acts and services have begun to have a more positive impact upon the fishing industry.

The National Marine Fisheries Service

The National Marine Fisheries Service (NMFS) reports through the National Oceanic and Atmospheric Administration (NOAA), which was established in October of 1970 in the U.S. Department of Commerce (USDC). The NMFS affects buyers in the following ways:

- It administers the Fishery Conservation and Management Act of 1976 (see the following discussion).

- It provides voluntary in-plant sanitary inspection, compliance, and grading services.

- It publishes *Fishery Market News Report* and other statistical data relating to catch sizes, trends, and prices.

- It promotes the use of fish products.

The NMFS provides a vital source of information for the buyer. Its consumer affairs branch, located in Washington, D.C., generally provides information, conducts workshops, and develops recipes and educational data to better acquaint the public with fish and shellfish. It is a central source from which the buyer can obtain much of the information detailed previously.

Large buyers can gain knowledge of comparable services in foreign nations that export to the United States. In addition, buyers can obtain much information helpful in the buying process from the NMFS publication *Fishery Market News Report*.

The Fishery Conservation and Management Act of 1976

As already noted, the FCMA has greatly changed the world fishing industry. It provides the United States with the opportunity to manage its fish populations. Every foreign nation wishing to fish within the U.S. Fishing Conservation Zone (FCZ) must apply for and receive authorization through a process that ultimately requires the approval of Congress. These agreements state the amount of fish that can be caught, include a fee schedule, and provide for on-board inspection by U.S. observers. Allocations are made only for quantities that American vessels do not intend to catch. Quotas are reviewed each fishing season and may be altered if conditions change. The intent is to harvest optimal yields, while permitting American vessels first right of refusal.

The FCMA established eight regional fishery management councils; their primary function is to prepare fishery management plans for the fisheries under their jurisdictions. These plans are intended to reflect the composite thinking of the various states in the zone, the fishing industry, foreign political interests, and the American public—a formidable task and obviously one that requires compromise. A steady stream of jurisdictional and operational issues arises in the process, but on balance the 1976 act and the council management program have had a positive effect on the fishing industry in this country.

The Fishery Products Inspection Service

Inspection of fish products for wholesomeness, prior to interstate shipment, is not required by federal statute as it is for meat and poultry. Plants are required to produce clean, healthy items under federal standards set by the Food and Drug Administration (FDA), but inspections are irregular at best. The NMFS offers a voluntary program, available to processors for a fee, which provides some buyer protection.

Phase I of this service includes inspection of the facility to determine if it meets minimum USDC and FDA sanitary requirements. It includes consultation and technical advice to assist in meeting these requirements. Phase II builds on Phase I, providing for a minimum of 12 hours per month of sanitation inspections. After meeting certain standards, plants then become official establishments, operating under an FDA/NMFS memorandum of understanding and listed in an NMFS biannual publication (*USDC Approved List of Sanitary Inspected Fish Establishments*) available to buyers. Plants that meet the specified requirements submit a label to NMFS. Upon approval, these plants can display a stamp on their package that reads "Packed under Federal Inspection." Exhibit 3 displays this stamp as well as a federal grading stamp.

Voluntary product grading is available to processing plants in NMFS programs which offer U.S. grade standards. These grades are general and should be supported by specific buyer requirements. They do, however, provide some measure of protection. NMFS inspectors must be present to provide this grading service. Often, the plant's quality control program becomes an extension of the NMFS program in meeting standards. The two programs work closely together to prevent inferior products from reaching the market.

Exhibit 3   Federal Inspection and Grading Stamps

Other available services include lot inspection, which may be called for by either buyer or seller. The inspector provides the client with a certificate spelling out quality and condition of the lot. The service is available nationwide. The NMFS also has official responsibility for the inspection of fish/shellfish exports and imports.

Sanitation standards are established in Federal Standard 369—Sanitation Standard for Fish Plants. This standard is incorporated into the USDC Fishery Products Inspection and Safety Program which provides ongoing sanitary inspections and quality grading in addition to the initial inspection service. All of these additional services are voluntary.

Fish and Shellfish Specifications

Industry specifications for fish and shellfish are deficient in many respects. In contrast to the precise definitions afforded by meat specifications, these specifications are rather ill-defined and lacking in uniformity.

This situation is caused by a number of problems unique to the fishing industry. Fish does not have the economic importance of beef. Consumer concerns have not been great enough to cause government and industry cooperation of the type that produced standards of quality and wholesomeness for meat. The fishing industry lacks an organization, either national or international, that is strong enough or representative enough to take on a job of this magnitude. Since fishing is an international industry, each nation sets its own standards, which are primarily based on traditional practices.

In the absence of generally agreed-upon specifications, the buyer has a difficult task to specify and receive items of the desired quality. However, buyers may gain some added assurance in making purchases by using the following methods.

Exhibit 4   Fish/Shellfish Terminology

Round:	the fish as it comes from the water. The head may be on or off.
Drawn:	the fish is completely eviscerated.
Steaked:	portioning by slicing steaks at right angles to the backbone, against the grain. Halibut, salmon, and swordfish are offered in this form. As with any portioning of this type, watch the end cuts.
Fillets:	portioning by cutting parallel to the backbone. Specify size and packaging, such as layer pak, snap pak, and cello wrap.
Sticks:	generally prebreaded, formed portions of any available fish variety. May be made from solid or minced flesh.
Count:	either count per pound (as in shrimp 16/20) or size for each unit. In the case of lobster tails, "4/6" means each tail is within the 4- to 6-ounce size range.
Butterflied:	an item that has been separated against the natural seams. Shrimp is butterflied when it is partially split. Fillets may be butterflied to give better plate coverage.
Headless Shrimp:	the same as "shell-on." The head has been removed and discarded, leaving the tail. These are green (raw) shrimp.

- Require that products, as a minimum, meet the equivalent of USDC Grade A standards maintained by the NMFS.*

- Examine the NMFS "approved" list to see if the supplier in question is producing in an inspected plant.

- Buyers should require that bacterial levels do not exceed those allowable under FDA guidelines, which primarily cover uncooked shellfish and mollusks. Some states have also set bacterial standards.[1]

- Learn fish terminology (see Exhibit 4). Many of these terms deal with methods of portioning, cutting, and processing. Other terms are concerned with count and size as well as packaging forms.

The NMFS publication *Institutional Purchasing Specifications for the Purchasing of Fresh, Frozen, and Canned Fishery Products* is an informative resource for buyers. It gives a rather general set of specifications for competitive bidding of products and provides a framework to which specific requirements may be added.

Exhibit 5 illustrates some common forms of fish, which vary in degree of processing. The following discussion considers quality factors of major interest to the commercial buyer.

---

*Such standards cover the following product classes: whole or dressed fish, frozen dressed whiting, frozen halibut steaks, frozen salmon steaks, general fish fillets, fresh or frozen cod fillets, fresh or frozen flounder and sole fillets, fresh or frozen haddock fillets, frozen fish blocks, frozen minced fish blocks, frozen raw fish portions, frozen raw breaded fish portions, frozen raw breaded fish sticks, frozen fried fish portions, frozen raw headless shrimp, frozen raw breaded shrimp, fresh or frozen raw scallops, and frozen fried and breaded scallops.

Exhibit 5   Fish Primer

	Form	Definition	Best Ways to Cook
	Drawn	Whole fish, eviscerated	Bake, poach, broil, fry, steam
	Dressed or pan-dressed	Ready to cook	Bake, poach, broil, fry, steam
	Steaks	Cross-section cuts of large fish	Bake, poach, broil, fry, steam
	Fillets	Meaty sides of the fish	Bake, poach, broil, fry, steam
	Butterfly fillets	Two single fillets held together by a small piece of skin	Bake, poach, broil, fry, steam
	Breaded fillets	Fillets with seasoned crumb coating	Oven finish, deep fry
	Breaded portions	Uniform serving portions. Cut from frozen blocks or fillets. Seasoned crumb coating.	Oven finish, deep fry
	Fish sticks and bite-size pieces	Uniformly cut from frozen blocks. Seasoned crumb coating.	Oven finish, deep fry

Reprinted courtesy of National Fisheries Institute

Quality Factors

There are some general standards that apply by product class. It is especially critically to carefully check the quality of fresh fish and shellfish when they are received. Several designations apply to these items.

Fresh Fish. To be considered fresh, fish should meet certain standards. The odor should be fresh and mild. The eyes should be clear, round, and bright (not dull or sunken). Gills should be clean and red (not sticky). Scales should shine and adhere tightly to the skin. Flesh should be firm, elastic, and free of slime. Fillets should be bright, moist, and firm; without bruises, blood spots, or browning; packed skin side down; and laid flat with paper separating layers of fillets. The product should be packaged in an airtight container and properly refrigerated at approximately 32°F (0°C).

Cod, haddock, and perch are the major imports in the category of fish fillets. Canada, Iceland, Korea, Denmark, and Norway are the major suppliers of fish fillets. The United States also catches these species, as well as other varieties such as mackerel, off the Atlantic and Pacific coasts. All are cold-water species except mackerel, which is caught from New England and California south into tropical waters.

Improvements in Seafood Quality

The quality of seafood is steadily improving. The use of factory ships at sea helps to ensure that fish are processed promptly. Recently, some American fishing crews began packing fish in ice-filled tubs at sea rather than storing them in bulk holding bins. Excess handling is avoided and quality is better, leading in part to an acceleration in fresh fish sales.

Cooperatives and government agencies are educating members of the fishing industry in procedures designed to preserve catch quality. The Grade A program of the NMFS is gaining in popularity because it delivers fresher products to the consumer.

Production from third-world nations also seems to be making strides. Competition provides the incentive and technology provides the knowledge to improve product quality. Technological factors, such as controlled atmosphere, refrigeration, handling, processing skill, packaging, irradiation, and international air transport, help to deliver products to the customer quickly and in fresh condition.

Fresh Shellfish. Live lobsters and crabs should be moving to be considered fresh. In addition, lobsters should have hard shells. Fresh shellfish should be shipped with a covering of moist seaweed or paper and maintained between 40°F (4°C) and 45°F (7°C). Oyster, clam, and mussell shells should be tightly closed or should close when tapped. All fresh shellfish must have the necessary documentation and tags.

Partially Processed Shellfish. This group includes such items as headless, green (raw) shrimp. This particular product should be consistent in color. The flesh, when pushed with the thumb, should be resilient enough to snap back to its original form.

Frozen Products. Frozen fish, when thawed, should have flavor, texture, and odor characteristics identical to their freshly caught counterparts. If the surface flesh has been exposed (as is the case with fillets or peeled and deveined shrimp), a thin protective ice-glaze should be present. Packaging should exclude air to prevent dehydration (freezer burn). The product should never have been thawed and refrozen (a condition that may be detected by excessive ice formation in one end of the box). The product should be from the current production season.

Various species of fish are frozen into blocks for ease of handling and shipped to the United States for further processing. U.S. production of blocks is practically non-existent as its catch goes into fresh or frozen-finished products. Canada, Iceland, Korea, Denmark, Norway, and Argentina are the major suppliers. Cod is the primary block frozen fish, followed by pollack, whiting, and haddock; whiting is fished worldwide, while the other three fish are North Atlantic species. Blocks are available in varying sizes.

IQF or block IQF. Individually quick frozen (IQF) means that each piece is frozen separately and then packaged. Block frozen means that the product is frozen into a solid block which may weigh five or more pounds. It is obviously much

---

Factors to Check When Receiving Fish

Excess ice—the case weight shown should be net of excess ice.

Breading—specify the percentage and check to see that the correct percentage is supplied.

Counts—buy by the pound, but sell by the portion. Portions per pound is the key.

Broken pieces—excessive broken pieces reduce portions and returns.

Additives—smell to determine if excess chemicals have been used.

Protection—frozen products should be ice-glazed and packaged to avoid dehydration (freezer burn).

Date—processed products should be from current production.

---

easier to check and work with IQF products (although many block frozen items are acceptable). Generally, ready-to-use items are IQF while commodity products are frozen in blocks. For example, peeled and deveined shrimp are typically IQF, but practically all headless shrimp come in 5-pound blocks.

The exterior carton should list two weights:

- Gross—includes ice; used in calculating transportation charges
- Net—free of ice; should be the weight shown on the invoice

Sampling is often used to confirm the weight of block products; it involves randomly selecting a 5-pound box (or unit), thawing it, and checking the net weight.

Glaze. Most frozen products with the protective covering (skin or shell) removed are lightly ice-glazed to protect the product from dehydration. This is a good means of quality control if it is not abused. However, the buyer should pay only for net weight (less ice-glaze weight). Wash the ice glaze off to check the weight. Remember that fish are high in water content (up to 80% for shrimp) and will lose a significant amount of weight when they are handled extensively.

Breading. Many fish products come in a breaded form. Specifications should state the amount of breading as a percentage of the finished product weight. For example, a 2-ounce fish portion with 40% breading has 1.2 ounces of fish and 0.8 ounces of breading. Generally, if a product has more than 50% breading, it must be labeled "imitation." In the case of imitation shrimp, the breading can be as much as 65% of the finished product weight.

The amount of breading is determined by following these steps:

1. Weigh a sample of frozen, breaded product, then wash the sample in a tepid water bath (about 75°F or 24°C) until the breading has been removed.

2. Blot the flesh with paper towels and allow it to drain for two minutes.

3. Next, weigh the remaining product.

4. Divide the remaining weight by the beginning weight and calculate the percentage of fish by multiplying by 100. The difference between this and 100% is the breading percentage.

Generally, these checks are done in the kitchen by the chef or cook, who then reports the results to the buyer. Products from new suppliers should be checked regularly until their reliability is established. While occasional deviations from weight standards may be tolerated, continual variations (especially those in favor of the seller) are cause for eliminating that supplier. If the violation involves substantial amounts of money, documentation of the short weights should accompany any claim for credit.

Soaking or Dipping. Many companies use alkaline phosphate during processing, a practice sanctioned by the FDA as an aid in preserving product integrity by retaining natural moisture in the fish. However, some buyers argue that natural moisture is replaced or supplemented by moisture containing the chemical and that this results in a mushy product with a chemical flavor.

This condition may be particularly apparent in products such as cut scallops, peeled and deveined shrimp, and cooked shrimp. It is not as noticeable in products such as fish fillets unless the practice is abused. Buyers should be aware of the manufacturing processes used by their supply sources. Processors may gain a pricing advantage due to the extra weight of added water.

Typical Specifications

Specifications should be designed to communicate all relevant information to the supplier. Some typical examples of specifications are shown in Exhibits 6 to 9. These specifications form the basis for the pricing examples found at the end of this chapter.

Processing, Marketing, and Distribution

The industry incorporates a complex series of steps, beginning with the initial harvest of the raw catch and ending with the distribution of the product to the end-user. Along the way, the product is processed, manufactured, and packaged into a usable, manageable form.

There may be as many as five basic elements in the distribution chain:

- The fishing crew catch the fish and may perform some processing on board.

- The packer, usually located off the shore of the United States, packs in blocks or some bulk form.

- The processor, located in the United States, performs further processing services such as breading, sizing, and/or cooking. The processor may use imported products from the packer or domestic products coming directly from the boats.

- The distributor, usually located in a major city, performs a distribution service for products manufactured or caught by others. The distributor may also carry out some manufacturing processes.

- The end-user is the retail outlet, commercial operation, or institutional food service operation.

Exhibit 6   Sample Specification #1: Green Headless Shrimp

Item:	16/20 green (raw) headless shrimp.
Grade:	U.S. Grade A, or must meet USDC "Packed Under Federal Inspection" requirements.
Packaging:	5-pound frozen boxes; 10 boxes to each 50-pound master carton. Label to identify product and packer, net and gross weights, count per pound, and date packed.
General Requirements:	Must not exceed bacterial levels allowable under FDA standards; either white or pink species; must be packed in accordance with good commercial practice.
Specific Requirements:	To average 18 shrimp per pound and have less than 1% broken pieces. Product to be from current year's production and have a minimum of 5% glaze.
Handling:	Receiving temperature to be no higher than 0°F (−18°C).

Exhibit 7   Sample Specification #2: Breaded Shrimp

Item:	16/20 breaded shrimp, 40% breading.
Grade:	U.S. Grade A, or must meet USDC "Packed Under Federal Inspection" requirements.
Packaging:	3-pound boxes; 8 boxes to each master carton of 24 pounds. Label to identify product and packer, count per pound, and date packed.
General Requirements:	Must not exceed bacterial levels allowable under FDA standards; either white or pink species; must be layer-packed in accordance with good commercial practice.
Specific Requirements:	From 21/25 green (raw) headless shrimp, machine-breaded, butterfly type, tail off, oriental-type breading from ABC Breading Company. To average 23 count per pound with no broken pieces. Product to be from current year's production.
Handling:	Receiving temperature to be no higher than 0°F (−18°C).

Exhibit 8   Sample Specification #3: Block-Frozen Sea Scallops

Item:	30/40 block-frozen sea scallops, Canadian or domestic.
Grade:	U.S. Grade A, or must meet USDC "Packed Under Federal Inspection" requirements.
Packaging:	5-pound boxes; 10 boxes to each 50-pound master carton. Label to identify product and packer, count per pound, and date packed.
General Requirements:	Must not exceed bacterial levels allowable under FDA standards; must be packed in accordance with good commercial practice.
Specific Requirements:	To average 35 pieces per pound, uniformly cut. Product to be from current year's production.
Handling:	Receiving temperature to be no higher than 0°F (−18°C).

Exhibit 9   Sample Specification #4: Frozen Cod Fillets

Item:	Frozen cod fillets, skinless and boneless, 6–8 ounces each.
Grade:	U.S. Grade A, or must meet USDC "Packed Under Federal Inspection" requirements.
Packaging:	Snap or layer pack; 10-pound box; 4 boxes to each 40-pound master carton. Label to identify product and packer, count per pound, and date packed.
General Requirements:	Must not exceed bacterial levels allowable under FDA standards; must be packed in accordance with good commercial practice.
Specific Requirements:	From Canadian or domestic sources. Product to be from current season's production.
Handling:	Receiving temperature to be no higher than 0°F (−18°C).

Not all steps may be required to move products through distribution channels. For example, large retail users may provide their own distribution services. Members of the fishing crew may be independent, part of a cooperative, or company employees. The company or cooperative may own processing facilities based on shore or at sea. In addition, some of the manufacturing steps may be combined. However, these are the basic functions performed.

Some specific examples follow which describe the marketing channels for distributing fish and shellfish.

Tuna. Tuna are generally frozen round (as the fish comes from the sea) aboard the vessel and delivered to shore-based processing facilities, where heads and guts are removed and the fish are cooked and canned. Tuna fishing is a deep-sea, high-investment enterprise, usually conducted in the United States by a combination of independent and company vessels. Foreign tuna fishing may be nationalized or may be done by cooperatives or independents.

The U.S. canning industry is concentrated in Puerto Rico, American Samoa, and California. At retail, tuna is a consumer brand item, so there is little opportunity to market products other than through the large consumer companies. Most food service operations use large sizes (for instance, 60-ounce cans); much of this is private label or has a foreign label not recognized by consumers. Large distributors have products labeled with their logo to help maintain continuity when they change suppliers. Tuna is sold to large users directly from domestic processors or importers. Smaller users obtain supplies from their distributors.

Shrimp. Domestic catches are often sold fresh. Breading, cooking, or further processing is done in the United States. Most domestic landings are made by companies operating 20 or more trawlers. Some of these vessels are owned by companies with shore-based processing facilities. Other fishing companies may contract with these processors to purchase all of their catch. Prices may be contracted but are generally based on the market or auction price at the port.

Many domestic companies are owners or partners in foreign ventures. These usually involve investment in vessels, personnel, and processing facilities. The product (usually green headless shrimp) is shipped to the United States where the shrimp are further processed. U.S. processing companies without foreign connections buy foreign-produced shrimp to supplement domestic catches.

Shrimp is headed and rough-graded on the vessels, then finish-graded at the processing plants where the value of the cargo is ultimately determined. Domestic and foreign production is generally sold through brokers, although some domestic companies have direct sales forces to sell to large users. Small users usually buy from local suppliers. Fresh shrimp are available in most major American cities, but are expensive due to special handling and high transportation costs (usually air). The number of local distributors handling fresh shrimp, or any fresh fish, is much less than those handling frozen products.

Cod, Haddock, Flounder, and Perch. The supply of these fish and other North Atlantic species is split between foreign and domestic vessels. Foreign imports to the United States come as blocks and in ready-to-use forms such as fillets, eviscerated whole fish, or cut and sized portions. As with shrimp, these imports may be further processed in U.S. plants. Blocks are sliced into required shapes and sizes. Fillets may be stuffed with crabmeat or other products. Any of these items may be raw or cooked.

Domestic catches generally go to the fresh or frozen fillet market, but some are used for breaded or cooked products. Sizing is a buyer concern and this relates to the quality control practices of the processor. Most North Atlantic fishing nations maintain adequate standards.

The domestic distribution network is similar to that for shrimp, although different brokers or sales agents may be used. Distribution of foreign products varies with the country of origin. Production in Iceland is nationalized and all exports are handled through two state-managed companies: Icelandic and Scandia. In turn, these companies own and operate further processing facilities in the United States. By contrast, Canada subsidizes individual companies with various incentives; some Canadian companies maintain further processing facilities in the United States. American buyers of these products have direct access to the original processors if the volume is adequate. This contact is usually made through brokers, and the products may be purchased and inventoried if desired. The network of distributors that handles shrimp typically carries selected brands of these products. Fresh North Atlantic products are available in most eastern and mid-American cities.

Pollack, Salmon, and Crab. The processing, marketing, and distribution systems for these items and other West Coast fish are similar to those used in the North Atlantic. Salmon is somewhat more difficult to follow as it is used in fresh, frozen, and canned forms. Most frozen and canned salmon comes from Alaska, while Washington and Oregon tend to produce more of the fresh supply.

King and snow crab are processed by relatively few companies. Pricing is tied directly to vessel prices as reported for various entry ports by the NMFS.

Lobster. North Atlantic (true) lobster fishing remains an individual endeavor. The price received is determined daily and depends upon supply and demand. Ex-vessel (at the boat dock) prices are reported for Maine and Massachusetts; market prices are used in Boston and New York. These products, shipped live, may be bought direct in Boston if the buyer can retrieve them from a nearby airport. Generally, they reach the buyer through a local fresh fish distributor (perhaps the same one handling shrimp and fresh fillets). Price is usually based on Boston price plus transportation and handling.

For spiny lobsters, fishing seasons are controlled and prices are determined by the amount of the catch and the demand. Fishing is generally conducted during warm weather; in the Southern Hemisphere, this takes place in November, December, January, and February. Northern Hemisphere production is reversed, although the season is longer. Products from South Africa, Australia, and New Zealand are considered "cold water" and command a price premium over "warm water" tails. South Africa markets its products through licensed organizations in both South Africa and the United States. The price is controlled by a limited U.S. network. Production from other countries comes through licensed stateside brokers, but there is usually a little more competition.

Oysters, Clams, and Local Crabs. Harvest and distribution of most of these products have not changed a great deal over the years. Consumption has primarily been in areas contiguous to their habitat. Oyster farming is on the increase, however, and these products can be available year-round if distributors stock them. They are more expensive when natural fishing stops during the warm months of May, June, July, and August. Fresh fish distributors carry these items.

Pricing and Yields

In order to effectively negotiate prices for these products, the serious buyer requires information about product inventories, the prices paid to boats, major market wholesale prices, forecasts of availability, and a vast amount of related data. There are three ways to gather such information: personally attend auctions, obtain information from suppliers, and/or subscribe to one or more market reporting services. Obviously, it is not practical for buyers to utilize all of these sources of data, although occasional visits to auctions are recommended.

Suppliers can be an excellent source of information despite being limited to the products carried by their own companies. The people actually involved in processing generally have better data than brokers or distributors; in comparison, processors tend to be closer to the markets and carry a narrower product line.

Foremost among the reporting services is the USDC's *Fishery Market News Report,* which reports activity in various fish centers around the country (see Exhibit 10). Other sources of independent data are also available. *The Erkins Seafood Letter,* which is published monthly, builds on NMFS market data and gives opinions on trends in consumption, landings, and price. Urner Barry Publications publishes *Seafood Price-Current* (see Exhibit 11). Prices are reported for a wide variety of fresh and frozen fish, landed at east, west, and gulf ports, and are generally based on sales in large lots by first receivers (the company which buys from the boat or imports the product).

In order to understand pricing systems, one must know more about the basic types of distributors:

- General, full-line distributors: These companies carry a wide line of frozen and dry items. Fish products are frozen or canned, and the selection is usually limited to popular items such as shrimp and cod fillets. For important customers, these distributors may carry additional items, but they generally require some assurance that these products will be used within a reasonable time period.

- Specialized distributors: These businesses are relatively small, independently operated companies buying fresh, frozen, and canned products. Such distributors carry fillets, whole fish, oysters, clams, crabs, and other products required by their markets. In many cases, these companies perform filleting, sizing, or other special services for customers.

Approaches to using these two types of distributors differ. If requirements can be met by a general, full-line company, buyers usually prefer to combine fish orders with non-fish items to make a package deal. The idea is to increase the

Exhibit 10 *Fishery Market News Report*

```
408 Atlantic Avenue, RM 141        UNITED STATES DEPARTMENT OF COMMERCE          Four Pages - 1
BOSTON, MA 02210-2203         National Oceanic and Atmospheric Administration    Wed., April 16, 1986
Tel.: (617) 223-8019                 National Marine Fisheries Service
223-8012 / 8017 /8018             FISHERY MARKET NEWS REPORT B-45
                                          BOSTON FISH PIER
LANDINGS AND SALES:  In 1,000 lbs. & $ per Cwt.  Hailing fares.  Prices are ex-vessel for first sales.
    Landings and prices are available daily by phone (617) 223-8013.
```

	Hadd	Scrd	WCod	NCod	Scrd	Cusk	Hake	Poll	OPch	Wolf	B	B Dabs	GryS	Dabs&GryS	SDab	Mixd	Total
TUESDAY 4/15:	$ 120	91	LCod 60	53	50	40	40	37	56	25	75 125	60 125	60 140	Small 60	-	-	-
*Act I.........	-	-	-	-	-	-	-	-	-	-	-	-	-	-	-	2	2.0
Captain Sam....	-	-	0.3	1.7	0.5	3	11	12.5	12.5	0.2	-	0.3	1.2	1.2	-	-	44.4
Hudson.........	0.2	-	-	3.5	1.5	0.5	5.7	1.7	1.8	0.3	-	2	6.8	-	-	0.2	24.2
Jason&Danielle.	1	0.2	5.3	3	0.2	0.2	0.2	10.5	-	0.1	-	15	4.6	-	-	-	40.3
*Nicholas B....	-	-	-	-	-	-	-	-	-	-	2.2	-	-	-	-	-	2.2
*Shannon III...	-	-	-	10.5	10	-	-	-	-	0.5	3	-	-	-	-	-	24.0
6 - Total.....	1.2	0.2	5.6	18.7	12.2	3.7	16.9	24.7	14.3	1.1	5.2	17.3	12.6	1.2	-	2.2	137.1
WEDNESDAY 4/16:	$ 160	91	65	60	60	35	37	32	50	25	Geo 125	64 115	62 130	64	26	-	-
Bagatell.......	0.5	-	0.1	0.3	0.1	6.3	9.5	15	11	0.2	0.2	0.3	0.5	-	0.2	-	44.2
Margot Ann.....	1	-	4	2.5	-	0.1	0.3	9	-	0.1	-	11	2.5	-	-	-	30.5
Miss Vicky.....	0.1	0.2	0.3	1	0.3	2.5	4.5	10	8.5	0.3	-	0.8	2.8	-	-	-	31.3
Olympia........	0.2	-	1	2.5	1	5	10.5	19	20	0.1	-	0.5	0.6	0.5	-	-	60.9
4 - Total.....	1.8	0.2	5.4	6.3	1.4	13.9	24.8	53	39.5	0.7	0.2	12.6	6.4	0.5	0.2	-	166.9

```
1/ Poll: Tues.: $37, Wed 37                  3/ GryS: Tues.: Lge $140, Med 116, Sml 60
2/ BB: Tues.: $75, Georges 125                        Wed.: Lge $130, Med 109, Sml 62
OTHER PRICES: Tues.: Whiting, Round Not Sold    *Carried over from Monday.
```

```
                         NEW BEDFORD, MASS.
LANDINGS & SALES:  In 1,000 lbs.  Ex-vessel prices in $/Cwt. for landings
  sold at the New Bedford selling room.  Landings and prices are available
  daily by phone (617) 997-6565.    PRIVATE AUCTION
SCALLOPS, SEA: TUES.: N O  L A N D I N G S
   WED.: 2 Scallopers Total 14.0 @ $475-479; Patience 10.5, Prowler 3.5
```

	Hadd	Scrd	Cod	B	B	LemS	Dabs	GryS	Y	T	Poll	SDab	Total
TUESDAY 4/15:	$ 100	60 80	40 55	90 110	& BB	80 125	90 125	95 125	15 20	21 66	-		
Bridget M.........	-		6	6.5	-	-	-	-	-	7.5	20.0		
Carevelle.........	-		19	6.5	-	-	-	-	-	1.5	27.0		
Faneca............	-		1	3	-	1	0.8	8.5	-	-	14.3		
Imigrante.........	3.5		19	-	1	2	-	4.8	0.2	8.5	39.0		
Kimbanda..........	-		0.3	3	-	-	-	1.3	-	6.5	11.1		
Min Flicka........	-		-	2.4	-	-	-	-	-	3.7	6.1		
Potpourri.........	-		-	8	-	-	-	-	-	6	14.0		
Triunfo...........	4		11.5	0.5	1.5	-	1	8.5	0.2	3	30.2		
8 - Total........	7.5		56.8	29.9	2.5	3	1.8	23.1	0.4	36.7	161.7		
WEDNESDAY 4/16:	$ 125	70 160	40 65	80 160	-	90 125	90 125	90 130	20 25	40 105	-		
Bell.............	3.5		21	-	1.5	-	-	-	-	-	26.0		
Faro.............	-		29	6.3	-	-	-	-	-	3.2	38.5		
Fisherman........	1		7.5	-	0.6	-	:	-	-	2	11.1		
Gen. George S.Patton	3		28.5	4	-	-	-	-	-	-	35.5		
Gertrude D.......	-		0.5	2.5	-	-	-	-	-	1	4.0		
Kilkenny.........	-		5.3	10.5	-	-	-	1	0.7	1.5	19.0		
Marilyn B........	-		0.5	1	-	1.5	2	8.5	-	0.5	14.0		
Nancy&Christine II	-		11	7	-	-	-	-	-	-	18.0		
Ocean Spray......	0.4		12.2	-	11.5	0.4	-	-	2	2	28.5		
Unicorn..........	-		-	3	-	-	-	-	-	7	10.0		
Wanderer.........	-		1	3.5	-	-	-	-	-	12	16.5		
11 - Total.......	7.9		116.5	37.8	13.6	1.9	2	9.5	2.7	29.2	221.1		

```
1/ Cod: Tues.: Whale & Lge $40-45, Mkt 50-55, Scrd 41-50
   Wed.: Whale $50, Lge 40-50, Mkt 50-65, Scrd 40-60
2/ BB: Peewee: Tues.: $60-65;  Wed.: $60-100
3/ LemS & BB: Tues.: LemS $155-170, Lge BB 130-140, Sml BB 120, PW 60-100
   Wed.: LemS $120-170, Lge BB 100-150, Sml BB 80-125, PeeWee 40-60
```

```
PROVINCETOWN, MASS.
LANDINGS IN 1,000 lbs.
MONDAY & TUESDAY:
Cod.................. 4.8
Flounder: BB........  2.8
         Dabs.........  3.4
         Dabs, Sand...  1.7
         Fluke........  0.1
         Sole, Gray...  1.8
               Lemon...  0.1
         Yellowtail...  9.2
Haddock.............  0.1
Ocean Pout..........  6.0
Pollock.............  0.3
Red Hake (Ling).....  0.7
Whiting, Round......  0.7
Mixed...............  15.2
34 Otter Trawlers... 46.9
```

```
POINT JUDITH, R.I.
LANDINGS IN 1,000 lbs.


No Report Received
```

```
NEWPORT, R.I.
LANDINGS IN 1,000 lbs.
MONDAY & TUESDAY:
SCALLOPS, SEA:
  1 Scalloper Total 7.8
Cod................. 25.3
Flounder: BB........  1.5
          Dabs.......  1.6
```

Exhibit 11 Urner Barry's Seafood Price-Current

Saltwater Shrimp Complex
FIRST RECEIVERS—EX-WAREHOUSE • DELIVERED NEW YORK METRO (Mid-Atlantic)

COUNTS	Mexican No.1 White Del. W. Cst.	Domestic Brown	Domestic White	No. Brazil & Colombia Pink	Ecuador Pond Raised White	COUNTS	Domestic Peeled	Domestic & Mexican P & D IQF	Taiwan/Phili-pines/Thailand Black Tiger	India/Pakistan
Under 10	8.10	8.10-8.45	8.10-8.50	—	8.45-8.50	Under 10	—	—	—	—
Under 12	7.00	7.10-7.25	7.10-7.60	—	7.10-7.30	Under 12	—	—	—	—
Under 15	6.90	6.50-6.75	6.80-6.90	7.00-7.10	7.00-7.05	Under 15	—	—	6.50-6.60	6.25
16-20	6.90	6.05-6.10	6.35-6.40	6.45-6.60	6.60-6.80	16-20	—	9.50	5.80-5.85	5.25
21-25	6.90	6.00-6.05	6.05-6.15	6.50-6.60	6.50-6.60	21-25	—	9.00-9.10	4.75-4.80	5.00
26-30	6.00	5.75-5.80	5.95-6.05	5.70-5.85	5.80-5.90	26-30	—	7.35	4.40-4.50	4.50
31-35	5.70	5.40-5.50	5.40-5.50	5.40-5.45	5.45-5.50	31-35	—	7.05	—	4.40
36-40	4.70	4.70-4.80	4.70-4.80	4.70-4.75	4.75-4.85	36-40	—	6.00	—	3.75
41-50	4.20	4.45-4.55	4.45-4.55	4.00	4.10-4.30	41-50	5.50-5.60	5.75	—	3.25
51-60	3.65	3.70-3.80	3.70-3.80	3.30	3.45-3.65	51-60	4.50-5.00	5.25	—	3.00
61-70	2.85	3.00-3.10	3.00-3.10	2.75	2.95-3.20	61-70	4.15-4.25	4.90	—	2.50
71-80	2.35	2.50-2.75	2.50-2.75	*2.35	2.55-2.75	71-80	*3.80-4.00	—	—	2.40
81-90	2.20	2.10-2.20	2.10-2.20	*2.35	2.45-2.55	81-90	*3.80-4.00	—	—	—
91-110	—	1.80	—	2.25	1.95-2.10	91-110	3.30-3.50	—	—	—
111-130	—	—	—	—	1.85-1.90	111-130	2.60-2.70	—	—	—
131-150	—	—	—	—	—	131-150	2.40-2.55	—	—	—
151-200	—	—	—	—	—	151-200	2.10-2.20	—	—	—
201-300	—	—	—	—	—	201-300	1.65-1.90	—	—	—
*71-90 count	—	—	—	—	—					

Freshwater Shrimp Complex
First Receivers—Ex-Warehouse • Del. New York Metro (Mid-Atlantic)

COUNTS	Bangladesh	Burma Singapore	Indonesia Taiwan Thailand
Under 5	7.75	7.75	—
Under 8	7.50	7.50	—
Under 12	6.75	6.75	—
16-20	5.50-5.75	5.50-5.75	—
21-25	5.25-5.40	5.25-5.40	—
26-30	4.55-4.65	4.55-4.65	—
31-40	4.20-4.40	4.20-4.40	—
41-50	3.80-4.05	3.80-4.05	—
51-60	3.50	3.50	—
61-70	3.05	3.05	—
71-90	2.25	2.70	—
		2.25	

Sea Scallop Complex
First Receivers—Ex-Warehouse • Del. New York Metro (Mid-Atlantic)

COUNTS	Japan	Peru	Canada	Domestic	W. Australia	Icelandic	Bay UK IQF
10/20	4.90	—	5.85-6.00+	5.95-6.00+	—	—	—
20/30	4.45-4.60	4.40	5.60-5.65	5.50-5.65	—	4.45-4.50	—
20/40	—	—	—	—	—	—	—
30/40	4.25-4.50	4.10-4.20	4.75-5.10	—	—	—	—
40/50	4.25-4.50	4.10-4.20	4.50	5.05	5.05	4.00	—
40/60	—	—	—	—	—	—	—
50/60	—	—	—	—	—	—	—
60-80	—	4.05-4.15	4.40	—	—	4.10-4.25	—
80-100	—	—	—	—	—	—	—
90-110	—	—	—	—	—	4.10-4.25	—
110-130	—	—	—	—	—	4.10-4.25	—

Eastern Fresh Fish
F.O.B. DEALERS DOCK

Fresh Fillets	Mid Atl.	New Eng.
Bluefish, jumbo	1.75	1.40
Large	—	—
Small	2.00	2.10
Cod, large	—	—
Market	1.60-2.25	1.75-1.90—
Scrod	1.60-2.00	1.60-1.80—
Cusk	—	1.50-1.55+
Yellowtail, large	5.00	—
Regular	3.00-3.50	3.05—
Large, mixed	4.75-4.85—	4.25—
Fluke, jumbo	5.00	—
Large	5.50—	—
Medium	4.55	—
Small	4.30+	—
B/B, large	3.10—	—
Mixed	5.00	—
Regular	3.90-4.75	4.50-4.85+
Dabs, Sea	2.90-3.00	4.00-4.65+
Mixed	5.00—	—
Regular	4.50	—
Sole, lemon large	3.00—	2.75-3.00+
Mixed	—	—
Sole, gray, large	6.00—	—
Mixed	5.00	5.50
Hake, white	1.50	4.65
Haddock	—	1.25-1.50
Haddock, Scrod	—	3.00
Monkfish	—	2.50-2.85
Pollock	2.80-3.50	2.75-2.90+
Ocean Perch	1.20+	2.20-2.95+
Salmon, Baby Coho, bnd	—	.90-1.15+
Tuna, Bigeye, Cuts	—	—
Tuna, Bluefin, Cuts	—	—
Tuna, Yellowfin, Cuts	—	5.00
Ocean Catfish	2.95	—
Weakfish	2.55—	1.15—

FRESHWATER FISH

	Mid Atl.	New Eng.
Shad, boned	3.00	—
Shad Roe, jumbo	3.50-4.00	—
Large	3.25	—

Exhibit 12   Percentage Yield in Processing Fish and Shrimp

Fish	Round to fillets
Cod (skinless)	40%
Haddock	44%
Haddock (skinless)	40%
Halibut (skinless)	65%
Pollack	46%
Flounder—Dabs (skinless)	34%
Flounder—Yellowtail (skinless)	38%
Flounder—Gray (skinless)	35%
Grouper (skinless)	40%
Ocean Perch	33%
Ocean Perch (skinless)	30%
Salmon (skinless)	65%
Red Snapper	40%

Note: Percentages vary somewhat with season and fish condition (fat or lean).

Shrimp	Green headless to:	
	Peeled and deveined, shell on	84%
	Peeled and deveined, shell off	75%
	Peeled and deveined, cooked	48/50%

purchase volume and thus reduce the markup. This method depends on the distributor's ability to secure sufficient quantities at good prices.

A specialized distributor is more difficult to deal with, but, in some cases, may be the only source for the fish products required. If the product is fresh, prices are subject to fluctuations in ex-vessel prices. Availability is sporadic and transportation costs can be high.

If more than one fresh fish supplier is acceptable, competition takes care of some concerns regarding specialized distributors. Efforts to build volume attract supplier interest. Knowledge of ex-vessel and first-receiver prices in the major ports also helps buying efforts. Large users want to know about the companies (usually in major port areas) that process the fish.

If the volume is sufficient, a cost-plus plan that considers yield can often be worked out. The purpose of this pricing strategy is to establish a base cost to which the distributor adds a fee for handling and delivery. This fee should be negotiated as cents-per-pound over cost rather than a percentage of cost. The upcharge varies with volume, payment practices, and services required, but helps diminish the impact of wide fluctuations in ex-vessel prices on menu prices.

If the distributor performs some manufacturing function, such as filleting from the round state, yields must be considered. The cost of these fillets can be checked against the prices given by the reporting services and through actual cutting tests. Exhibit 12 shows percentage yield for various fish as well as green headless shrimp.

The product needed determines the distributor used, but price checking is identical in either case. Buyers must know the cost of fish at the source and understand how the final price is determined. Two examples demonstrate how this can be done.

The primary source for prices in the following examples is the NMFS publication *Fishery Market News Report.* This information is used to show how "port" or "point of entry" prices translate into bids presented to buyers. Use of these formulas does not guarantee that buyers will be able to buy or that sellers will actually sell at these numbers. Formulas do, however, provide a reasonable reflection of what prices should be. Buyers must use the normal tools of specifications, bidding, and negotiation to arrive at final prices.

The following examples illustrate how prices may be estimated for various fish and shellfish items. The specifications given in Exhibits 6 to 9 form the basis for each pricing example. (Note, however, that the second example uses requirements identical to Specification #4 except that the fillets are fresh, not frozen.)

Example 1: Fresh cod fillets

Ex-vessel prices for market cod in round form are reported in Exhibit 10 as ranging from 53¢ to 60¢ per pound at the Boston Fish Pier and from 50¢ to 65¢ per pound at New Bedford.

Assuming a mid-range price of 56¢ per pound, an operator could estimate prices for fillets produced by a Boston processor and delivered to New York through a local distributor. The parties involved must agree on several factors such as using Wednesday's ex-vessel fish cost as a base number and 40% as the fillet yield. (Cost per pound filleted is determined by dividing cost per pound round by the fillet yield.) The total cost delivered to the New York operator is calculated as follows:

Yield to fillet (.56/40%)	$1.40/lb
Add: Boston processor cost	.60/lb
Freight to N.Y.	.06/lb
Cost delivered to N.Y. distributor	$2.06/lb
Add: Distributor charge	.40/lb
Cost delivered to N.Y. operator	$2.46/lb

The operator must negotiate a flat markup for processing, freight, delivery, and handling.

All fish delivered the following week would be at this agreed-upon price. As a means of comparison, *Fishery Market News Report* (N-46, called "Green Sheet," but not to be confused with *Hotel, Restaurant, Institution Meat Price Report,* similarly called "The Green Sheet") reported New York cod fillet prices as $2.25/2.30 and *Seafood Price-Current* listed prices at $1.60/2.25 for the same time period. Many variations are possible and a knowledge of the market enables buyers to more intelligently evaluate prices.

Example 2: Frozen green headless shrimp

Various market publications report shrimp prices for all of the world's producing areas. Exhibit 11, an excerpt from *Seafood Price-Current,* displays such information. These represent estimates of selling prices from first receivers, ex-warehouse, delivered to the mid-Atlantic region.

During the Gulf of Mexico harvest season (July through December), larger buyers should follow the landings reported for New Orleans in *Fishery Market*

News Report (O-45). Buyers who are willing to commit to specific quantities can lock in prices until the next season. Smaller buyers who are unable or unwilling to do this can use market data such as that shown in Exhibit 11.

Green (raw) headless prices are shown in a range depending on variety and country of origin. The range on domestic brown variety 16/20 count shrimp is $6.05/6.10 per pound. An operator could request that distributors quote a spread (markup) over the middle of the range each Thursday, to be effective for the next week's deliveries. The middle of the range in this example is calculated as follows:

$$\text{Mid-range price} = \frac{\text{High price} + \text{Low price}}{2}$$

$$\text{Mid-range price} = \frac{\$6.05 + \$6.10}{2}$$

$$\text{Mid-range price} = \$6.075$$

A negotiated spread is then added to this mid-range price. Assuming a spread of 50¢ per pound is agreed upon, the operator's cost would be:

Thursday, middle of the range	$6.075/lb
Spread	.50
Delivered cost	$6.575/lb

This system works well for many other products, including lobster tails and frozen fillets. Prices for other products requiring further processing are not shown in these market reports.

Example 3: 16/20 Breaded Shrimp, 40% breading from domestic brown shrimp

Buying breaded products is more complicated. Breaded shrimp are measured after processing; therefore, final counts per pound are not equivalent to green headless counts.

This specification requires 40% breading in the finished product, which is to average 18 shrimp per pound. To accomplish this, the processor starts with 21/25 count green headless shrimp. Middle of the range price for the domestic brown species shown in Exhibit 11 is $6.025. Starting with 100 pounds of 21/25 count shrimp (average 23 per pound), the operator may calculate the price as shown in Exhibit 13. The cost of 16/20 shrimp with 40% breading at the processor plant is $5.38 per pound and the count per pound is about 18.4 shrimp (2300 shrimp divided by 125 pounds, breaded). As in the previous example, freight and distributor's handling charges must be added to this figure. Buyers using the techniques shown in this example should negotiate the cost of the raw product using published information as a starting point.

Example 4: 30/40 Block frozen sea scallops

Scallop shell is discarded at sea and some size grading is done aboard the vessel. Exhibit 10 reports that two scallop vessels landed at New Bedford with a total of 14,000 pounds of scallops. The price is reported at $475 to $479 per hundred pounds. Exhibit 11 reports first receiver price (mid-Atlantic area) as $4.75/5.10 for Canadian

Exhibit 13   Price Calculation for Breaded Shrimp

	Weight	Count	$/lb	Total
Green Headless Shrimp	100 lb	2300	$6.025	$602.50
Peel loss	− 25 lb			
Peeled/deveined	75 lb			
Breading	+ 50 lb		.40 (1)	20.00
Processing cost				50.00 (1)
Breaded Shrimp	125 lb (2)	2300	$5.38 (3)	$672.50

(1) Breading and processing costs are estimated.

(2) $\text{Finished weight} = \dfrac{\text{Peeled/deveined weight}}{100\% - \% \text{ Breading}}$

$\text{Finished weight} = \dfrac{75 \text{ lb}}{100\% - 40\%}$

$\text{Finished weight} = \dfrac{75 \text{ lb}}{60\%}$

(3) Price per pound is calculated by dividing the total price ($672.50) by the total weight (125 lb).

and $5.05 per pound for domestic (30/40 count). Buyers can negotiate a spread over the mid-Atlantic price as previously discussed. They should also be familiar with the boat price, which can fluctuate widely due to weather and harvest size. The New England boat prices are usually reflected in metropolitan markets within the week, but knowledge of the markets is helpful in ensuring that this is the case.

Buying Systems in Review

There are several purchasing systems for fish and shellfish. The system chosen depends on numerous factors including purchase volume, supplier capability, and items needed.

Ride the Market. If the decision is to purchase in this fashion, a program similar to that for meat is required. A weekly bid is received from approved suppliers and the low total bid (considering all items) is awarded the order. This system is only practical in major cities where there are several qualified vendors; even then, buyers find "out of stocks" a common occurrence.

Cost-Plus. A cost-plus arrangement should be negotiated with local distributors with an add-on based on cents-per-pound. If one or more manufacturing functions are performed, these should be priced on a yield and labor basis. If the volume is great enough, processors can be contacted directly and the fish priced at that point. Products can then be handled by the local distributor for an agreed-upon fee.

An understanding of ex-vessel prices, manufacturing yields, and other costs is necessary to manage a cost-plus program. While these cannot be obtained precisely, using data from the NMFS and other sources is adequate to maintain the

---

Correct Purchasing Saves Dollars

Fish products are bought by the pound and sold by the portion. Count per purchase unit is, therefore, critical. If 2-ounce fish portions are specified, then 8 portions per pound should be provided for sale. Assume the following details regarding the purchase of cod: 40% breading, 2-ounce portions, and a cost of $1.50 per pound. Assuming the selling price for a sandwich is 75¢, the return is:

Income:	8 (2.0-oz) sandwiches @ 75¢ each	=	$6.00
	Fish cost (per pound)		− 1.50
	Return before other costs		$4.50

Now assume that the processor made the portion 2.5 ounces rather than 2 ounces. The total number of portions is reduced from 8 to 6.4 per pound.

Income:	6.4 (2.5-oz) sandwiches @ 75¢ each	=	$4.80
	Fish cost (per pound)		− 1.50
	Return before other costs		$3.30

The return has dropped $1.20 ($4.50 − 3.30) per pound because incorrect portion sizes were used.

Counts for shrimp must be watched very closely. They are sold in ranges such as 16/20 or 21/25 per pound; a 16/20 count may range from 16 to 20 individual shrimp per pound, but should average 18. Assume the specification requires 16/20 count shrimp at a cost of $6.00 per pound. Assume the selling price is $4.00 per portion of 4 shrimp. If 18 shrimp per pound are received, 4.5 portions are obtained.

Income:	4.5 portions (4 shrimp) @ $4.00 each	=	$18.00
	Shrimp cost (per pound)		− 6.00
	Return before other costs		$12.00

Now assume that 16 shrimp per pound are received; 4 portions are available for sale.

Income:	4 portions (4 shrimp) @ $4.00 each	=	$16.00
	Shrimp cost (per pound)		− 6.00
	Return before other costs		$10.00

The return has dropped $2.00 ($12.00 − 10.00) per pound because of count problems.

---

program. The buyer should (1) select one day of the week or an average of days to determine the base bid, (2) identify the base information source, such as "Green Sheet" or "Blue Sheet" (*Fishery Market News Report*, B-45), and (3) make the agreement and adhere to it.

Buy-and-Inventory. The harvest of fish and shellfish is seasonal and prices are almost always lower in the harvest season. High-volume buyers should develop their buying strategies at that time. If a buying program seems profitable from an inventory position, the purchase decision can be made and the product can be further processed and distributed. Purchasers can calculate the carrying charges, add an estimated amount for risk, and compare the figure against the price forecast.

There is little help available in developing price forecasts. Carry-in inventories (supply prior to the beginning of harvest season) help in some cases and estimates of economic conditions can also be helpful, but price forecasting for these products is usually reduced to a judgment based on experience. The best pattern to follow is to:

- Monitor inventories, consumption, and landings
- Talk to processors
- Evaluate the company's need to maintain constant supply
- Remember the handling charges

In today's financial environment, 1% per month represents the minimum charge required to carry the investment and 2% should be used to cover some risk.

The quantity purchased depends upon both the company's philosophy and the market conditions. Annualized, a $6.00 per pound item may cost about 60¢ per pound to store and finance for one year, so a 10% price increase must occur to break even. Many companies spot-buy for shorter periods of time (for example, on a month-to-month basis when the market is steady, then for 3 or 4 months as a dip occurs). Buying and storing is quite common with fish and shellfish, but it has its risks.

Long-Term Contract. There are opportunities in this area of purchasing to write long-term contracts under certain circumstances. The price is agreed upon and a carrying charge is added. However, these deals are seldom available with the first receiver from the boat. In most cases, a second party (usually a speculator, trader, or importer) offers to handle the financing for a fee. Long-term contracts also apply to the formula arrangements. There is no futures market to assist in forecasting the prices of fish and shellfish. No one really knows if the fish are there until the fishing begins, or what the amount of the harvest will be until the fishing ends.

Endnotes

1. The National Fisheries Institute publication, *Handbook of State and Federal Microbiological Standards and Guidelines,* details bacterial standards.

REVIEW QUIZ

When you feel you have covered all of the material in this chapter, answer these questions. Choose the *best* answer. Check your answers with the correct ones found on the Review Quiz Answer Key at the end of this book.

True (T) or False (F)

T (F)   1. The supply of seafood is large, with no expected shortages in the near future. *easy to good* *f*

(T) F   2. Fresh seafood deteriorates rapidly after harvesting, and requires prompt processing. *not fresh* *T*

T (F)   3. Grade standards for seafood are precisely defined. *F*

(T) F   4. The size categories used for marketing shrimp are based on count per pound. *T*

(T) F   5. Haddock and cod are both called "scrod" at times. *T*

(T) F   6. Halibut, flounder, and sole are all types of flatfish. *T*

123 T (F)   7. The Fishery Conservation and Management Act of 1976 gave the United States control of fish only as far as 100 miles from its coastline. *F* *200*

(T) F   8. The quality of shrimp is more related to its feeding habits and handling after catch than to its variety. *T*

(T) F   9. "Perch" can refer to either freshwater or ocean varieties of fish. *T*

(T) F 10. Specifications for fish are ill-defined and lacking in uniformity. *T*

(T) F 11. A voluntary grading service is available to those plants in the NMFS programs. *T ?*

193 T (F) 12. Prior to interstate shipment, fish products must be inspected for wholesomeness according to federal statute. *is not required.* *F*

(T) F 13. Fish may be lightly glazed with ice to prevent dehydration. *T*

(T) F 14. If breading exceeds 50% of total weight, the product usually must be labeled "imitation." *T*

(T) F 15. Knowing the ex-vessel cost of fish is helpful in determining what the final price should be. *T*

Multiple Choice

16. A fish that has had only its entrails removed is termed:

    a. round.
    (b.) drawn.
    c. steaked.
    d. filleted.

17. Fresh fish should have all of the following traits *except*:

    a. sunken eyes.
    b. elastic flesh.
    c. red gills.
    d. tight scales.

18. Prawns are:

    a. flatfish.
    b. mollusks.
    c. large shrimp.
    d. freshwater fish.

19. Salmon are:

    a. migratory fish.
    b. lean fish.
    c. trash fish.
    d. none of the above.

20. Rock lobster is commonly caught in all of the following areas *except*:

    a. Australia.
    b. New Zealand.
    c. South America.
    d. Iceland.

Chapter Outline

Types of Poultry and Game Birds
    Chickens
    Turkeys
    Other Poultry and Game Birds
USDA Role in Poultry Marketing
    Poultry Inspection
    Poultry Quality Grading
Poultry Specifications and Quality Control
    Buyer's Refinements
Marketing and Distribution Channels
Poultry Pricing
    Price Sources
    Geographical Differences
    Price References
    Determining Costs
Price Forecasting
    Forecasting Example
USDA Role in Egg Marketing
Considerations in Purchasing Eggs
    Fresh Eggs
    Processed Eggs
Buying Systems for Eggs
    Distribution
    Pricing and Yields

Learning Objectives

1. Differentiate types of chicken and turkey, describing their major characteristics.

2. Describe other poultry and game birds of importance to the hospitality industry.

3. Summarize the major areas of governmental control affecting the poultry industry.

4. Describe the system for grading poultry.

5. Explain the basic factors included in poultry specifications.

6. List sources used in pricing poultry and summarize factors affecting prices.

7. Summarize the major areas of legislation affecting eggs.

8. Describe purchase considerations for various forms of eggs.

11

Poultry and Eggs

POULTRY REFERS TO birds that have been domesticated for their meat and egg production. Poultry includes chickens, turkeys, ducks, geese, and pigeons. By contrast, game birds are those that forage for themselves and live in the wild. Some types of game birds are also raised domestically.

Per capita consumption of poultry products has increased at a much greater rate than beef and pork. Chicken, in high demand by the fast-food industry, is the fastest-growing protein source in the United States. Concern about nutrition, health, and wellness has also spurred interest in poultry; fat and cholesterol content of red meats work against their consumption by diet-conscious consumers.

The short production cycle enables processors to react promptly to demand. Twenty-one days are required from egg to chick, then another 6 to 9 weeks in the "grow-out" stage, depending on the size required. By comparison, marketable weight hogs require 6 to 10 months and cattle require 2 to 3 years.

The costs of poultry production are considerably lower than those of pork or beef production. Since it takes about two pounds of feed to produce one pound of chicken, the feed-to-weight ratio is 2:1. By comparison, the feed-to-weight ratio for pork is approximately 3.5:1, and the feed-to-weight ratio for beef is 7:1. With corn and soybean meal at 5¢ and 8¢ per pound, respectively, the economic advantages of poultry production over pork and beef production become obvious.

One major development in the growth of the poultry market has been consolidation and integration of the various stages of production and marketing. Many broiler firms have their own hatcheries, feed mills, and processing plants. As illustrated in Exhibit 1, a feed mill provides breeder feed to hatching farms or to growers raising broilers. The hatching farm, which can be company-owned or under contract with the broiler firm, provides eggs to a hatchery which, in turn, provides more breeders to the hatching farm and supplies broiler chicks to contract growers or company farms. The contract growers or company farms care for the birds until they reach marketable weight, when they are moved to the processing plant and then into market distribution channels.

Like poultry production, egg production has been aided by large, highly specialized flocks. Hens live in controlled environments with automated feeders, waterers, ventilators, conveyors, and devices for candling (passing the egg over a light source and checking the yolk, air space, and any imperfections). Fortified feed has increased production and yield. In the 1950s, average annual production per hen was 120 eggs; by the 1980s, it was approximately 260.

In previous years, most egg products were marketed in shell form. Today, a large portion of production goes to processed egg products—frozen whole, yolk, or whites; liquid eggs; table-ready frozen eggs; hard-cooked, peeled eggs; tube

Exhibit 1 Functions of an Integrated Broiler Firm

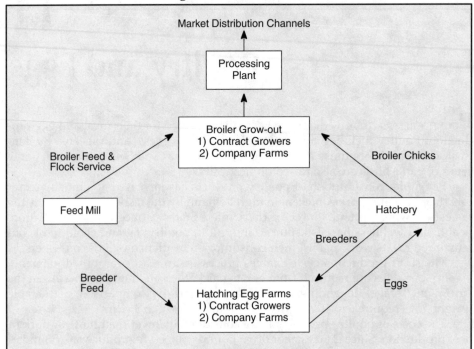

eggs; and dried eggs. Annual demand per person in the United States has remained fairly constant for all forms of eggs. Price changes generally are caused by supply increases or shortages.

Types of Poultry and Game Birds

The USDA has grouped poultry into classes based primarily on maturity. Young birds have tender meat and are suitable for roasting, broiling, frying, barbecuing, and baking. Mature birds have tougher meat which should be simmered, steamed, or braised to be made tender. Practically all mature birds are further processed by mass-producers into items such as soups, pot pies, and stews. Since food service operations use young birds, the discussion focuses on this class. USDA classifications form the basis of the following descriptions.

Chickens

A limitless variety of processed chicken is available in products which may be boned, breaded, marinated, minced, rolled, and/or cooked. Chicken is categorized into a number of different classes depending on such factors as age and sex.

Broilers or Fryers. This category includes young chickens of either sex, usually between 9 and 13 weeks of age. They are tender-meated with soft, pliable, smooth-textured skin and flexible cartilage. They are purchased in both fresh and frozen forms and may be whole eviscerated (with or without necks and giblets), halved, quartered, or cut-up (8 or 9 pieces).

Roasters. Roasters are young chickens of either sex, usually between 12 and 20 weeks of age. They have identical eating characteristics to broilers, but the cartilage is less flexible. They usually weigh between 4 and 7 pounds and are fatter than broilers. Roasting is typically the preferred method of cooking. Processing is usually whole eviscerated (with or without necks and giblets).

Capons. Capons are castrated male chickens, usually under 8 months of age, weighing between 6 and 9 pounds. The surgery retards the capon's muscular and sexual development and results in fat marbling throughout the muscle structure. These birds are large breasted, with a better ratio of breast to bone than fryers. They are usually marketed whole eviscerated (with or without necks and giblets) and are primarily used for roasting.

Hens, Fowls, or Stewing Chickens. This category includes female birds, usually more than 10 months of age, weighing from 4 to 7 pounds. They generally come from egg-laying operations and have been retired from production. Their general use is for soups and stews. The availability of these birds in the market is sporadic; when available, they are relatively inexpensive. Many large soup and further processors use these birds in preparing their products.

Rock Cornish or Cornish Game Hens. Members of the chicken family, Rock Cornish or Cornish game hens are prepared from Cornish chickens or from cross-breeding Cornish chickens and another breed of chicken. Rock Cornish hens are the most generally available. They are young, immature chickens (usually 5 to 6 weeks) weighing not more than 2 pounds. They are usually served bone-in and are available whole eviscerated, whole stuffed, halved, quartered, or in pieces—either fresh or frozen. Yield in edible meat from a 24-ounce bird, dressed and ready-to-cook, is about 45%.

Turkeys

Unlike chickens (which were brought to America by early settlers), turkeys are native to North and Central America. Extensive breeding in Europe eventually resulted in the "broad-breasted bronze or Beltsville" turkey which was reintroduced to America in the 1930s and has since become the most popular commercial variety.

In comparison to lighter hens and fryers, the heavy toms (male turkeys) are of greater importance since they account for approximately 90% of annual U.S. production. Consumption of turkey, like chicken, depends to some extent on the prices of competing beef and pork. While turkey production is spaced throughout the year, heaviest sales occur during the Thanksgiving and Christmas seasons.

Heavy-breed toms are preferred by boning facilities and processors. More mature, heavier birds return a better meat-to-bone ratio than smaller birds since the bone structure remains essentially constant beyond 20 pounds. However, the feed required per pound increases dramatically as the bird matures.

Exhibit 2 demonstrates this fact. The percent yield (ready-to-cook) of live weight increases from 77% of the 17.5-pound bird to approximately 80% of the

Exhibit 2   Turkey Growth and Yield Chart

Bird Age (Weeks)	Average Feed Consumption to Date	Average Live Weight	Percent Yield (1)	Ready-to-Cook Weight	Boneless Percent Yield (2)	Boneless Edible Meat Weight	Ratio of Feed:Edible Meat (3)
18	51 lb	17.5 lb	77%	13.5 lb	41%	5.6 lb	9.1 to 1
26	100 lb	26.8 lb	80%	21.5 lb	51%	11.0 lb	9.1 to 1
38	195 lb	36.0 lb	80%	28.8 lb	58%	16.7 lb	11.7 to 1

(1)   Percent Yield $= \dfrac{\text{Ready-to-Cook Weight}}{\text{Average Live Weight}} \times 100\%$

(2)   Boneless Percent Yield $= \dfrac{\text{Boneless Edible Meat Weight}}{\text{Ready-to-Cook Weight}} \times 100\%$

(3)   Ratio of Feed:Edible Meat $= \dfrac{\text{Average Feed Consumption to Date}}{\text{Boneless Edible Meat Weight}}$

larger sizes. The boneless edible (cooked) meat yield greatly improves as the bird grows older and larger (from 42% for an 18-week bird to 58% for a 38-week bird). The ratio of feed to edible meat, however, increases from 9.1 (pounds of feed to a pound of cooked meat) for the smaller sizes to 11.7 for the 38-week birds—a negative factor for the grower.

Most of the weight gain in the older birds is in breast and thigh meat (which bring more money than the wings, drums, and other parts). All of these factors, in addition to investment and related costs, determine the weight and selling price at the time of processing.

Fryer-Roaster Turkeys. Fryer-roaster turkeys are young, immature birds of either sex that are tender-meated with soft, pliable, smooth-textured skin and flexible breastbones. They are usually under 16 weeks of age, eviscerated with neck and giblets included, and generally sold whole.

Young Turkeys. These birds are tender-meated with soft, pliable, smooth-textured skin and flexible breastbones. They may be of either sex; young tom turkeys or young hen turkeys may be specified. Toms are usually processed by 8 months of age. Heavier birds (more than 20 pounds) are used to make boneless cuts for both retail and food service. Hens are normally processed between 18 and 22 weeks and dress out between 12 and 16 pounds. Practically all are sold as whole birds in chain stores.

Yearling and Mature Turkeys. Yearlings are usually under 15 months, while mature birds are over 15 months of age. Both have coarser, tougher meat and normally are further processed into such items as soups and pot pies.

Processed Forms. Turkey products are available in many processed forms. Of primary interest to food service buyers are natural and formed breast meat, thigh meat, and combinations. Price range varies greatly, from natural oven-roasted breasts (toward the top end) to formed rolls made from scrap pieces (near the bottom of the range). Products are available in raw fresh, raw frozen, cooked fresh, and cooked frozen forms. Rib bones may be left in or the breast may be completely free of bones.

Many convenience turkey products are also available. Diced and pulled meat may be used for stews and pot pies. Other products include turkey ham, turkey bologna, and turkey franks.

Other Poultry and Game Birds

In addition to the major categories of turkey and chicken, other types of poultry are available. Ducks, geese, and pigeons are categories from which hospitality operations may purchase. Purchasers may also find game birds available.

Ducks. Broiler ducklings or fryer ducklings are young birds under 8 weeks of age and usually weigh under 5 pounds. Roaster ducklings are over 8 but under 16 weeks of age and weigh under 7 pounds. The bill and windpipe in these classes should be soft and easily dented. Eviscerated ducks are available whole or split, usually frozen. Duck is also available precooked with sauce packed separately. Practically all production is in the white Peking strain (also known as "Long Island Duckling").

Geese. Young geese may be of either sex, but should have tender meat and a windpipe that can be easily dented. They are available whole and eviscerated, either fresh or frozen. They range in size from 6 to 14 pounds, but most weigh around 8 to 10 pounds.

Pigeons. Pigeons are mature birds of either sex, with coarse skin and toughened flesh. Squabs are young, immature pigeons of either sex and are extra tender-meated. They are usually under 4 weeks of age, and weigh about 1 pound before boning. These birds have dark meat and are low in fat.

Game Birds. This category includes such birds as pea-fowl, swans, quail, wild ducks or geese, and pheasants. Except in the fall season, when they have stored fat for winter, game birds are leaner and tougher than domestic foul and, therefore, require different cooking methods. Banding or wrapping the bird with bacon or other fat is often used to retain moisture and to help baste during roasting.

Pheasant should have flexible bone cartilage. Domestic pheasant is less flavorful than wild pheasant and must be cooked with more flavorings. Dressed weight is usually 2 to 4 pounds. Pheasants are normally available frozen.

Quail are available bone-in, split, whole, whole drawn, partially boned, or stuffed.

USDA Role in Poultry Marketing

The USDA enforces several laws applicable to poultry, mainly in the areas of inspection, grading, and quality control. Those involved in purchasing management must be aware of these regulations since they have an impact upon the manner in which products move through market channels and the quality of products received.

Poultry Inspection

The Poultry Products Inspection Act was passed in 1957. It addresses sanitary conditions in poultry processing plants and also regulates additives and labeling. The act covers poultry prepared for both interstate and foreign commerce. Since 1968, the Wholesome Poultry Products Act has required that state inspection programs for intrastate (within state) shipments be at least equal to federal programs. Those states not maintaining at least "equal to" programs must have federal inspections. The 1968 act also strengthened enforcement of standards of poultry imported into the United States. Inspection is mandatory; costs are paid by the processing plant, which then passes these costs on to the next element in the distribution channel.

A "voluntary quality control system" became effective in 1980. Under this program, some processing plants are not required to have continuous on-site inspections but must be able to demonstrate that internal quality control programs are at least equal to those required by the USDA. On-site inspections by USDA personnel at irregular intervals are also conducted.

Most processing plants have adequate quality control programs responding to consumer concerns and competition. However, there is always a danger that "short cuts" may be taken in response to economic pressures. Voluntary quality control programs should not result in any loss of quality. Only further processing plants (those which manufacture other items besides the poultry products) may apply for these programs. Slaughter plants are still required to have on-location federal inspection, or state inspection, if approved. One of the key areas checked in these voluntary programs is wholesomeness (fitness for human consumption). The wholesomeness of raw materials is verified upon arrival at the plant and again before use. Also checked are: temperature of cooking oven or vessels; percentages of ingredients; accuracy of the weight of the finished product; storage temperatures; and sanitation of utensils, production lines, and packaging equipment. Plants with approved programs may display the stamp shown in Exhibit 3.

Poultry Quality Grading

The grading of poultry is a voluntary service. All poultry receiving quality grades must have been previously inspected for wholesomeness, although this inspection has no effect on the quality grade assigned. Costs of grading are paid by the party requesting the service. Thus, processors/sellers may have products graded if they want to display the USDA grade shield (see Exhibit 3) on their packages, and buyers may have grading performed if they want to assure that contract commitments have been satisfied. Federal grading is authorized by the Agricultural Marketing Services Act of 1946 and administered by the Food Safety and Inspection Service of the USDA.

Poultry grades are classified as USDA Grade A, B, or C. Standards of quality define the factors which determine the grade and include fat covering, fleshing, exposed flesh, discolorations, conformation of the bird, presence of pin feathers, and freezing defects (if the product is frozen). USDA grades are primarily appearance standards. They do not identify eating qualities. Thus, a mature chicken can be

Exhibit 3   USDA Inspection Stamp and Grade A Shield

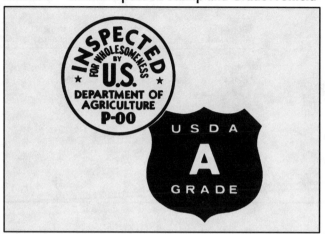

Grade A, while a young, more tender chicken can be Grade B. As a practical matter, few birds below Grade A receive a grade. If the birds do not "make grade," they usually are further processed. Game birds may be inspected for wholesomeness and graded for quality; however, this is not mandatory under the 1946 act.

Many chicken processing plants today do not use the USDA grading service. Their products are usually sold directly to large hospitality customers or distributed as private label items purchased by chain stores. These customers have their own specifications and contracts with the processor and, in some cases, may also have their own inspectors in the plants. Many of these processing plants identify the product as "Plant Grade A." Since it costs about one cent per pound for the USDA grading service, quality grading done by the plant can be less expensive for the buyer.

Turkey processing plants may pack graded or ungraded products. Some ungraded products are marketed under retail private labels. Other ungraded products are further processed into such items as turkey rolls, hot dogs, sausages, and cooked breasts. These plant-graded birds are identified in the trade as "canner pack" and are shipped in carload or truckload lots without necks and giblets.

Poultry Specifications and Quality Control

As a result of USDA involvement in the processing of poultry, there is a great deal of standardization. Buyers writing purchase specifications for poultry should begin with USDA data. Some quality factors should be addressed as poultry specifications are developed. For example, although all poultry must be inspected for wholesomeness as required by the Poultry Inspection Act, this should still be specified by the buyer.

In terms of the quality grade, if a processor has paid for USDA quality grading, it will be shown on the package. However, buyers generally have somewhat different concerns depending on whether whole birds or poultry parts are purchased.

Exhibit 4   Breakdown of Chicken Parts by Weight and Percentage

	Bone-in Weight (oz)	Percentage Bone-in	Cooked Meat Boneless (oz)	Percentage Cooked Meat
Breast	15.1	33.6%	6.6	
Thigh	13.1	29.1%	5.2	
Drumstick	6.4	14.2%	2.7	
Wing	+5.4	+12.0%	+1.8	
Total for shell	40.0	88.9%	16.3	40.8%
Neck	3.0	6.7%	0.5	
Giblets	+2.0	+4.4%	+1.0	
Total for other parts	5.0	11.1%	1.5	30.0%
Total	45.0	100.0%	17.8	

If whole birds are intended for food service use, graded birds may carry a USDA grade or plant grade depending on the distributor. Small users should require the USDA grade. Large users may buy plant grade (which is less expensive); however, USDA Grade A equivalent should always be specified if the highest quality is desired.

Poultry parts generally carry the same grade as the bird before it was cut. The parts may be bone-in or boneless. The cuts must be made skillfully; parts must be similar in general appearance before and after cutting. Exhibit 4 gives a breakdown of various chicken parts by weight.

Buyer's Refinements

After developing specifications around existing USDA standards, buyers add the specific requirements of their companies. Clearly written specifications help ensure effective communication between buyers and sellers. Sample specifications are presented in Exhibits 5 to 8. Possible refinements to USDA standards may include such considerations as sizing, preservation and temperature, and cutting.

Sizing. The buyer should state the required size by weight. Five-ounce chicken breasts should not weigh six ounces. At 10¢ per ounce, this means 10¢ higher cost per portion and 10¢ lower profit by order. Remember that operators buy by the pound, but sell by the portion!

Preservation and Temperature. Improvements in refrigeration technology have aided poultry production, raising quality levels of products reaching the hospitality operator. As late as the mid-1960s, practically all chicken was refrigerated by use of chunked or shaved ice. Today, vacuum-sealed packaging is flushed with carbon dioxide (CO_2) gas to maintain quality and extend shelf life.

Poultry products are offered in several packs depending upon customer requirements. If purchased fresh (unfrozen), the product may be specified as ice pack, chill pack, or vacuum CO_2-flush. Some precooked chicken may be packaged fresh also. Ice pack is simply the traditional method of packing in crushed ice. Chill or dry pack involves cooling (in some cases actually freezing the bird about one-fourth

Exhibit 5 Sample Specification #1: Fresh Whole Broilers

Item:	Fresh whole broilers, weighing 2.75 pounds each, plus or minus 2 ounces
Grade:	USDA Grade A
Packaging:	Packed two birds per vacuum-sealed, CO_2-flushed bag; ten bags to each master carton; USDA data and production date to be displayed on exterior of carton
General Requirements:	Without necks or giblets
Specific Requirements:	Birds to be received within three days of processing
Handling:	Receiving temperature (internal product) not to exceed 34° F (1° C)

Exhibit 6 Sample Specification #2: Fresh Cut-Up Broilers

Item:	Fresh cut-up broilers, weighing 2.75 pounds each, plus or minus 2 ounces
Grade:	Plant Grade A
Packaging:	Packed two birds per vacuum-sealed, CO_2-flushed bag; ten bags to each master carton; USDA data and production date to be displayed on exterior of carton
General Requirements:	Without necks or giblets; eight-cut with keel bone split; separated at natural joints by using knives (no saw)
Specific Requirements:	Birds to be received within three days of processing
Handling:	Receiving temperature not to exceed 34° F (1° C)

Exhibit 7 Sample Specification #3: Fresh Turkey Breast/Thigh Roasts

Item:	Fresh, raw, boned, and tied breast/thigh roasts made from young tom turkeys; each roast to weigh 8 pounds, plus or minus 8 ounces
Grade:	USDA Grade A
Packaging:	One roast per vacuum-sealed, CO_2 flushed package; five roasts to each master carton; USDA data and production date to be displayed on exterior of carton
General Requirements:	Composed of 60% breast, 40% thigh meat; all solid pieces to be used only from these two parts
Specific Requirements:	No skin, fillers, binders, or seasoning

Exhibit 8 Sample Specification #4: Frozen, Oven-Roasted Turkey Breasts

Item:	Fresh, oven-roasted turkey breasts from young tom turkeys; finished weight of 9 pounds, plus or minus 8 ounces
Grade:	USDA Grade A
Packaging:	Each roast individually vacuum-sealed; frozen at minus 40° F (4° C) or lower; four roasts to each master carton; USDA data and production date to be displayed on exterior of carton
General Requirements:	Natural shape; hand formed; no more than three solid pieces to each roast; breast meat only
Specific Requirements:	Skin-on; no broth or fillers

inch from the outside), packing in poly-bags, and then maintaining storage and transportation temperatures of about 30° F (−1° C) throughout the distribution cycle. This is difficult to do; some processors sprinkle CO_2 (pellets or flakes) into poultry cases before sealing in order to eliminate oxygen, inhibit bacterial growth, and maintain temperature. Bags can also be vacuum-sealed using a CO_2-flush to eliminate the oxygen. However packed, the internal product temperature should not exceed 34° F (1° C).

The bird should appear fresh, with firm, clean, and clear flesh; the skin should be dry and smooth with no stickiness. Likewise, there should be no odor from the skin or cavity and no blood should be present. Be sure to check the joints for blood traces as this may be evidence of storage at improper temperatures. If the product is frozen, it should be packaged to exclude air; there should be no discolored flesh or bones. After thawing (slowly in a refrigerator), the characteristics described above should still be present. The production date should be stenciled on the exterior of the carton.

Cutting. The fast-food industry usually buys broilers in a cut-up form: a standard eight-cut or the Kentucky Fried Chicken nine-cut (which separates the breast into 3 pieces). A few operations still buy whole broilers and portion them on-site. Poultry can also be purchased quartered and in other market forms. Most hospitality operators have little use for the neck and giblets; they generally buy only the shell (chicken carcass minus the neck and giblets). As with sizing, weight range is critical to portioning.

If cut poultry is required, the method must be specified. For fryers, should the keel bone be left in or removed? Should the tail be left on or off? Should the cuts be made by hand (with a knife) or by saw? What should the tolerance level be for miscuts (saw cuts that miss the joint)?

Other Considerations. If the item is breaded, the proportion of breading to product must be specified. If precooked or browned, the degree of each must be stated. If a cooked roast is required, the method of cooking should be addressed (for instance, dry roasted, steam-injected, or water-cooked).

Breast and thigh roasts should be made from solid pieces of these parts. Rolls may be of smaller formed pieces and generally have more binder in the form of broth, emulsified skin, and gelatin. Rolls with practically the same label can vary from good to virtually inedible; breast roast has a narrower tolerance. In the case of a mixed roast, the percentages of white and dark meat should be included, paralleling the percentages of the whole bird: about 65% white meat and 35% dark meat.

Marketing and Distribution Channels

The traditional local poultry distributor carried a variety of products which, in addition to poultry, included fresh eggs, cheeses, and other dairy items. This distributor carried out some further processing in the form of cutting and boning. As the fast-food chains emerged and grew in the 1950s and the 1960s, some became distributors for these chains and carried additional items, for instance, chicken patties. Other distributors concentrated on the remaining food service accounts available to them, while still others de-emphasized distribution and concentrated more heavily on making further processed items, such as boneless breasts, patties, cutlets, and chicken Cordon Bleu.

Today, slaughter plants are also specializing. Many of these plants are still in the retail-chain commodity-broiler business, but others concentrate on cutting and sizing according to fast-food chain demand. Some plants provide prebreaded and/or precooked items, again in response to the food service chains.

Traditional poultry distributors also carried turkeys, with practically all sales concentrated around the Thanksgiving and Christmas seasons. Because of the growing trend toward further processing, turkey sales are now spread more evenly throughout the year. Since cooked turkey products generally are frozen, area distributors of frozen foods carry them in competition with distributors specializing in poultry. Manufacture of these items is on a mass production-line basis; local companies have been unable to produce them competitively.

Other poultry (for instance, ducks and geese) and game birds continue to be available through the traditional distributor. An exception is Cornish game hens: their popularity has caused many frozen food distributors to stock them.

Distributor markups vary with the size of the customer's orders and the type of service required. Generally, cents-per-pound over cost can be negotiated on fresh commodity products while percentage markups are used for further processed items. As with any cost-plus program, the costs must be known in order to manage the program.

Poultry Pricing

Until the mid-1960s, auctions for live chickens were fairly common throughout the United States. The prices established at these auctions were public information and provided buyers with a base from which to judge the cost of their processed broilers. As the industry consolidated and integrated its operations, however, there were no longer any meaningful auctions. Buyers were left with competitive bids as the only means to determine prices.

The present situation requires that buyers be knowledgeable about poultry pricing methods. They must use reliable price references and understand geographical differences in poultry pricing. The examples given in this section provide buyers with a framework for establishing their own systems. Buyers must develop systems which best complement their companies' needs.

Price Sources

The hospitality buyer has access to a number of price sources for broilers. Most local newspapers carry daily quotes as does *The Wall Street Journal*. Buyers should understand that these broilers are intended for the retail chain stores; the neck and giblets are retained in the cavity of the bird and the added weight is reflected in the price. The hospitality buyer can use these numbers as a reference, but generally not in negotiations with local distributors.

Two market reports are frequently used although others are available. *Poultry Market News Report* is published three times weekly by the Agricultural Marketing

Exhibit 9 *Poultry Market News Report,* **Friday, April 11, 1986**

PRELIMINARY REPORT of prices negotiated for trucklot sales of ready-to-cook icepacked and CO_2 packed Broiler/Fryers to be delivered to first receivers at major market areas week of April 14–18, 1986 (Cents Per Pound)

U.S. GRADE A (Includes Branded Product)

MARKET AREAS	MAJORITY
BOS/NEW ENGLAND	46.50–50.00
CHICAGO	46.00–47.00
CINCINNATI	Too Few
CLEVELAND	Too Few
DENVER	51.50
DETROIT	47.00
LOS ANGELES	52.00
NEW YORK	49.00–50.00
PHILADELPHIA	Too Few
PITTSBURGH	47.00
ST. LOUIS	Too Few
SAN FRANCISCO	52.50

SOUTHEASTERN AREA FOB DOCK EQUIVALENT

MISSISSIPPI	47.00–48.00

WOG BROILERS—(Without giblets)—Prices Paid Per Pound in Trucklot and LCL Quantities Delivered First Receivers Week of April 14, 1986

MARKETING REGIONS	MAJORITY	WTD. AVG.	LOADS
East	52.00–53.00	52.56	39
Central	51.75–53.00	53.21	84
West	56.50–58.00	57.59	96

Source: USDA, Agricultural Marketing Service, Poultry Division.

Service of the USDA. This publication reports national pricing for broilers and turkeys, and also gives prices for some raw components (Exhibit 9). *Urner Barry's Price-Current* by Urner Barry Publications is published five days each week. In addition to broiler and turkey information, it reports prices and market data for a number of other items, including cooked poultry, eggs, and dairy products (Exhibit 10).

Geographical Differences

Poultry pricing is developed independently in the major producing areas around the country. For instance, *Poultry Market News Report* identifies the primary producing areas as: Southeast, South Central, West, and Delmarva (Delaware, Maryland, and Virginia).

Exhibit 10 *Urner Barry's Price-Current,* **Friday, April 11, 1986**

CHICKENS (Trucklot)

Prices delivered warehouse based on current negotiations. (Deliveries 1–7 days.)

	Northeastern Area		Midwestern Area	
	Today	5 Day Avg	Today	5 Day Avg
Plant Grade, 2 1/4 lbs. & up	.4700	.4500	–	–
U.S. Grade A, Sized 2–3 1/2 lbs	.4800	.4600	.4700	.4500
U.S. Grade A, 3 1/2 lbs & up	–	–	–	–
Canner Pack, Trim or Better	–	–	–	–

WOG CHICKENS   CUT-UP CHICKENS

(Without Giblets)		Eight Piece Cut	Nine Piece Cut
2 1/4–2 1/2 lbs	.5500	.5900	.5900
2 1/2–2 3/4 lbs	.5500	.5900	.5900
2 3/4–3 lbs	.5500	.5900	.5900

CHICKEN PARTS

TRUCKLOT prices delivered warehouse—based on current negotiations.
(Deliveries three to seven days.)

	Northeastern Area	Midwestern Area
Breasts	.95	–
Breast, front halves	.75	.75
Legs	.39	.38
Leg quarters	.30	.30

Source: Urner Barry Publications, Inc., Toms River, New Jersey. Reprinted with permission.

Labor cost advantages are the major reason for rural producers' expansion into further processed items. In addition, they can add more product value at the source and reduce transportation costs by removing inedible matter (bones, fat, and cartilage) before shipping over long distances.

Producers closest to a metropolitan area have a freight advantage over producers in rural areas, but may also have higher production costs. Prices for poultry, regardless of where it is produced, tend to equalize in the major metropolitan consumption areas. For instance, Arkansas producers competing in California tend to have lower prices FOB their plants (prices prior to distribution) than California producers, who are often faced with higher labor and overhead costs. Similarly, producers in the Delmarva region (closer to the major Eastern markets) normally have higher prices FOB their plants than Georgia or Alabama producers who compete in the same markets.

Within the producing areas, prices trade in a narrow range on an FOB basis. For example, Alabama and Mississippi poultry are often very close in price. When an imbalance does occur, it is typically caused by unusually high or low production in one of the areas. This is generally caused by weather affecting an area of consumption, transportation, or production.

Price References

Exhibit 9 (toward the top half of the exhibit) gives price quotations for USDA Grade A broilers for eight major market areas. Four other cities are reported as "Too Few," which means that the reporter was unable to get information. Note the comment "Includes Branded Product," which means that prices for advertised brands are averaged into the quotations. Hospitality buyers normally have little interest in branded products.

The need for pricing data gave rise to "dock prices" for different parts of the country. Dock prices are USDA estimates of prices FOB the processing plant and reflect sales to major retail chains. Immediately below the market area quotes given in Exhibit 9 can be seen "Southeastern Area FOB Dock Equivalent," then "Mississippi 47.0–48.0." This range is intended to approximate poultry prices (in cents per pound) at Mississippi processing plants after subtracting freight costs from the major markets. A buyer may ask a poultry supplier to quote a cents-per-pound spread over dock price; the size of the spread depends on the location of the buyer's company.

A better price reference is WOG broilers (WOG means "without giblets"), which appears just below "Southeastern Area FOB Dock Equivalent" in Exhibit 9. Prices are quoted delivered to East, Central, and West marketing regions. Buyers can request quotations from local suppliers based on their section of the country. For example, the buyer may solicit quotes based on $2^{3/4}$ pound broilers, price quote to be cents-per-pound over the weighted average price for East marketing region shown in *Poultry Market News Report*. In this case, the USDA price shown is 52.56¢ per pound and the supplier would quote an upcharge to cover handling and profit.

While the USDA report does not quote prices for cutting, *Urner Barry's Price-Current* does provide this information (see Exhibit 10). Quotations shown are:

Cut-up chickens	59¢/lb
WOG chickens	− 55¢/lb
Difference or spread	4¢/lb

This report indicates that the cost to cut a chicken is 4¢ per pound. Using this figure, buyers could estimate costs for cut-up broilers using WOG broiler prices listed in *Poultry Market News Report* (all figures in cents per pound):

Marketing Region	Weighted Average WOG Broilers		Cutting Cost		Estimated Supplier Cost
East	52.56	+	4.0	=	56.56
Central	53.21	+	4.0	=	57.21
West	57.59	+	4.0	=	61.59

To these figures, the local distributor's charges for handling and profit are added. Both parties must agree on the base number, with the spread determined by competitive bid in the local market. Many variations on this system are used by large hospitality companies. These buyers often agree with the processor on price FOB the plant plus add-ons (for example, transportation).

Determining Costs

The purpose of developing cost information is to establish a base point for negotiations. In purchasing poultry products, the buyer has three options available to establish prices:

- Accept the supplier's quotation with or without negotiation.

- Take competitive bids, generally once each week, from two or more acceptable suppliers and award the order to the lowest bidder.

- Negotiate a cost-plus arrangement with a supplier based on some independent market pricing source acceptable to both parties. This arrangement begins with a bid between two or more suppliers in which they are asked to quote a spread (or cost-plus figure) over the price shown in the market report.

The preferred system involves cost-plus pricing, but the major problem remains identification of costs. Most of the major processors are fully integrated, owning grain supplies, feed mills, hatcheries, egg-processing facilities, and related enterprises. The costs incurred by these components within the company ultimately affect the price of the poultry. No two companies are alike and none want to disclose operating costs, least of all to a buyer.

The following examples develop estimates of delivered prices using the cost-plus option. Both examples demonstrate that special requirements add costs to the base price—costs which must be negotiated with processors.

Example 1: Fresh Whole Broilers

Refer to Sample Specification #1 given in Exhibit 5, which stated typical quality requirements for fresh whole broilers. Each factor is fairly standard except for the requirements regarding size and lack of necks and giblets. Since the Southern dock price does not reflect these two restrictions, they must be negotiated with the processor. A large user negotiates directly with the processor while a small user may negotiate through a distributor.

Suppose that Friday's Mississippi dock price is to be used (middle of the majority range) for the following week's delivery. Exhibit 9 reports majority USDA Grade A, Mississippi dock at 47.0 to 48.0¢ per pound. Middle of the range is 47.5¢ FOB Mississippi. Assume the following: a premium of 0.5¢ per pound has been negotiated for sizing and 4¢ per pound is added for removal of the neck and giblets; the user is in New York City, freight is 3¢ per pound to New York City, and distribution cost from the local warehouse to the hospitality operation is 8¢ per pound. Exhibit 11 shows the calculations needed to determine delivered cost. Once established, a successful cost-plus program must be consistent over the long term.

Example 2: Fresh Cut-Up Broilers

Let's look at a second example of the use of specifications and market data in the pricing decision. Refer to Sample Specification #2 given in Exhibit 6, which states

Exhibit 11   Pricing Example for Fresh Whole Broilers

	(cents/pound)
Mississippi dock; Friday, April 11, 1986	47.5
Add for sizing (1)	0.5
Add for removing neck/giblets (1)	+ 4.0
Cost FOB dock	52.0
Add freight to New York	+ 3.0
Cost delivered to New York warehouse	55.0
Add distribution to operation (2)	+ 8.0
Cost delivered to property	63.0

(1) Costs which are negotiated with processor
(2) Costs which are negotiated with distributor

typical quality requirements for fresh cut-up broilers based on plant grade. The same pricing procedure is used here as with the whole bird. Many buyers negotiate prices for plant grade chicken by agreeing to a standard discount from Grade A prices. This can vary somewhat depending on supply and demand.

Since *Poultry Market News Report* does not quote plant grade prices in its publication, *Urner Barry's Price-Current* must be consulted. Exhibit 10 indicates that the price of "Chickens (Trucklot)" in the Northeast during this period is 48¢ per pound for Grade A and 47¢ per pound for plant grade. For purposes of this example, assume the buyer has negotiated a one-cent spread (discount) and the cutting premium previously established as 4¢ per pound. Costs for removing necks and giblets, sizing, freight to New York warehouse, and distribution to the hospitality operation are identical to those given in Example 11. Exhibit 12 shows the calculations needed to determine delivered cost.

Price Forecasting

Price forecasting is imperative for companies when poultry represents a significant amount of their total sales. However, price forecasting is an inexact science. Poultry prices are interrelated with both beef and pork (although the correlation to pork is closer). Consumers make judgments based on their perception of the relative values among these three meats. Unpredictable events, such as bad weather, cause supply disruptions and price fluctuations. Although prices cannot be forecasted for specific days, given relevant information, judgments can be made which cover specific periods of time. Three important sources of information for forecasting prices are:

- Historical records of the hospitality operation

- Judgments of suppliers

- Judgments of independent forecasting firms

Exhibit 12 Pricing Example for Fresh Cut-Up Broilers

	(cents/pound)
Mississippi USDA Grade A	47.5
Minus allowance for plant grade	− 1.0
Plant grade whole broiler price	46.5
Add for sizing (1)	0.5
Add for cutting (1)	4.0
Add for removing necks/giblets (1)	+ 4.0
Cost FOB dock	55.0
Add freight to New York	+ 3.0
Cost delivered to New York warehouse	58.0
Add distribution to operation (2)	+ 8.0
Cost delivered to property	66.0

(1) Costs which are negotiated with processor
(2) Costs which are negotiated with distributor

Exhibit 13 Forecasting Firm's Summary of Production and Prices

SUMMARY OF QUARTERLY LIVESTOCK AND POULTRY PRODUCTION AND PRICES

	1984				1985				1986			
	JFM	AMJ	JAS	OND	JFM	AMJ	JAS	OND	JFM	AMJ	JAS	OND
PRODUCTION (% Change from Year Ago)												
Commercial Pork	+7.3	−2.7	−8.3	−6.0	−3.2	+1.9	+5.9	−3.7	−0.6	−2.2	−3.1	−3.0
Commercial Beef	+3.3	+4.9	−1.1	−0.7	−0.3	+1.7	+3.6	−2.7	+1.5	−3.5	−5.6	−4.9
Fed. Inspected Broilers	+0.7	+2.3	+6.4	+10.4	+4.7	+4.7	+4.3	+3.2	+4.2	+4.6	+4.0	+3.6
AVERAGE CASH PRICES												
Hogs, B&G Omaha ($/cwt)	$47.74	$48.64	$51.05	$47.45	$47.30	$43.09	$43.58	$44.86	$43.00	$42.00	$47.00	$45.50
Pork Bellies, 12–14 lb Midwest ($/cwt)	$58.28	$61.04	$62.07	$58.71	$65.49	$62.24	$56.53	$53.99	$55.60	$57.00	$63.00	$61.00
Broilers, 12 city (¢/lb)	61.77¢	56.37¢	54.10¢	49.97¢	51.08¢	50.96¢	50.56¢	50.29¢	50.50¢	48.00¢	50.00¢	45.00¢
Choice Steers, Omaha ($/cwt)	$67.54	$66.00	$64.28	$63.28	$62.40	$57.66	$52.25	$61.16	$57.25	$62.00	$65.00	$64.00

Source: Agri-Commodities, Inc., Andover, Massachusetts. Reprinted with permission.

Buyers should always start with historical data from their own operations. What happened during a specific time frame in past years? What were the prices of competing products such as ground beef and pork loin? After answering these questions, the buyer looks to outside sources for information: suppliers are considered first. What do they think will occur? Generally, more than one supplier is contacted and a consensus of their opinions is formed. There are a number of paid services available that provide price forecasting on one or more parts of the poultry complex.[1] Exhibit 13 illustrates how one company presents its estimates.

Forecasting is an ongoing process and some schedule should be established to update information. The schedule should fit the company's needs, but forecasting should take place at least quarterly; many companies update monthly. Processors,

Exhibit 14   Forecasted Price for Cut-Up Broilers

	(cents/pound)	
	July	October
Grade A Broiler Prediction	52.0	47.0
Add: Sizing	0.5	0.5
Removing necks/giblets	4.0	4.0
Cutting	+ 4.0	+ 4.0
Cost delivered to city	60.5	55.5

of course, constantly update forecasts since their accuracy usually means the difference between profit and loss.

Forecasting Example

Assume that a forecast is to be developed for broilers. A hospitality company uses cut-up broilers and negotiates price on a cost-based formula such as that described in the previous section. First, the price of broilers must be forecast for the periods of July and October. Suppose that as of April 15, 1986, the price of USDA Grade A broilers is 48¢ per pound delivered to New York in truckloads. Past history shows that prices in July tend to be higher than in April and that prices decrease into the fall season. Three suppliers are contacted and their predictions regarding the price of broilers are averaged as 52¢ per pound in July and 47¢ per pound in October. Next, the company considers the following predictions reported by three forecasting firms:

	Firm #1	Firm #2	Firm #3	Average
July	.50/lb	.49/lb	.55/lb	.513/lb
October	.45/lb	.46/lb	.48/lb	.463/lb

After considering historical records, suppliers' opinions, and forecasting firms' estimates, the hospitality operation can now make a reasonable prediction of future poultry prices. All of the information collected by the company can be summarized as follows:

	Suppliers' Opinions	Forecasting Firms' Estimates	Purchaser's Predictions
July	.52/lb	.513/lb	.52/lb
October	.47/lb	.463/lb	.47/lb

The purchaser's information regarding the price of broilers combines opinions from all sources with added weight placed on the source that gives the buyer the most confidence. The purchaser's prediction is only an estimate, but it is an *informed* estimate based on the facts available. The buyer can now add the necessary costs to calculate the cut-up broiler price (see Exhibit 14). Costs must be negotiated with the processor for sizing, cutting, and removing necks and giblets. Remember, this predicted price includes delivery to Chicago or New York; no freight needs to be added.

USDA Role in Egg Marketing

Much legislation has been enacted to regulate the marketing of eggs and egg products. Several federal and state regulations also apply to the edibility, quality, and grading of eggs. Buyers must become familiar with the regulations for each state in which they conduct business. Some important federal laws are as follows.

Farm Products Inspection Act (1917). This act is the original legislation providing authority for establishing voluntary grades and grading service.

Agricultural Marketing Act (1946). This act amended the 1917 act. It grew from the experiences gained during World War II and, in effect, regulated the practices then in place for military procurement. The act provided for a voluntary program, administered by the USDA and paid for by the user. It introduced terms such as "Fresh Fancy," "Grade A," and "Large," which have become familiar and widely accepted by the public.

Federal Food, Drug and Cosmetic Act (amended in 1938). This act covers all food products and is intended to prevent the shipment of adulterated or mislabeled foods in interstate commerce. Its application to eggs is primarily in relation to further processed products and to tolerances of a certain percentage of loss due to breakage in the case of shell eggs.

Egg Products Inspection Act (1970). This act requires and provides for the continuous inspection of egg processing and also controls the handling and disposition of restricted eggs in intrastate, interstate, and foreign commerce. Restricted eggs include loss, leakers, inedibles, rejects, dirties (soiled shells), and checks (shell cracked but not leaking). This act also establishes uniform standards, grades, and weight classes for interstate shipment.

Dirties and checks may move to official egg-breaking plants, but other restricted eggs must be destroyed or used for purposes other than human consumption. When released into normal consumer channels, all processed products are required to test negative for *Salmonella* bacteria (the *Salmonella* genus includes a number of infectious microorganisms). Processed products may be shipped unpasteurized to a further processing plant where they are pasteurized or stabilized prior to release. (Pasteurization kills harmful organisms through a process of controlled heating, thus extending a food's shelf life and destroying disease-causing organisms.)

Considerations in Purchasing Eggs

Eggs may be purchased in both fresh and processed forms. For fresh eggs, quality grading and size are important factors in the purchase decision. Processed eggs have legal standards regarding processing and preservation, but lack quality grades. Whether buying fresh or processed, purchase specifications must closely match the products' intended uses.

Fresh Eggs

Quality in egg products relates to uniformity of size and the absence of defects. For shell eggs, quality relates to fresh products stored below 45° F (7° C) at all times. They should be clean and have minimal breakage, blood spots, or other internal defects. Egg shells are porous and permit air to transfer between the interior and exterior of the egg. As this occurs, the firm white contracts and weakens, and the yolk becomes spread out. Loose white (albumen) and a weak yolk are usually indications of an overaged egg or one that has been subjected to high temperatures.

One grading procedure involves measuring the air cell inside the egg to identify age, since the air cell increases as the egg ages. The candling process (passing the egg over a light source) enables graders to check air cell size, detect impurities and cracks, and examine the yolk for freshness.

Oil spraying (or dipping) is a preservation technique used to retard deterioration of shell eggs by excluding air. After washing, a light spray of edible oil is applied to the egg to seal the shell. However, the albumen of an oiled egg may become cloudy or stick to the shell of hard-cooked eggs.

There is no physical or chemical difference between white or brown eggs besides color, which merely identifies the species of the laying hen. Certain markets, however, have preferences. Boston, for example, historically prefers brown eggs while New York favors white ones.

Quality Grading of Eggs. There are three consumer quality grades of shell eggs: USDA Grade AA (or Fresh Fancy), USDA Grade A, and USDA Grade B. Exhibit 15 displays egg standards.

Not every egg in a single case needs to be of the grade shown. Tolerances shown in Exhibit 16 are quality requirements for point of origin as well as destination. In the first set, requirements pertain to lots of two or more cases. In the second set, requirements relate to individual cases within a lot. Generally, plants try to produce above the minimum USDA standards to ensure that they can ship the grade required, as market price varies substantially between grades. Buyers can usually specify at least 90% within a grade and receive this with little problem and at no price penalty.

Exhibit 17 displays the USDA grade marks. Cases carrying the official shield stamp must be lot numbered to identify the packing date. To qualify as fresh, the eggs must be less than 30 days of age. As a practical matter, most eggs are shipped within three or four days after they are laid, but buyers should know that the lot number date is the date of pack. Generally, hospitality buyers receive shell eggs packed in cases containing 15 or 30 dozen. Each case must carry data indicating grading lot number. When the USDA's Acceptance Service is used, the delivery is accompanied by a grading certificate, which gives date of inspection and other pertinent information.

Size Designations. There are standard size designations for fresh shell eggs, although size is unrelated to the quality grade. Six classes of shell egg sizes are jumbo, extra-large, large, medium, small, and peewee. Weights of egg classes are shown in Exhibit 18.

Exhibit 15   USDA Standards for Quality of Individual Shell Eggs

	Specifications for Each Quality Factor		
Quality Factor	AA Quality	A Quality	B Quality
Shell	Clean Unbroken, practically normal	Clean Unbroken, practically normal	Clean to slightly stained Unbroken, may be slightly abnormal
Air Cell	$1/8$ inch or less in depth May show unlimited movement and may be free or bubbly	$3/16$ inch or less in depth May show unlimited movement and may be free or bubbly	$3/8$ inch or less in depth May show unlimited movement and may be free or bubbly
White	Clear Firm	Clear May be reasonably firm	Clear May be slightly weak
Yolk	Outline slightly defined Practically free from defects	Outline may be fairly well defined Practically free from defects	Outline may be well defined May be slightly enlarged and flattened May show definite but not serious defects

Source: USDA, *Regulations Governing the Grading of Shell Eggs and U.S. Standards, Grades and Weight Classes for Shell Eggs,* 7CFR, Part 56.

Exhibit 16   Grading Tolerances for Eggs in Cases

	Quality Required for Lots of 2 or More Cases		Quality Required for Individual Cases in a Lot	
USDA Grade	At Origin	At Destination	At Origin	At Destination
Grade AA (Fresh Fancy)	85% AA	80% AA	75% AA, 15% A, 10% B	70% AA, 20% A, 10% B
Grade A	85% A	80% A	75% A, 25% B	70% A, 30% B
Grade B	85% B	80% B	75% B	70% B

Source: USDA, *Regulations Governing the Grading of Shell Eggs and U.S. Standards, Grades and Weight Classes for Shell Eggs,* 7CFR, Part 56.

Processed Eggs

Many buyers purchase further processed products such as frozen whole eggs and cooked peeled eggs. These products may be made from shell eggs that do not qualify for the consumer grades just described, but qualify as wholesome. They also come from raw products that are never intended for consumer shell grading.

Exhibit 17   Federal Grade Marks

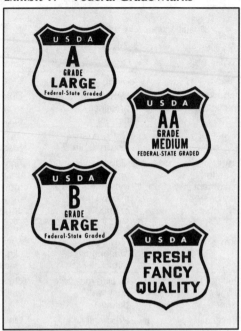

Exhibit 18   Shell Weight Classes

Weight Class	Minimum Net Weight (oz/doz)	Minimum Net Weight (lb/30 doz)	Minimum Weight for Individual Eggs (oz/doz)
Jumbo	30	56.0	29
Extra-Large	27	50.5	26
Large	24	45.0	23
Medium	21	39.5	20
Small	18	34.0	17
Peewee	15	28.0	—

An average lot tolerance of 3.3% in the next lower weight class is permitted as long as no individual case exceeds 5%.

Source: USDA, *Regulations Governing the Grading of Shell Eggs and U.S. Standards, Grades and Weight Classes for Shell Eggs*, 7CFR, Part 56.218 (Table I).

All processed egg products must be produced and packed under continuous federal inspection for wholesomeness. There are no quality grades; however, labeling must be accurate and must reflect net weights. The raw materials used must be wholesome, the manufacturing process must be sanitary, and the product must be free of *Salmonella* bacteria. Interplant sales or transfers of unpasteurized products are permitted, but the product must be free of *Salmonella* bacteria prior to release to the trade.

Exhibit 19 Weight Equivalents for Processed Eggs

	Number of Large Eggs/Pound
Whole eggs (fresh or frozen)	9.3
Yolks	25
Whites	15
Whole eggs (dried)	32
Yolks (dried)	54
Whites (dried)	100

Exhibit 20 Sample Specifications for Egg Products

Specification #1

Item: USDA Grade A Large fresh eggs

Packaging: 30-dozen cartons; cartons carry appropriate shield stamps and lot number identifications

Requirements: 90% Grade A or better (no C's or checks) and 97% Large or better (no small eggs); delivered within two days of inspection

Handling: Cartons identified in USDA standards and carrying appropriate shield stamps and lot number

Specification #2

Item: Frozen whole eggs

Grade: Packed under continuous USDA inspection with certificates furnished

Packaging: 30-pound cans

Requirements: Pasteurized; negative for *Salmonella* bacteria; Color Level Three (Whole eggs and yolks are sold with different color levels, which carry different prices. More color, up to a point, commands a higher price.)

Specification #3

Item: Frozen yolks—45% solids

Grade: Packed under continuous USDA inspection with certificates

Packaging: 30-pound cans; yolks packed with a percentage of sugar or salt, ranging from an average of 2% to as high as 12% (the percentage must be indicated)

Requirements: Pasteurized; negative for *Salmonella* bacteria; Color Level Four

Specification #4

Item: Table-ready egg blend—30/32% solids

Grade: Produced within last six months in inspected plant

Packaging: Packed in eight 4-pound pure pack cartons; shield stamp on exterior carton

Requirements: All egg solids (no milk, sugar, salt, or other ingredients)

If any ingredient is added to the egg product, it must be identified on the label. Total egg-solids content may in no case be less than 24.7% of the total weight if the item is identified as a whole egg product. It is particularly important to know this when comparing costs of various products such as scrambled egg mixes.

The weight equivalents of large shell eggs to processed forms are given in Exhibit 19. Dried equivalents are approximate since the residual moisture in the purchased products varies, but should be no more than 5% as purchased. These products absorb moisture if exposed to air and can deteriorate very rapidly. Packaging must properly protect the product.

Exhibit 20 shows four sample specifications covering fresh, frozen, and processed egg products.

Buying Systems for Eggs

While egg distributors are generally quite competitive, prices change rapidly; egg distributors can make extra profits when prices increase. When the distributor receives notice of a price increase from the processing plant, the standard practice is to immediately raise the price to the hospitality buyer, thus making extra money on lower-priced existing inventory. When prices fall, the reverse is true.

Buyers should have some source in addition to their distributor to keep them informed regarding price changes. If increased prices are forecasted, inventory can be stockpiled, if desired, on shelf-stable products. Fresh products must be rotated regularly, but markup levels can be determined to remove some of the guesswork.

Distribution

Before 1960, eggs moved from the farm into large metropolitan terminal markets. These markets provided a mechanism to establish prices as well as to perform grading functions. As quality control improved at the farm level and wage pressures increased in the metropolitan areas, such markets gradually disappeared. The egg-producing industry consolidated into larger plants.

Local multi-purpose distributors evolved who carried fresh eggs, processed egg products, cheese, butter, and chicken. Large hospitality buyers with their own commissaries often took direct deliveries; smaller users depended on these local distributors. Determining the price became a problem as there was no open auction which reported the results of buying and selling. Large chain grocery stores chose from among bids offered by several packers in various parts of the country.

Buyers for small operations did not, and still do not, have that luxury. They can and should, however, bid among local distributors. Some purchasers use formula buying. A good sources for information on which to base formula trades is *Urner Barry's Price-Current*. Exhibit 21 displays a sample section applicable to eggs and egg products. The numbers shown in such market reports, if used properly, can help hospitality purchasers negotiate fair prices.

Exhibit 21 reports egg prices in a section entitled "Regional Table Grade Eggs." Immediately below this section, prices for "Breaking Stock" (products intended for further processing) are also shown. Exhibit 22 displays this same data three weeks later. The five-day average price for large shell eggs in the Northeast has dropped from 87.0¢ to 67.8¢ and similar price reductions have occurred in other parts of the country. Such price fluctuations are not at all unusual; they are sometimes caused by supply disruptions and much less frequently by extraordinary demand. In this particular instance, egg prices have advanced in anticipation of Easter and then drop dramatically afterwards.

Now examine frozen and dried egg prices under "Egg Products" in Exhibits 21 and 22. There was very little change in the frozen products and only about a 4% decrease in the whole plain egg solids (dry). Liquid eggs (whole) have decreased approximately 8% (as would be expected since they are from current production), but this compares to a 22% decrease in the fresh shell product. Prices for egg products used in further processing do not respond sharply to short-term market disruptions, either up or down.

Exhibit 21 *Urner Barry's Price-Current,*
Friday, March 21, 1986

URNER BARRY'S
Price-Current
Established • 1858

Number 56 — Friday, March 21, 1986 — Volume 129

REGIONAL TABLE GRADE EGGS

	Northeast			Midwest	Southeast			So. Central	
	Spot Mkt	5-Day Avg	WHITES	Spot Mkt	5-Day Avg	Spot Mkt	5-Day Avg	WHITES	Spot Mkt	5-Day Avg
	.88	.880	Jumbos	.87	.870	.87	.870	Jumbos	.87	.870
	.87	.870	Extra Large	.86	.860	.86	.860	Extra Large	.86	.860
	.87	.870	Large	.86	.860	.86	.860	Large	.86	.860
	.74	.740	Mediums	.74	.740	.74	.740	Mediums	.75	.750
	.55	.550	Smalls	.55	.550	.56	.560	Smalls	.56	.560
	.74	.740	Off Gr Large	.73	.730	.73	.730	Off Gr Large	.72	.720
			BROWN					BROWN		
	.88	.880	Extra Large	.89	.890	.89	.890	Extra Large	.89	.890
	.87	.870	Large	.88	.880	.88	.880	Large	.88	.880
	.74	.740	Mediums	.74	.740	.74	.740	Mediums	.74	.740

Breaking Stock

Cents Per Dozen - General Trading Prices
Nest Run - Delivered - Net Weights - Material may or may not be included.

Northeast		Midwest	Southeast		So. Central
-	42-44 lbs	-		42-44 lbs	
.50-.53	48-50 lbs	.50-.53	.51-.54	48-50 lbs	.51-.52
.52-.54	50 lbs. & up	.52-.54	.52-.54	50 lbs. & up	

UNDERGRADES
B, C, Stains, 46-47 lbs. Picked Up

NE	Avg.	MW	Avg.	SE	Avg.	SC	Avg.
.45	.450	.45	.450	.45	.450	.45	.450

CHECKS
45-46 Lbs. Picked Up

.43	.430	.43	.430	.43	.430	.43	.430

GRADEABLE NEST RUN

Cents Per Dozen — elivered
Packing Material Included

Class	Trading Level	Conver Cost	tCtn Mkt Quote
	NORTHEAST		
1	$.7300	$.2235	$.9550
2	.6800	.2535	.9350
3	.5300	.2134	.7450
4	.6300	.1213	.5500
	MIDWEST		
1	$.7100	$.2208	$.9300
2	.6700	.2487	.9200
3	.5300	.2142	.7450
4	.4400	.1214	.5600
	SOUTHEAST		
1	$.7100	$.2207	$.9300
2	.6700	.2482	.9200
3	.5500	.2120	.7600
4	.4500	.1249	.5750
	SOUTH CENTRAL		
1	$.7100	$.2192	$.9300
2	.6700	.2448	.9150
3	.5400	.2159	.7550
4	.4500	.1223	.5700

EGG PRODUCTS

Trading in frozen and dried is light. Liquid activity is reasonably good. Whites are firm but yolk products are weak. Some commitments on salted yolks for April-May delivery reported at 63-64 cents per pound, some lower.

Urner Barry Quotations

FROZEN -
30 Lb. Cans, Per Lb. L.TL. 25 Can Mix Trucklots

	L.T.L.	Trucklots
Whole, Actual 3	-	.580-.590
Actual 2	-	.540-.550
No color	.540-.570	.500-.510
Whites	.370-.400	.330-.350
Yolk, 45% solids -		
Actual, 4	-	1.09-1.10
Actual 3	-	1.04-1.05
Nepa 3	-	1.00-1.01
Under Nepa 3	.93-.94	.88-.89
Yolk sugar 43% solids-		
No color	.73-.78	.69-.71
Yolk, salt, 43% solids -		
No color	.68-.70	.65-.67
Blend -		
30-32% egg sol.	.72-.75	.69-.70
27-29% egg sol.	.60-.65	.58-.59

EGG SOLIDS -	L.T.L.	Trucklots
Whole plain	1.60-1.75	1.60-1.65
Yolk	1.65-1.75	1.60-1.65
Albumen, spray	2.80-2.90	2.75-2.80
Blends	1.36-1.40	1.30-1.35

LIQUID EGGS	Tank Carlots Track Per Lb.
Whole, Unpasteurized	.360-.365
Custom Pack, Pasteurized	.480-.500
Whites, Unpasteurized	.280-.290
Custom Pack, Pasteurized	.290-.300
Yolk, 43% solids, Unpasteurized	.610-.620
Custom Pack, 43% Pasteurized	.680-.690
Yolk, Salt 43% solids, 10% salt	-

INSTITUTIONAL PACKS — FROZEN
PURE PAK Containers 30-32 Lb. Case Wt

Delivered	L.T.L.	Trucklots
Whole	.620-.650	.580-.600
Whites	-	
Yolk, sugar	-	
Blend -	-	
30-32% egg solids		

Fluid Milk

TRUCKLOTS DELIVERED MET N.Y.
Bottling quality per 40 qt unit $11.78-12.04
Bottling Quality per Cwt. 13.87-14.17

Condensed Skim Milk

DELIVERED METRO NEW YORK
Per lb. Solids (SNF) in tnklts .8150-.8300

Fluid Cream

CLASS II or MANUFACTURING
SPOT SALES DELIV. NORTHEAST
Butterfat per lb. in tanklots $1.7650-1.7850

Source: Urner Barry Publications, Inc., Toms River, New Jersey. Reprinted with permission.

Pricing and Yields

There are three common systems for buying egg products: cost-plus, formula, and open bid. These three systems may also be used in combination. Very large users

Exhibit 22 *Urner Barry's Price-Current, Friday, April 11, 1986*

URNER BARRY'S Price-Current

Established • 1858 •

Number 70 Friday, April 11, 1986 Volume 129

REGIONAL TABLE GRADE EGGS

Northeast			Midwest		Southeast			So. Central	
Spot Mkt	5-Day Avg	WHITES	Spot Mkt	5-Day Avg	Spot Mkt	5-Day Avg	WHITES	Spot Mkt	5-Day Avg
.67	.688	Jumbos	.66	.676	.67	.688	Jumbos	.68	.692
.66	.678	Extra Large	.65	.666	.66	.678	Extra Large	.67	.682
.66	.678	Large	.65	.666	.66	.678	Large	.67	.682
.59	.600	Mediums	.59	.598	.60	.610	Mediums	.60	.610
.49	.496	Smalls	.49	.494	.50	.506	Smalls	.50	.506
.54	.556	Off Gr Large	.54	.554	.54	.556	Off Gr Large	.55	.560
		BROWN					BROWN		
.73	.740	Extra Large	.74	.750	.74	.750	Extra Large	.74	.750
.72	.730	Large	.73	.740	.73	.740	Large	.73	.740
.61	.620	Mediums	.61	.620	.61	.620	Mediums	.61	.620

Breaking Stock

Cents Per Dozen - General Trading Prices
Nest Run - Delivered - Net Weights - Material may or may not be included.

Northeast		Midwest	Southeast	So. Central
-	42-44 lbs			42-44 lbs
.39-.41	48-50 lbs	.39-.41	.39-.41	48-50 lbs	.39-.41
.41-.43	50 lbs. & up	.41-.43	.41-.43	50 lbs. & up	-

UNDERGRADES
B, C, Stains, 46-47 lbs. Picked Up

NE	Avg.	MW	Avg.	SE	Avg.	SC	Avg.
.34	.356	.34	.356	.34	.356	.34	.356

CHECKS
45-46 Lbs. Picked Up

.32	.336	.32	.336	.32	.336	.32	.336

EGG PRODUCTS

Market steady on whites, unsettled on the balance. Buyers are cautious, anticipating lower values due to decreases in raw material costs.

EGG SOLIDS -	L.T.L.	Trucklots
Whole plain	1.59-1.69	1.54-1.59
Yolk	1.55-1.65	1.50-1.57
Albumen, spray	3.10-3.20	2.95-3.05
Blends	1.28-1.33	1.23-1.27

Urner Barry Quotations

FROZEN		
30 Lb. Cans, Per Lb.LTL 25 Can MinTrucklots		
Whole, Actual 3	-	$.580-.590
Actual 2	-	.540-.550
No color	.500-.530	.450-.470
Whites	.380-.410	.350-.360
Yolk, 43% solids -		
Actual, 4	-	1.07-1.09
Actual 3	-	1.02-1.03
Nepa 3	-	.96-.99
Under Nepa 3	.90-.91	.85-.86
Yolk sugar 43% solids-		
No color	.71-.76	.67-.69
Yolk, salt, 43% solids -		
No color	.64-.67	.62-.64
Blend -		
30-32% egg sol.	.72-.75	.69-.70
27-29% egg sol.	.60-.65	.58-.59

LIQUID EGGS	Tank Carlots Track Per Lb.
Whole, Unpasteurized	.330-.340
Custom Pack, Pasteurized	.440-.450
Whites, Unpasteurized	.290-.305
Custom Pack, Pasteurized	.310-.320
Yolk, 43% solids, Unpasteurized	.590-.600
Custom Pack, 43% Pasteurized	.650-.660
Yolk, Salt 43% solids, 10% salt	-

INSTITUTIONAL PACKS — FROZEN		
PURE PAK Containers 30-32 Lb. Case W1		
Delivered	L.T.L.	Trucklots
Whole	.590-.620	.560-.570
Whites	-	
Yolk, sugar	-	
Blend -		
30-32% egg solids	-	

BUTTER

URNER BARRY QUOTATIONS

Based on extensive country-wide trade reports & other terminal market wholesale transactions.

TRUCKLOTS BULK	SALT	SALES FROM WAREHOUSES	
Deliv East (Spot Mkt.)		1 Pound Solids	1 Pound Quarters
$1.4200	....93 Score (AA)...	$1.4300-1.5300	$1.4700-1.5700*
1.4150	....92 Score (A)....	1.4250-1.5250	1.4650-1.5650*
1.3725	....90 Score (B)...	1.3825-1.4825	1.4225-1.5225

Midwest

Loads & Pool Loads Delivered (Bulk)

93 Score	92 Score	90 Score
$1.3900	$1.3850	$1.3425

*Should have read same since March 14th

CHEESE

CHEDDARS —WHOLE MILK —POUNDS

	EX SHARP	SHARP	MEDIUM	MILD
Blocks	$1.82-2.18	$1.6750-1.7950	$1.59-1.75	$1.3750-1.8125
Daisies			1.75-2.05	1.5375-1.5900
Splits				1.5000-1.5800
Midgets		1.78-2.18	1.73-1.85	1.4825-1.6700
Flats	1.93-2.18	1.79-1.83		
		(CURRENT)		
Proc. 5 lb loaf	-		-	1.3450-1.5200
Proc. 5 lb sliced	-		-	1.3850-1.6800
Muenster	-		-	1.4050-1.6775

Source: Urner Barry Publications, Inc., Toms River, New Jersey. Reprinted with permission.

generally use cost-plus to ensure a steady supply of raw materials. For example, extensive quantities of frozen and fresh liquid eggs are used by national baking companies specializing in sweet goods. Large users occasionally make speculative purchases, but more often these companies have regular supply sources, which set prices on some prearranged system.

Certain buying systems may be applied to the purchase of fresh shell eggs and frozen whole eggs. The following examples are based on Sample Specifications #1 and #2 given in Exhibit 20.

Example 1: Fresh Shell Eggs

Assume a New York coffee-shop operator uses 50 cases (30 dozen each) of eggs per week, delivered twice a week (25 cases each delivery). The operator selects three distributors and asks them to quote a weekly price based on *Urner Barry's* 5-day average for large eggs. The operator will accept the low bid with a guarantee of business for one year, provided service and quality are satisfactory. The operator receives the following bids:

Company	Bid
A	5-day average flat (same quote as *Urner Barry's*)
B	5-day average minus 2
C	5-day average plus 1

Price bids are to be effective for purchases made Monday through Friday of the following week. Exhibit 21 indicates that the 5-day average (Northeast) for large eggs on the date of report was 87.0¢ per dozen. Company A then bid 87.0¢, Company B bid 85.0¢, and Company C bid 88.0¢. The buyer accepts Company B's proposal and establishes Friday as the day to make the price for the following week. Exhibit 22 (Friday, 4/11/86) shows the 5-day average at 67.8¢ so the price for the following week is 65.8¢ (67.8¢ − 2¢ = 65.8¢).

The buyer has established a pricing level based on competitive bids and has locked this to market reports. The buyer is dependent on the accuracy of *Urner Barry's* report but, as a relatively small user, the buyer feels confident that the basis for a fair price over the next year has been established. The buyer must periodically seek bids from qualified suppliers to ensure that the spread (2¢ under flat market) is still valid.

Example 2: Frozen Whole Eggs

Most food service units use this product in relatively small amounts. A bid establishing a price level related to *Urner Barry's* quotes is effective. For the large-volume user, the selection of the distributor is important. Certain distributors specialize in these items and can probably buy them in larger quantities and at a better price than general distributors. It is not uncommon for the general distributor to have prices over 20% higher than those of the specialty supplier simply because the distributor does not buy the item correctly.

Endnotes

1. Three price forecasting services are:
   - Agri-Commodities, Inc., Andover, Massachusetts
   - Sparks Commodities, Inc., Memphis, Tennessee
   - Live Stock Business Advisory Services, Inc., Kansas City, Missouri

REVIEW QUIZ

When you feel you have covered all of the material in this chapter, answer these questions. Choose the *best* answer. Check your answers with the correct ones found on the Review Quiz Answer Key at the end of this book.

True (T) or False (F)

T   F   1. A food buyer may specify modifications in the standard poultry product.

T   F   2. Specifications for poultry should not indicate pack.

T   F   3. Mature turkeys have better yields than younger ones, in terms of proportion of meat to bone.

T   F   4. Poultry is inspected for wholesomeness before and after slaughter.

T   F   5. "Plant Grade A" is an official USDA grade for poultry. *don't use*

T   F   6. Brown-shelled eggs are nutritionally superior to white-shelled eggs.

T   F   7. Egg size is integrated into egg grading standards.

Multiple Choice

no grading

8. Possible factors that are checked in USDA quality grading for poultry are:

    a. exposed flesh.
    b. discoloration.
    c. eating quality.
    d. a and b.

9. Which of the following terms denotes an immature pigeon?

    a. fryer
    b. squab
    c. yearling
    d. broiler

10. Fresh eggs are normally received in cases containing:

    a. 30 dozen.
    b. 12 dozen.
    c. 15 dozen.
    d. a and c.

11. Which of the following is *not* an egg size?

    a. colossal
    b. jumbo
    c. extra-large
    d. small

Chapter Outline

Dairy Production and Distribution
A Closely Regulated Industry
Milk
Processed Milk
Cheese
Butter
Frozen Desserts
Sources for Dairy Products
Pricing Structures and Yields

Learning Objectives

1. Summarize the major areas of legislation affecting the dairy industry.

2. Describe milk from the standpoints of processing, standards, and specifications.

3. Briefly describe varieties, designations, and standards for cheeses.

4. Describe butter in terms of processing, packaging, quality, and pricing.

5. Explain problems associated with specifications for frozen desserts.

6. Summarize factors which affect the pricing of dairy products.

12

Dairy Products

MILK AND DAIRY PRODUCTS can represent a significant portion of food costs in hospitality operations. These costs may be significantly reduced when purchasers take advantage of market price alternatives. To accomplish this task, purchasers must know how these commodities move through distribution channels. Effective purchasing also demands that buyers thoroughly understand the quality requirements of their operations and how these may be affected by the extensive government regulation of dairy products. Both buyers and sellers of milk and dairy products experience restraints that are unlike those placed on other commodities.

Dairy Production and Distribution

While some dairy production is found today in almost every state, most processing is concentrated in the dairy-intensive states of Wisconsin, Minnesota, California, and New York. These states produce roughly half the cheese and butter used in the United States; Wisconsin alone accounts for about one-fourth of total production.

Historically, the short shelf life of dairy products prevented the shipment of fresh fluid products from states with surpluses to supply-deficient areas. Because of the perishable nature of these products, production and consumption were local and purchase contracts for multi-unit operations were negotiated on a city-to-city basis.

The economic impact of new technology within the dairy industry is of tremendous importance. Technological advances in refrigeration and processing methods have yielded greater product stability, extended the shelf life of fluid products, and enabled more widespread distribution. Surplus products can be shipped around the country with reduced spoilage and greater savings in production costs. Although fluid milk is still, for the most part, bought and sold locally, improvements in milk production and distribution systems have increased product availability and led to cost savings for the purchaser.

A Closely Regulated Industry

The consumer protection movement of the 1920s led to improved sanitation practices in milk production. Today each state has enacted individual statutes, and all states follow the minimum standards of the U.S. Public Health Service Milk Ordinance and Code administered by the U.S. Food and Drug Administration (FDA). Legislation also requires that health standards be maintained within dairy herds and applies to interstate shipments and to foreign imports as well. These laws help to ensure a consistently high level of wholesomeness and quality of dairy products sold within the United States. Sanitary regulations have also encouraged the cooperative distribution of milk by producers and, over the years, a consolidation of dairy producers and handlers has emerged.

State and federal legislation greatly influences dairy product pricing. Unfortunately, the supply and demand of dairy products is never well-balanced. For example, cows produce greater quantities of milk during spring and summer; however, the demand for milk remains relatively constant throughout the year. Price-stabilizing regulations help the dairy industry cope financially with alternating cycles of undersupply and overproduction.

State and federal legislation, introduced during the early 1930s (and amended many times since), still remains in effect. For example, federal marketing orders establish the prices that milk producers receive for their products. Marketing orders are published monthly by USDA personnel for each jurisdiction covered. Many states establish resale prices and impose penalties if a handler provides discounts below cost or illegal incentives to lure large-volume users.

Congress passed legislation in 1948 requiring that the government buy all surplus dairy production in the form of butter, cheese, or dry milk in order to maintain farmers' purchasing power and to guarantee a continuing supply. To regulate the dairy industry, the government established parity, basically an index of farmer costs. Parity is the equivalence between farmers' current purchasing power and their purchasing power at a selected base period, maintained by governmental support of agricultural commodity prices. This complicated legislation attempts to establish fair and reasonable prices for dairy products as well as to balance production and consumption. However, this balance is difficult to sustain because government purchases of surplus products often encourage overproduction. Also, rate changes over the years have resulted in enormous government purchases and further widening of cost spreads between U.S. and world dairy products. For example, under its support programs, the U.S. government currently pays about $1.40 per pound for butter while the world market price is under $.50.

Federal and state statutes also provide price supports. These price supports are designed to equalize prices and increase competition within the industry. The price supports help smaller, local producers compete with larger companies that may enjoy considerable cost advantages.

Milk

Governmental regulations concerning sanitation extend to all dairy products at every stage of production and distribution. Federal standards require that fluid whole milk be free of any undesirable taste, contain no less than 8.25% non-fat solids and 3.25% butterfat, and be unadulterated (pure and unmixed).

Processing. A process known as HTST (high temperature, short time) pasteurization is required to destroy undesirable bacteria. In this process, milk is heated to 161° F (72° C) and held at that temperature for 15 seconds. Allowable bacteria counts within milk vary from state to state; however, all states follow minimum standards to protect the public. Most standards pertaining to whole milk (excluding

Exhibit 1   Minimum Butterfat and Non-Fat Milk Specification Requirements

	Minimum Butterfat (%)	Minimum Non-Fat Milk Solids (%)
1. Fluid whole milk	3.25	8.25
2. Homogenized	3.25	8.25 Fat uniformly distributed
3. Vitamin "D"	3.25	8.25 Minimum of 400 USP Vitamin "D" units per quart
4. Skimmed	0.50	7.75
5. Low fat	0.2 to 2.0	8.25
6. 2%	2.00	10.00 Generally
7. Buttermilk	0.50	8.25
8. Evaporated whole milk	7.5	18.00
9. Evaporated skim milk	0.2	18.00
10. Sweetened condensed	8.5	19.5 Sugar added
11. Non-fat dry milk	1.5	In the dry product—5% moisture max.
12. Whole dry milk	26.0	In the dry product—5% moisture max.
13. Half & half	10.5	8.25
14. Table cream	18.0	8.25
15. Sour cream	18.0	8.25 Culture added 0.2% acidity
16. Light whipping cream	30.0	8.25
17. Heavy whipping cream	36.0	8.25
18. Ice cream	10.0	10.00 Plus sugar, flavor, stabilizers
19. Frozen custard	10.0	10.0 Plus egg yolks and ice cream ingredients
20. Fruit sherbet	1.0 to 2.0	2.0 to 5.0 Total milk solids
21. Milk shakes	3.25	8.25
22. Butter	80.00	

Source: USDA Food Safety and Quality Service, *Federal and State Standards for the Composition of Milk Products.* Agricultural Handbook No. 51. Washington, D.C., January 1, 1980.

butterfat requirements) also apply to non-fat milk, buttermilk, cream, half and half, and other dairy products.

Homogenization was introduced during the 1930s and today most fluid milk products are homogenized. This involves a process that breaks fat globules of milk into finer particles which remain permanently suspended in the fluid and do not recombine and rise to the top as cream. Some minimum standards for butterfat and non-fat milk solids are shown in Exhibit 1. This data can be helpful to buyers in developing purchase specifications.

Standards. Milk and milk product standards are updated and published annually by the federal government. These standards represent minimum requirements and many processors make products which exceed them. For example, the minimum butterfat content for ice cream is 10%, but "super premium" ice cream products are available at 12%, 14%, and even higher levels. In some cases, the milk solids may be higher in quality than dictated by minimum requirements. Each hospitality operation should establish its own quality levels and develop a system for maintaining these requirements.

Fat content is specified for different types of milk (whole, skim, 2%, low-fat), but can sometimes be misunderstood. The terms "light cream," "heavy cream," and "whipping cream" should indicate specific ranges of butterfat content. If the buyer desires coffee cream containing 13% butterfat, that percentage should be specified.

Exhibit 2   Typical Specifications for Dairy Products

Specification 1	Fluid milk—Grade A 1 gallon whole milk
Specification 2	• Butter, 92 score (A): 1-lb prints; 30-lb carton • Butter, 92 score (A): 72-count chips; 24-lb carton • Butter, 92 score (A): 90-count reddies; 24-lb carton • Butter, 92 score (A): whipped, 30% overrun; 7-lb tubs

Specification 3   Milk shake mix
Weight per gallon = 9 lb

Butterfat	3.5 %
Non-fat dry milk solids	12.0 %
Cane sugar	8.5 %
Stabilizer (not to exceed)	0.35%
Total solids	24.35%

Specification 4   Bulk vanilla ice cream—3-gallon container
Weight per gallon = 4.5 lb

Butterfat	12.0%
Non-fat dry milk solids	13.0%
Cane sugar	13.0%
Stabilizer	0.5%
Flavoring	2.0%
Overrun	100.0%

Specification 5	Regular processed American cheese 27% milkfat, 30% non-fat solids, 43% moisture, no aged cheese 160 slices per 5-lb package
Specification 6	Sharp processed American cheese 27% milkfat, 30% non-fat solids, 43% moisture, aged cheddar added for flavor 160 slices per 5-lb box
Specification 7	Regular processed cheese food 23% milkfat, 23% non-fat solids, 44% moisture 160 slices per 5-lb box

The relative content of fat and vitamins may be altered in the processing of milk. Fat is removed from many milk products, either partially (as is the case with 2% milk) or almost entirely (as with skim milk). Milk products may be fortified with vitamins and other types of nutrient supplements. Vitamin D is a particularly common additive to fluid milks. Vitamin A is removed in the defatting process and is frequently added back into skim milk.

Specifications. Because of the government's close involvement in regulating standards within the dairy industry, specifications for dairy products are relatively straightforward. Typical specifications for dairy products are shown in Exhibit 2. Note that each identifies and quantifies major factors important in determining quality parameters for products, and specifies packaging and weight requirements as well.

For most natural fluid products (such as whole milk, low-fat milk, skim milk, half and half, and cream), federal or state standards are satisfactory in purchase specifications. However, caution should be exercised when buying products such as chocolate milk, milk shake mixes, and eggnog, which contain substantial amounts of added ingredients. Since the manufacture of these products alters the basic percentages of solids and fats, buyers should know the standards for the milk used and should also consider the quality of added ingredients.

The "Grade A" rating for fluid milk products indicates wholesomeness (fitness for consumption) rather than quality; it is generally adequate by most operations' standards. For other manufactured products, such as butter, selected cheeses, and dry milk products, quality designations have been developed. Also, the label "Quality Approved" is available for products such as sour cream and cottage cheese. All of these designations are USDA standards developed primarily for the retail customer, but they can also help the quality-conscious purchaser uphold product standards.

Considerable quantities of milk are processed into butter, cheese, frozen desserts, and other dairy products. Approximately 45% of all milk production is retained in a fluid form, while the remaining 55% is used to manufacture other dairy products. Cheese and butter account for approximately 80% of these other dairy products.

Processed Milk

Processed milk constitutes a considerable portion of the total milk supply. Through processing, these products have been evaporated, dried, sweetened, and/or defatted. Most of the milk dried in the United States is manufactured by a spray process in which milk is vaporized and evaporated under vacuum conditions.

Dried milk powders are extensively used in baking and frozen desserts and are becoming more widely used within the hospitality industry. All dried milk products must be uniform in color and pleasing to the taste. Products should be stored in a cool area and when opened should be used immediately to prevent absorption of moisture.

Minimum federal standards are available for selected dairy products. Such information can be helpful in developing specifications. USDA grade designations exist for dry milk and dry buttermilk products.

There are no grades for canned milk products. Specifications for sweetened condensed skim milk are identical to the non-skim sweetened condensed milk except that butterfat requirements are eliminated. Condensed skim milk is used in the baking and frozen dessert industries, and is generally available only in bulk containers.

Cheese

The distinctive nature of each variety of cheese adds to its appeal and is an outgrowth of its development. Methods for processing cheese evolved independently in many parts of the world. Most of the cheese varieties commonly used in the United States have European origins. Many similar types of cheese are known by different names, usually associated with the region of production. Roquefort, for example, was made from ewe's milk in the village of Roquefort in southern France. Similarly, other cheeses were named for the towns of Gorgonzola in Italy and Stilton in England. Production techniques were often jealously guarded.

Raw material, texture, ripening process, and length of cure period determine the variety of cheese. Cheddar is tightly compressed resulting in a firm texture. The interior of Swiss cheese is ripened by bacteria which produce gas and form its characteristic holes. Curds (the thick part of coagulated milk) are stretched to produce the thread-like texture of Provolone and Mozzarella. Roquefort, Gorgonzola, and Bleu are mold-ripened throughout, providing each variety with a unique color and distinctive flavor.

Commercially, the most popular variety of cheese in the United States is processed American. This cheese variety was developed and patented by the founders of the Kraft Company, who enjoyed a single source advantage for many years until those patents expired; now, all major processors produce this variety. Processed American is popular for several reasons: (1) the texture, color, and flavor are consistent; (2) the processing method inhibits bacterial growth and makes the product shelf stable; and (3) the product melts quickly and evenly.

Designations. To be labeled either natural or processed, cheese products must meet certain federal standards for moisture, fat, and other factors. Products labeled "cheese food"—a third designation for cheese—have been available for many years. These products generally have less fat and more moisture than the natural or processed products. They are nutritious, flavorful, and inexpensive, and may be acceptable for cooking purposes in some food service operations.

Imitation or synthetic products are usually made from imported casein (dried milk protein), vegetable oil, flavoring, and coloring. The U.S. dairy industry is concerned about imported casein, which is brought into the country duty-free and supplants American products. When we compare butterfat at approximately $1.78 per pound and vegetable oil at $.19 per pound, the cost advantages of the synthetic product become apparent. This situation is similar to the oleo margarine-butter controversy of many years ago. Today, butter costs approximately six times more than margarine. Many consumers buy margarine because of its cost savings.

Standards. Standards for cheese vary according to variety, processing method, and age. Current federal standards for maximum moisture and minimum butterfat for some popular varieties are shown in Exhibit 3.

The USDA has established general standards for domestic varieties of natural cheeses and has inspectors available to the industry who, for a fee, will establish grades and affix the USDA shield. For example, grading standards for natural cheddar are shown in Exhibit 4. Wisconsin, the leading state in cheese processing, has developed separate grading standards. Wisconsin State Brand is its highest designation, comparable to USDA Grade AA.

Butter

Butter is produced by pasteurizing milk, treating it with a milk acid to cause curdling, then churning the product into butterfat. At that point, the butterfat is processed, colored, and, if necessary, flavored to achieve the desired product.

Butter is packaged in many forms, including tubs, blocks, one-pound prints (smaller blocks), and 1/4-pound-sticks. Butter is also available in a whipped form

Exhibit 3 Moisture and Milkfat Standards for Cheese

Variety	Maximum Moisture (%)	Minimum Milkfat in Solids (%)	Minimum Milkfat in Cheese (%)
Cottage—regular	80	—	4
Cream	55	—	33
Camembert	—	50	25
Limburger	50	50	25
Bleu	46	50	27
Monterey	44	50	28
Muenster	46	50	27
Roquefort	45	50	27.5
Cheddar	39	50	30.5
Colby	40	50	30
Gouda	45	46	25.3
Swiss	41	43	25.4
Parmesan	32	32	21.8
Romano	34	38	25.1
Mozzarella—regular	52/60	45	18
Mozzarella—low moisture, part skim	45/52	30/45	14
Provolone	45	45	24.8
Pasteurized Processed Cheese	43	47	27
Processed Cheese Food	44	—	23
Cold Pack Cheese	42	47	27
Cold Pack Cheese Food	44	—	23

Source: USDA Food Safety and Quality Service, *Federal and State Standards for the Composition of Milk Products.* Agricultural Handbook No. 51. Washington, D.C., January 1, 1980.

Exhibit 4 Grading Standards for Cheddar Cheese

AA   Meets federal standards for fat and moisture content. The cheese has a fine, highly pleasing cheddar flavor, a smooth compact texture, uniform color, and attractive appearance. The plant in which the cheese is produced must meet USDA sanitary requirements.

A   Same as AA, but there may be some variation in flavor and texture between packages.

All packages carrying the USDA grading shield must also show the cure category:

Mild	partly cured (usually 2 to 3 months)
Mellow Aged	moderately ripened (4–7 months)
Sharp	fully ripened (8–12 months)

Any product aged over 12 months may be labeled "very sharp."

Source: USDA Food Safety and Quality Service, *Federal and State Standards for the Composition of Milk Products.* Agricultural Handbook No. 51. Washington, D.C., January 1, 1980.

which incorporates air in the product. When packaged properly, butter may be frozen without fear of deterioration.

Butter chips and butter reddies are used by many operations since they are convenient and lend themselves to portion-control costing. Chips are square, individual portions on a liner surface (usually cardboard); reddies are identical to

Exhibit 5 Descriptions of Quality Grades for Butter

U.S. Grade AA (93 Score)
.... Delicate, sweet flavor, with fine highly pleasing aroma.
.... Made with high-quality, fresh sweet cream.
.... Smooth texture, with salt completely dissolved.

U.S. Grade A (92 Score)
.... Pleasing flavor, made from fresh cream; fairly smooth texture.

U.S. Grade B (90 Score)
.... May have slightly acid flavor; generally made from sour cream.

Butter bearing USDA Grade Shields must be produced in a sanitary plant approved by the USDA.

Source: USDA Food Safety and Quality Service, *Federal and State Standards for the Composition of Milk Products.* Agricultural Handbook No. 51. Washington, D.C., January 1, 1980.

chips, but have paper covering each portion. Individual portions of butter are also packaged in plastic cups and may be foil wrapped.

For packages, count (number of portions) per pound should be specified. Chips and reddies are available in 72 and 90 count per pound; cups and foil wraps are approximately 50 count per pound. Whipped butter is widely used in seven-pound tubs.

Grading. Federal standards require that butter contain 80% butterfat solids, 17% moisture, 2% salt, and 1% artificial coloring and other solids.[1] Practically all butter is packed under USDA supervision for quality and wholesomeness. Descriptions of quality grades for butter are presented in Exhibit 5. Grading shields for butter, which also apply to some cheese varieties, are also illustrated.

Butter grades are rated by letter and numerical designation based upon flavor, body, color, and salt content. Grades are: AA = 93 score, A = 92 score, B = 90 score. The quality of butter depends to a great extent on the quality of the raw materials (milk and cream) used in its manufacture. Butter is generally salted, but is also available without salt (sweet butter).

Pricing. Butter processors are attempting to counteract the increased popularity of margarine by offering blended butter-margarine products. These mixtures, usually 40% butter and 60% margarine, are generally of good quality. Assuming butter is priced at $1.60 per pound and margarine at $.30, the blend cost per pound would be:

Blend Cost = (40% × Butter Cost) + (60% × Margarine Cost)
Blend Cost = (40% × $1.60) + (60% × $.30)
Blend Cost = (.40 × 1.60) + (.60 × .30)
Blend Cost = .64 + .18
Blend Cost = $.82 per pound

Cost savings of the blended butter ($.82 per pound) over the 100% butter product ($1.60 per pound) are substantial. While the blended product cannot be identified as butter on the menu, it may be acceptable for cooking purposes in some properties and it may actually be preferred for table use by diet- and health-conscious consumers.

Exhibit 6   Minimum Standards for Frozen Desserts

Product	Milkfat (%)	Total Milk Solids (%)	Minimum Weight (lb/gal)
Plain ice cream	10	20	4.5
Chocolate or flavored ice cream	8	16	4.5
Frozen custard	10	20	4.5
Milk shake mix	3.25	11.5	
Sherbet—minimum	1	2	6.0
standard	2	4	6.0

Source: USDA Food Safety and Quality Service, *Federal and State Standards for the Composition of Milk Products.* Agricultural Handbook No. 51. Washington, D.C., January 1, 1980.

Frozen Desserts

Exhibit 6 indicates minimum standards for frozen desserts imposed by federal and state regulations with regard to butterfat, milk solids, and minimum weight per gallon. Unfortunately, there are no in-plant inspection programs or grading designations for these products. In such instances, taste testing may be advisable to determine quality. Manufacturers, however, are bound by truth-in-labeling and weights/measures legislation to meet required standards.

Specifications for frozen desserts such as cream pies and cakes and items with cream fillings offer more challenge for the buyer. The federal specifications for primary ingredients, such as milk, provide a base for predictions, but quality and price are affected by the specific combination of ingredients. These products may contain butterfat, non-fat milk solids, sugar, flavorings, stabilizers, and a wide range of other ingredients, many of which do not have legislated standards of quality.

Overrun is another important consideration in purchasing frozen dairy products. Overrun is the percentage (by volume) of air mixed into the product during the freezing process. A gallon of ice cream mix (an unfrozen liquid) with an 80% overrun will produce 1.8 gallons of frozen product. In purchasing frozen items such as ice cream and sherbet, specifications should indicate the preferred level of overrun and per gallon weight should be checked at receiving to gauge overrun. Milk shake mix is delivered unfrozen to retail units, with overrun added by the freezing equipment of the hospitality operation.

Sources for Dairy Products

The distribution of fresh fluid products such as milk are normally handled by dairies selling within a localized area. Frozen desserts, by contrast, have a wider distribution area because they pose fewer potential problems in relation to sanitation and quality control.

Processing companies, rather than distributing companies, frequently deliver dairy products to hospitality operations. Frozen dessert products tend to be more fragile than regular frozen merchandise (for example, french fries) and cannot be handled in the same manner as other frozen items. Specialized distribution of these products is necessary.

Cheese is available through standard distribution channels. It is carried by full service distributors as well as by specialty companies, such as egg dealers. Freight cost is a major factor in the pricing of cheese; a distributor buying in large quantities has a price advantage that can be passed on to buyers. Prices are also influenced by the area of production and, in particular, by the support price for that area.

Pricing Structures and Yields

Three pricing structures form the basis for dairy product pricing:

Class I	Fluid milk consumed as a beverage.
Class II	Milk intended for further processing into cream, eggnog, cottage cheese, milk shake and ice cream mixes, and yogurt.
Class III	Milk used to produce cheese; butter; and dry, evaporated, and condensed forms of milk.

Some simple formulas can be used to determine if prices are competitive. However, a complicating factor is the government support program, which applies to butter, cheese, and dry products and is triggered by Class II prices.

Dairy Market News (Exhibit 7) is a comprehensive USDA weekly publication. *Urner Barry's Price-Current* (Exhibits 8 and 9) is another helpful source of pricing information. Data from these reports are used in the pricing examples which follow. The USDA Agricultural Marketing Service also offers a good data source for purchasers.

Example 1: Fluid Whole Milk

To estimate the price of fluid whole milk, the buyer must compute the cost of the milk and add estimates for packaging, processing, and delivery charges. While differentials can be negotiated, they are best established by bid.

The role of federal marketing orders in establishing farmers' milk prices was previously discussed. Current information is always available to buyers through local area dairies. The publications mentioned previously offer this information in a more readily available, condensed form.

The section titled "Fluid Milk" in Exhibit 8 quotes New York fluid milk (Class I or bottling quality) prices at $13.87–14.17 per hundredweight (cwt). Market orders are quoted "per cwt," so buyers may wish to convert from these units to gallons. First, find the average of the two prices:

$$\text{Average Price} = \frac{\text{Upper Range} + \text{Lower Range}}{2}$$

$$\text{Average Price} = \frac{\$13.87 + 14.17}{2}$$

$$\text{Average Price} = \frac{\$28.04}{2}$$

$$\text{Average Price} = \$14.02/\text{cwt}$$

Exhibit 7 *Dairy Market News,* **Week of March 24—28, 1986**

```
WEEK OF MARCH 24 - 28, 1986              DAIRY MARKET NEWS              VOLUME NO.  53  REPORT NO.  13
```

NATIONAL DAIRY MARKET AT A GLANCE

At the Chicago Mercantile Exchange, Grade AA Butter held steady at $1.3825, Grade A was unchanged at $1.3775, and Grade B stayed at $1.2925. At the National Cheese Exchange in Green Bay, 40¢ Blocks were unchanged at $1.2350 and Barrel Cheese stayed at $1.1850. The supplemental funding bill (H.J.R. 534) for CCC purchase programs was signed by President Reagan on March 24. The assessment rate to offset reductions mandated by Gramm-Rudman will be between 10 and 12 cents per cwt. effective April 1. Also on April 1, a 40 cents per cwt. assessment will be implemented to partially fund the Dairy Termination Program. Announcements will be made on March 28 about the bids USDA will be accepting from producers to terminate milk production for five years under the Dairy Termination Program. The consumer price index (CPI) for February for all food was up 1.9% from last year. For dairy products, the CPI was down 0.7%. Milk was down 1.8%, butter was down 0.9%, and cheese was unchanged. The U.S. cold storage report for February indicates that butter and cheese inventories were mixed from the previous month, but down from last February. Butter stocks were reported at 243.9 million pounds, an increase of 18.3% from January 1986 and a decrease of 15.7% from February 1985. Natural American Cheese stocks were at 726.4 million pounds, a decrease of 2.1% from the previous month and a decrease of 13.9% from last year. For the period March 24 - 26, CCC purchased 3.5 million pounds of butter, 8.8 million pounds of cheese, and 14.2 million pounds of nonfat dry milk. The milk equivalent, on a milkfat basis, is 159.8 million pounds. This compares to 238.1 million pounds last year and 242.1 million pounds last week. CCC soldback 2.0 million pounds of standard grade nonfat dry milk for animal feed use at prices ranging between $.4650 - .5433 per pound. The U.S. dairy cow slaughter figures for the week ending March 8, indicate the East slaughtered 19,300 dairy cows, the Central 29,800, and the West 12,600, for a total of 61,700. This compares to 55,100 last year and 63,500 the previous week. The all cow figure is 129,900 compared to 126,600 last year.

BUTTER MARKETS

CHICAGO BUTTER: With no trading activity occurring at the Chicago Mercantile Exchange, all grades of bulk butter held steady. Bulk butter markets regained stability this week following the signing of the Dairy Assessment bill late last week. Trading stocks are generally in balance for all current orders. Churning schedules are seasonally heavy, but the call for cream for Class II products is gaining momentum. Buying interest this past week has been good as most buyers have reentered the market. Now that Easter orders have been placed, contacts feel that the butter business will return to seasonal light levels. During the 3 days of March 24 - 26, Midwestern sources offered CCC 1,187,769 pounds of excess bulk butter.

WHOLESALE SELLING PRICES - DOLLARS PER POUND - TRUCKLOT - BULK IN FIBER BOXES - DELIVERED METROPOLITAN AREA
(Prices include Government CCC purchase price whenever bulk butter is moving to CCC from the Midwest area)

DATE	MARCH 25	:	MARCH 27	:	MARCH 28
GRADE AA	$1.3825-1.3975	:	$1.3825-1.3975	:	
		:		:	NOT AVAILABLE
GRADE A	$1.3775-1.3975	:	$1.3775-1.3975	:	

BUTTER TRANSACTIONS ON THE CHICAGO MERCANTILE EXCHANGE: THURSDAY, MARCH 27, 1986   (CARLOT UNIT = 40,000 - 42,000 LBS.)

		MARCH	AVERAGES	GRADE	:	PRICE CHANGE	:	LAST SIGNIFICANT TRANSACTION		
		1986	: 1985							
SALES:	NONE	$1.3825	: $1.4150	AA	:	N. C.	:	$1.3825	: OFFER	02/28/86
BIDS UNFILLED:	NONE		:							
		1.3775	: 1.3925	A	:	N. C.	:	$1.3775	: BID	03/07/86
OFFERS UNCOVERED:	NONE		:							
		1.2925	: 1.3400	B	:	N. C.	:	$1.2925	: BID	03/21/86

The above is the last significant trading action with the sale, offer or bid and date indicated.

CHEESE MARKET

TRANSACTIONS ON THE NATIONAL CHEESE EXCHANGE, INC. 1/   THURSDAY, MARCH 27, 1986   (CARLOT UNIT = 38,000 - 42,000 LBS.)

2/SALES ON BIDS:	1 CAR 40¢ BLOCKS @ $1.2350	MARCH	AVERAGES	CHEDDAR/STYLES	:	PRICE CHANGE	:	LAST SIGNIFICANT TRANSACTION	
		1986	: 1985		:		:		
		$1.1838	: $1.2615	BARRELS	:	N. C.	:	$1.1850	: SALE 3/27/86
2/SALES ON OFFERS:	1 CAR 40¢ BLOCKS @ $1.2300			(White) 3/	:		:		:
	2 CARS 40¢ BLOCKS @ $1.2275	1.2350	: 1.2870	40¢ BLOCKS	:	N. C.	:	$1.2350	: SALE 3/27/86
	1 CAR 40¢ BLOCKS @ $1.2350			(Colored) 4/	:		:		:
	1 CAR BARREL CHEESE @ $1.1850								
BIDS UNFILLED:	NONE								
OFFERS UNCOVERED:	1 CAR 40¢ BLOCKS @ $1.2350								
	2 CARS BARREL CHEESE @ $1.1850								

1/ Exchange meetings held at 10:00 a.m. (Central Time) each Friday at Green Bay, Wisconsin. 2/ Sales are FOB sellers warehouse or nearest rail siding. 3/ Equivalent WI State Brand, USDA Extra Grade or better. 4/ Equivalent WI State Brand, USDA Grade A or better. Prices do not include permissible allowances for transportation, freight differential, adjustments for moisture content, clearing charge, barrel deposit, etc. Barrels and 40¢ Blocks are subject to price adjustments for moisture content.

Source: USDA, Agricultural Marketing Service, Dairy Division.

Next, convert from hundredweight units to 40-quart units. A conversion factor of 0.85 is used. The price of $14.02 per cwt is equivalent to $11.92 per 40-quart container. (This price may be developed independently by calculating the mid-range price for 40-quart units, quoted at $11.78–12.04 in Exhibit 8.)

Using the conversion factor of 4 quarts per gallon, the cost of milk to bottlers in New York can be calculated as follows:

Exhibit 8 *Urner Barry's Price-Current,* **Friday, March 21, 1986**

URNER BARRY'S
Price-Current

Established · 1858 ·

Number 56   Friday, March 21, 1986   Volume 129

REGIONAL TABLE GRADE EGGS

Northeast			Midwest		Southeast			So. Central		
Spot Mkt	5-Day Avg	**WHITES**	Spot Mkt	5-Day Avg	Spot Mkt	5-Day Avg	**WHITES**	Spot Mkt	5-Day Avg	
.88	.880	Jumbos	.87	.870	.87	.870	Jumbos	.87	.870	
.87	.870	Extra Large	.86	.860	.86	.860	Extra Large	.86	.860	
.87	.870	Large	.86	.860	.86	.860	Large	.86	.860	
.74	.740	Mediums	.74	.740	.74	.740	Mediums	.75	.750	
.55	.550	Smalls	.55	.550	.56	.560	Smalls	.56	.560	
.74	.740	Off Gr Large	.73	.730	.73	.730	Off Gr Large	.72	.720	
		BROWN					**BROWN**			
.88	.880	Extra Large	.89	.890	.89	.890	Extra Large	.89	.890	
.87	.870	Large	.88	.880	.88	.880	Large	.88	.880	
.74	.740	Mediums	.74	.740	.74	.740	Mediums	.74	.740	

Breaking Stock

Cents Per Dozen - General Trading Prices
Nest Run - Delivered - Net Weights - Material may or may not be included.

Northeast		Midwest	Southeast		So. Central
-	42-44 lbs	-		42-44 lbs	-
.50-.53	48-50 lbs	.50-.53	.51-.54	48-50 lbs	.51-.52
.52-.54	50 lbs. & up	.52-.54	.52-.54	50 lbs. & up	-

UNDERGRADES
B, C, Stains, 46-47 lbs. Picked Up

NE	Avg.	MW	Avg.	SE	Avg.	SC	Avg.
.45	.450	.45	.450	.45	.450	.45	.450

CHECKS
45-46 Lbs. Picked Up

.43	.430	.43	.430	.43	.430	.43	.430

GRADEABLE NEST RUN

Cents Per Dozen — elivered
Packing Material Included

Class	Trading Level	Conver Cost	tCtn Mkt Quote
NORTHEAST			
1	$.7300	$.2235	$.9550
2	.6800	.2535	.9350
3	.5300	.2134	.7450
4	.4300	.1213	.5500
MIDWEST			
1	$.7100	$.2208	$.9300
2	.6700	.2487	.9200
3	.5300	.2142	.7450
4	.4400	.1214	.5600
SOUTHEAST			
1	$.7100	$.2207	$.9300
2	.6700	.2482	.9200
3	.5500	.2120	.7600
4	.4500	.1249	.5750
SOUTH CENTRAL			
1	$.7100	$.2192	$.9300
2	.6700	.2448	.9150
3	.5400	.2159	.7550
4	.4500	.1223	.5700

Fluid Milk
TRUCKLOTS DELIVERED MET N.Y.
Bottling quality per 40 qt unit $11.78-12.04
Bottling Quality per Cwt... 13.87-14.17

Condensed Skim Milk
DELIVERED METRO NEW YORK
Per lb. Solids (SNF) in tnklts .8150-.8300

Fluid Cream
CLASS II or MANUFACTURING
SPOT SALES DELIV. NORTHEAST
Butterfat per lb. in tanklots $1.7650-1.7850

EGG PRODUCTS

Trading in frozen and dried is light. Liquid activity is reasonably good. Whites are firm but yolk products are weak. Some commitments on salted yolks for April-May delivery reported at 63-64 cents per pound, some lower.

Urner Barry Quotations

FROZEN -		
30 Lb. Cans, Per Lb.	**LTL 25 Can Min**	**Trucklots**
Whole, Actual 3	-	$.580-.590
Actual 2		.540-.550
No color	.540-.570	.500-.510
Whites	.370-.400	.330-.350
Yolk, 45% solids -		
Actual, 4	-	1.09-1.10
Actual 3		1.04-1.05
Nepa 3		1.00-1.01
Under Nepa 3	.93-.94	.88-.89
Yolk sugar 43% solids-		
No color	.73-.78	.69-.71
Yolk, salt, 43% solids -		
No color	.68-.70	.65-.67
Blend -		
30-32% egg sol.	.72-.75	.69-.70
27-29% egg sol.	.60-.65	.58-.59

EGG SOLIDS -	L.T.L.	Trucklots
Whole plain	1.65-1.75	1.60-1.65
Yolk	1.65-1.75	1.60-1.65
Albumen, spray	2.80-2.90	2.70-2.80
Blends	1.36-1.40	1.30-1.35

LIQUID EGGS	Tank Carlots Track Per Lb.
Whole, Unpasteurized	.360-.365
Custom Pack, Pasteurized	.480-.500
Whites, Unpasteurized	.280-.290
Custom Pack, Pasteurized	.290-.300
Yolk, 43% solids, Unpasteurized	.610-.620
Custom Pack, 43% Pasteurized	.680-.690
Yolk, Salt 43% solids, 10% salt	-

INSTITUTIONAL PACKS — FROZEN		
PURE PAK Containers 30-32 Lb. Case Wt		
Delivered	L.T.L.	Trucklots
Whole	.620-.650	.580-.600
Whites	-	-
Yolk, sugar	-	-
Blend -		
30-32% egg solids	-	-

Source: Urner Barry Publications, Inc., Toms River, New Jersey. Reprinted with permission.

Exhibit 9 *Urner Barry's Price-Current*, **Friday, April 11, 1986**

URNER BARRY'S Price-Current

Established • 1858 •

Number 70 Friday, April 11, 1986 Volume 129

REGIONAL TABLE GRADE EGGS

Northeast			Midwest	Southeast			So. Central		
Spot Mkt	5-Day Avg	WHITES	Spot Mkt	5-Day Avg	Spot Mkt	5-Day Avg	WHITES	Spot Mkt	5-Day Avg
.67	.688	Jumbos	.66	.676	.67	.688	Jumbos	.68	.692
.66	.678	Extra Large	.65	.666	.66	.678	Extra Large	.67	.682
.66	.678	Large	.65	.666	.66	.678	Large	.67	.682
.59	.600	Mediums	.59	.598	.60	.610	Mediums	.60	.610
.49	.496	Smalls	.49	.494	.50	.506	Smalls	.50	.506
.54	.556	Off Gr Large	.54	.554	.54	.556	Off Gr Large	.55	.560
		BROWN					**BROWN**		
.73	.740	Extra Large	.74	.750	.74	.750	Extra Large	.74	.750
.72	.730	Large	.73	.740	.73	.740	Large	.73	.740
.61	.620	Mediums	.61	.620	.61	.620	Mediums	.61	.620

Breaking Stock

Cents Per Dozen - General Trading Prices
Nest Run - Delivered - Net Weights - Material may or may not be included.

Northeast		Midwest	Southeast	So. Central	
-	42-44 lbs			42-44 lbs	-
.39-.41	48-50 lbs	.39-.41	.39-.41	48-50 lbs	.39-.41
.41-.43	50 lbs. & up	.41-.43	.41-.43	50 lbs. & up	-

UNDERGRADES
B, C, Stains, 46-47 lbs. Picked Up

NE	Avg.	MW	Avg.	SE	Avg.	SC	Avg.
.34	.356	.34	.356	.34	.356	.34	.356

CHECKS
45-46 Lbs. Picked Up

.32	.336	.32	.336	.32	.336	.32	.336

EGG PRODUCTS

Market steady on whites, unsettled on the balance. Buyers are cautious, anticipating lower values due to decreases in raw material costs.

EGG SOLIDS -	L.T.L.	Trucklots
Whole plain	1.59-1.69	1.54-1.59
Yolk	1.55-1.65	1.50-1.57
Albumen, spray	3.10-3.20	2.95-3.05
Blends	1.28-1.33	1.22-1.27

Urner Barry Quotations

FROZEN -

30 Lb. Cans, Per Lb.	LTL 25 Can Min	Trucklots
Whole, Actual 3	-	$.580-.590
Actual 2	-	.540-.550
No color	.500-.530	.450-.470
Whites	.380-.410	.350-.360
Yolk, 45% solids -		
Actual, 4	-	1.07-1.09
Actual 3	-	1.02-1.03
Nepa 3	-	.98-.99
Under Nepa 3	.90-.91	.85-.86
Yolk sugar 43% solids-		
No color	.71-.76	.67-.69
Yolk, salt, 43% solids -		
No color	.64-.67	.62-.64
Blend -		
30-32% egg sol.	.72-.75	.69-.70
27-29% egg sol.	.60-.65	.56-.59

LIQUID EGGS	Tank Carlots Track Per Lb.
Whole, Unpasteurized	.330-.340
Custom Pack, Pasteurized	.440-.450
Whites, Unpasteurized	.295-.305
Custom Pack, Pasteurized	.310-.320
Yolk, 43% solids, Unpasteurized	.590-.600
Custom Pack, 43% Pasteurized	.650-.660
Yolk, Salt 43% solids, 10% salt	

INSTITUTIONAL PACKS — FROZEN

PURE PAK Containers 30-32 Lb. Case Wt

Delivered	L.T.L.	Trucklots
Whole	.590-.620	.550-.570
Whites	-	-
Yolk, sugar	-	-
Blend -		
30-32% egg solids	-	-

BUTTER

URNER BARRY QUOTATIONS
Based on extensive country-wide trade reports & other terminal market wholesale transactions.

TRUCKLOTS BULK Deliv East (Spot Mkt.)	SALT	SALES FROM WAREHOUSES 1 Pound Solids	1 Pound Quarters
$1.4200	.....93 Score (AA)	$1.4300-1.5300	$1.4700-1.5700*
1.4150	.....92 Score (A)	1.4250-1.5250	1.4650-1.5650*
1.3725	.....90 Score (B)	1.3825-1.4825	1.4225-1.5225

Midwest
Loads & Pool Loads Delivered (Bulk)

93 Score	92 Score	90 Score
$1.3900	$1.3850	$1.3425

*Should have read same since March 14th

CHEESE

CHEDDARS —WHOLE MILK —POUNDS

	EX SHARP	SHARP	MEDIUM	MILD
Blocks	$1.82-2.18	$1.6750-1.7950	$1.59-1.75	$1.3750-1.8125
Daisies	-	-	1.75-2.05	1.5375-1.5900
Splits	-	-	-	1.5000-1.6800
Midgets	-	1.78-2.18	1.73-1.85	1.4825-1.6700
Flats	1.93-2.18	1.79-1.83	-	
		(CURRENT)		
Proc. 5 lb loaf	-	-	-	1.3450-1.5200
Proc. 5 lb sliced	-	-	-	1.3850-1.6800
Muenster	-	-	-	1.4050-1.6775

Source: Urner Barry Publications, Inc., Toms River, New Jersey. Reprinted with permission.

$$\text{Price per gallon} = \text{Price per 40 quarts} \times \frac{4 \text{ quarts}}{1 \text{ gallon}}$$

$$\text{Price per gallon} = \$14.02 \text{ (mid-range)} \times \frac{4 \text{ quarts}}{1 \text{ gallon}}$$

$$\text{Price per gallon} = \$1.402$$

The buyer then can request competitive quotations from bottlers at a markup (or spread) over this base figure of $1.402. Assuming that packaging, processing, overhead, and distribution costs total $.60 per gallon:

Base cost	$1.402/gallon
Packaging, processing, overhead, and distribution	.60/gallon estimated
Approximate delivered cost, Metro New York area	$2.002/gallon

Example 2: Butter

Fresh butter is traded on the Chicago Mercantile Exchange. Exhibit 7 shows that the price is $1.3825–1.3975 per pound for AA quality butter in truckloads. Exhibit 9 quotes the price for the Midwest at $1.39. The Chicago price reflects surplus production from Wisconsin and Minnesota and provides the driving force behind butter prices all over the country.

Exhibit 9 shows truckload bulk (delivered east—spot market) butter AA quality at $1.42 per pound. The 3¢ premium over the Chicago price ($1.39) represents transportation costs. Midwest butter prices should be used as a base for cost calculations, but local production conditions must also be taken into consideration.

For example, the cost of $1.39 per pound in Exhibit 9 is a bulk price. The butter must be transported to the buyer's area, converted to its serving form, and delivered when needed. Therefore, there are four cost elements to consider: (1) cost of the bulk butter (which relates to support prices); (2) transportation costs; (3) processing costs to convert the bulk butter to serving forms; and (4) local distribution costs. Buyers should negotiate markups or spreads over these base prices as explained in the fluid milk example.

Example 3: Cheese

Urner Barry's Price-Current publishes price quotes which can be used as a cost guide for a number of cheese varieties. For example, processed cheese (5 pounds sliced) is quoted in Exhibit 9 at $1.385–1.68. Because of its color and melting qualities, processed cheese is the standard product used for cheeseburgers. Flavor can vary a great deal among the products offered by different processors; actual tests should determine how well specific cheeses meet an operation's needs.

Imported natural cheeses are usually more expensive than similar varieties produced domestically. However, the quality differences may not always support the cost differences. Buyers must test products to guarantee that flavor and other characteristics meet their properties' quality requirements.

Buyers must know their needs, communicate them to suppliers, and check incoming products against purchase specifications. For instance, mozzarella is a popular cheese variety with pizza restaurant operators. When purchasing mozzarella, operators should realize that cheese made from whole milk is more expensive than that made from skim milk and that moisture content affects prices.

Synthetic or imitation products seem destined to take a larger market share. Buyers can expect to find costs of imitation products below those of their "natural" counterparts. At the moment, imitation cheeses are making their biggest inroads in replacing mozzarella and processed American cheeses. Imitation products are also being promoted directly to consumers as low in cholesterol.

As with the purchase of any product, procedures for buying dairy products depend on an operation's volume requirements and the purchasing system used. A thorough understanding of how prices are developed and adjusted enables the buyer to make better purchases.

For dairy products, government involvement tends to stabilize prices, at least in the short run. The best overall procedure by which a purchaser can ensure the lowest price is to schedule products for bid periodically, perhaps annually. As previously explained in this chapter, buyers should request that bids be based on a known market indicator. For fluid milk, the best indicator may be the Class I price in the applicable support-price area. For items such as butter and cheese, consulting a Midwest commodity exchange price may be useful. Market indicators act as a baseline for judging price increases in the bids received. During the life of the bid, price changes may be linked to changes in the price of raw materials reflected in these market indicators.

Endnotes

1. *Federal and State Standards for the Composition of Milk Products.* Agricultural Handbook No. 51, USDA Food Safety and Quality Service. Washington, D.C., January 1, 1980.

REVIEW QUIZ

When you feel you have covered all of the material in this chapter, answer these questions. Choose the *best* answer. Check your answers with the correct ones found on the Review Quiz Answer Key at the end of this book.

True (T) or False (F)

(T)   F   1. Pasteurization is a method of making milk safe for human consumption.

T   (F)   2. The milk industry is loosely regulated and seldom inspected.

T   (F)   3. There are no products that can be successfully substituted for dairy foods.

T   (F)   4. The relative content of fat and vitamins remains unchanged in processing milk.

(T)   F   5. Federal standards require that butter contain at least 80% milk fat.

(T)   F   6. States may establish resale prices for milk.

(T)   F   7. Grade A for milk denotes wholesomeness rather than quality.

Multiple Choice

8. Fat globules in whole milk are broken into finer particles and permanently suspended in fluid by a process known as:

    a. pasteurization.
    b. evaporation.
    (c.) homogenization.
    d. fortification.

Chapter Outline

Government Regulation of Fresh Produce
    Specifications and Quality Control of
        Fresh Produce
Fresh Fruits
    Apples
    Apricots
    Avocados
    Bananas
    Berries
    Cherries
    Citrus Fruits
    Coconuts
    Grapes
    Melons
    Nectarines
    Peaches
    Pears
    Pineapples
    Plums
    Fruit Sections and Salad Mixes
Fresh Vegetables
    Artichokes
    Asparagus
    Beans
    Broccoli
    Brussels Sprouts
    Cabbage
    Carrots
    Celery
    Corn
    Cucumbers
    Salad Greens
    Onions
    Peppers
    Potatoes
    Sweet Potatoes
    Tomatoes
Distribution of Fresh Produce
Pricing and Yields of Fresh Produce
    Iceberg Lettuce
    Repack Tomatoes
    Baking Potatoes
    Pricing Factors
The Processed Fruits and Vegetables
    Industry
    Government Regulation
    Specifications and Quality Control
    Distribution
    Pricing and Yields
    Price Forecasting

Learning Objectives

1. Explain government regulation of the fresh produce industry.

2. Outline the major categories of fresh fruits, focusing on varieties, growing areas, maturity, and storage factors.

3. List important characteristics of citrus fruits.

4. Describe principal types of melons.

5. Outline the major categories of fresh vegetables in terms of growing areas, availability, and quality factors.

6. Distinguish among various types of salad greens.

7. Explain the marketing of fresh produce.

8. Describe fresh produce in terms of distribution options, processing, and packaging.

9. Explain the pricing of fresh produce and the influence of yield on costs.

10. Identify various organizations within the processed fruits and vegetables industry.

11. Describe government regulation of the processed fruits and vegetables industry.

12. Explain the need for specifications and quality control when buying processed fruits and vegetables.

13. Describe distribution patterns for processed fruits and vegetables.

14. Explain the pricing of processed fruits and vegetables.

13

Fruits and Vegetables

THE UNITED STATES, with over 2.3 billion acres devoted to agriculture, efficiently produces a wide variety of fruits and vegetables in great abundance. California, while containing less than 3% of the nation's farms, produces between 25 and 30% of the United States' table food.

Fresh fruit and vegetable production is seasonal. From October through March, the East Coast of the United States draws from outside sources, purchasing items from Florida, Texas, Mexico, and California. During the summer, these same eastern states—New Jersey, New York, Ohio, and the mid- Atlantic states—supply fresh products to other areas. This seasonal pattern is repeated throughout the country.

Certain crops are produced only once annually (for instance, berries, peaches, pears, and apples). They are harvested within a relatively short time and, depending upon their harvest volume and holding qualities, may not be available year-round. The price for these items is established during harvest and varies based on storage costs and availability. Crop prices for multi-annual vegetables can fluctuate dramatically depending on their availability, which is greatly affected by the weather.

When the weather is good, availability is high and prices are low. When the weather is poor, availability is low and prices are high. Products harvested when the fields are wet may be dirty, prematurely rotted, and undersized due to lack of sunlight. Ironically, this is usually when prices are highest because demand exceeds supply.

Supply and demand of fresh produce affects the canning and frozen food industries as well. The food processing industry is small and tightly knit. The number of companies is shrinking as consolidation occurs. There are few secrets concerning such factors as pack intentions (expected production levels) and plant capacity. Employees are constantly moving between companies within the industry. Buyers must have contacts within the processing industry to develop a feel for the business.

Government Regulation of Fresh Produce

Government involvement in the marketing of fresh fruits and vegetables attempts to (1) ensure fair competition, (2) establish standard terminology to improve communications between buyers and sellers, (3) develop protective legislation to help correlate production with demand, and (4) produce consumer legislation concerned with unfair supplier practices and the purity of products.

The Federal Trade Commission (FTC) helps protect the free enterprise system. Although the FTC has in some cases been concerned with fresh product marketing (primarily in the relationships between principals, brokers, and buyers), fresh fruits and vegetables are not a major concern of this agency. Instead, the USDA's Agricultural Marketing Service (AMS) is involved in grading produce, establishing standards, and stabilizing prices.

The Perishable Agricultural Commodity Act of 1930 defines marketing terms and terminology. Standards for appearance, condition, and product quality grew out of this act and now form the basis for trading. Almost every product has U. S. standards, and some may have state requirements as well. Florida oranges, Idaho potatoes, and Washington apples are subject to state standards that are generally more restrictive than federal levels.

Terminology with regard to fruits and vegetables is important. For example, "quality" refers to specific product characteristics, maturity, color, and lack of blemishes. "Condition" relates to factors that change (such as decay). The product's "grade" is the sum of specific factors checked at inspection.

The Agricultural Marketing Agreement Act of 1937 authorizes "marketing orders," which attempt to balance production with demand. Some orders provide funds to expand markets and others establish minimum grades that can be shipped. Establishing minimum grades requires compulsory inspection to determine grades at the time of shipment. Some states have their own "orders" which operate in a similar fashion to the federal orders. Buyers sometimes view marketing orders as devices which restrict production and therefore hamper competition. Growers, on the other hand, view them as a means to protect investments and to maintain profit levels.

Both the USDA and the FDA have some legislative responsibility to protect the public from contaminated products. Pesticide residues must be kept below defined levels and insect infestation must be controlled. Freezes which damage products may cause temporary embargoes. The best consumer protection device, however, may be free competition within the marketplace which eliminates marginal or low-quality producers. Buyers must protect their companies by issuing clear specifications and by performing intensive inspections when products are received.

Specifications and Quality Control of Fresh Produce

Buyers should base specifications on USDA standards. Two or more grades have been established for most products. Generally, the top grade is U.S. #1, U.S. Fancy, or U.S. Extra Fancy. Shippers are not required by law to continuously inspect and establish grades. However, inspectors are located in the major producing areas and perform specific shipment inspections at the buyer's request. The request is transmitted through the supplier and some delay in shipment may occur if the inspector is not located on-site.

The remainder of this chapter provides information helpful in developing specifications and in understanding government standards.

Fresh Fruits

Hospitality operations use a great variety of fresh fruits. Because fruits are highly perishable, their purchase requires constant attention in order to obtain and preserve quality. The following section discusses the most popular types of fresh fruits. Exhibit 1 gives U.S. grades, typical pack sizes, and storage characteristics for most of these fresh fruits.

Apples

Major varieties of apples include Red Delicious, Golden Delicious, McIntosh, Rome, Jonathan, York, and Winesap. Apples should be selected according to use, such as freezing, baking, making into sauce or pies, or eating fresh. Some varieties are considered all-purpose (for instance, Winesap, McIntosh, and Jonathan), while others are best suited for a single purpose (for example, the Delicious varieties, which are principally eaten fresh).

The largest producers of apples are Washington, New York, Michigan, California, Pennsylvania, and Virginia. Controlled atmosphere storage using CO_2 gas permits year-round availability. Apples may be stored for a long time, but storage conditions affect quality.

USDA grades cover color, maturity, and condition. Condition is determined by inspection for blemishes, conformation (shape), and general appearance. Maturity relates to the time of the apple harvest and is checked by means of a pressure test. Refractometers can be used to measure sugar levels, which indicate the degree of maturity. Grades may be used in combination. Only consecutive grades can be packed (for example, U.S. Fancy and U.S. #1) and the lot must have at least 50% of the higher grade.

Apricots

Primary varieties of apricots are Moorpack, Royal, and Tilton. Moorpack is a sweet, medium-sized apricot with light amber flesh. Royal is a small apricot with sweet, reddish-yellow flesh. Tilton is a large apricot with light flesh and a tart flavor. Blenheim, King Derby, and Perfection are other popular varieties. Fresh apricots are primarily grown in California and are available from June through August.

Golden orange color, plumpness, and firmness are indications of good quality. Apricots develop flavor and sweetness on the tree and should be mature but firm when picked. A greenish tint implies immaturity as does overly firm fruit. Dull appearance, mushiness, and wrinkled texture all indicate overmaturity. Apricots are fragile and should be used within ten days after harvest. The ripening process may be accelerated by temperatures from 65°F (18°C) to 75°F (24°C).

Avocados

There are over 500 different varieties of avocados. The most popular include Fuerte, Hass, and Booth 7 and 8. Fuerte is a California-grown avocado that is pear-shaped with thin, pliable green skin. It generally weighs from 8 to 16 ounces and its season lasts from October to March. Hass is a California summer variety with medium-thick, leathery, rough skin. It is green at maturity but turns black when ready to eat. Hass is more nearly round than the Fuerte variety. Booth 7 and 8 are Florida-grown varieties. Booth 7 is rounded and bright green, while Booth 8 is oblong and medium green.

Exhibit 1   Fresh Fruit—U.S. Grades, Pack Sizes, and Storage Characteristics

Product	U.S. Grades	Pack Sizes	Storage Characteristics
Apples	Extra Fancy, Fancy, #1, and Utility	Loose in cartons weighing 38 to 40 pounds, or tray pack cartons weighing 40 to 45 pounds. Counts range from 48 to 198 per carton.	Soften rapidly in warm temperatures. Store at temperatures around 30°F (−1°C).
Apricots	#1 and #2	Lugs weighing 24 to 26 pounds.	Store at temperatures from 32°F (0°C) to 36°F (2°C).
Avocados	#1, Combo, #2, and #3 (grades for Florida only)	California packs—one-layer flats weighing 12 1/2 pounds with counts of 9 to 35 per flat. California and Florida pack double-layer 25-pound lugs with counts of 18 to 96.	Ripen at room temperature, then refrigerate until use.
Bananas	No U.S. grades	Cartons of 40 pounds in assorted sizes; some markets offer a uniform 150 count per carton in petite size.	Bananas should be purchased at the ripeness stage that will hold until anticipated usage.
Blackberries/ Raspberries	#1 and #2	Normally packed in 12-pint flats with overfilled baskets.	Store at 32°F (0°C) with 90% relative humidity.
Blueberries	#1	Shipped in 12-pint flats with overfilled baskets.	Store at 32°F (0°C) with 90% relative humidity.
Cantaloupes	Fancy, #1, Commercial, and #2	Half crates weighing 38 to 41 pounds; 2/3 crates weighing 53 to 55 pounds; and full crates weighing 75 to 85 pounds. Counts range from 12 to 46 depending on container size.	Store at 40°F (4°C).
Cherries	#1 and Commercial	Normally shipped in 20-pound lugs.	Refrigerate at 34°F (1°C).
Coconuts	No U.S. grades	Usually sold by the dozen.	Refrigerate at 34°F (1°C).
Cranberries	#1	Typically packed in cartons of 24 one-pound units and 25-pound bulk.	Store at 32°F (0°C) with 90% relative humidity.
Grapefruit	Fancy, #1, Combo, #2, and #3	All areas—7/10 bushel cartons weighing between 38 and 42 pounds with counts ranging from 23 to 64.	Store at 50°F (10°C).
Grapes	Fancy, #1 Table Grapes, and #1 Juice Grapes	Weights vary by shipping area. Normally shipped in flats weighing 17 to 20 pounds and lugs weighing 20 to 26 pounds.	Store near 32°F (0°C) with 90% relative humidity.
Honeydews	#1, Commercial, and #2	Bliss cartons (29 to 32 pounds) or 2/3 cartons (5 to 10 melons with total weight of 30 to 34 pounds)	Honeydews may have to be pre-ripened by letting stand in a warm room for several hours (or days).
Lemons	#1, #1 Export, Combo, and #2	Standard cartons described for grapefruit, weighing between 37 and 40 pounds. Standard counts range from 63 to 235 per carton (115, 145, 165, and 200 counts are most popular).	Store at 50°F (10°C).

Exhibit 1 *(continued)*

Product	U.S. Grades	Pack Sizes	Storage Characteristics
Limes	#1 and Combo	Cartons weighing 10, 20, and 40 pounds. Counts range from 72 to 126 for 20-pound cartons (96 and 108 counts are most popular).	Store at 50°F (10°C).
Nectarines	Fancy, Extra #1, #1, and #2	Generally packed in two-layer lugs of 20 pounds. Counts range from 50 to 84.	Refrigerate at 35°F (2°C).
Oranges	Fancy, #1, Combo, and #2	Standard fruit cartons with counts ranging from 48 to 162 (mandarin orange counts generally 176 or 210).	Refrigerate at 35°F (2°C).
Peaches	Fancy, Extra #1, #1, and #2	Boxes weighing 17 to 18 pounds with counts ranging from 40 to 65; Los Angeles Lug (two-layer) weighing 18 to 23 pounds with counts ranging from 50 to 80.	Peaches ripen rapidly at room temperature. Refrigerate at 32°F (0°C).
Pears	Extra #1, #1, Combo, and #2	Cartons weighing 44 to 45 pounds with counts ranging from 80 to 165; 100 count is a popular eating size.	Store at 40°F (1°C).
Pineapples	Fancy, #1, and #2	Cartons weighing 40 pounds with counts of 8-9-10-12-14-16; ½ cartons weighing 20 pounds with counts of 4-5-6-7.	Store at room temperature to ripen, then hold at 45°F (7°C).
Plums	#1	Usually packed in 28-pound lugs with counts ranging from 126 to 225.	Refrigerate at 34°F (1°C).
Strawberries	#1, Combo, and #2	Normally packed in 12-pint flats with baskets heaped.	Store at 32°F (0°C) with 90% relative humidity.
Watermelons	Fancy, #1, and #2	Usually sold individually with a minimum weight specification of 20 pounds recommended.	Store at 65°F (18°C).

Avocados are primarily grown in California, Florida, and Mexico. They are available year-round with some short supply occurring during the summer. Like bananas, avocados continue to ripen after they are picked. They should be purchased green, ripened at room temperature, and then refrigerated until use. An avocado is ripe if it yields to gentle pressure or if a toothpick can be inserted into the stem cavity easily and without forcing. Fruit with dark sunken spots or cracks should be avoided.

Bananas

The leading banana variety is the Cavendish. Bananas for U.S. consumption are produced primarily in Costa Rica, Honduras, Ecuador, and Mexico; they are available year-round. Bananas ripen and develop flavor after picking and, therefore, are picked green. Controlled conditions of temperature and humidity are required to properly time the ripening process. Trade designations identify the stages of ripeness by color number:

Number	Characteristics
1	Green peel color
2	Light green peel, breaking slightly toward yellow
3	Yellowish-green peel
4	Greenish-yellow peel, more yellow than green
5	Yellow peel with green tips
6	Yellow peel
7	Yellow peel, flecked with brown

Cooling slows the ripening process, but temperatures of less than 50°F (10°C) cause the skin to turn dark. While the flesh may not be affected, the appearance is unacceptable to most consumers. Other quality concerns include uniform size and lack of blemishes.

Berries

Generally, the term "berry" refers to a fleshy fruit of small size, irrespective of its structure. (Actually, true berries include the banana, grape, and tomato; however, we will use the term in its general sense.) Berries are fragile and have a short shelf life.

Blueberries. Blueberries are generally available from the Northwest, Michigan, and New Jersey from May through September. Maine and Nova Scotia ship a wild variety which is smaller, firmer, more tart, and has better holding characteristics.

Berries should be plump, firm, dry, mold-free, and uniform in size. Look for dark blue color and a silvery bloom. Signs of deterioration include dull appearance, softness, and mold.

Strawberries. Strawberry varieties and appearance vary by production area. Mexican berries are small, contain excess seeds, and may be less well-formed. Florida ships small berries which are usually cleaner and more flavorful. California ships the best "holding" berries. Strawberries are often available year-round.

Fruit should be bright and dry without mold. Unlike other berries which lose their hulls, the strawberry's "cap" (calyx) should remain attached when properly mature.

Blackberries and Raspberries. Blackberries and raspberries are usually available only on a local basis for very short periods of time. They have the same general appearance, and are more fragile than strawberries. Berries should be firm, plump, and free of hulls.

Cranberries. Massachusetts and Wisconsin are the primary producers of cranberries, which are available from September through January. Color designates maturity but different varieties mature at different color levels. Berries should be firm and packs should contain minimal leaf and twig residue. Watch for worm damage.

Cranberries hold particularly well in storage and keep longer than other berries, but should be refrigerated nonetheless.

Cherries

The principal sweet cherry varieties are Bing and Lambert, and primary growing areas include California, Oregon, Washington, and Idaho. Sour cherry varieties include Montmorency and English Morello; Michigan is a major producer of sour cherries. Cherries are available May through July. Many varieties are used for freezing and canning.

Cherries are delicate and must be handled with care to avoid bruising the fruit. Fresh, firm, juicy, and flavorful fruit is of prime quality. Dull appearance, shriveling, and softness are indicative of overripe fruit.

Citrus Fruits

The buyer should look for certain characteristics in all citrus. Heavy weight is a desirable characteristic, while rough skin and misshapen fruit are indicators of poor quality. All citrus should be mature and ready to use when picked.

Grapefruits. The best grapefruits are grown in Florida, whose season runs from October to June. The Marsh seedless is the most popular Florida-grown variety. The Rio Grande Valley area in Texas has a fruit season roughly parallel to Florida's and grows the same varieties, though in much smaller quantities. Summer grapefruit is available from California and Arizona, but this product usually has a heavy rind, is more pulpy, and is less flavorful than Florida varieties.

Quality is best determined by weight and appearance. Grapefruit should be well-formed; rough or uneven skin and bulges (particularly at the stem end) denote thick skin. Fruit with such bulges is termed "nosey" and should be avoided. There should be no soft spots, which indicate decay. A desirable characteristic is heavy fruit, a sign of juiciness. Light or puffy fruit generally has pulpy, tasteless flesh. Exterior skin coloring may be important for plate appeal but has little bearing on fruit quality. Grapefruit is never artificially colored.

While a $^7/_{10}$ bushel carton is the standard packing size, Texas ships some fruit in $1^2/_5$ bushel double cartons. Florida also uses a 45-pound, $^4/_5$ bushel. Care should be taken to specify carton size because of its effect on count and, therefore, size.

Lemons. California and Arizona grow most of the U.S. supply of fresh lemons. Florida produces lemons for processing into beverages and food products. Supplies of fresh lemons are available year-round.

Best quality is exhibited by well-formed, bright yellow lemons with a tight waxy skin. A greenish cast usually indicates very fresh fruit with higher acidity. Deep yellow lemons are usually more mature than lemons with lighter color. Coarse or rough skin indicates thick skin and less juice. Fruit should be free of sunburn, scars, or decay. Large, puffy fruit is generally lacking in flavor.

Limes. There are two principal lime types: Tahiti and Mexican. Persian is the most extensively grown commercial variety of Tahiti. Tahiti types are large, seedless, and light greenish-yellow when ripe. By contrast, Mexican types have small fruit with thin rinds; the Key lime is an example. Mexican import varieties are green when picked and turn yellow when ripe. Limes mature more or less throughout the year, but the primary season for Mexican types is late fall to spring.

Oranges. Florida is the primary source of oranges but California and Arizona produce some excellent varieties for eating fresh. Much of Florida's production is further processed into juice or salad mixes. California and Arizona fruit generally have heavier rinds than Florida varieties. Early season fruit is usually more tart and higher in acid content, while later varieties are sweeter.

Valencia is the premier juice orange. Juice labels provide worthwhile information on juice composition. "100% fresh" means that the product was made from fresh oranges while "100% Valencia" means that the product was made from that variety only. "From concentrate" means the product was reconstituted from frozen concentrate, which could have been produced in the United States or imported from a foreign source.

Russeting (spotting) on Florida fruit does not denote a quality problem; however, fruit with dull, dry skin and soft, spongy texture should be avoided. Regreening (a chlorophyll transfer to the skin) does not indicate a quality problem, but some customers find it objectionable. Florida growers may dip fruit in a dye to yield the typical orange color. Fruit so handled must be labeled "color added."

State associations of orange growers, aided by USDA personnel, control quality and are very careful not to permit below-grade merchandise to be shipped to other states. However, different growing areas may use different size cartons; 64 count per carton oranges from Florida may be a different size compared with the same count from Arizona. A good eating size is California 88s. Typical salad sizes are Florida 64s or 80s.

Mandarins. This category is generally divided among three classifications of oranges: Tangerines, Satsumas (the primary Japanese variety), and miscellaneous hybrids such as the Tangelo (a grapefruit/tangerine cross) and the Tangors (a group which includes the Temple). Mandarins are easily peeled fruits that come primarily from Florida. Store at temperatures between 38°F (3°C) and 40°F (4°C).

Coconuts

Coconuts come to the United States year-round, with peak availability in October, November, and December. Growing areas include Mexico and Central America.

Good quality coconuts are heavy for their size. Shake the coconut to hear the milk inside. Coconuts without milk have spoiled. Also avoid coconuts with wet or moldy "eyes" (the three soft spots at the top of the shell).

Grapes

California grape varieties, originally imported from Europe, today constitute the primary commercial production in the United States. Imports fill the gap in American production from February to May.

There are two major categories of domestic grapes: Eastern types (American) and Western types (European). Western types have tight skins, and the seeds are easily removed. They have good flavor and can be stored for up to four months under the proper conditions. Primary varieties include:

- Thompson Seedless—A sweet, white-green grape with a small olive shape. It is probably the most important variety.

- Flame Tokay—A sweet, bright red grape which is large and round and contains seeds. A seedless hybrid is also available.

- Cardinal—A sweet, bright red grape which contains seeds.

- Emperor—A large, sweet grape with a cherry flavor. Emperor is the main storage variety of fresh grapes. It is dark red in color and seeded.

Eastern types have a loose skin, but the seeds adhere to the pulp. They do not keep well in storage and are used primarily for juice and jellies. Primary varieties include:

- Concord—A sweet, seeded grape which is blue or black. It is the principal American variety.

- Delaware—A small, pink, seeded grape.

- Catawba—A large, purplish-red grape with seeds. It is used primarily for juice and wine.

Grapes should be picked near maturity since they do not ripen further when removed from the vine. Color is a good indicator of ripeness: mature red grapes show no tinge of green, and white varieties should have an amber color. Grapes should be soft to the touch and the seeds should be brown (not green). Select bunches that are well-formed and have a uniform appearance. Stems should be green and easily bent; in storage, however, stems become brown and brittle. No wet berries or mold should be present.

Melons

Melons represent a large and diverse group of fruits. Newly developed varieties continue to be introduced into the market. The following types of melons are of particular interest to buyers.

Cantaloupes. There are many different varieties of cantaloupes (sometimes called muskmelons). Hales Best is the most popular commercial variety. California, Arizona, and Texas are the primary growers of cantaloupes, which are generally available May through September. Mexico provides fruit early in the season.

Melon maturity is judged by the following characteristics:

- The stem should be completely gone leaving a smooth, shallow basin (called full slip). If part of the stem remains (half slip) or the entire stem remains (green), the melon was picked before maturity. Specify full slip.

- Netting on the rind should be coarse, heavy, and raised.

- The rind between the netting should be a buff brown or pale yellow.

A full, ripe melon has a pleasant odor and may yield slightly to pressure at the blossom end. Its seeds may rattle if shaken.

Casaba. This melon is harvested in California and Arizona from late June to November. Shaped like a pumpkin, it has a ridged and furrowed rind. When ripe, the outside is yellow and the flesh is white. It is sweet and juicy, weighing from 6 to 8 pounds. The stem does not separate from the melon and must be cut when harvested. Casaba melons may be packed in Bliss cartons (4, 5, or 6 melons weighing a total of 32 to 34 pounds) or flat crates (5 or 6 melons weighing a total of 48 to 51 pounds).

Crenshaw. Crenshaw melons are grown in California and are available July through October. Some fruit is imported from Mexico in the off-season. Fruit should be picked at the full slip stage. The rind should be a deep golden yellow with lighter yellow flecks, and the flesh should be orange. The fruit should yield slightly to pressure at the blossom end and have a slight aroma. Weight averages from 4 to 9 pounds. Crenshaw melons may be packed in Bliss cartons (4, 5, 6, or 8 melons weighing a total of 32 to 34 pounds) or in flat crates weighing 35 to 50 pounds.

Honeydews. Primary producing areas are Texas, Mexico, Arizona, and California with some off-season fruit coming from South America. The best fruit usually comes from the western California valleys. Normal availability is from June to October with imports available part of the off-season.

Honeydew is a smooth-rinded melon, oval to round in shape and weighing 4 to 8 pounds. Melons vary from creamy white to creamy yellow with a slight oily film on the exterior. The flesh is mild, green-tinted, and firm.

Maturity is determined at time of picking, and the melon should be full or half slip. Honeydews ripen after picking, yielding melons with a distinct, pleasing aroma. Mature fruit has a velvety feel, and ripeness is determined by pressure tests and aroma of the fruit. Large melons usually have the best flavor.

Watermelons. There are many watermelon varieties but the Charleston and Thurmont Gray are among the most important. The East Coast receives watermelons from Florida, Georgia, North and South Carolina, Virginia, and Maryland. California produces most of the western fruit, but Texas, Arizona, and Mexico also ship their production. Domestic supplies are available from May through September with imports extending the season somewhat.

Appearance, size, and variety determine watermelon quality. Melons should have a velvety, glossy finish. The underside should be a yellowish-white color. Fruit should be well-formed and free of sunburn, hail marks, or "hollow heart" (a white, hard core running though the fruit). Mature fruit generally has black or brown seeds.

Nectarines

Nectarines are stone fruits with the stone (pit) either cling or free. Nectarines are closely related to peaches; in fact, many nectarine varieties have been cross-bred with peaches to achieve large size and firmness. California is the primary nectarine producer. Nectarines do not become sweeter after harvest and must be mature when picked. Red colors do not indicate ripeness; look instead for yellow between the red areas, fullness, and moderate hardness.

Peaches

There are hundreds of peach varieties grown. The freestone is most commonly used for eating fresh. The Fay Elberta is probably the best known freestone variety. Primary peach-producing areas are California, Georgia, West Virginia, and Michigan. Availability is from May (California) to October (Washington).

Fruit should be plump and well-formed with a yellow to reddish blush. Green color indicates immaturity. Spots, bruises, or resin accumulations detract from quality.

Peaches are highly perishable with a shelf life of two to three weeks after picking. Many shippers pick just prior to maturity and then "hydrocool" (shower with ice water) to retard ripening and reduce decay in transit. Buyers should specify precooled products and should cut a sample peach to determine its condition.

Pears

Pears primarily come from California, Oregon, and Washington. Four varieties of pears account for most U.S. production:

- The Bartlett, known as the summer pear, is bell-shaped, with a thin skin which is clear yellow when ripe. The flesh is white and juicy. This pear is available July through November.

- The D'Anjou has a short stem end, yellow-white flesh, and a spicy sweet flavor. When mature, this pear may be yellow, yellow-green, or green. It stores well and is available from October to May.

- The Bosc has a dark yellow, cinnamon color, with a long tapered stem end and juicy yellow-white flesh. Good for eating fresh and baking, it is available from September to February.

- The Comice has greenish-yellow skin and a round shape, with very fine and juicy flesh. It is available from September to February.

Pears are picked green but mature; they continue to ripen off the tree. Maturity before picking is determined by refractometer readings and firmness. Ripeness is also judged by color.

Pineapples

Hawaii, Mexico, Central America, and the Philippines are the primary suppliers of pineapples to the United States. Hawaiian products are generally better since fruit from the Caribbean areas has higher acidity and is less sweet. Pineapples are available year-round but their peak season is between April and June.

Pineapples are picked green but fully mature, and do not sweeten after harvest. Appearance and aroma are the best ripeness indicators. The fruit should be dry with no bruise spots. It should yield under slight pressure, but should not be overly soft on the butt end. It should be golden brown with a slight piney aroma. Storing pineapples after harvest results in softening and a change of color, which is often equated with "ripeness." Pineapples have three stages of ripeness:

- Hard—green fruit, may require seven days to ripen

- Half ripe—turning (ripening), three or four days needed

- Full ripe—brown, ready to eat

Size is not an indication of maturity but large fruit is generally sweeter and provides a better yield. Eyes should be firm and the spikes or leaves should be fresh and green. Caribbean fruit is usually a pale brown. Pacific fruit develops a darker shade.

Plums

There are two major varieties of plums: Japanese and European. Japanese plums are medium to large and never blue or purple. European plums are smaller than the Japanese variety and always blue or purple. About 75% of the world's supply of plums is grown in California. Plums should have good color for the variety and should be soft enough to yield to slight pressure.

Fruit Sections and Salad Mixes

Many different types of fresh, peeled fruit are available. The most popular are orange, grapefruit, and pineapple sections. Primary considerations are types of fruit, method of peeling, and type of preservative. Cold rather than hot peel is considered best. Sodium benzoate is the usual preservative but if too much is used, it affects taste. Most of these products are shelf stable when stored at 38°F (3°C) for extended periods of time. They can help bridge the summer season quite nicely.

Fresh Vegetables

Fresh vegetables are increasingly being served in food service operations ranging from hotel food service to fast-food operations. In the following pages, the most commonly used vegetables are discussed. In addition, Exhibit 2 gives U.S. grades, typical pack sizes, and storage characteristics for most of these fresh vegetables.

Artichokes

The main artichoke variety is Green Globe. California is the primary producer of artichokes, which are available year-round. Good green color and plump globes are the most important quality considerations.

Asparagus

Asparagus is available from March through June, primarily from California and New Jersey. Different terminology is used to identify the various sizes. California sizes are used most often and include:

Exhibit 2   Fresh Vegetables—U.S. Grades, Pack Sizes, and Storage Characteristics

Product	U.S. Grades	Pack Sizes	Storage Characteristics
Artichokes	#1 and #2	Cartons weighing 20 to 25 pounds with counts ranging from 18 to 60.	Store at 38°F (3°C).
Asparagus	#1 and #2	Bunched (approximately 12 bunches of 2 pounds each per crate) or loose (30 pounds per case).	Packed upright in crates with a moist base to preserve quality.
Beans	Fancy, #1, combo, and #2	Cartons or baskets weighing from 26 to 31 pounds.	May be held for short period between 45°F (7°C) and 50°F (10°C).
Broccoli	Fancy, #1, and #2	Half cartons containing 14 to 18 bunches (each weigh 1 1/2 pounds).	Store at 34°F (1°C).
Brussels Sprouts	#1 and #2	Pint containers (12 per tray, or about 9 pounds); 25-pound cartons.	Store at 34°F (1°C).
Cabbage	#1 and Commercial	Cartons or bags weighing 50 to 60 pounds; Savoy cabbage normally packed in 40-pound cartons.	Store at 34°F (1°C).
Carrots	A, B, #1, and Commercial	Varies, most commonly packed as 48 one-pound units and bulk bags weighing 25 to 50 pounds.	Store at 34°F (1°C).
Celery	Extra, #1, and #2	Cartons or wire bound crates of 60 pounds, with counts of 18, 24, 30, 36, or 48 bunches.	Store at 32°F (0°C).
Corn	Fancy, #1, and #2	Wire bound crates of 50 pounds; counts range from 54 to 66.	May be stored at 32°F (0°C) for a short time period.
Cucumbers	Fancy, Extra #1, #1, #1 Small, #1 Large, and #2	Packed in lugs, West Coast lugs, and cartons.	Store at 45°F (7°C).
Iceberg Lettuce	Fancy, #1 Commercial, and #2	West—varies in weight per case from 35 to 55 pounds; normally 18, 24, or 30 heads per standard western carton.	All varieties of lettuce may be stored at 34°F (1°C).
Leaf Lettuce	Fancy	Varies, but mostly in 24-quart hampers weighing about 10 pounds.	
Boston Lettuce	#1	Varies, best to purchase by the pound.	
Onion	#1, Combo, #2, and Commercial	Usually packed in 50-pound mesh fiber bags.	Should be stored under dry conditions.
Romaine	#1	Western lettuce cartons holding 24 heads and weighing approximately 40 pounds.	Store at 34°F (1°C).
Sweet Peppers	Fancy, #1, and #2	Bushels with various counts; 80 count is a good size for stuffing.	Store between 46°F (7°C) and 48°F (9°C), with relative humidity of 85%.

(continued)

Exhibit 2   *(continued)*

Product	U.S. Grades	Pack Sizes	Storage Characteristics
Potatoes	Extra #1, #1, and #2	Cartons with counts ranging from 60 to 120 per carton.	Store in cool, dry, dark area. Raw potatoes should *not* be refrigerated.
Sweet Potatoes	Extra #1, #1, Commercial, and #2	Normally packed in bushel baskets of approximately 50 pounds.	Store at 50°F (10°C) with low humidity and use promptly.
Tomatoes	#1, Combo, #2, and #3 (field grading standards; grade identification is lost in repacking)	Sold by the box, which may contain 10, 20, 25, or 30 pounds; weight may vary by 10%.	Bring to full color at 55°F (13°C). Store between 40°F (4°C) and 50°F (10°C) until used.

Term	Stalks per pound
Colossal	7
Jumbo	8
Extra Select	9
Select	10
Extra Fancy	11
Fancy	12

Asparagus is highly perishable and should be cut when mature, hydrocooled, and then shipped quickly. Stalks should be straight and fresh, with compact pointed tips that are dry and bright in color and show no mold or decay. About an inch of white stalk should show, and it should be moist. Stalks should be about 7 inches when trimmed and should yield easily to fingernail pressure. Watch for sand, which is difficult to wash out.

Beans

Green beans are of two types—bush beans and vining (pole) beans. Pods should be long, straight, and crisp enough to snap easily. Lima beans come in two varieties, small (called potato or baby) and large (butter or fordhook). Lima beans should have clean, well-filled pods of dark green color and plump greenish beans with tender skins. Garbanzo beans, also called chick-peas, are really members of the pea family. Fresh cut and snapped beans are also available in most major terminal markets.

Broccoli

California is the primary broccoli producer but Texas, New Jersey, Oregon, Florida, and other states also grow large quantities of broccoli. Broccoli is available year-round, but the smallest supply corresponds to the hottest months—July and August. The color should be dark green with no yellow showing; the head may have a purplish cast and should be tightly bound and free of insect damage. Stems should not be tough or thick, and leafy broccoli should be avoided. Broccoli should be purchased by weight.

Brussels Sprouts

California is the major grower of brussels sprouts. The primary season for brussels sprouts is October to March. Sprouts should be firm, compact, and bright in appearance and should have a good green color. Wilted or yellowing leaves are signs of aging.

Cabbage

There are three major varieties of cabbage: Common green, Savoy (similar to Romaine), and Red. Another variety, Celery cabbage (Chinese cabbage) is primarily used for salad greens. Almost every state grows cabbage, but Florida, New Jersey, New York, and Texas are the major producers.

Green cabbage varieties are the most important commercially and are available year-round. Heads tighten and become heavier for their size as the season advances. Watch for excess leaves, decay, worm damage, and seed stems, all of which reduce yields as does internal rot. External condition, trim, and weight are the primary value indicators.

Carrots

California and Texas are the primary producers of carrots, but Arizona and Michigan also have good production. Carrots are in large supply all year and may be stored in good condition for many months using proper temperature and moisture controls.

The best sized carrots have diameters not less than $3/4$ nor more $1\,3/4$ inches. The ends should be blunt, not tapered; the carrot should be well-formed, not misshapen. Carrots should be crisp and firm with bright color (not pale or washed out). Carrot tops should be removed since they draw moisture from the carrots. Watch for "sunburn" which is evidenced by green at the top which must be trimmed. Carrots develop root straglets and a woody characteristic when overly mature.

Celery

Celery production is centered in California, Florida, Michigan, and New York, with supplies available every month of the year. Pascal (green) is the major variety and is almost "stringless" (lacking tough strands). Stalks should be well-formed, tight, trimmed, and crisp. Leaves should be fresh (not wilted) and branches should be almost brittle. The heart should be whitish-yellow and free of decay. Avoid "hollow heart" (a pithy hollow center), "black heart" (brown or black spots), and "seeders" (long thick seed stems).

A good size is 16-inch bunches weighing approximately $1\,3/4$ pounds each, packed 30 bunches per carton. Celery hearts are packed in plastic bags of 1 to 2 pounds each, in 25-pound master cartons.

Corn

Over 200 varieties of sweet corn are grown in the United States. Corn is available year-round with the heaviest supplies produced from May to September. Winter production is provided by Florida and California. The husk should be a fresh green color. Rows should be well-formed and kernels full and moist.

Cucumbers

There are three types of cucumbers—common (field grown), hothouse, and pickling varieties. Florida, North and South Carolina, and California are the largest producers. Cucumbers are produced year-round with the greatest availability occurring from May to August. Look for a bright green color and firm condition. Most establishments specify slicing cucumbers (U.S. #1) which are also called super selects. They weigh $1/2$ to $3/4$ pound each.

Salad Greens

Many types of salad greens are available, which vary in color, flavor, and form. Salads can be more interesting if prepared from a variety of greens. The most important categories of salad greens are iceberg lettuce, leaf lettuce, Boston lettuce, romaine, escarole, chicory, and endive. Salad greens are available on a year-round basis.

Iceberg or Head Lettuce. The principal growing areas of iceberg (head) lettuce are California's Salinas Valley (May to October) and Imperial Valley (December to April), as well as the Yuma area of Arizona (October to March).

The product should be well-trimmed with no more than five or six wrapper leaves. Heads should be firm but not hard (which implies overmaturity). Color varies by season but should be green to light green. The cut end should be bright but can have some brown color, which is caused by oxidation. If a reddish tinge shows, the lettuce may contain "rust." Cut a head to see if this condition is present throughout the plant.

Watch for a "nosey" condition (bumps) on the head which could mean that a seeder stem runs through the plant. Check for "seeders" by sharply rapping the cut end to loosen and remove the core. Gauge its size and the loss that will be suffered. Also check for tip burn (slight discoloration on tips of outer leaves caused by heat or cold shock) which leads to rapid deterioration. A slight discoloration of the wrapper leaves is typically not a problem.

Between harvest and delivery, iceberg lettuce used on the East Coast takes a minimum of eight days by rail or four to five days by truck. It is highly perishable, so buyers should specify vacuum cooling. Prices fluctuate dramatically and usually are highest when quality is poorest.

Leaf Lettuce (Garden or Hothouse). Leaf lettuce is available in-season from local markets, and shipments are often available by air during off-seasons. This plant does not grow as a tight head, but rather as a series of broad, loosely connected leaves. Watch for tip burn, discolored leaves, or interior decay.

Boston Lettuce. Sometimes called "Butterhead," this variety includes Bibb lettuce (erroneously called "limestone" lettuce). Boston lettuce is smaller, lighter, and softer than iceberg lettuce. Its outer leaves are light green while the inner leaves are a light yellow. Use the same quality checks as with iceberg lettuce. Packages vary so make purchases by the pound to ensure that value is obtained.

Romaine (Cos). Although it is grown in every area of the country, romaine is produced in greatest quantity in California. California products have leaves which are large and uniform.

This elongated plant has stiff, coarse, well-ribbed leaves. Inner leaves should be smaller and pale yellow-green. Its flavor is stronger than iceberg lettuce but is pleasing. Use the same condition checks as for iceberg lettuce. This variety is less fragile than other lettuces. Weights and case counts vary, so check before buying.

Escarole, Chicory, and Endive. Terminology is confusing with these varieties. Escarole is a flat spreading plant with broad, slightly curly leaves and a white center. Exterior leaves are a deep green.

Curly leaf endive and curly leaf chicory are the same plant. It is somewhat more upright than escarole with smaller, curly leaves. The head is bunched and the center is a yellowish-white.

French or Belgium Chicory is often called "true," "Belgium," or "French" Endive. This plant is completely different from the others; it has tightly wrapped leaves and an elongated, solid head. It is grown away from sunlight to preserve its bleached appearance.

There is only one federal grade for escarole, curly chicory, and curly endive—U.S. #1. Use the same condition checks used for iceberg lettuce. These vegetables may be held briefly at 32°F (0°C), and keep better with crushed ice in or around the package. Check counts per case and weights to ensure that value is received.

Onions

Three basic types of onions are available in the U.S. market: Early, Main, and Yellow Sweet Spanish. Early (Bermuda-Granex-Grano hybrids) are mild, large-sized onions with a short shelf life. Main (domestic or yellow globe) are grown heavily in the Northwest and are the primary storage type. Yellow Sweet Spanish onions, also from the Northwest, are globe-shaped and flavorful, but do not store well.

There are three main production seasons for onions: March to June (primarily Texas, New Mexico, Arizona, and the Imperial Valley); July and August (California); and September to December (northwestern United States, Colorado, Michigan, and New York). Onions are stored for use later in the year, although some onions are imported from Chile and Peru in the off-period.

Onions should be well-shaped and dry enough to crackle, with thin necks and bright, hard bulbs. Decay usually begins at the stem so check there for wetness. Seed stem growth or "seeders" reduce yields but are difficult to detect from the exterior.

Peppers

Garden peppers may be classified in two categories: mild or sweet-fleshed varieties, and hot or pungent-fleshed varieties. Within each category are a vast array of shapes, sizes, and colors. The Bell (California Wonder) is the primary variety of sweet pepper. Peppers are produced in all areas (California, Florida, and Texas ship in the winter season). Best quality peppers are bright in color with no blemishes or rot. Pale color and soft seeds indicate immature fruit.

Potatoes

Potatoes are the most important vegetable crop in the United States. There are several basic types of potatoes. The Russet and Long White types are of primary commercial importance for fresh use. Maine, Idaho, Washington, and California are the leading producers. The primary fresh potato demand in hospitality operations now is for bakers. The famous "Idaho potato" is the Russet Burbank, which is ideal for baking. California Long Whites are a reasonable substitute for Russets and often must be used in the summer when Russet storage supplies are depleted. (It is not practical to expect Russet availability year-round, and buyers should anticipate this situation.)

Type of soil, method of moisture application, and growing temperatures govern potato quality. Storage also is an important consideration. Potatoes sprout if held at high temperatures, yet convert starch to sugar if temperatures are too low. High starch is desirable in bakers. As a result, bakers are generally shipped in refrigerated transport but stored by local distributors at ambient temperatures to prevent further starch loss. Wet spots or moisture showing through the skin indicates high sugar content and poor potatoes for baking.

Dump and count a box routinely to ensure that quantity and size requirements are met. Examine the potatoes for uniformity of size and condition. In addition to sizing, look for cuts and bruises, sprouting, freeze damage, hollow heart, and wetness. Hollow heart appears as dark, hollow sections in the interior, a result of too rapid growth. As with any fresh item, appearance is the best indicator of quality. Federal grade standards deal with sizing and condition. Supplement the federal standards with count size when developing specifications.

Sweet Potatoes

The two most popular types of sweet potatoes are Jerseys and Porto Ricos. Jerseys are drier and less sweet with lighter meat color. Porto Ricos (also called Nancy Halls, but commonly known as yams) have moist, darker meat and a sweeter flavor.

Sweet potatoes are grown in California, Texas, Louisiana, North Carolina, Florida, and New Jersey. Some imports are received from Puerto Rico and the Dominican Republic. Sweet potatoes are available year-round.

Sweet potatoes are very perishable. Buy thick, chunky potatoes that are firm and well-formed; tapered toward ends; and free of bruises, cuts, decay, and insect damage.

Tomatoes

Locally grown, vine-ripened tomatoes are generally more flavorful and less expensive than hothouse-grown and shipped tomatoes. Unfortunately, local tomatoes are only available for short periods of time in most areas. During the rest of the year, tomatoes are grown in Florida, Texas, Mexico, or California. These tomatoes are picked mature but green, and then shipped to major metropolitan areas for repacking by size and color.

When purchasing tomatoes, buyers should specify color. Trade terminology includes green (no red showing), turning (a trace of color), pink (more than 50%

color), hard ripe (fully colored, but hard, not ripe), and full ripe (ready to use). Most buyers specify pink or hard ripe. External appearance is important. Watch for shoulder scars, puffiness, cracks, and handling damage.

Sizing of tomatoes is important for cost control. This is accomplished by counting the number of tomatoes per layer in a standard tomato box. The most common repack sizes are a 10-pound one-layer box and a 20-pound two-layer box, but larger box sizes are available. Thus, a 10-pound box of 5×5 tomatoes contains approximately 25 tomatoes in one layer, and a 20-pound box of 5×5 tomatoes contains 50 tomatoes in two layers. The 25-pound box is normally loose pack, unsized, and often unsatisfactory.

The best sized cherry tomato is $1 1/2$ inches. The same quality standards apply as for regular tomatoes, but sizing may be a problem. They are generally packed in flats of 12 pounds.

Distribution of Fresh Produce

Production of fresh fruits and vegetables is a major commercial enterprise conducted by large organizations. Some seasonal production is available adjacent to urban communities, but the country depends on the major growing areas for steady annual supplies. Those hospitality companies located close to these areas have a distinct advantage because transportation represents a large part of fresh produce cost. The following sections discuss the system by which products move from the grower, or importer, to the consumer.

Marketing. Land under production is either farmed by the owner or leased. Traditionally, products were sold through auctions located in the growing area. Brokers or consolidators purchased from the grower and sold to urban area distributors and retail chain stores. Often the product was shipped "open" (unsold) and sold while en route. The grower had little influence over prices. In response to this situation, cooperatives were formed to market products for groups of growers. Cooperatives believed that higher prices would result from these marketing efforts. The products were still traded as commodities, but new efforts were directed at building brand recognition by consumers.

Consistent quality and a regular, predictable flow of merchandise is required to obtain and retain consumer support of brands. This support has been developed to at least some extent for oranges, grapefruits, strawberries, and lettuce. While expensive, these marketing efforts have been successful, hastening the entry of large corporate organizations into the field to compete with the cooperatives. Thousands of acres worth of production is sold through these channels.

Auctions, however, still play a vital role and many growers remain independent. Many products purchased by hospitality companies are affected by the auction process; if not actually bought at auction, they may be sold at auction prices. While brand recognition is primarily a concern of retail stores, growers and their agents tend to favor sales to brand companies because of the higher prices paid. In times of shortage, this can become a problem for the hospitality buyer; caution should be exercised when establishing specifications and agreements with local distributors.

Distribution. Distributors buy from any of these marketing organizations depending on price, availability, and customer specifications. There are at least two types of distributors in most urban terminal markets: primary distributors, sometimes called first receivers, and secondary distributors. Primary distributors may specialize in one or two specific products (for instance, tomatoes sorted by color and size and repacked from field boxes). Primary distributors attempt to buy in sufficient quantity to command the best FOB prices and freight rates. This generally means taking delivery of a truck or carload of products.

Smaller, secondary distributors often find it advantageous to purchase from the first receiver rather than to negotiate directly with sources. In some cases, a first receiver may be the exclusive distributor for certain growers, leaving secondary distributors with no other options if they want the product. Imported products, most of which come from Mexico, are often sold through primary distributors after customs clearance. Buyers should deal with primary distributors if at all possible, since their products are likely to be fresher and their prices probably lower.

If consumption is adequate to make use of full truckloads of products, hospitality buyers can purchase through growers' auctions. Agents on the scene locate the items, consolidate the billing, and arrange transportation, all for a fee. Buyers considering this method must have adequate storage facilities.

Many distributor companies in urban terminal markets also process fresh produce into a convenience form. For example, they may prepare salad ingredients, peel potatoes and carrots, cut beans, or slice orange rounds. Companies in the growing areas also perform these activities when the product's shelf life can be maintained. Many distributors of canned and frozen products have added fresh produce to their lines, sometimes processing these items further. This development is a response to customer pressure for one-stop shopping, and is viewed by these distributors as a means to increase order sizes and profit margins.

Choice of supplier is affected by purchase volume. Large users with their own distribution capabilities may buy some products directly from the growing area and obtain other needed produce items from primary distributors in the local terminal markets. Large users who do not operate their own facilities depend on the market to acquire, store, and deliver products. Because their purchase volumes are less, small users may be forced to pay the higher prices associated with secondary distributors.

Packaging. Counts and weights per package are often inconsistent from one growing area to another, and may even differ among growers in the same area. Many fresh products are sold in non-denominated units (a "bag" of cabbage or a "flat" of strawberries). A distributor may receive similar products from many different growing areas, whose particular conditions and practices are reflected in varied types of packaging. A crate of romaine lettuce may hold 15 heads, 18 heads, or 24 heads, depending on the point of shipment. The buyer, dealing almost exclusively by telephone, must have specifications on record with the supplier to help ensure good communication.

Although no universal weight standards exist, weight is considered the best standard. Obviously, a 50-pound carton of potatoes should weigh 50 pounds. Standard cartons and counts per standard carton are the next best control. For example, 88 count California navel oranges should be packed in standard West Coast fruit cartons containing 88 oranges. Difficulties arise when items are sold on a volume basis, such as spinach (sold by the bushel) or strawberries (sold by the flat of 12 pints). The buyer should take all precautions and select suppliers who have the best reputations for delivering what is desired.

Pricing and Yields of Fresh Produce

There are two sets of prices that buyers must consider—FOB growing area prices and terminal market prices. FOB prices are related to auction prices. Buyers using FOB prices intend to bypass local distributors and have the merchandise delivered directly. Agents may consolidate shipments and arrange transportation for the items. An ongoing relationship between buyer and agent is important, with at least weekly communication recommended; neither party should take advantage of the other.

Buyers purchasing from terminal market distributors may use either a bid or cost-plus system. Those utilizing a bid system can check FOB price data to measure the reasonableness of the quotations they receive. Those using cost-plus can expect the local distributors to follow FOB prices, adjusting for in-transit time and adding transportation costs. Buyers should have information on supply and price conditions in the growing area in order to gauge prices in the local terminal market.

Yields greatly affect value in fresh products. Therefore, specifications are necessary to establish communications with suppliers, and careful inspections are required to ensure that the products received actually meet specifications. Sample specifications, yield calculations, and pricing examples for three products are presented in the following sections.

Iceberg Lettuce

A carton of iceberg lettuce of U.S. Grade #1 or better is ordered. The minimum acceptable weight is 45 pounds per carton (24 heads per carton). The lettuce is to be well-trimmed with no more than seven wrapper leaves. It should be dark green in color and have no overmature heads or field rust.

Yield. Lettuce is bought by the carton and sold by the portion. Assume that the usable yield is 80% of purchased weight and that the price is $12.00 per carton. If the specified weight of 45 pounds is received, the cost per pound (usable) is calculated as follows:

$$\text{Cost per lb (usable)} = \frac{\text{Price per carton (as purchased)}}{\text{Pounds purchased} \times \text{Yield}}$$

$$\text{Cost per lb (usable)} = \frac{\$12.00}{45 \text{ lb} \times 80\%}$$

$$\text{Cost per lb (usable)} = \frac{\$12.00}{36 \text{ lb}}$$

$$\text{Cost per lb (usable)} = \$.33$$

Exhibit 3   Summary of Pricing Information for Three Products

Date	Source	Specification 1 Iceberg Lettuce	Specification 2 Repack Tomatoes	Specification 3 Baking Potatoes
3/19	USDA FOB	$6/7	Mexico—3 layer $4.00 Florida—25 lb $4.00	$ 7.75
3/22	USDA FOB	$6/7	Mexico—3 layer $4.00 Florida—25 lb $3.50	$ 7.75
3/26	USDA FOB	$11/13	Mexico—3 layer $4.50 Florida—25 lb $3/350	$ 7.75
3/29	USDA FOB	$15	Mexico—3 layer $5.00 Florida—25 lb $4.50	$ 7.75
4/2	USDA FOB	$15/20 Mostly $18	Mexico—3 layer $7.00 Florida—25 lb $4.50	$ 7.75
4/7	USDA FOB	$8/12 Mostly $10	Mexico—3 layer $8.00 Florida—25 lb $4.50	$ 7.75
		ALL ABOVE PRICES ARE FOB SHIPPING AREAS		
3/22	USDA—Philadelphia	$11/11.50	Florida—25 lb $6.00 Repack—20 lb $9.50	$ 11.25
3/23	USDA—Philadelphia	$11	Florida—25 lb $7.00 Repack—20 lb $9.50	$ 11.25
3/26	USDA—Los Angeles	$12.50	Mexico—3 layer $6/7	$ 9.50
3/29	USDA—Los Angeles	$15/16	Mexico—3 layer $7.00	$ 9.50
3/29	USDA—Philadelphia	$16/17	Florida—25 lb $6.00 Repack—20 lb $8.50	$ 11.25
3/30	USDA—Philadelphia	$18/20	Florida—25 lb $6/6.50 Repack—20 lb $8.50	$ 11.25
4/5	USDA—Dallas	$19/22	Mexico—3 layer $7/9 Repack—3 layer $7/9	$ 10.50
4/8	USDA—Dallas	$14	Mexico—3 layer $10/10.50 Florida—25 lb $7.50 Repack—3 layer $9.00	$ 10.50
		ALL ABOVE PRICES ARE SALES BY PRIMARY DISTRIBUTORS IN TERMINAL MARKETS		

Estimates of Freight from Shipping Points to Terminal Cities

Destination	Specification 1	Specification 2	Specification 3
Philadelphia	$3.15	$1.35	$2.00
Dallas	$2.00	$ .75	$1.50
Los Angeles	$ .75	$ .75	$ .75

Received weight is the first check. If the cartons actually weigh only 35 pounds, cost increases by almost 30%. Of course, quality factors (such as seeders and rot) should be considered. If yield is reduced to 67% due to rot, cost increases by almost 20%.

Pricing. Exhibit 3 summarizes pricing information drawn from terminal markets in Philadelphia, Los Angeles, and Dallas. Dates range from March 19 through April 8, 1986. Both terminal market and FOB shipping area prices are shown. Referring to the upper half of the exhibit (FOB shipping area prices), it can be seen that lettuce prices dramatically fluctuate. FOB prices started at $6/7 ($6 to $7 range) per carton on March 19, went up to $15/20 on April 2, and down to $8/12 on April 7.

Two reasons may account for these fluctuations. First, production decreases seasonally as the harvest is completed in the southern Imperial Valley of California and in the Arizona desert. (Production later moves northward into the central California valleys around Salinas.) Second, heavy rains affected the growing area during this period, causing the harvest to be curtailed. The overall result is that the FOB price more than doubled in a very short period of time.

How did the terminal markets react to these conditions? Philadelphia (at least four days' travel time from California) serves as an example:

3/19 FOB cost $6/7	$6.50/ctn (average)
Freight to Philadelphia	3.15/ctn
Computed cost	$9.65/ctn
3/26 FOB cost $11/13	$12.00/ctn (average)
Freight to Philadelphia	3.15/ctn
Computed cost	$15.15/ctn

By looking at the lower half of Exhibit 3 (terminal prices), we can see that the Philadelphia distributors increased prices (and markups) when they received news of higher FOB prices. Their markups may be calculated as follows:

3/23 Terminal resale price	$11.00/ctn
Computed cost	−9.65/ctn
Computed markup	$1.35/ctn
3/30 Terminal resale price $18/20	$19.00 (average)
Computed cost	−15.15/ctn
Computed markup	$3.85/ctn

This is a common practice in the fresh produce market. The buyer must use a consistent system to monitor the prices or bids received. Large buyers, purchasing from growing area shippers, are aware of supply conditions and can manage their prices accordingly. Other buyers depend on terminal market distributors for their supplies.

One pricing system is to negotiate a markup per carton over the supplier's cost and add a provision that the cost must not exceed the USDA reported primary distributor price for that market. If the supplier pays less than the reported price, the buyer's price should be adjusted down accordingly. While the buyer will not know the supplier's cost, at least a ceiling has been established. Benchmarks such as this coupled with regular competitive bids between suppliers should enable buyers to maintain a fair price structure.

Repack Tomatoes

In this example, we compare U.S. #1 repack tomatoes in 10-pound cartons of 6×7 and 6×6 count. The tomatoes should be mature pink with no decay or surface mold and minimal blemishes. California tomatoes are preferred and Florida, Texas, or Mexico tomatoes are second choices.

Yield. For tomatoes, count and condition determine yield. A 10-pound box of 6×7 repack tomatoes should contain approximately 42 tomatoes, and a 10-pound box of 6×6 tomatoes should contain 36 tomatoes. In some markets, 6×7 tomatoes are slightly less expensive than 6 × 6 tomatoes. For comparative purposes, assume the prices are equal. At $.50 per pound ($5.00 per 10-pound box), costs are as follows:

$$6 \times 6 \text{ box: } \frac{\$5.00}{36 \text{ tomatoes}} = \$.139, \text{ or approximately } 14¢/\text{tomato}$$

$$6 \times 7 \text{ box: } \frac{\$5.00}{42 \text{ tomatoes}} = \$.119, \text{ or approximately } 12¢/\text{tomato}$$

If five slices are obtained from both sizes of tomatoes, costs can be calculated as follows:

$$6 \times 6 \text{ box: } \frac{\text{Cost per tomato}}{\text{Number of slices}} = \frac{14¢}{5} = 2.8¢/\text{slice}$$

$$6 \times 7 \text{ box: } \frac{\text{Cost per tomato}}{\text{Number of slices}} = \frac{12¢}{5} = 2.4¢/\text{slice}$$

The difference of 0.4¢ divided by the cost of the less expensive slice (2.4¢) represents a 17% cost difference. If an extra slice can be obtained from the larger (6 × 6) tomato, then the costs would be approximately equal.

Pricing. Look at Exhibit 3 and follow the FOB shipping area prices for tomatoes. Note that FOB Mexico prices have doubled while FOB Florida prices have remained quite steady.

Now examine terminal prices in the lower half of Exhibit 3. Los Angeles reports 3-layer Mexican prices. Applying the freight rates for Los Angeles, a buyer can estimate distributors' markups by comparing FOB and terminal prices for 3-layer Mexican tomatoes (prices in dollars per pound):

Date	FOB Price	Freight	Total	Terminal Price	Difference
3/26	4.50	.75	5.25	6.00/7.00	.75/1.75
3/29	5.00	.75	5.75	7.00	1.25

In this small sampling, the primary distributor's average markup is calculated as approximately $1.25 per carton.

Baking Potatoes

In this example, U.S. Grade #1 Russet Burbank baking potatoes are ordered. The potatoes are shipped in 50-pound cartons with 90 count per carton. No field damage or sprouts should be present. Idahos are preferred, but Washingtons will be accepted as a second choice.

Yield. Verify the condition of the potatoes and, if satisfactory, check the count. Menu prices are established based on a predicted quantity of 90 potatoes per carton, and buyers must ensure that correct counts are received. If costs are $12 per carton, each potato costs approximately 13¢ ($12 divided by 90 potatoes). If 80 count potatoes are actually received, each potato costs 15¢ ($12 divided by 80

Exhibit 4   Example of Price Calculations for Baking Potatoes

	Philadelphia	Dallas	Los Angeles
70/90 FOB Idaho (50-lb cartons)	$ 7.75	$ 7.75	$ 7.75
Freight (estimated)	2.00	1.50	.75
Delivered cost to terminal	$ 9.75	$ 9.25	$ 8.50
	Philadelphia	Dallas	Los Angeles
Terminal market price	$ 11.25	$ 10.50	$ 9.50
Delivered cost to terminal	− 9.75	− 9.25	− 8.50
Apparent markups	$ 1.50	$ 1.25	$ 1.00

potatoes). This 2¢ difference (15¢ − 13¢) represents a food cost increase of approximately 15%:

$$\text{Price increase} = \frac{\text{Price difference}}{\text{Original price}} \times 100\%$$

$$\text{Price increase} = \frac{2¢}{13¢} \times 100\%$$

$$\text{Price increase} = 15.4\%$$

A medium size restaurant can easily use 20 cartons (1,800 potatoes) each week. Over time, this 2¢ difference adds up to a considerable loss:

1,800 potatoes × $.02 each = $36 per week
$36 per week × 52 weeks = $1,872 per year

Pricing. According to Exhibit 3, the FOB shipping area price for bakers is $7.75 for Philadelphia, Dallas, and Los Angeles. Exhibit 4 develops delivered cost to the terminal market and calculates the apparent markups of primary distributors. These markups are fairly consistent. Variations from one distributor to another may be due to normal volatility in terminal market prices, differences in price opinions, freight factors, or cost variations between original and repacked merchandise.

Pricing Factors

Prices must be interpreted properly to be useful, but over time patterns do evolve. Freight costs supplied under cost-plus arrangements should be verified. Purchase volume, services required, and payment practices all contribute to the price. No one system is best for every hospitality operation, but an informed buyer with knowledge of how products are marketed and priced will obtain greater value.

Pricing information is available from several sources. A number of wire services provide data on supply and price conditions. The USDA publication *National Shipping Point Trends* provides price estimates (FOB growing area) and reports of activity in the major metropolitan areas.[1] Industry publications such as *The Packer* (a national weekly business newspaper of the fruit and vegetable industry) also provide useful information. Daily updates of market condition are generally available by telephone from both USDA and industry publication sources. Local competition is always a potential source of information for buyers.

Prices of fresh fruits and vegetables are volatile due to short production cycles, weather, transportation costs, and limited shelf life. Prices are generally highest when product conditions are worst, which only adds to the confusion. This price volatility presents the vendor with the opportunity to increase profits. If the weather is bad in California causing FOB prices to rise, a New York vendor with several days' inventory may increase prices immediately and make the extra profit. Conversely, if prices drop in California, the same vendor may sell the remaining inventory at the higher price. Buyers must avoid being caught on the wrong side of such price shifts.

The Processed Fruits and Vegetables Industry

Most fresh fruits and vegetables can be processed into another form and stored for future consumption. Growers market their produce through distribution channels to be either sold fresh or further processed. Fresh products represent a fast day-to-day business, while processed products follow seasonal patterns. Buyers of processed products can give more consideration to market studies because supplies are more predictable. Decisions need not be made as rapidly with processed products, but capital requirements are greater.

Several large cooperatives dealing in canned products have developed in California. These are grower-owned organizations with processing and marketing facilities. Growers of products intended for freezing form a smaller group, but they also bargain collectively with processors to establish prices.

Over the years, a number of specialized organizations have evolved to represent buyers and sellers more effectively. Three broad types are:

- The corporate buying office, whose staff deals directly with the processor and represents only one company.

- Field brokers, who represent a wide range of processors for a fee. They sell directly to retailers, distributors, and large hospitality companies. They match buyers with processors in direct competition with the traditional broker.

- The member-owned buying office, an organization which typically evolves from a distributor cooperative. One such organization is National Institutional Food Distributor Associates (NIFDA).

Most processors have headquarters with marketing and sales staffs as well as service representatives. Many have national networks of brokers located in major metropolitan cities, some concerned only with food service sales.

Government Regulation

The FDA and the USDA are the two federal agencies most involved with the fruit and vegetable processing industry. The FDA is primarily concerned with consumer protection and product contamination or adulteration. It deals with package labeling and standards of product identity, quality, and fill.

The USDA is involved in aiding farmers in their marketing activities. This agency helped develop U.S. grades to maintain and convey standards to consumers, who rely on grades as a means of quality assurance. The grades were developed jointly by industry and government to assess physical characteristics including color, texture or character (maturity), defects, and uniformity of size and appearance.

Certain states, growing areas, and industries developed quality terms prior to the USDA system and these were incorporated into the standards. A relatively uniform point system has evolved to define levels of quality. The chart below correlates the two and provides the point scores necessary to meet grade requirements. The minimum point scores for each grade vary from product to product and many exceptions exist to these designations:

Government designation	Industry designation	Point score
Grade A	Fancy	90 to 100
Grade B	Extra Standard or Choice	80 to 89
Grade C	Standard	70 to 79
Grade D	Substandard	Below 70

Practically no products are packed that score below Grade C. "No-grade" merchandise is converted into items such as soups, sauces, purees, and condiments.

USDA grades provide standards for processed products, but there are some conditions with which buyers should be familiar. For example, Grade A tomatoes from California may not be the same quality as Grade A tomatoes from Indiana. Grades also vary throughout the season. Quality varies from year to year and the grades themselves change. In practice, the tendency is to give the top grade to the best of what is available that year.

Grade marks may be shown on the package if the plant is approved and if a recognized inspection program is in effect. The products must meet both FDA and USDA requirements. Plants with an approved quality control program may qualify to perform self-inspections and to assign grades. These programs must have USDA approval and production records must be kept for auditing by government personnel. For a fee, USDA inspectors will examine products in lot inspections and issue grade certificates on this basis. The USDA encourages good quality control programs, and many plants have installed programs with standards more stringent than those of the USDA.

Specifications and Quality Control

Exhibit 5 provides U.S. grades, packing seasons, and production areas for many popular processed fruit and vegetable items. A wide range of individual factors must be addressed when writing specifications for particular items. These include:

- Count, sieve size (peas), or other size designations

- Variety—for example, Rio-Oso-Gem freestone peaches, Russet Burbank french fries, or Northern Spy apples

Exhibit 5   Processed Fruits and Vegetables—U.S. Grades, Packing Seasons, and Producing Areas

Product	U.S. Grades	Primary Packing Season	Primary Producing Area
Apples—Canned	A or Fancy (85) C or Standard (70)	October to December	Michigan, Washington, Virginia
Apples—Frozen	A or Fancy (85) C or Standard (75)	October to December	MIchigan, Washington, Virginia
Apple Juice—Canned	A (90) B (80)	October to December	Michigan, Washington, Virginia
Applesauce—Canned	A or Fancy (90) B or Choice (80)	October to December	Michigan, Washington, Virginia
Apricots—Canned	A or Fancy (90) B or Choice (80) C or Standard (70)	June and July	California
Asparagus—Canned	A or Fancy (85) C or Standard (70)	April to July	California, New Jersey, Michigan
Asparagus—Frozen	A or Fancy B or X-Standard	April to July	California, New Jersey, Michigan
Beans, Green & Waxed—Canned	A or Fancy (90) B or X-Standard (80)	June to October	Northwest, Wisconsin
Beans, Green & Waxed—Frozen	A or Fancy (90) B or X-Standard (80) C or Standard (70)	June to October	Northwest, California
Beans, LIma—Canned	A or Fancy (90) B or X-Standard (80) C or Standard (70)	August to October	California, East Coast
Beans, Lima—Frozen	A or Fancy (90) B or X-Standard (80) C or Standard (70)	August to October	California, East Coast
Beets—Canned	A or Fancy (85) C or Standard (70)	August to December	California, Northwest, Michigan, New York
Berries—Frozen	A or Fancy (85) B or Choice (70)	June to August	Northwest, California
Broccoli—Frozen	A, B	June to August	California
Brussels Sprouts—Frozen	A, B, C	June to August	California
Carrots—Canned	A or Fancy (85) C or Standard (70)	August to May	California, Texas
Carrots—Frozen	A or Fancy (90) B or X-Standard (80)	July to October	California, Northwest, Texas
Cauliflower—Frozen	A or Fancy (85) B or X-Standard (70)	June to September	California
Cherries, Red—Frozen	A or Fancy (90) B or Choice (80) C or Standard (70)	June to July	New York, Pennsylvania, Michigan
Corn on Cob—Frozen	A or Fancy (90) B or X-Standard (80)	June to August	Northwest
Corn, Whole Kernel—Canned	A or Fancy (90) B or X-Standard (80) C or Standard (70)	August to October	Northwest, Wisconsin, Minnesota
Corn, Whole Kernel—Frozen	A or Fancy (90) B or X-Standard (80) C or Standard (70)	June to August	Northwest, Wisconsin, Minnesota
Cranberry Sauce—Canned	A or Fancy (85) C or Standard (70)	October to January	Massachusetts, New Jersey
Fruit Cocktail	A or Fancy (85) B or Choice (70)	June to September	California
Fruit Jelly	A (90) or B (80)	Year-round	California, Virginia, Michigan, Ohio
Fruit Preserves—Jam	A (85) or B (70)	Year-round	California, Virginia, Michigan, Ohio

Exhibit 5 *(continued)*

Product	U.S. Grades	Primary Packing Season	Primary Producing Area
Mushrooms—Canned	A or Fancy (90) B or X-Standard (80)	Year-round	Pennsylvania, North Carolina
Olives, Green—Canned	A or Fancy (90) B or X-Standard (80) C or Standard (70)	Year-round	California, Spain
Olives, Ripe—Canned	A or Fancy (90) B or X-Standard (80) C or Standard (70)	October to February	California
Onion Rings—Breaded Frozen	A or Fancy (85) B or X-Standard (70)	April to December	Various states
Onions—Canned	A or Fancy (85) C or Standard (70)	April to December	Various states
Peaches—Frozen	A (90) B (80) C (70)	July to September	California, Virginia, Pennsylvania, Georgia
Peaches, Clingstone—Canned	A, B, C	July to September	California
Peaches, Freestone—Canned	A, B, C	July to September	California
Pears—Canned	A or Fancy (90) B or Choice (80) C or Standard (70)	July to November	Northwest California
Peas—Canned	A or Fancy (90) B or X-Standard (80) C or Standard (70)	July to August	Wisconsin, Minnesota
Peas—Frozen	A or Fancy (90) B or X-Standard (80) C or Standard (70)	June to July	Northwest, Wisconsin, Minnesota
Peas & Carrots—Canned	A or Fancy (90) B or X-Standard (80) C or Standard (70)	June to August	Northwest, Wisconsin, Minnesota
Peas & Carrots—Frozen	A or Fancy (90) B or X-Standard (80) C or Standard (70)	June to July	Northwest, California
Pickles—Canned	A or Fancy (90) B or X-Standard (80)	Year-round	Michigan
Pineapple—Canned	A or Fancy (90) B or Choice (80) C or Standard (70)	January to September	Puerto Rico, Hawaii, Philippines
Pineapple—Frozen	A or Fancy (90) B or Choice (80) C or Standard (70)	January to September	Puerto Rico, Hawaii, Philippines
Pineapple Juice—Canned	A or Fancy (85) C or Standard (70)	January to September	Puerto Rico, Hawaii, Philippines
Plums—Canned	A or Fancy (90) B or Choice (80) C or Standard (70)	July to September	California, Northwest
Potatoes, French Fry—Frozen	A or Fancy (90) B or X-Standard (80)	September to May	Idaho, Washington, North Central, Maine
Potatoes, White—Canned	A (90) B (80)	September to March	Various states
Potatoes, Hash Brown—Frozen	A (90) B (80)	September to May	Northwest, North Central, Northeast
Sauerkraut—Canned	A or Fancy (90) B or X-Standard (80) C or Standard (70)	Year-round	New York, Pennsylvania
Spinach—Canned	A or Fancy B or X-Standard	June to October	California, Texas

(continued)

Exhibit 5 *(continued)*

Product	U.S. Grades	Primary Packing Season	Primary Producing Area
Spinach—Frozen	A or Fancy (90) B or X-Standard (80)	June to October	California
Strawberries—Frozen	A or Fancy (90) B or Choice (80) C or Standard (70)	May to July	California, Northwest, Mexico
Sweet Potatoes—Canned	A or Fancy (90) B or X-Standard (80)	July to March	Southeast
Tomatoes—Canned	A or Fancy (90) B or X-Standard (80) C or Standard (70)	July to November	California
Tomato Catsup—Canned	A or Fancy (85) B or X-Standard (85) C or Standard (70)	Year-round	California
Tomato Juice—Canned	A or Fancy (93) C or Standard (80)	July to February	California
Tomato Juice, Concentrate—Canned	A or Fancy (85) C or Standard (70)	July to February	California
Tomato Paste—Canned	A or Fancy (90) C or Standard (80)	July to November	California
Tomato Puree—Canned	A or Fancy (90) C or Standard (80)	July to November	California
Tomato Sauce—Canned	A or Fancy (85) C or Standard (70)	July to November	California
Vegetables, Mixed—Frozen	A or Fancy (90) B or X-Standard (80) C or Standard (70)	Year-round	California, Northwest

- Preferred growing area
- Time of pack—early or late pack (time of harvest) may be important to some buyers
- Can or package size
- Method of pack—dry, water added, in syrup, sugar added (ratio of fruit to sugar)
- Drained weight—the quantity of solids remaining after removal of excess liquid
- Any special requirements such as size tolerances, variance from federal standards, or IQF (individually quick frozen)

Sampling by can cutting is one way to check the quality of canned products. Frozen fruits and vegetables can also be sampled. However, sampling is a subjective judgment, and the buyer has no guarantee that the product delivered will equal the sample submitted. Approving samples by production lot can add assurance. Processors identify production lots (called "runs") with a code that denotes the day and plant in which the item was produced. The buyer can approve a sample with the requirement that the shipment come from the same lot as the sample. A problem with this method is that the preferred lot may have already been sold when the buyer makes the request. In that case, the sampling procedure must be repeated.

Exhibit 6   Sample Specifications for Processed Fruits and Vegetables

Specification #1 (Frozen Orange Juice Concentrate)

- U.S. Grade A (Fancy); minimum point score of 95
- 32-oz cans of 12 per case
- 3:1 concentrate; no sugar added
- Minimum of 50% Florida Valencia orange solids
- Pulp added, 4 to 8 grams per 6 oz (concentrate basis)
- Sugar/acid ratio—range from 14.5:1 to 16.5:1
- Brix—44.8 to 45.8 degrees
- Proof of grade required

Specification #2 (Frozen French Fry Potatoes)

- U.S. Grade A (Fancy)
- Blast frozen ($-40°$ both F and C)
- Extra Long; $3/8'' \times 3/8''$ with at least 90% over 2''
- Minimum of 10% under 2'' pieces (measured per carton)
- Oil blanch; uniform color (no high sugars)
- From Russet Burbank variety; minimum of 32% solids
- 6 bags (4.5 lb each) per carton

Specification #3 (Canned Tomatoes)

- U.S. Grade B (Extra Standard); minimum point score of 85
- California 145 coreless variety; packed in natural juice
- 66 oz minimum drained weight measured by case
- Number 10 size cans, 6 per case
- Proof of grade required

Specification #4 (Canned Peach Halves)

- California clingstone; packed in heavy syrup
- Number 10 size cans, 6 per case; 35/40 count
- USDA Grade A; minimum point score of 9
- Minimum drained weight—65 oz per number 10 size can
- Good yellow color; minimum breakage; uniform size

Specification #5 (Frozen Peas)

- N.W. Pack—12 packages (2.5 lb each) per case
- USDA Grade A (Fancy); minimum point score of 94
- Less than 5% pieces; good green color
- 3 to 5 sieve size

Review the sample specifications given in Exhibit 6. Each guideline has elements which exceed federal standards. Note that Specification #2 requires that no less than 90% of the fries be over two inches in length. Long strips are more desirable to the guest. An additional consideration is that longer strips fill the container with less weight than shorter pieces, which fit more compactly and weigh more. Since portion yields and sizes are calibrated closely, any deviation in potato strip length is cause for operator concern.

Buyers must be careful not to construct specifications for specific products that exclude good suppliers. This may become a problem with blended products and nationally advertised merchandise such as chili, tomato sauce, and catsup for which each supplier has a specific formula. Many of these products have excellent consumer acceptance based on recognized labels, advertising, and home use. These formulas are protected by producers and the buyer may find it difficult to stimulate competition among suppliers. Sometimes the "or equal" approach is used in which a stated brand *or* its equal is specified. The "or equal" judgment is a subjective one and may not be possible given strong brand preferences.

The best approach is to construct specifications using federal standards and modify these standards in specific areas as necessary. If branded merchandise is required, the buyer may be put at a distinct disadvantage due to the nature of such negotiated purchases. Market price may be estimated by pricing comparable non-branded merchandise and then making value comparisons. Using this information as a negotiating tool, the buyer has a better chance of reaching a favorable agreement on branded merchandise.

Distribution

With a few exceptions (notably, potatoes and onions), produce must be processed immediately after harvest. The processing season is usually quite short (as little as 6 weeks for some vegetables grown in the Northwest). In fact, out of the entire year, processing plants may be used only during that brief period. The amount of capital required to support the investment in both the plant and finished inventory is immense.

Tomato products provide a good example of how items cycle through processing and marketing channels. Large cooperatives or independent canners of tomatoes, catsup, paste, puree, pizza sauce, juice, and other tomato products plan their anticipated production far in advance of the season. They consider factors such as anticipated carry-in (inventory at the beginning of the harvest season), grower's intentions, labor and plant conditions, economic outlook, and capital availability.

Canners then negotiate with growers for a "field" or "contract" price. At this point, both parties usually hedge their positions. Processors seldom contract for their entire anticipated production and many growers leave part of their harvest open. Both are gambling that prices will move in their favor. This practice is especially prevalent with crops that can be stored, such as potatoes and onions.

Few processing plants produce all the items they sell. They are primary packers of some items and fill out their lines by purchasing other items. For example, a tomato canning plant packing whole tomatoes, juice, puree, and paste may buy catsup and pizza sauce from another processor. The plant may even provide the paste from which these products are made to another packer and buy back finished products. These buy-and-sell transactions are known as "interpacker trading."

The quotations which processors cite at the beginning of the season are called "opening prices." If supply and demand are well balanced or if supplies are low, prices increase throughout the season in response to storage and carrying costs. If there is excess supply, prices normally drop to increase sales. In some years, buyers can profit by buying and taking possession at the time of harvest. If this is to be done successfully, all costs, possible risks, and other pertinent factors must be weighed. Most buyers do not have access to all of the data required to make such decisions.

More often large buyers will "book." This is an informal procedure in which the buyer states the intention to use a certain quantity of merchandise and the processor states the intention to reserve that quantity for the buyer. The price agreement may be: opening price firm, opening price modified by market changes during the year, opening price plus increases throughout the year to cover carrying costs, or another specified arrangement.

The buyer's intent is to guard against market declines. The processor's intent is to keep the processing plant running at full capacity and to obtain price increases. Although bookings are contracts, breaches are seldom prosecuted unless the financial losses are significant. Buyers may book with more than one processor to help ensure the best price and/or an adequate supply. Processors regularly overbook their capacity because they know the buyer may not keep the commitment. If a shortage develops during the year, processors allocate production to their advantage. An item produced to a buyer's personal specification (such as a pizza sauce with a unique formula) requires a firmer contract, which is more strictly enforced and commits performance by both parties.

Distributors have no way to forecast sales precisely and prefer the flexibility of booking their requirements. As a result, they are subject to market price fluctuations. Buyers who use distributors can obtain firm prices if they wish, but must commit to the processor through the distributor. This is usually practical only for large-volume users.

Some large-volume users may contract for an item directly with the processor and arrange for distribution, but some legal and marketing issues are involved with this type of transaction. Briefly, the seller must provide equal pricing to buyers with the same volume and service requirements. A direct buyer, however, may have different specifications or service requirements than a distributor. The distributor's account may then be billed at one price and the direct buyer's account at a different price. Disclosure must be made and agreements reached among processor, distributor, and buyer so that potential conflicts are avoided.

Buyers should know from whom their distributors purchase. Various field broker organizations and buying cooperatives market processed products. From the buyer's perspective, the product should pass through as few hands as possible before reaching the metropolitan distribution system, since each step can add costs. However, these marketing systems exist to fill a need and in many cases provide valuable services such as product consolidation for freight economies, inventory management, and improved warehouse turnovers.

Freight can be a major element in the cost of processed goods. For instance, tomatoes are largely produced on one coast and consumed on the other. While costs for distribution by truck are higher than those for railroad transport, delivery time is reduced. To compete with trucks, the railroads have offered an "in transit" system which involves consolidating products in a warehouse closer to the user. While some cost is added, the distributor's inventory turns are improved.

Pricing and Yields

Buyers must have access to data in order to measure prices. Packers' FOB price lists, distributors' price lists, USDA publications, and *The Wall Street Journal* can all provide useful information. *The Food Institute Report* gathers data and reports conditions and prices for a variety of products.[2] This report is quite accurate and may be used as a base point from which to begin negotiations. It also provides data on changes throughout the year which can be used to measure price performance by suppliers. Large buyers close to the packing industry may negotiate prices before these data are even published. The average buyer, without such contacts, should use these reports as a benchmark. The remaining discussion deals with pricing factors for the products detailed in sample specifications given in Exhibit 6.

Frozen Orange Juice Concentrate. Review Specification #1 for frozen orange juice given in Exhibit 6. A juice packer may request a higher price for this product than that quoted in the trade publications since this specification exceeds federal standards. Assume that Florida statistics show the following:

	End of April (million gallons)	Change from year earlier
Pack to date	125	− 8%
Sales movement into distribution	130	− 6%
Stock on hand	95	−18%
Imports to date	44	−39%

The packing level is down, reflecting heavy production and imports in the previous year. Sales are also down as a result of competition and economic conditions.

At the same time, frozen bulk concentrate is trading on the New York Cotton Exchange (CTN) at approximately $1.00 per pound, down from $1.50 per pound one year earlier. This price is depressed and any increase in consumption is likely to trigger a price increase. Contracting now appears to be prudent.

Processors must be found who are willing to blend and pack to this specification. Most juice is made from bulk concentrate, domestically produced throughout the season from various orange varieties. Large quantities of foreign-produced concentrate are imported and combined with domestic product by some processors. The specification requires 50% Valencia, a variety which is not harvested until late spring. Negotiations will take place in April and May and a processor will be selected by June.

The buyer has three options for pricing: firm, accelerating, and market. With the firm option, the price is set by bid or negotiation and the product is paid for upon completion of pack. With the accelerating option, the buyer agrees to buy a fixed quantity within one year. A base price is established by bid to which carrying charges (storage and interest) are added during the contract year. With the market option, the price fluctuates with the market or trading level.

Assume the trading level reported by *The Food Institute Report* is $19.19 FOB Florida (a dozen 32-ounce cans per case), with some discounts available for large-volume orders. This trading level is used as a benchmark to evaluate bids. The specified product may be priced higher than trading levels for the standard product, but the premium (difference between the prices) should remain constant through the life of the contract. For example, if a $1.00 per case premium is negotiated, the price should be $20.19 per case (19.19 + 1.00 = 20.19).

Distributors also have these three buying options, but they generally prefer to purchase at the market. A buyer using a distributor can select the firm or accelerating options, but negotiation then is between three parties: processor, distributor, and buyer.

Probably of greater importance to buyers purchasing from distributors is the distributor's policy regarding promotions and inventory pricing. *Promotions* in the form of trading level reductions are a common occurrence. *Floor protection*, at the time of a price decrease, allows credit to the distributor for a part of the floor stock. *Buy-in*, at the time of a price increase, permits the distributor to purchase some quantity at the lower price. How these factors will be reflected in the buyer's price should be a matter of prior agreement.

Frozen French Fry Potatoes. Review Specification #2 for frozen french fries given in Exhibit 6. The specification is slightly more restrictive than regular industry standards. However, this item is frequently produced by potato processors and represents an acceptable standard to request.

Trading levels are established at the time of harvest (which begins in September and is completed in December), fluctuating throughout the year in response to supply and demand. Buyers should concentrate their research efforts during this time and attempt to establish a pricing level that will remain constant until the following season. Beginning inventory, harvest estimates, and demand predictions all influence cost.

Potato processors publish price lists and trading levels evolve from these lists. Some idea of relative value can be obtained by comparing raw and processed costs. Assume processors buying bulk potatoes are paying about 4¢ per pound to growers in the West and 5¢ per pound in the East. About 55 pounds of blanched potato strips are obtained from 100 pounds of raw product (55% yield). Without considering processing or other production costs, the value of potato strips can be determined by dividing the price per pound by yield (expressed as a decimal):

$$\text{Value} = \frac{\text{Price per pound}}{\text{Yield}}$$

$$\text{Value (West)} = \frac{4¢}{.55} = 7.3¢$$

$$\text{Value (East)} = \frac{5¢}{.55} = 9.1¢$$

The actual cost of potato strips may be less than half of the trading level price for processed fries. Processed fries are priced at what the market will bear, not just on the basis of what they cost to produce. Alert buyers find ways to capitalize on this wide spread. Buyers should inquire about promotional activities and allowances. The spread may also be reduced by introducing competitive products or using nearby sources. Buyers should consider consolidating purchases to strengthen their bargaining position with the processor.

Canned Tomatoes. Refer to Specification #3 given in Exhibit 6. The specification calls for Extra Standard. This quality level is higher than that of the typical product quoted in trade publications, so a price increase may be expected.

Assume that canned tomato inventories are down 20% from a year earlier and prices are firm. Also assume that this year's field price is not expected to change from last year's levels, but anticipated production is predicted to be up 32%.

At the beginning of the season, supply and prices are likely to be unpredictable. Therefore, the buyer should not make long-term contracts but instead should spot buy for immediate needs. In this particular example, the buyer should wait until the harvest is well under way, opening prices are announced, and perhaps until trading levels are established, to determine if a firm price contract is in order.

Canned Peach Halves. Refer to Specification #4 given in Exhibit 6. Assume that *The Food Institute Report* shows this item to be trading at list price ($13.00) less a 50¢ promotional discount to net at $12.50. Also assume that in early April, before the current season peak, food service stocks are at 4.4 million cases (1% over a year earlier) and that retail inventories are up 6% to 16.7 million cases. Processors are offering discounts to get the inventory carry-in down so that opening prices can be maintained or increased from current levels.

Commitment before completion of harvest is a gamble for the buyer. However, in this case, there are two reasons for making a commitment that did not exist in the tomato example discussed earlier. First, peach prices are weak. Second, the peak harvest is forecasted to be smaller than the previous year. The decision could be made to purchase enough to last until the harvest is complete. The decision could then be re-evaluated at that time.

Frozen Green Peas. Refer to Specification #5 given in Exhibit 6. Assume that inventories are 22% less than the previous year and 25% less than the five-year average for this date. Twelve 2.5-pound cases FOB West Coast are quoted at 10¢ per pound more than last year. Also, assume that 2% fewer acres are expected to be planted in peas during the coming year. If the weather is unfavorable, prices could increase further.

The top price for peas is controlled by competing vegetables which can replace peas on the menu. The buyer might make a modest purchase to assure an ample supply until the new pack is available. All indicators point to existing or higher prices. Therefore, buyers could take a more aggressive position by purchasing supplies for the next six months. Buyers must calculate the cost/risk benefits and include the cost of carrying inventory as part of the product cost.

Price Forecasting

A large-volume buyer must gather as much information as possible before making price forecasts. Projected yields per acre, inventory carry-in, business forecasts, and industry capacity are all woven into the price forecast. Exhibit 7 shows an example of a production and supply forecast.

Buyers should follow the pack season closely, watching such factors as weather, predicted harvests, old pack prices, and opening prices for the new pack. Excessive cost increases in labor and energy can have an effect on price forecasts,

Exhibit 7   Sample Forecast of Production and Supply Levels

Production/Supply Forecast	Million Pounds
Carry-in (last September)	500
Production (last season)	+ 4000
Available	4500
Reduction (sales, distribution and inventory— last season)	− 3800
Carry-in (1)	700
Production (1)	+ 4000 (2)
Available (1)	4700
Reduction (1)	− 3800 (3)
Carry-out (1)	900 (4)

(1) Estimated this year.
(2) Production estimate based on acreage estimates, processors' intentions, and other forecasts.
(3) Reduction is based on forecasts of general business levels which predict that the next year will be flat (i.e., it will have the same usage levels as last year).
(4) The carry-out (which will be the carry-in for the succeeding year) is up substantially from the previous two years, indicating a weak market.

but their impact on prices of finished goods is considered insignificant. Time spent gathering facts prior to purchase will contribute to better buying judgments.

Endnotes

1. *National Shipping Point Trends* is published by the USDA's Agricultural Marketing Service (Fruit and Vegetable Division) in cooperation with various state departments of agriculture.

2. *The Food Institute Report* is published weekly by the American Institute of Food Distribution, Inc., 28-12 Broadway, Fair Lawn, NJ 07410.

REVIEW QUIZ

When you feel you have covered all of the material in this chapter, answer these questions. Choose the *best* answer. Check your answers with the correct ones found on the Review Quiz Answer Key at the end of this book.

True (T) or False (F)

T   F   1. California is a major producer of numerous commodities in both winter and summer.

T   F   2. Ultimately, the weather may have a dramatic effect on the prices of fresh produce.

T   F   3. States may not impose their own standards for fresh produce if federal standards already exist.

T   F   4. Agricultural marketing orders may in some cases establish minimum grades which may be shipped.

T   F   5. USDA standards should be used as a basis for developing specifications for fresh produce.

T   F   6. Practically all of Florida's orange crop is used for eating fresh.

T   F   7. Eastern grapes are most often used for processed products.

T   F   8. Casabas and Crenshaws are types of peaches.

T   F   9. The Russet Burbank is considered the ideal potato for baking.

T   F   10. Lettuce with a "nosey" condition means the product has a bad odor and is deteriorating.

T   F   11. Tops of carrots should remain attached since this helps the carrot retain moisture.

T   F   12. Primary distributors may specialize in one or two specific products and generally buy in truckload lots.

T   F   13. Packaging practices are identical in all growing areas.

T   F   14. The FDA is concerned with labeling and standards of identity, quality, and fill.

T   F   15. Can cutting is not an appropriate way to check the quality of canned products.

Multiple Choice

16. The government agency concerned with grading fresh fruits and vegetables is the:

   a. Federal Trade Commission.
   b. Agricultural Marketing Service.
   c. Federal Drug Administration.
   d. none of the above.

17.   Which of the following is *not* a good determinant of quality in grapefruit?

   a. weight
   b. skin color
   c. skin texture
   d. shape

18.   Early, Main, and Yellow Sweet Spanish are all types of:

   a. peppers.
   b. potatoes.
   c. onions.
   d. tomatoes.

19.   Specifications for processed fruits and vegetables may incorporate:

   a. count or other size designations.
   b. time of pack.
   c. preferred growing area.
   d. all of the above.

20.   When the buyer states the intention to use certain quantities of merchandise and the processor states the intention to reserve those quantities, the arrangement is called:

   a. booking.
   b. open price.
   c. hedging.
   d. field price.

Chapter Outline

Baked Goods
    Distribution and Pricing Patterns
    Specifications for Baked Goods
Grain-Based Products
    Wheat Flour
    Rice and Other Grains
Fats and Oils
Mayonnaise and Dressings
Sweeteners
Spices and Condiments
Field Products

Learning Objectives

1. Describe the major categories of baked goods distributors.

2. Characterize specifications for baked goods.

3. Identify different types of wheat flours.

4. Explain the major uses of fats and oils.

5. Describe specifications and pricing for fats and oils.

6. Describe the primary types of sweetener-based products.

7. Identify characteristics and categories of spices.

8. Describe quality checks used in the purchase of dried vegetables and nut products.

9. Differentiate between the two types of olives and list factors useful in their purchase.

10. Differentiate between the two types of pickles and list factors useful in their purchase.

14

Baked Goods and Miscellaneous Food Products

Baked goods and miscellaneous food products, often classified as grocery items, warrant special attention by the purchaser. While the dollar volumes may be considerably less than those for meat and poultry, the impact of purchase decisions on customer acceptance should not be underestimated.

Just as important as quality considerations is selection based on intended use. Many grocery items within the same category cannot be used interchangeably. For example, a cake flour may be totally unsuitable for preparing bread products; similarly, a cake shortening may produce disastrous results when used for deep frying.

Our discussion ranges from finished baked goods to raw ingredients such as grains and oils, and includes a number of other products which do not fit conveniently into previous categories. To the extent practical, these items must be carefully selected to ensure that value is received for the purchasing dollars spent.

Baked Goods

The general trend toward fresh foods is quite evident in the area of bakery products. Guests enjoy products that are baked fresh daily on the premises, and hospitality operations are capitalizing on the marketing implications of this fact. This trend runs counter to those that spawned the fast-food industry, which emphasized ready-made components, including baked goods, for assembly under controlled conditions at the retail unit.

Freshly baked bread can be quite appealing to guests, but may be too costly to produce. Utility, cleanup, and other costs are high relative to the value of the finished product. Bakery equipment is expensive and space-intensive. With the exception of highly automated plants, bread production requires a great deal of skilled labor. Each operation must decide whether to prepare bread on-site or choose from a number of convenience alternatives.

In this century, the bakery industry concentrated its efforts on specialization and mass production. High-volume operations with automated facilities developed, placing a premium on standardization and efficiency. To maintain volumes, these operations expanded their sales range to a regional and sometimes national level, oriented themselves toward consumers, and promoted products directly to end-users (primarily independent retailers, retail chains without bakeries, and food service operations).

As volumes used by food service operations increased, so did the influence of these operations on the bakery industry. Package sizes changed, new delivery and payment systems were devised, and special products were formulated.

Distribution and Pricing Patterns

Knowledge of distribution and pricing procedures can help purchasers become more effective in negotiating for baked goods. Procedures vary with the type of baking company used. Our discussion examines the basic means of distributing baked goods.

Traditional, Retail-Oriented Bakers. These bakers may use a "route salesperson" approach to distribution. Trucks are loaded each morning, with the driver as the salesperson. At the end of the day, the truck inventory is reconciled and the driver is compensated with a flat-base rate plus a sales commission. This system works well for retail sales where the driver stocks shelves and rotates products.

As both retail and hospitality sales have grown, however, distribution needs have changed. For some companies, the services of a driver/salesperson are unnecessary; store employees order, restock, and take inventory. This trend, coupled with the growth in contract baking for fast-food operations, has led to changes in pricing methods.

Bakery companies traditionally sold their products from a price list, with costs directed at moderately sized operations requiring a range of items. With the emergence of chain operations, sellers have restructured this pricing system to more closely reflect the cost of servicing the various accounts. The general pattern in the bakery industry involves establishment of a series of off-invoice discounts on a "service-needed" basis. Such practices may raise discriminatory pricing issues under the Robinson-Patman Act, however, and should be reviewed by legal counsel.

Limited-Line, High-Volume Bakers. These bakers stress good buying practices, an efficient manufacturing operation, and bulk-handling procedures for distribution. Such operations set product prices on the basis of specific time frames and various cost factors.

Since these bakers essentially operate on a cost-plus system, their effectiveness as buyers should be a major concern to end-users. A purchaser may contract on the basis of a pricing formula that includes the costs of ingredients, labor, energy, maintenance, and overhead. Exhibit 1 is an example of a pricing formula. Note that raw ingredient cost at 36¢ represents the largest single element in the price of hamburger buns—a cost which must be effectively managed by the baker.

Different approaches may be taken to manage ingredient costs. A baking firm may evaluate the market, decide that forward contracting is advisable, and consult with the end-user to gain concurrence. The raw material price is then firm for the duration of the contract. Other bakers, rather than speculate, fix prices for 60 days and, after that time, recompute costs based on the market price.

Once the product is fully cost-allocated for production, actual service costs must be assessed and agreed upon. In dealing with a particular supplier, the purchaser has to consider such factors as delivery frequency and range.

Exhibit 1   Pricing Example for Hamburger Buns

Component	Cost (¢/doz)
Ingredient cost	36.0
Packaging	2.5
Wages	9.0
Plant maintenance	3.0
Utilities	4.0
Other plant overhead	2.5
Administrative expenses	5.0
Supervision and markup	6.0
Cost per dozen—FOB dock	68.0¢

Other Distribution Options. Traditional local specialty bakers use various distribution and pricing methods. Negotiation takes place at the local level with no nationwide pattern to use as a guide.

Component manufacturers and national producers of shelf-stable items primarily distribute full-line and specialty products. Prices are usually obtained from published lists, starting with minimum order quantities and working down through price brackets. These brackets reflect cost economies as order size increases. Some manufacturers will produce a specific formula or a private-label product upon request.

Specifications for Baked Goods

In order to maintain consistency and quality, specifications are required for baked goods. Since these products contain a number of different ingredients, a standard set of specifications is difficult to develop. Decisions are based on more or less subjective determinations of product appearance and taste. In a frozen pie, for example, the amount and type of filling can be defined, yet unspecified procedures for handling and baking may also contribute to the acceptability of the finished product.

Therefore, baking specifications generally focus on physical characteristics (weight per dozen, slices per loaf, slice size, or fruit weight per pie), which can and should be measured. General specifications for several products illustrate how descriptions for bakery items might be developed.

- Bread, sandwich type: $1^{1/2}$ pounds baked weight; slice size $4^{1/4}$ to $4^{1/2}$ inch square; 25 slices per loaf; sealed polybag packaging; delivered within one day of baking.

- Bread, toast type: $1^{1/2}$ pounds baked weight; slice size 4×4 inch with round top; 28 slices per loaf; sealed polybag packaging; delivered within one day of baking.

- Hamburger bun, single slice, sesame-seeded: 26 ounces per dozen baked weight; $3^{1/2}$ inches diameter; 2 inches high; minimal amounts of misshapen products, excess pan flour, or internal holes; sealed polybag packaging; delivered within one day of baking.

"Day-Old" Products

What about "day-old" products? Items in this category are often one day out of a retail operation; they may actually be a week old. While such products are perfectly acceptable for some uses (bread crumbs, for example), operators and buyers should not misinterpret the designation "day-old." Know what you are buying and ensure that it really provides value to the food service operation.

Standards are in effect for bread and flour shipped in interstate commerce and labeled as "enriched." Such products must contain specified amounts of thiamine, riboflavin, niacin, and iron on a per pound basis. Calcium and Vitamin D are two optional ingredients used to enrich bread and flour.

Grain-Based Products

The cereal grains dominate world agriculture, occupying over 70% of total farm acreage. Wheat is considered the world's most important grain product. Rice runs a close second with corn trailing as a distant third. Other grain crops include oats, barley, rye, millet, and sorghum. Rye is second only to wheat as a major bread-making grain.

Since similar items may vary greatly in composition and baking characteristics, it is essential to match the correct product with the intended use. Let's look at some common grain products.

Wheat Flour

Grinding or milling of wheat for food has been practiced for thousands of years, and the basic techniques for processing wheat have not changed a great deal over time. The first flours were whole grain (or whole wheat as they are commonly known today).

A kernel of wheat has three edible parts: the bran, the germ, and the endosperm. The bran is the outer covering, which composes about 14.5% of the kernel. The germ is the sprouting section, which constitutes about 2.5% of the kernel. The endosperm, which is the source of white flour, composes approximately 83% of the kernel. The term "patent," still used today, refers to white flour of a fine grade produced by a patented process which separates these three parts.

Types of Wheat. The type of wheat used bears heavily on the products made from its flour. Three main types of wheat are:

Type	Protein in Flour
Hard Spring	11 to 16%
Hard Winter	9 to 14%
Soft	7 to 10%

High-protein (hard) flours are used in bread doughs. When combined with liquids and kneaded, a chewy desirable texture is achieved. Low-protein (soft) flours are used for biscuits, cakes, and crackers. The terms "bread flour" and "pastry flour" refer to specially formulated flours. All-purpose formulas have been developed for home use. Commercial bakers often use flour especially formulated for the end product.

Hard durum wheat is used to make macaroni products. The high-protein flour derived from this grain is ideal for the manufacture of products that must retain their shape during cooking. Egg noodles are durum flour noodles with approximately 5.5% egg solids added.

Distribution and Pricing. Wheat trading is big business. It was the first commodity traded in the United States on the Chicago Board of Trade. Exchanges are also located in Minneapolis and Kansas City. These futures exchanges offer an opportunity for buyers and sellers to meet and make transactions. The major uncertainties in such exchanges are harvest size and export volume.

The average buyer cannot use wheat prices to estimate flour costs; simply too many variables exist in the wheat market. For instance, wheat is used extensively in animal feed as well as in flour. Therefore, wheat prices reflect the market demand for both livestock and flour. Freight is also a significant cost factor for flour. Kansas City flour delivered to the eastern United States may have freight costs ranging from 3¢ to 6¢ per pound depending upon shipment size and method of transportation.

Flour prices are kept competitive because a sufficient number of flour manufacturers serve the market. In addition, these prices are a matter of public record. (*The Wall Street Journal* is one source for flour prices.) The large-quantity flour buyer should establish a spread between the price of the product delivered to the operating unit and the market price, recognizing that different flours have different cost structures.

Rice and Other Grains

Rice is produced primarily in the south-central part of the United States, although some is also grown in the West. Of the several types of rice available, food service operations generally use converted rice, which has been steamed and enriched.

In the United States, rice products are marketed in one of two ways: with an advertised consumer label or as a commodity. The variation in prices between these marketing approaches is substantial. On a recent day, a consumer brand product was offered at 45¢ per pound while #2 milled rice was quoted in *The Wall Street Journal* at 18¢ per pound FOB mill.

Products such as oats, barley, rye, and corn are usually not of great significance to hospitality buyers, but pricing techniques similar to those previously described for rice and wheat can be applied if these products are required.

The cost to produce breakfast cereals seldom has any relationship to their selling prices. Competition between several top producers yields the most reasonable prices for the majority of buyers. If the volume is significant, buyers can have their own formula produced. These private-label products are significantly less expensive than the branded products.

Fat and Oil Manufacturing Terms

Purchasers should understand the meaning of terms used to describe various processes in the manufacture of fats and oils.

Refining—Removing various amounts of free fatty acids, gums, color pigments, and perhaps seed particles.

Bleaching—Removing some color pigments and minor amounts of cleansing agents remaining after the refining process. It is a physical process rather than a chemical one. The oil is heated, agitated, and then filtered.

Hydrogenation—Adding hydrogen to unsaturated fatty acids in the oil, done for two purposes: (1) to retard fat interaction with oxygen and thus reduce rancidity, and (2) to raise the melting point, changing liquid/solid properties.

Winterization—Removing fatty acids that are of high molecular weight and more saturated, so that the oil will remain fluid and not become cloudy at refrigerator temperatures.

Deodorization—Heating under pressure, injecting steam, and removing materials which could contribute objectionable flavor or odor. The oil is left bland and colorless.

Formulation—Altering the manufacturing process or using additives so that the end product is better suited for its intended use.

Fats and Oils

Baking a simple mixture of flour and water would yield a tough, inedible product without the addition of special fats called shortenings. Shortening has unique properties that contribute to the tenderness of baked goods.

Fats and oils constitute an important part of our diets. Many fats are present, though not always apparent, in meat and dairy products. Other fats, such as frying oil and margarine, generate significant costs in operating a food service unit. The purchase of fats and oils may represent 4% of total food expenditures.

Sources and Primary Uses. Generally, fats come from animal sources and are solid, while oils come from plant sources and are liquid. The following is a list of seven raw materials used to produce the fats and oils that purchasers most often require, roughly in order of quantity produced:

- Soybean oil
- Cottonseed oil
- Corn oil
- Peanut oil
- Butterfat
- Lard
- Coconut oil

Exhibit 2   Common Frying Problems

Problem 1: Foods do not brown properly.
Check these factors:

- Breading—Improper breading can affect product color.
- Oil temperature—Is it too low?
- Recovery—Is basket overloaded, causing the temperature of oil to drop?
- Foaming—Oil could be breaking (decomposing). How long has it been in use?

Problem 2: Foods are too brown.
Check these factors:

- What types of foods have been fried? (For example, potatoes cause dark oil when sugar/starch is released into the oil and caramelizes.)
- Has the oil broken or been improperly filtered?

Problem 3: Objectionable fat flavor.
Check these factors:

- Does fresh oil (or food) have odor? What type of food (for example, fish) has been fried?
- Condition of oil in fryer—Is it old? Has it deteriorated? (For example, soy oil reverts unless treated, causing a beany or fishy flavor.)
- Has exhaust system dripped into the kettle?
- Were cleaning materials left in the kettle?

Problem 4: Excessive oil absorption.
Check these factors:

- Was food fried from thawed state?
- Improper drainage.
- Oil temperature—Is it too low?
- Was product incorrectly blanched by processor?
- Calibration of fryer.

Problem 5: Oil smoking or foaming.
Check these factors:

- Oil temperature—Is it too high?
- Was all gum/carbon removed from the kettle during cleaning?
- Has oil been freshly filtered?
- Excessive moisture in the raw material.

These materials are blended with other products (and sometimes with each other) to form specific food items, which vary widely in oil content. For instance, products intended for frying and baking are practically 100% oil, while salad dressing may have only 30% oil. Products must be evaluated both in terms of purchase costs and operating performance.

Buyers should discuss particular needs in fats and oils with those staff members who actually use the products. Buyers should also recognize the reasons for common problems that arise. Many relate to frying and are reviewed in Exhibit 2.

Baked goods. The final product determines the properties required in a fat. Major bread and roll bakeries typically use a liquid oil (primarily stabilized soybean oil), since it is much easier to handle and measure. Pie dough requires the good shortening properties supplied by a firm fat with a high level of saturated fatty acids. Fats used for cakes generally are further refined (texturized or pre-creamed) to provide a smooth texture. Emulsifiers are added to fats in order to stabilize the fat-water mixture and provide special characteristics such as stability in icings.

Frying fats/oils. In order to be stable at high temperatures, products used for frying must contain fatty acids with high molecular weights. When fat breaks down, it takes on an undesirable flavor and may foam. Flavor is a critical factor since oil content may be as high as 35% of the finished fried product. Frying fats should also possess a high smoke point—the temperature at which a fat or oil gives off a thin bluish smoke.[1] The smoke point of a fat used for deep fat frying decreases with use.

Low-volume frying operations reuse fat for longer time periods. Many high-volume, fast-food operations do so much deep frying that the product never gets old—it simply gets replaced. Cleaning the deep fryer then becomes a primary function, with regular filterings recommended.

Mayonnaise and dressings. These products are primarily made from soybean oil, although cottonseed and corn oils are also widely used. These oils require less processing than those used for baking or frying and should be less expensive. The oils are combined with other ingredients, such as eggs, cheese, buttermilk, sour cream, vinegar, spices, and lemon juice; the end product must remain stable after emulsification.

Margarine. Margarine generally refers to a product made from fats of either vegetable or animal origin. Today, vegetable oils are by far the most widely used in preparing margarine. By weight, margarine is 80% fat, 17 to 18.5% skim milk, and 1.5 to 3% salt. Products with less than 80% oil must be labeled "imitation."

In addition to the standard bulk and stick forms, margarine is available whipped with air, as chips, and in liquid and semi-liquid forms. Its price should closely follow the bulk oil market. Quality relates to the formula and manufacturing process used, salt level, melt characteristics, and blending ability.

Specifications. The fats and oils industry is dominated by large marketing-oriented companies, selling on the basis of better performance, longer product life, and training assistance. The buyer's mission is to find cost-saving alternatives within the range of options. The buyer must either have specifications that can be put out for bid or else have more than one brand approved for use.

Specifications provide a common basis for product comparisons, a necessary element in order to purchase fats and oils effectively. The major alterations to the basic specifications include the use of additives (such as methyl silicone to increase frying life) and/or modifications in processing (such as changing the molecular weight of fatty acids to improve frying properties).

Exhibit 3 gives sample specifications for baking and frying fats, as well as for salad oil and margarine.

Yields and Pricing. Soybean oil is produced by crushing soybeans and extracting the oil. Soybean meal (used for animal feed) is produced concurrently, so the prices of oil and meal are interrelated. Processors will crush primarily for oil or meal

Exhibit 3   Sample Specifications for Common Fats and Oils

Specification #1: Baking Fat

Solid fat index:	At 70°F (21°C), 20.5 to 22%
	At 80°F (27°C), 17 to 19%
	At 90°F (32°C), 14 to 16%
	At 104°F (40°C), 6 to 8%
Wiley melt point:	115–119°F (46–48°C)
Color:	As specified
Free fatty acid:	0.06%
Minimum smoke point:	325°F (163°C)
Emulsifier:	2.9 to 3.1%
AOM stability:	100 hours minimum*

Either plasticized or liquid. Packaging as specified.

Specification #2: Frying Fat

Solid fat index,	
Summer range:	At 70°F (21°C), 27 to 31%
	At 92°F (33°C), 13 to 16%
	At 104°F (40°C), 2%
Winter range:	At 70°F (21°C), 22 to 24%
	At 92°F (33°C), 6.5 to 8.5%
	At 104°F (40°C), 0 to .05%
Wiley melt point:	105–110°F (40–43°C)
Melt point:	106°F (41°C)
Congeal point:	86.5°F (30.3°C)
Minimum smoke point:	465°F (240°C)
Free fatty acid:	0.025%
Flavor:	Neutral and bland
AOM stability:	180 hours minimum*

Either plasticized or liquid. Packaging as specified.

Specification #3: Salad Oil

Oil:	Refined soybean oil
Free fatty acid:	0.05%
Peroxide value:	1.5
Color:	Neutral
Flavor:	Bland
Chill test:	More than 100 hours at 32°F (0°C)

(All major oil suppliers make a "refined salad oil.")

Specification #4: Margarine

Fat:	80% minimum (soybean oil and/or cottonseed oil)
Moisture:	16.1 to 16.3%
Nonfat milk solids:	1.3% minimum
Solid fat index:	At 50°F (10°C), 28.5% ± 1.5%
	At 70°F (21°C), 17.5% ± 1.5%
	At 90°F (32°C), 4.2% ± 0.8%
Free fatty acid:	0.05% maximum
Salt:	2.4 to 2.6%

Fortified with vitamins as labeled.

*AOM stands for active oxygen method. It is a technique for measuring fat stability—how long before a fat becomes rancid.

Sources: Specifications #1 and #2 are modifications of specifications established by Lever Brothers Co., Industrial Division, 390 Park Ave., New York. A specification used by C & T Refinery, Inc., Richmond, VA, forms the basis of Specification #3. The U.S. Food and Drug Administration has established standards for margarine, essentially those shown in Specification #4.

depending upon which product has the best profit margin. This obviously affects the supply of the other product.

Buyers should have crude oil prices available when making purchase decisions. Both *The Yellow Sheet* and *The Wall Street Journal* report current crude oil prices. Large buyers of refined oil products often work out price spreads with refiners based on a specified cents-per-pound over the reported crude oil price. Decatur crude oil cash price often forms the basis for these calculations. (Decatur is a central point in the soybean harvest region.)

Exhibit 4 is a pricing example which develops spreads for some common fats and oils (based on Specifications #1, #2, and #3 given in Exhibit 3). Buyers should set specifications or identify several manufacturers whose products are satisfactory, then negotiate price spreads on the basis of a reported price indicator (for instance, Decatur crude oil). The buyers should seek agreement that this spread will hold for a fixed term, ideally for at least a year. Spreads established during a depressed oil market perform better as prices advance.

Buyers should also follow the prices of soybeans, soybean meal, and soybean oil in the futures exchanges (the Chicago Board of Trade, for example). Because of futures activity, prices of soybean products very closely reflect a pure supply and

Exhibit 4   Spreads on Fat/Oil Specifications

Specification	Private Label		Decatur Price	Spread		
	Low (1)	High (2)	(3)	Low (1 − 3)		High (2 − 3)
Baking fat	32	36	18.5	13.5	to	17.5
Frying fat	30	34	18.5	11.5	to	15.5
Salad oil (bulk)	25	28	18.5	6.5	to	9.5
Salad oil (pkg.)	28	32	18.5	9.5	to	13.5

All figures are in cents per pound. To calculate the spreads, use the Decatur high price (column 3) and deduct it from the low (column 1) and high (column 2) sides of the range. For example, note that the low and high prices for baking fat are, respectively, 32¢ and 36¢. By deducting the Decatur price (18.5¢) from those ranges, the low side of the spread is 13.5¢ (the difference between columns 1 and 3) and the high side is 17.5¢ (the difference between columns 2 and 3).

Source: Private label prices were estimated by the author for purposes of example only. Decatur prices are published widely; one source is *The Wall Street Journal.*

demand relationship. Buyers can trade in these markets, or have their suppliers do so, with confidence that the prices reflect actual conditions.

Futures prices are affected by a premium paid over and above the futures price itself; for example, reported futures prices might be increased by 1¢. These premiums can vary, so it is best to get a precise quote from the supplier. After establishing the cash crude oil price for the futures month, the agreed-upon spread is added. Some processors of branded products are willing to negotiate with these techniques, while others are not.

The decision to use or not to use brands obviously relates to more than just purchase cost. Life of the product, quality of finished goods, and similar factors bear on purchase decisions. The time and effort devoted to developing specifications or other supply sources can pay off.

Mayonnaise and Dressings

Mayonnaise, salad dressings (similar to mayonnaise, but with a starch base), and table dressings form a diverse group of food service items. One ingredient common to many of these products is vegetable oil, as discussed previously in this chapter.

Oil requirements, as established by federal standards of identity, provide a gauge of cost changes related to this ingredient. Because these emulsified products are blended with other ingredients, however, the specific formula used by a manufacturer ultimately determines the cost. To further complicate matters, the selling price may have little relation to ingredient costs; rather, it is a question of what the market will bear.

The major marketing companies that sell these products work from price lists and offer price concessions based on volume and other factors. Knowledge of ingredient costs does not have a great impact on pricing, although it helps buyers evaluate the relative qualities of products. To use ingredient costs more effectively, buyers

Exhibit 5   Pricing Examples for Mayonnaise and Salad Dressing

Cost Estimate: Heavy Mayonnaise

Components	Cost ($/lb)
70% refined oil @ 27¢	= 0.189
15% eggs @ 60¢	= 0.09
Other ingredients	= 0.06
Ingredient cost	= 0.339
Processing (25%)	= 0.085
Total cost	= 0.424

Refined oil weighs about 7.7 pounds per gallon. Mayonnaise is somewhat lighter due to the other ingredients and the emulsification process. Assuming 7.25 pounds per gallon, cost is estimated as follows:

Cost/gallon = pounds/gallon × cost/pound
Cost/gallon = 7.25 pounds/gallon × $0.424/pound
Cost/gallon = $3.074/gallon

Cost Estimate: Salad Dressing

Components	Cost ($/lb)
40% oil @ 27¢	= 0.108
10% eggs @ 60¢	= 0.06
Other ingredients	= 0.08
Ingredient cost	= 0.248
Processing/overhead	= 0.084
Total cost	= 0.332

Assuming 7.25 pounds per gallon, the cost is estimated as follows:

Cost/gallon = pounds/gallon × cost/pound
Cost/gallon = 7.25 pounds/gallon × $0.332/pound
Cost/gallon = $2.407/gallon

must first know the formula. Fortunately, mayonnaise and salad dressings have simple formulas that allow cost estimations. Exhibit 5 illustrates the costing process.

When comparing table dressings, the buyer should look at weight per gallon, source of flavorings (natural or artificial), and quantity of eggs used. The industry offers formulas varying widely in price, usually a reflection of quality. If quantities used are large enough, formulas can be developed. Many individual operators make their own dressings without knowing actual costs. While the product may be better, buyers should still attempt to accurately measure costs.

Sweeteners

Sweeteners and products made with sweeteners constitute 5 to 10% of the total food expenditures for a food service operation. Much of this volume is in sweetener-intensive products such as soft drinks, pastries, and toppings. Sugar (sucrose) is the major sweetener but, in many manufactured products, it has been replaced by corn syrup (dextrose). The primary reason is economic: domestic corn syrup is priced 10 to 20% below sugar.

Sugar. Sugar is produced from sugar cane and sugar beets. Sugar cane is a member of the tropical grass family. U.S. production is centered toward the Gulf of Mexico. Sugar beets, on the other hand, grow in the temperate zones. While both sources yield sugar of equal quality, the cost to produce beet sugar is higher. Since world sugar production exceeds consumption, competitive pressures have caused the closing of many domestic plants which processed beet sugar.

The United States imports about 40% of its sugar. The countries of origin and their quotas are designated by legislation, amended annually upon the President's recommendation and Congress's concurrence. Legislation has been in place for many years to protect the domestic producer through subsidies, import duties on foreign products, and platforms below which the government will buy to maintain prices. World sugar prices have little effect on U.S. prices.

U.S. sugar prices are quoted in a number of publications, among them *The Wall Street Journal.* On a recent day, prices were as follows:

Refined can sugar—New York	$.326/lb
Raw cane sugar—New York	−$.220/lb
Refining spread	$.106/lb

The spread between New York refined and New York raw prices is called the refining spread.

Large-quantity buyers should attempt to base their costs on raw prices and negotiate a refining spread. The best way is to compare bids and decide between two acceptable refiners. Prices for raw sugar as well as refined products may vary around the country, usually due to freight differentials or possibly resulting from variances in supply and demand.

Small buyers must depend on their suppliers to make wise purchasing decisions. Such buyers can still challenge the fairness of the supplier's price by keeping abreast of the market. Local suppliers or distributors generally place their markups on top of the refined price.

Classifications for raw sugar are coarse, sanding grade, standard granulated, fine granulated, and very fine granulated. Below the very fine class, the sugar carries an "X" designation, the finest available being 10X. Brown sugar simply contains a percentage of molasses. The color of brown sugar determines its trade designation as light, medium, or dark.

Liquid Sugar. This form of sugar is used in many manufacturing operations. Price for liquid sugar should be based on the ratio of sucrose to water. Clear liquid sugar is available, but the amber form may be less expensive since it requires less processing.

Non-Caloric Sweeteners. Non-caloric sweeteners are important items for many food service buyers. Controversy surrounding their approval by the FDA is long-standing; buyers must be careful not to purchase questionable products. Most operations use individual portion packages, choosing between a consumer brand

and a distributor label. For this tabletop item, the operator must determine the value of brand recognition when compared with the added cost.

Honey. Honey is another source of pure sweetener. The USDA grades assigned to this product relate to uniform color, flavor, aroma, and clarity. Grade A (or Fancy) is the top quality, while Grade B (or Choice) is of slightly lower quality. Food service operations generally use portion packs of approximately one-half ounce each, an item carried by most jelly packers. The buyer should run comparative tests for preference among grades.

Jellies, Jams, Preserves, and Marmalades. These products may be sweetened by either natural sugars or non-caloric sweeteners, but must be at least 45 parts of fruit or fruit juice to 55 parts sweetener by weight. Products failing to meet the composition requirement must be labeled "imitation." The label must identify the source of sweetener.

In cooperation with industry, the USDA has developed grade standards for these products. Grade A (or Fancy) and Grade B (or Choice) must meet certain standards in terms of consistency, color, and flavor.

These products are available in a number of package sizes and quantities, including #10 size cans or glass jars of various sizes. The cost per ounce or pound should be calculated when comparing product costs. Many institutional buyers use portion packs, which are available in a variety of sizes and usually priced by the hundred or thousand. Package attractiveness, product quality, fill per unit, and brand recognition are points for the buyer to consider closely in deciding on portion packs.

Maple Sugar. Maple sugar was probably the first sweetener produced in North America and is still popular today. Most maple sugar is produced in Canada, but the northern United States still supplies some quantities. Many imitation maple flavorings are available and pure maple syrup may also be blended with less expensive sweeteners. Pure maple syrup is classified by the following USDA grades:

Light Amber	U.S. Grade AA
Medium Amber	U.S. Grade A
Dark Amber	U.S. Grade B

Dessert Toppings and Flavored Syrups. These sweetener-based products may be of interest to hospitality buyers. While lacking federal grades and standards of identity, the finished products must be made with wholesome ingredients and may be subject to inspection prior to use; state or local laws may also apply. An ingredient declaration must be prominently displayed on the label.

Chocolate fudge is the most popular dessert topping. Products of high quality usually include cocoa or chocolate, whole milk, sucrose, and stabilizer. Characteristics to check include stability, viscosity (degree to which a liquid resists flow), smoothness, and uniformity of color and texture. Most processors offer a variety of chocolate products with similar names and appearance, but in different price categories. The buyer must examine these products carefully to see which one gives the required quality at the lowest cost per serving. Weight per can may be another indicator of value.

Products generally fall into two categories:

- Toppings—Semisolid products; may require heating before serving.

- Flavored syrups—Less viscous products compared to toppings; may be used as they come from the container.

Any of these products may have either artificial or natural flavorings and a combination of different sweeteners. (A flavoring is the actual substance that gives a product its taste qualities.) While ingredients must be listed on the label in order of relative weight, there are no requirements that percentages of ingredients be shown. The buyer should ask the supplier for percentages, then establish specifications that ensure uniform products are purchased.

A wide assortment of flavored syrups are available, including strawberry, cherry, vanilla, and coffee. They may be used as drink flavorings (shakes and sodas) and ice cream toppings. Compared to synthetic flavorings, natural flavorings are more expensive and generally superior in taste. The value of flavored syrups is primarily based on the proportion of water to ingredients (in particular, flavoring and sugar).

Formulas can be developed, but most buyers do not consume adequate volumes to generate processor interest. The remaining option is to test products, determine how well they meet operational requirements, and request bids from potential suppliers. Buying is usually restricted to negotiation after the preferred product has been selected.

Spices and Condiments

Spices differ from flavorings in that spices are produced directly from naturally occurring plant substances. Flavorings (also called extracts) may be made from either natural or artificial sources, and represent a highly processed form.

Spices and condiments do not represent a large expenditure for food service operations. However, their use often determines the success of a dining experience. Therefore, buyers should not take risks in selecting specific suppliers.

Many of our spices originated in the Far East, either in China, India, or Indonesia. Today, many of these products are produced in other areas around the world. The United States produces some, but imports the vast majority. Three items—sesame seed, mustard seed, and black pepper—account for more than 60% of the total.

Several classifications fall within the spice category. Major groups and some examples follow:

- True spices—Pepper, cloves, and cinnamon.

- Herbs—Plant leaves such as sage and mint.

- Seeds—Caraway, celery, and mustard.

- Vegetable flakes—Dehydrated products such as onions, celery, and parsley.

- Blends—Combinations of the above (for example, spice salts, which are blends of table salt and dehydrated vegetable flakes).

Many other flavor developers or enhancers are not spices, strictly speaking. For example, monosodium glutamate (MSG) is the sodium salt of glutamic acid, a derivative of the wheat milling process.

The quality of a seasoning is reflected in its taste and smell. Grinding releases volatile oils in the product, resulting in a more pronounced fragrance; however, flavor content tends to dissipate more rapidly in ground spices. Packages of spices should be vacuum-sealed and used within a reasonable time. The best quality assurance for these products is choosing a reputable supplier.

Relatively few spice packers are located in the United States. They generally fall into either of two categories: a consumer label packer or a private label packer. Most retail chain stores carry both the consumer label and products packed under their chain brand name. Pricing of branded products is fairly consistent around the country given similar service records and quality specifications.

Prices for some raw unprocessed spices are published daily. For example, *The Wall Street Journal* has a daily spot cash price for whole black peppercorns, FOB New York City. A very large-volume user might be able to negotiate a cost-plus arrangement based upon published prices.

Buyers can usually obtain a spice processor's price list with little difficulty, even though they may be buying through a distributor. Examination of that list reveals a fairly standard pricing pattern. Using black pepper as an example:

- Whole black peppercorns in large containers FOB the processing plant have the lowest price.
- There are accelerating add-ons as the package size diminishes.
- There are add-ons for additional processing (for example, grinding).
- Freight cost (per unit basis) accelerates as the shipment size diminishes.

Some cost savings can be obtained through periodic reviews to ensure that proper container sizes are used by the hospitality operation. Informed buyers will know when to take advantage of promotions offered by many brand manufacturers throughout the year.

Field Products

This "catch-all" group includes such diverse products as dried vegetables, nuts, olives, and pickles. Buyers must know the intended use of a product before purchasing in order to secure the best value. The following section discusses some general categories of field products.

Dried Vegetables. These include members of the bean family (navy, red kidney, pinto, and lima beans). Other dried vegetables include peas (green and yellow, split and whole), garbanzo beans (chick-peas), black-eyed peas, and lentils.

Federal and state grades are available for some of these products. The best assurance of quality, however, is an inspection check. Products should be uniform in size and should retain some of the original fresh color. They should also be clean, containing a minimal number of broken seeds. No sticks, rocks, or other debris should be present.

Exhibit 6   Olive Sizes and Counts

Type	Green Count*	Ripe Counts** Whole	Ripe Counts** Pitted
Small	737	557	578
Medium	644	466	486
Large	539	404	402
X-Large	457	338	334
Mammoth	385	288	278
Giant	312	228	245
Jumbo	253	192	199
Colossal	199	152	163
Super-Colossal	172	128	—

* Approximate count per gallon container.
** Approximate count per #10 size can.

The Food Institute Report is a source of market information for dried vegetables. This report can be used by buyers to judge the reasonableness of distributor pricing.

Nut Products. The major types are almonds, walnuts, pecans, and peanuts. Walnuts usually refer to the light-skin English walnut, although black walnuts are used by some food service operators. Walnuts are primarily a California crop. On the other hand, peanuts and pecans are southeastern crops. There are three types of peanuts: Virginians, Spanish, and Runners (the predominant variety). Peanut butter is the end product for about half of the total peanut harvest.

The USDA has published standards for the most popular nut varieties as well as peanut butter. Inspectors assign official grades, which provide a good quality assurance tool. Many acceptable products are packed without USDA inspection; in these cases, visual inspections become all the more important.

Olives. Olives are available in two basic types: green and black. Most green olives are of the Spanish variety, imported from Spain and other Mediterranean countries. Green olives may be purchased whole, pitted, and stuffed.[2] Black olives undergo an oxidation process to yield their uniformly dark color. Practically all domestic production of black olives is located in California, while imports come from Greece. Exhibit 6 lists the sizes and approximate counts for green and black olives. In addition, various combinations of broken pieces are quite acceptable for certain uses.

USDA grades have been established for both types of olives, although imports will probably not carry a USDA grade shield. Olives are classified as Grade A (or Fancy), Grade B (or Choice), Grade C (or Standard), and Substandard. Color, texture, character, defects (or absence thereof), and uniformity of size and appearance are the standard USDA criteria used to establish grades.

The Food Institute Report contains some information relating to availability and pricing. Buyers should use this data to measure prices, taking into account any sales promotions.

Exhibit 7 Pickle Sizes and Counts

Size	Count (per gal)	Diameter
Midget	270 or more	$3/4''$ or less
Small Gherkin	135 to 269	Up to $15/16''$
Large Gherkin	65 to 134	Up to $1\,1/16''$
Small	40 to 64	Over $1\,1/16$ to $1\,3/8''$
Medium	26 to 39	Over $1\,3/8$ to $1\,1/2''$
Large	18 to 25	Over $1\,1/2$ to $1\,3/4''$
X-Large	12 to 17	Over $1\,3/4$ to $2\,1/8''$

Pickles. Pickles serve as condiments which supplement major meal items. They are processed in various areas of the country, but the majority of production has long been in the Midwest. This area produces ideal cucumbers for pickling. Small sizes are derived from immature cucumbers, and increased handling accounts for their relatively high cost.

The terms "cured" and "fresh-pack" are used to differentiate between processing types. Cured pickles are stored for a period of time in a brine and flavoring solution before packing. Fresh-pack pickles are immediately packed in a brine and flavoring solution, then put through a heat process to preserve the product.

Established standards for pickles relate to terminology, proportions of ingredients in mixed products, fills (minimum pickle content in containers), sizes, counts, and quality factors. USDA grades for pickles are Grade A (Fancy), Grade B (Extra Standard), and Substandard. Color, uniformity, defects, and texture are scored in grading. Scores of 90 and up are Grade A; scores of 80 to 90 are Grade B; and scores below 80 are Substandard. The uniformity factor is fairly restrictive regarding size, both for whole and cuts.

Buyers should be aware of grading information but should also realize that the process of selecting one product over another often involves a subjective decision requiring comparative tests. When purchasing pickles, the buyer should consider cost on the plate, appearance, and taste characteristics. Buyers must specify counts per container when ordering sliced pickle products. Exhibit 7 notes standard counts per gallon for whole pickles.

Particular attention should be given to pricing at harvest time when availability becomes known. Pickles should be selected after products from competitive suppliers are evaluated. If the quantity required is significant, contracts should be negotiated in late summer when the harvest is complete.

Endnotes

1. The smoke point for refined soybean oil is 492°F (256°C). Other descriptive terms for fat/oil properties include:

   Flash point—Temperature at which the mixture of vapor and air will ignite: 618°F (326°C) for refined soybean oil.

   Fire point—Temperature at which the substance will sustain a continued combustion: 673°F (356°C) for refined soybean oil.

Many fires begin in kitchen deep fryers. Safety concerns are of obvious importance as purchasers select fats and oils for deep frying.

2. Pitting and stuffing of olives was once done in the United States at ports of entry (POE) such as New York, but today, it is practically all done in the country of origin. Some repacking into various package sizes is still done in the United States.

REVIEW QUIZ

When you feel you have covered all of the material in this chapter, answer these questions. Choose the *best* answer. Check your answers with the correct ones found on the Review Quiz Answer Key at the end of this book.

True (T) or False (F)

T   F   1.   Quality is the most important factor in selecting grocery items.

T   F   2.   Products within the same general category may be used interchangeably; for example, cake flour may be used in place of bread flour.

T   F   3.   Limited-line, high-volume bakers essentially operate on a cost-plus basis.

T   F   4.   The three edible parts of wheat are the bran, the endosperm, and the germ.

T   F   5.   In general, soft wheat flours are higher in protein and lower in starch than hard wheat flours.

T   F   6.   Durum wheat flour is used for making macaroni products.

T   F   7.   Wheat prices provide a reliable, straightforward means of estimating flour prices.

T   F   8.   Fats come from animal sources and are solid at room temperature, while oils come from plant sources and are liquid at room temperature.

T   F   9.   Fats for frying should contain fatty acids with high molecular weights in order to be stable at high temperatures.

T   F   10.   Mayonnaise and salad dressings have simple formulas that allow cost estimations.

T   F   11.   Corn syrup (dextrose) is an economical replacement for sugar (sucrose) in many manufactured products.

T   F   12.   Jams and jellies with less than 45 parts of fruit or fruit juice to 55 parts sweetener (by weight) must be labeled "imitation."

T   F   13.   The best means to ensure quality of spice products is to select a reputable supplier.

T   F   14.   The two basic types of olives are green and black.

T   F   15.   Fresh-pack pickles are stored for a period of time in a brine and flavoring solution before packing.

Multiple Choice

16. The type of distributor most closely associated with a route salesperson system of delivery is a:

   a. component manufacturer.
   b. traditional retail-oriented baker.
   c. national producer of shelf-stable items.
   d. limited-line, high-volume baker.

17. Specifications for baked goods should focus on:

   a. physical characteristics.
   b. quality of the flour.
   c. packaging.
   d. none of the above.

18. The specific process by which fatty acids are removed so that oil will remain fluid and clear at refrigerator temperatures is called:

   a. refining.
   b. hydrogenation.
   c. bleaching.
   d. winterization.

19. Flavorings differ from spices because:

   a. flavorings come strictly from artificial sources.
   b. flavorings are highly processed substances.
   c. spices have grade standards.
   d. spices have had a volatile oil removed.

20. Which would *not* be considered a field product?

   a. dried vegetables
   b. nuts
   c. spices
   d. olives

Chapter Outline

Scale of Convenience Foods
Evaluating Convenience Foods
Categories of Convenience Foods
The Make-or-Buy Analysis
    Roles in the Make-or-Buy Analysis
    Steps in the Make-or-Buy Analysis
An Example of a Make-or-Buy Decision

Learning Objectives

1. Describe convenience foods.

2. Evaluate convenience foods in relation to their non-convenience counterparts.

3. List categories of convenience foods.

4. Explain the process involved in the make-or-buy decision.

15

Convenience Foods

CONVENIENCE FOODS ARE DESIGNED to reduce labor, time, and costs for the hospitality operation. A product may be classified as a convenience food if the labor involved in making the item is provided elsewhere. Its counterpart requires more on-site preparation and production labor.

Sometimes difficult to define, convenience foods have been referred to as efficiency or ready-service foods, minimally or partially processed foods, fast foods, and prepared foods. For some people, the term refers to frozen menu items which need only to be heated before service. For others, a traditional product such as tomato catsup represents a convenience food, since on-site labor is not required to process fresh tomatoes into catsup.

Historically, quality problems have negatively affected managerial decisions about the use of some convenience foods. The stigma surrounding convenience foods may have begun with the manufacture and processing of frozen "TV dinners" during the 1950s and early 1960s.

Today, the quality of certain convenience foods is still unacceptable; however, many new options are now available to the purchaser. In order to take fullest advantage of these options, the purchaser must first consider such factors as quality, cost, customer attitudes and preferences, space, equipment, impact on back-of-the-house operating procedures, and related management concerns.

With the variety of convenience foods available, purchase selections have become increasingly complex. Decisions to use convenience foods must be made on an item-by-item basis. Purchasers must determine whether and to what extent convenience items should be used.

During a time of increased competition, greater guest demand for value, and ever-increasing costs, it has become all the more difficult to obtain a satisfactory bottom line. The purchaser, by selecting convenience foods that reduce operating costs without sacrificing quality, can contribute to the success of the hospitality operation.

Scale of Convenience Foods

Almost any item could be classified as a convenience food since hospitality properties do not maintain dairy herds, grow wheat for flour, or raise trout on fish farms. Rather, purchasers frequently buy items which have been manufactured, processed, or prepared to some extent.

A more realistic view of convenience foods considers the amount of labor required on-site for preparing, cooking, and serving the menu item. A scale that takes these factors into account is illustrated in Exhibit 1. At each point in the scale,

315

Exhibit 1   Scale of Convenience Foods: Bread

All Preparation On-site				No Preparation On-site
Raw ingredients (flour, yeast, lard, etc.)	Pre-weighed and measured dry bread dough mix	Frozen bread dough	Baked bread (unsliced)	Ready-to-serve bread (sliced)

different levels of preparation for the same end product are shown. This scale can be applied to the purchase of a variety of products.

Assuming that the menu requires a loaf of bread, the purchaser has several alternatives offering increasing levels of convenience:

- Raw ingredients of the proper quality (flour, yeast, fat, and all other ingredients) according to the standard recipe developed by the baker and approved by the food and beverage manager. This option involves every step in preparing bread: weighing, measuring, combining, proofing, baking, and portioning.

- Pre-weighed and measured dry bread dough mix containing all ingredients required for bread dough except water. When this product is used, initial weighing and measuring of ingredients are not required.

- Frozen bread dough. This alternative eliminates the need to combine required ingredients with water.

- Baked, unsliced bread. Use of this option eliminates on-site proofing and baking.

- Ready-to-serve, sliced bread. On-site labor is required only to remove the item from its wrapping, since portioning has already been completed.

Bread can be purchased in many other forms as well. The purchaser has a number of options available for each menu item.

Evaluating Convenience Foods

Compared to on-site food production, convenience foods have a number of advantages and disadvantages. Purchasers must weigh these factors when judging the potential impact of convenience products on the operation.

Convenience foods allow broader menu choices since they require less time, labor, and equipment. Less equipment may relieve facility restrictions by making more space available; by the same token, capital/depreciation costs may be decreased. Convenience foods are usually easier to control in terms of portion, size, and cost. Purchasing, receiving, storing, and issuing costs may be lowered (e.g., when a frozen beef stew is purchased, none of the raw ingredients needed to prepare the stew on-site are required).

However, items produced on-site may be higher in quality. In addition, marketing approaches tend to favor "fresh" items made on-site as an important promotion point. Moreover, some raw ingredients are more consistently available

Fewer Differences Between Industries

A traditional difference between manufacturing industries and food and beverage operations has been the need in the latter to undertake a broad range of activities. For example, a plant which manufactures automobiles or clothing specializes in a specific task. After manufacture, products are shipped to another business in a different location specializing in selling and servicing the product. With this approach, the manager of the manufacturing operation can specialize in that activity; others take on the marketing and distribution responsibilities after production.

By contrast, think about a typical food and beverage operation. The manager must be an expert in the manufacture, purchase, storage, marketing, and distribution (service) of products (menu items). Managers traditionally needed a much wider knowledge base since specialization was not an option.

Today, with an increasing variety of quality convenience food items available, differences have decreased between manufacturing operations and food and beverage operations. Specialists in food production can prepare items off-site, and others can arrange for their distribution to the food and beverage outlet. At that point, the unit manager can focus more attention on market-oriented activities and can concentrate time and effort on specialized areas of responsibility.

from a wide range of suppliers than are convenience items, thus providing greater assurance of continued supply. Finally, if a specific menu item is required but is unavailable because of inferior quality or lack of a supply source, the operator may have no alternative to on-site preparation.

The use of convenience foods also has implications for employees. If equipment is already available and staff members can schedule the time, on-site preparation may be a cost-effective way to prepare required items. However, employees may resist the introduction of new convenience items, since they may fear job loss and/or reduced working hours.

Capital costs for space and equipment may not be decreased by the use of convenience foods, if, for example, space and equipment are required for other items prepared on-site. The use of convenience products may require additional freezer or refrigerator storage space. Convenience foods can be most cost-effective when labor schedules and equipment use are optimized.

One potential problem with convenience foods is that a guest visiting several establishments using the same convenience products may receive identical meals. How does an operation distinguish its convenience products from those of another property?

Manufacturers and processors of these products suggest that convenience foods merely be used to form the base of the final product served to guests. For example, the addition of select herbs and spices, sauces, and garnishes, as well as the way food is presented, can all help transform a mass-produced item into something unique. Given both the variety of products available and the many creative ways they may be differentiated, hospitality managers can resolve these potential concerns before they become problems.

It is impossible to generalize about the use of these products. Rather, specific decisions must be made by the property according to its individual requirements.

Categories of Convenience Foods

As previously mentioned, many items are commonly classified as convenience items, ranging from minimally processed foods to fully prepared items.

Fresh foods. Even fresh foods can sometimes be considered convenience items, since limited processing may reduce the amount of labor and preparation time. Examples include sliced cabbage for coleslaw; various chopped, diced, and shredded vegetables for salads; apples, oranges, and other fruits sliced for salads and garnishes; and, of course, "fresh-squeezed" fruit juices. Each of these fresh products has at least one factor in common: it can be served more easily and quickly because some labor has been applied off-site to prepare it for service. The alternatives (for instance, shredding and dicing fresh vegetables, baking bread, or squeezing juice) require more on-site labor.

Canned foods. Canning, as a way to preserve foods, has been practiced for over two hundred years. The preserved foods that Napoleon's soldiers carried with them contributed to their ability to cross mountains and conquer armies. Today, canned products include fruits which can be served immediately; vegetables which may only need to be heated; soups, sauces, and entrées; casserole items such as ravioli, stew, and hash; and juices, snack foods, and even wine.

Frozen foods. Frozen foods may present the widest variety of convenience food products. Many frozen items are pre-portioned to control costs and to ensure consistency (a mark of value from the customer's perspective). Frozen convenience foods probably come closer to the quality level of their fresh counterparts than do any other convenience foods. Of course, in order for quality standards to remain high, proper storage and handling (before and after products reach the food and beverage operation), preparation, and service procedures are necessary.

Seafood, beef, poultry, lamb, pork, and many pasta and casserole products lend themselves to freezing. An increasing variety of specialty entrées, diet and "exotic" appetizers, snacks, and hors d'oeuvres is available in the frozen state.

Dehydrated foods. Dehydrated foods enjoy some popularity in commercial and institutional food and beverage operations. Mixes for soups, sauces, and gravies are popular, as are dehydrated vegetables. Dehydrated beverage mixes include freeze-dried coffee and instant tea.

The Make-or-Buy Analysis

Convenience foods may or may not be appropriate for a particular operation. The buyer must first conduct careful make-or-buy analyses and take this information into consideration before reaching a final decision.

Deciding whether to use a product made on-site from scratch ("make") or to purchase it in a convenience form ("buy") is difficult and time-consuming. For this reason, many operators fail to place the proper emphasis on analysis. Professional purchasers, however, understand that a make-or-buy study is required in several different situations.

Convenience Foods: Not an "All or Nothing" Decision

Few, if any, hospitality operations use either convenience foods or on-site pre-pared items exclusively. Consider today's fast-food operations and their use of con-venience foods. The trend toward help-yourself salad bars may necessitate preparing salad greens, shredding cheese, chopping hard-cooked eggs, and preparing many other items. While it is possible to purchase these items ready for service, this may not be an option for many properties whose guests believe that "fresh is best." By contrast, it is highly unlikely that "gourmet" properties with high check averages will totally exclude convenience foods from their menu. Premium ice creams with high fat content, prepared seasonings and flavorings, and other items are purchased in a ready-to-use form.

Generally, purchasers working with food and beverage management and the culinary staff conduct make-or-buy analyses to determine whether products should be prepared on-site, purchased in a ready-service food form, or prepared from a minimally processed form. Since at least some items are prepared from scratch, most properties must have the expertise and equipment necessary for on-site production. The extent to which these resources are used depends primarily upon the planned menu and the market form of products that will satisfy the property's requirements.

When menu changes require new food items. This is when make-or-buy analyses are most commonly undertaken. If, for example, an operator wants to add a new item to the menu, many factors must be assessed. Will the guests enjoy the item? Does it fall within the operation's pricing structure? Can it be purchased and prepared at the desired level of quality? How do equipment, space, storage condi-tions, personnel, or related factors affect the property's ability to consistently offer the product in the desired quality and quantity?

Modification of existing products. Products currently in use may be causing problems. For instance, inconsistent quality; space, equipment, or volume prob-lems; or sporadic supplies of products may lead operators to look for alternatives. In such cases, a study of the continued use of the product, along with the make-or-buy analysis, may be in order.

Supplier performance problems. Operators always strive to minimize the possibility of supply shortages. Supplier performance is especially critical with re-gard to convenience foods. If a particular product is available from only one sup-plier, there is a heightened need to decide whether the product should be made on-site or dropped from the menu altogether.

Changes in required volumes. Convenience foods are sometimes purchased because large quantities are needed, and equipment, personnel, or space may not be available to prepare required items on-site. If the quantities served decrease over time, the decision to purchase a particular convenience item should be reconsidered.

Personnel considerations. If the availability of experienced production staff changes, it may have a significant impact upon earlier decisions to make or buy specific items.

A number of situations call for a make-or-buy analysis to ensure that the products purchased are best suited to the property. Conducting these studies is an integral and ongoing part of the purchaser's job.

Roles in the Make-or-Buy Analysis

Managers in production departments and personnel in the purchasing department each have some responsibility for the make-or-buy analysis. Purchasing staff act in an advisory capacity to managers in the food and beverage department. As such, they may be expected to provide significant technical expertise as the make-or-buy analysis is conducted. For example, purchasing personnel can:

- Identify suppliers who are able to provide the required raw ingredients or appropriate convenience foods.

- Obtain samples and help evaluate the quality of convenience foods as well as other related factors.

- Acquire and develop information required in the make-or-buy analysis.

- Obtain cost estimates of products made on-site and their convenience food counterparts.

- Participate in taste panels and otherwise provide support to management as make-or-buy analyses are conducted and purchasing decisions made.

What role do managers in production departments play as make-or-buy analyses are undertaken? First, these staff members plan the menus which, in turn, dictate purchase requirements. Managers are required to meet cost and profit objectives and the expectations of their supervisors. They must also develop work schedules, plan and implement standard operating procedures, and otherwise control the preparation, production, and service of all items.

Managers, chefs, and other personnel in the food and beverage department must contribute significant input to the make-or-buy analysis, exerting great influence over the process. In this capacity, they can request assistance from the purchasing staff, provide suggestions about eligible suppliers and acceptable products, participate in taste panels, and provide estimates of factors which must be assessed in cost studies. Management personnel, not purchasers, should make the final decision about whether food items should be produced on-site or purchased in a convenience form.

Steps in the Make-or-Buy Analysis

The make-or-buy analysis consists of several steps. Purchasers must be aware of these steps and understand the proper procedures to apply as each step is performed.

Step 1: Identify Specific Problems. As the make-or-buy analysis is conducted, individual problems must be identified and considered. In so doing, factors useful in evaluating alternatives will be better defined.

For example, if the objective is to assess whether a proposed new menu item should be produced on-site or purchased from an external source, the focus will be on marketing aspects to determine which is the better value from the guest's perspective. By contrast, if the objective is to reduce operating problems, the make-or-buy analysis goes beyond marketing concerns in considering whether current problems can be resolved or minimized by changing the form in which the product is purchased.

Additional steps in problem definition involve identifying all factors pertinent to the make-or-buy analysis and assessing the roles of affected persons and departments. Time constraints and the operation's priorities should be considered, as well as the opinions and attitudes of key personnel.

Step 2: Consider Quality Concerns. Quality is a critical concern from a guest's perspective and must therefore be considered in the make-or-buy analysis. For example, if a specific item is proposed for the menu but is not available in the correct quality or quantity from a supplier, the operator really has only two alternatives: either to prepare the product on-site or not to offer it at all. Conversely, if the food service operation lacks the expertise or proper equipment to prepare a menu item, the operator is again faced with two alternatives: either to purchase the product in a convenience form or not to include the item on the menu.

Quality supersedes all other factors. If products of the proper quality are available in convenience form, a make-or-buy analysis can be conducted. However, if convenience products of the proper quality cannot be found, no further analysis regarding cost or other factors is necessary. The product cannot be used if quality standards are not met.

Relationships between the purchasing staff and line managers must be considered when quality factors are addressed. Managers and other personnel in the food and beverage department make the final decision about quality standards in convenience products and their on-site counterparts. Line managers with day-to-day contact with guests are better able to understand their preferences and to establish acceptable quality levels.

Quality is more than an abstract concept. Objective taste tests, ideally with input from the guests themselves, help management and staff assess whether products of the required quality are available. Securing samples from suppliers is usually a purchasing responsibility. Purchasing staff should help evaluate products when they are received. However, the guest is the final judge of product quality. Guest input must be solicited and used in the decision-making process.

Step 3: Assess Cost Concerns. Given a choice between acceptable products that can be prepared on-site or purchased ready-made, decision-makers must consider the costs associated with each alternative. Typically, the costs involved in the purchase of convenience foods are easier to assess than are the costs associated with items prepared on-site. The major costs of convenience foods are obtained from supplier quotations; incidental garnish, sauce, or other product costs used to enhance these products are generally small and easily estimated. While handling costs are incurred for convenience foods in preparation, reconstitution, reheating, and service, these charges are much lower than those associated with on-site preparation.

Many expenses must be quantified to assess the costs involved in on-site prep-aration. Labor, supplies, energy, and related expenses must be determined in addi-tion to direct product costs. While some energy is needed to reheat convenience food items, it usually costs much less to reheat an item than to prepare it on-site.

Unfortunately, some expenses associated with on-site preparation are very difficult to quantify (for instance, management/supervision costs and employee training). Moreover, convenience foods allow management to spend more time on activities other than food preparation. While employees must still be trained when convenience foods are used, their training can usually focus more on sanitation, guest relations, and other activities and less directly on food preparation.

Capital costs for equipment and space also pose problems during many make-or-buy analyses. The decision to make or buy is not an "all or nothing" proposi-tion. If specialized equipment is required to reheat a convenience product, space and money for the equipment must be allocated. (A make-or-buy study shown later in this section provides an example of the detailed cost analysis helpful in the decision-making process.)

Step 4: Consider Other Related Factors. After quality and cost elements have been reviewed, other factors should be considered.

- Will convenience products be accepted by employees? Concerns about re-duced hours and/or loss of jobs may produce resistance among employees.

- Is the packaging of convenience foods acceptable? For example, if frozen products are used, their packaging must be suited to the property's storage conditions.

- Is the unit size of packaging acceptable? For example, a convenience food item may be unacceptable if it is available only in a very large amount and the op-eration needs individual portions.

- Can convenience food suppliers meet the property's needs? Suppliers should be judged on their ability to provide the desired products and required techni-cal information. Properties should also take past experiences with suppliers into consideration.

- Are portion sizes consistent in size and weight? When items are purchased in a portion-controlled form, consistent portioning is an important concern. When products are purchased in bulk quantities, the weight of the individual units should be considered.

- Is the convenience product compatible with the operation's existing facilities, space, and equipment?

Step 5: Make Comparisons Between Alternatives. If on-site items and those pur-chased in convenience form meet the minimum quality standards of the property, comparisons may be narrowed to cost and related factors. Cost comparisons per-mit an objective analysis, while an evaluation of other factors (see Step 4) further develops the impact of the make-or-buy decision. Purchasing staff members pri-marily provide suggestions and advice. Final decisions about product acceptabil-ity rest with line management in the food and beverage department.

Purchasers should recognize that the same convenience item may be available in a number of forms, ranging from minimally processed to ready-to-serve. For example, if on-site bread preparation is causing problems, the make-or-buy analysis can consider bread products already baked and sliced, as well as bread products in other stages of preparation.

Step 6: Implement the Decision. If products are to be made on-site, it is necessary to develop purchase specifications, make arrangements with eligible suppliers, and establish operating procedures. By contrast, if items are to be purchased in a convenience form, specifications (if applicable) and agreements with eligible suppliers must be negotiated. Regardless of the type of product purchased, it is necessary to follow the basic principles of purchasing management, to train all staff in handling procedures, and to monitor employees and products to ensure that correct procedures are consistently followed.

Step 7: Evaluate the Decision. No matter how thorough the initial analysis is, subsequent evaluation of the make-or-buy decision is necessary. Generating comments from guests, observing plate waste, asking questions of preparation staff, and conducting sensory (visual, smell, and taste) tests of the products are good indicators of the appropriateness of a particular product.

The process of conducting make-or-buy analyses is cyclical. It begins with an evaluation of alternatives and ends with an evaluation of decisions previously made. This process eventually leads to further refinement of decisions and additional make-or-buy analyses.

An Example of a Make-or-Buy Decision

A typical example of a make-or-buy decision made by hospitality operators is whether to make "stock" from scratch or to use a convenience food base.

Stock is a seasoned broth made from liquid used to boil meat, poultry, fish, seafood, or vegetables; it forms the basis for soups, sauces, and gravies. Soup is a liquid food prepared from stock, sometimes combined with a milk or cream sauce as well as various other ingredients. A sauce is any flavorful liquid dressing or relish served as an accompaniment to food, while a gravy is a type of sauce made from the juices of a cooked meat.

A stock provides the foundation of any soup, sauce, or gravy; therefore, the make-or-buy decision regarding stocks is very important. One of the "foundation" stocks used in these three items is beef stock. Consider the preparation of a 5-gallon recipe of beef stock using either the "stockpot" method (Option A) or the food base method (Option B).

A standard recipe for 5 gallons of beef stock is presented in Exhibit 2. Note that the recipe gives the product name (beef stock); yield (5 gallons); and a sequential listing of ingredients, quantities, and steps in preparation. This information can be used to evaluate the make-or-buy decision.

If the stock is produced from scratch (Option A), the calculations shown in Exhibit 3 can be made. The stockpot method requires constant simmering, with a total preparation time of 7 to 8 hours.

Exhibit 2   Beef Stock Recipe

Standard Recipe: Beef Stock; Yield = 5 Gallons

This is a classic recipe for 5 gallons of beef stock. Ingredients are cooked from scratch in a stockpot.

INGREDIENTS

Bones, cut small	30 lb	Thyme	$1/2$ tbsp
Onions	1 lb	Bay leaves	7–10 each
Celery	1 lb	Salt	$1/2$ tsp
Leeks	1 lb	Tomato paste	optional
Cold water	6.5 gal		

METHOD

1. Place the bones in a large roasting pan and brown in preheated oven at 375°F.
2. Turn bones occasionally to brown uniformly.
3. Remove bones from pan and place in stockpot.
4. Drain fat from pan and reserve.
5. Deglaze roasting pan with part of the water.
6. Cover bones with water and deglazing liquor and bring to a boil.
7. Reduce heat and simmer 3 to 4 hours.
8. Sauté vegetables for mirepoix in reserved fat until browned.
9. Add mirepoix, tomato paste (optional), thyme, bay leaves, and salt to stock.
10. Simmer for an additional 3 to 4 hours.
11. Strain through china cap and cheesecloth.
12. Cool, then refrigerate. Use as required.

TIME REQUIRED: 7–8 HOURS

Exhibit 3   Option A: Make from Scratch

	Cost of 5 Gallons
Ingredients	
Bones (30 lb @ $.70)	$21.00
Onions (1 lb @ $.39)	.39
Celery (1 lb @ $.44)	.44
Leeks (1 lb @ $.99)	.99
Cold water	.00
Thyme ($1/2$ tbsp)	.01
Bay leaves (7–10 each)	.01
Salt ($1/2$ tsp)	.01
Tomato paste (optional)	.00
TOTAL Standard Recipe Cost	$22.85
Labor cost (2 hours @ $10/hour including 10% fringe benefits)	20.00
Energy cost	2.00
TOTAL Cost	$44.85

$$\text{Cost per ounce} = \frac{\text{Total Cost}}{\text{Total Volume (oz)}}$$

$$\text{Cost per ounce} = \frac{\$44.85}{5 \text{ gallons} \times 128 \text{ oz/gal}}$$

$$\text{Cost per ounce} = \$.07$$

Exhibit 4   Option B: Use Food Base

	Cost of 5 Gallons
Ingredients	
Food base (1 lb)	$5.00
Water	.00
TOTAL Standard Recipe Cost	$5.00
Labor cost (15 minutes @ $6/hour including 10% fringe benefits)	$1.50
Energy cost	$ .25
TOTAL Cost	$6.75

$$\text{Cost per ounce} = \frac{\text{Total Cost}}{\text{Total Volume (oz)}}$$

$$\text{Cost per ounce} = \frac{\$6.75}{5 \text{ gallons} \times 128 \text{ oz/gal}}$$

$$\text{Cost per ounce} = \$.01$$

Option A results in a cost of $44.85, or $.07 per ounce of finished beef stock. One of the advantages of this method is that it makes use of bones and scraps of meat, poultry, fish, seafood, or vegetables that otherwise may be discarded. Option A's disadvantages include the time and energy involved, the need for a highly trained worker earning $10 per hour, the costly raw materials if scraps are not available (bones are expensive and in limited quantity today), the possible sanitation risks, the costly equipment and valuable space required, and the inconsistent finished product (in terms of appearance and flavor).

Option B involves simply combining the correct amount of food base with boiling water. The mixture is stirred until it is well dissolved. Costs may be determined as in Exhibit 4. The food base method requires a total of 15 minutes of preparation time.

Option B results in a 5-gallon recipe cost of $6.75, or $.01 per ounce of finished beef stock, as compared to $.07 per ounce by the stockpot method. The advantages of this method include: time and energy efficiency, ease of preparation, lower cost, better sanitation, minimal need for equipment and space, and consistent quality.

When considering the number of gallons used annually, the cost savings of Option B may be substantial. Moreover, one of the primary advantages of using food bases is their consistency—a characteristic that is not quantifiable in terms of dollar savings.

REVIEW QUIZ

When you feel you have covered all of the material in this chapter, answer these questions. Choose the *best* answer. Check your answers with the correct ones found on the Review Quiz Answer Key at the end of this book.

True (T) or False (F)

T   F   1. The limited variety of convenience foods restricts the number of menu choices.

T   F   2. Convenience foods vary greatly in degree of preparation necessary.

Multiple Choice

3. Make-or-buy analyses are most commonly undertaken as a result of:

   a. menu changes.
   b. equipment breakdown.
   c. supplier problems.
   d. increased volume requirements.

4. The first step in the make-or-buy analysis is to:

   a. consider quality concerns.
   b. identify specific problems.
   c. assess cost concerns.
   d. make comparisons between alternatives.

Chapter Outline

Trends in Alcoholic Beverage Consumption
Liquor
    Market Types
    Measures and Storage
Beer
    Classes
    Storage and Service
Wine
    Wine Terminology
    Countries of Origin
Purchasing Alcoholic Beverages
Quality Considerations for Non-Alcoholic
    Beverages
Coffee
    Background
    Specifications
    Coffee Pricing
Tea
Cocoa
Soft Drinks
    Historical Development
    Purchasing and Distribution

Learning Objectives

1. Outline differences in liquor brands.
2. Describe systems for controlling liquor storage and dispensing.
3. Differentiate between various types of beers.
4. Define common terms used in the wine industry.
5. Identify wines by place of origin and common designations.
6. Describe some common forms of packaging for wines.
7. Describe typical pricing patterns for alcoholic beverages.
8. Outline forms of distribution for alcoholic beverages.
9. Describe coffee from the standpoints of varieties, quality, stages of processing, and pricing.
10. Describe tea in terms of types, quality and grading, distribution, and pricing.
11. Identify cocoa sources and designations.
12. Describe the soft drinks industry.

16

Alcoholic and Non-Alcoholic Beverages

A NUMBER OF FACTORS make the purchase of beverages unique. Most beverages are purchased by brand, so the brand itself becomes the purchase specification. If food and beverage managers know their guests' preferences, they can specify the desired brands, reducing the time and effort required for purchasing activities.

The purchasing and marketing of beverages cannot be separated in most operations; because of this, the buyer may play a smaller role in the purchase of these items compared to other products. Therefore, this chapter emphasizes the marketing and operations aspects in great detail. The purpose is twofold: to highlight the need for line and purchasing staff to work cooperatively as beverage purchase decisions are made and, secondly, to focus on factors influencing the effectiveness of marketing decisions.

Trends in Alcoholic Beverage Consumption

Changes in our society have influenced the purchase and consumption of alcoholic beverages. Concerns about dram shop laws (third-party liquor liability) exert significant pressure upon the hospitality industry. Liability insurance may be difficult to obtain in some cases, and rates have increased rapidly.

Managers are offering and promoting non-alcoholic beverages as an alternative for guests. Public interest in health and well-being, concern for accident prevention, and changing lifestyles (including a decline in social drinking throughout the United States) are factors which have affected the beverage industry.

While per capita consumption of liquor is decreasing, the sale of alcoholic beverages continues to be an important part of the dining experience and the social habits of many guests. Guest preferences are shifting away from "hard" liquors to wines, wine coolers, and specialty drinks containing smaller quantities of alcohol. Also on the upswing are "mocktails," drinks containing no alcohol, but developed as eye-appealing, tasty substitutes for alcoholic beverages.

The marketing and sales implications of these trends are important to hospitality managers. Focusing on guests is essential to effective beverage management. Hospitality operations should develop creative ways to take advantage of the high contribution margins (gross revenue minus product costs) associated with beverage sales.

Liquor

Liquor represents a large, diverse group of distilled spirits including whiskey, brandy, schnapps, gin, rum, and vodka. For our purposes, a broad discussion of the subject will be sufficient.

Market Types

Liquor is identified by either "call" or "house" brands. "Call" brands (also known as "pour" brands) are those used when a guest requests a specific label such as Johnny Walker Black Label with soda or Canadian Club with water. When the guest orders "scotch and soda" or "whiskey and water" without requesting a specific brand, the establishment can supply any brand. Historically, "house" brands (also known as "well" brands) have been non-promoted labels purchased at lower cost than the "call" products. There may not be a difference in product quality, but the "call" brand costs more and receives greater recognition and status because of advertising and other distiller promotions. Acceptable, unadvertised brands can be used for guests without a brand preference. This is the operator's decision and it should be based upon quality, value, and guest satisfaction.

The trend today is toward greater use of recognized brands as a means of communicating quality to the customer. The cost differential is a cost-effective part of the marketing plan for many operators, who provide products of recognized labels at the bar in much the same manner that they supply condiments with familiar labels at the dining table.

Measures and Storage

The metric system is now generally in use for the purchase of spirits and wine, but most properties still measure in the familiar ounce system. Distributors can usually provide conversion tables upon request.

Many types of automated dispensing devices are available to control the alcoholic content (portion size) of prepared drinks. Using "measured shots" and interfacing automatic drink preparation equipment with cash registers can help control beverage costs and track bar income. Use of these devices enables the operator to buy in larger containers which provide a savings in packaging costs.

Storeroom managers, who often act as purchasers, should establish storeroom par levels, maintain perpetual and physical inventories, and keep supporting records for liquor products. Sales should form the basis of par levels, to be exceeded only with proper authorization. If purchases exceed par levels but are warranted by discounts, documents should note the reason for excess purchase size and the length of time the supply will last.

Like other beverage products, liquor should be stored at the proper temperature; 60°F (16°C) is ideal. Temperature extremes must be avoided. Inventory dollar levels and turnover standards for the storeroom must be set. These vary according to the buying policy, but they should be pre-established and regularly measured. For example, some companies use a one-week inventory as standard, providing 52 turns per year; stated another way, the cost of liquor in storage, on the average, equals approximately one week's beverage cost. Other companies specializing in wide selections of items may manage on the basis of four or five turns per year. It is important to calculate the effect of carrying costs (value of money and inventory taxes, for example) to be sure that the costs are recovered or, at least, understood.

Beer

Most Americans drink domestic beer produced by a handful of major U.S. producers. These producers have acquired over 70% of the market through manufacturing efficiencies which permit massive and innovative advertising campaigns. Beer is typically ordered by brand and is generally purchased by the bottle or can. Approximately 15% of total beer volume is sold in kegs and dispensed through taps identifying the brand. In many hotels and upscale restaurants, imports are becoming very popular, as are specialty, low-volume domestic beers. Americans generally prefer light-bodied, light-colored beers with dry aromatic characteristics.

Classes

Quality in beer is determined largely by the quality of the components used in making it. The brewing process also has a major influence on the finished product. Beers with typical (bottom) fermentation can be classified into several groupings.[1]

- Lager: Lager beer accounts for the majority of malt beverage production in the United States. Lager beers are light-bodied.

- Bock: This is a heavy, dark-colored beer, sweeter and richer in flavor than lager. Traditionally prepared to herald the arrival of spring, true bock beer is only available for about six weeks of the year.

- Dark Beer: This beer is made from malt toasted to a darker color than normal. It is often confused with bock beer, but it does not have the sweetness of true bock.

- Pilsner: This is a beer of the style of Pilsen, Czechoslovakia. Pilsner has a pronounced flavor of hops, a light body, and a light color.

- Bavarian: Bavarian is also light in body and color. Bavarian-type hops are used which give the beer its own distinctive character.

Other beer types are classified as top-fermentation because the yeasts that ferment the basic mixture rise to the surface instead of remaining on the bottom. Beverages in this category include:

- Ale: Ale is characterized by its more pronounced hops flavor, which makes it more bitter than lager beer. Ales are much favored by the English and Canadians.

- Porter: This is similar to ale, but is heavier and darker, with a rich and heavy foam. In flavor, it is sweeter, tastes less like hops, and possesses a distinctive malt character. Very dark malt is used in the brewing.

- Stout: This brew is closest to porter, but even darker and heavier, with more of a hops flavor.

- Weiss: Weiss is brewed from wheat malt and further differentiated by a second fermentation in the package.

Storage and Service

Some buyers make the mistake of assuming beer is a highly stable product. Quite the reverse is true—beer is a very perishable product. It is, in fact, a food product, being made from grains, yeasts, and hops, and should be treated as such. Finished and packaged beer leaving the brewery is at the peak of its flavor and aroma. It must be handled properly or else it may deteriorate. Beer does not age after packaging, but ages prior to that, in the lagering vats. Consequently, it must be kept fresh.

The sooner that beer is served, the better its taste, so FIFO (first in, first out) stock rotation is very important. Cool storage temperatures are desired because a lower temperature prolongs the storage time. If beer is stored at too high a temperature, it can significantly reduce the time that the beer retains top quality. The storage temperature can range between 40°F (4°C) and 70°F (21°C). The storage area must be clean and dry. Dampness can cause carton damage and, in extreme cases, rust on bottle caps.

Light is an enemy of beer freshness. Light-struck beer has an undesirable taste and aroma. Storage rooms should not have natural sources of sunlight; electric lights should be turned off when not in use. Beer bottles are dark-colored for this reason. Canned beer is not subject to light damage, but sunlight can cause heat buildup which may also cause damage.

Because they are not pasteurized, draught beers (pronounced draft) are preferred by many consumers. Since they yield greater profits, they are also preferred by many operators. Modern kegs are easy to tap and serving staff can be readily trained in the proper handling of the equipment. Whether serving canned, bottled, or draught beer, there are some fundamental procedures and rules to follow.

One fundamental condition that must be met is chilling to the proper temperature. Beer should be chilled to 36–38°F (2–3°C) before serving. Unpasteurized draught beer can spoil if held above 45°F (7°C). Canned or bottled beer won't spoil, but requires holding at that temperature in order to be served properly. Beer served too cold will be flat (the CO_2 is trapped) and perhaps cloudy. Beer served too warm will be "wild" and foam excessively.

Wine

Wine can help create an elegant dining atmosphere. The opportunities to improve the guest's experience and the unit's profitability concurrently are almost limitless. The server, who is the link between the operator and the guest, must be knowledgeable about the product. Some distributors, distillers, and vintners (wine producers) offer special services, such as constructing a wine list or training employees in wine service. Operators should use training programs to teach servers simple basics (how to open a bottle of wine, the name of house brands, and so forth) along with general information about wines.

Exhibit 1 Some Common Red and White Grapes

White Types

Chardonnay—Sometimes called Pinot Chardonnay, these grapes are the source for white burgundy. Originally from Champagne, France, they are considered the best white wine grape in California.

Chenin Blanc—One of the leading French white grapes, it is also found extensively in California. However, its quality is typically lower than its European counterpart.

Gewurztraminer—This is a spicy tasting grape from Alsace, France. California is now producing some excellent products.

Pinot Blanc—Originally from France and California, this grape is a close second to Chardonnay.

Riesling—Sometimes called Johannesberg Riesling, Rhine Riesling or White, it is Germany's leading variety of grape and is also grown in France and California.

Sauvignon Blanc—Also called Fume Blanc, these grapes originally came from France. This grape is now found in California.

Red Types

Cabernet Sauvignon—This is the leading red grape of California.

Carignane—This is the largest volume red grape of France and is used to make "ordinaire" wine; it is a large volume non-varietal in California.

Gamay—This Beaujolais grape is referred to as "Napa Gamay" in California.

Gamay Beaujolais—In California, it is from the Pinot Noir variety.

Grenache—Grown in France, California, and Spain, it is used primarily for Rosé wines.

Pinot Noir—While this is an excellent French red from Burgundy, it is of lesser quality in California.

Sangiovese—This primary Italian variety is used to produce Chianti wine.

Zinfandel—This is an excellent California red.

With the improvement in the quality and variety of domestic products, increased wine consumption is likely to continue. Wine is now available in bulk containers (similar to those used for fluid milk). These containers allow wines to be dispensed at the bar through a tap system much like that used for beer. Regardless of whether wine is required for large banquet groups or more intimate dining applications, there truly are wine products for everyone's taste.

Thousands of grape varieties have evolved from all parts of the world. Buyers should be aware that wine from similar grape varieties may have different names according to the region or country in which the grapes are grown. Several common varieties are shown in Exhibit 1.

Wine Terminology

Buyers must understand basic wine terminology. Some common terms applicable to wine purchasing are included in this discussion.

Vintages. Part of the wine mystique, vintages rate the quality and potential of the year's production. Historically, vintages primarily applied to France and Germany. However, wines from California and Italy now carry vintage information. Vintages had their origin in the past when quality varied substantially from year to year and region to region, depending on weather, processing procedures, and other factors.

Variations still occur but have been modified to some extent by modern production techniques. For the vast majority of wines sold, vintages have no application.

Varietals. This is a term unique to California and describes the primary grape variety in the bottle. Cabernet Sauvignon and Pinot Chardonnay are considered varietals. Some of this varietal production may carry vintage dates, which are the pride of the California vintners.

Generic. This is a general California term describing wines merchandised as European types (Burgundy, Chablis, Chianti, and others). Some are quite good; lower grades are generally called "jug wines." A somewhat similar term in France is "vin ordinaire" which defines common (ordinary) wine, with no origin shown and identified only as red, white, or rosé.

Blending. This practice involves combining different wines to achieve some purpose, usually to maintain consistency over time, but occasionally to utilize a product which otherwise might not be marketable. In California, most generics are blends.

Countries of Origin

While wines are produced in many countries, several areas are best known for their history and quality in wine production.

France. The French were the original wine makers and have the most honored tradition. Wine is made by thousands of vineyards around the country. A system of controlled labeling has developed which helps to preserve the integrity of the wine industry. The term "Appellation Controlee," when appearing on the bottle, means that the product qualifies for a controlled label designation. This term identifies the geographical origin of the product and implies that traditional production methods and grape varieties were used. While not a quality designation, the better wines usually come from areas under an "Appellation Controlee," which may cover one small vineyard or an entire district. For example, Burgundy has scores of small and quite precise Appellations which are recognized by wine buyers. In Bordeaux, the actual chateau in which the wine is produced is considered the best identification. For example, "Lafite-Rothschild" is a famous Bordeaux wine. The label might appear as follows:

- Chateau Lafite-Rothschild—The name of the producing Chateau (or estate)

- Grand Cru Classe—A Bordeaux rating for growths

- Appellation Pauillac Controlee—The controlling Appellation

- Mise en bouteilles au Chateau—The place of bottling (at the Chateau)

Wine regions that have not qualified for an Appellation may be labeled "V.D.Q.S." for Vins Delimites de Qualite Superieure. These can be good, well-made wines. Such ratings and designations have developed over hundreds of years and are the source of great and justified pride to the French.

Germany. The Germans have an elaborate and complicated system of assigning quality classifications and a well-defined labeling process which gives the buyer a great deal of information. They assign quality on the basis of sugar to acid ratio at the time of harvest. The more developed the sugar, the better the grade. The top grade is designated "QMP" for Qualitatswein Mit Praedikat (translated, this means "quality wine with special attributes"). Wines in this grade range from dry to very sweet. A further classification within the grade defines natural sugar content.

- Kabinett—best of vintage

- Spatlese—from riper grapes

- Auslese—sweet

- Beerenauslese—sweeter

- Trockenbeerenauslese—sweetest

There are two other grades, "Qualitatswein" (quality wine) and "Tafelwein" (table wine). Some very good products are bottled under the quality wine designation. Table wine is usually consumed within the country and is similar to the French vin ordinaire.

Geographical identifications have been developed to help in marketing German wines. Wine production is clustered along the Rhine and Moselle Rivers and practically all labels identify the area of origin. Wine from the Rhine may be made of Riesling or Sylvaner grapes. Rheingau and Rheinhessen, two regions within the Rhine, contribute most of the export product.

A label well known to Americans which comes from the Rhine region is Liebfraumilch, a generic term which identifies a type of product—not a specific estate or grape variety. It is produced by a number of different vintners with varying success.

The Riesling grape is used exclusively with Mosel wines. Labels usually show Moselle-Saar-Ruwer identifying the three rivers. In much the same manner that Rheingau describes an area in the Rhine, Bernkasteler describes the Moselle area. This name is well-known throughout the world as a good Riesling product from the Moselle. In similar fashion, Rheingau Johannisberger Riesling identifies a Riesling product from the Rhine. In addition, if German wine is bottled by estate or grower, the label will so state. German labels, then, provide the buyer with much information.

Italy. Italy produces more wine than any other country in the world. Much production is consumed within Italy where per capita consumption is the world's highest. There are wide variations in quality levels and a seemingly infinite number of producers. "Vino locale" is produced and generally consumed in the same village. "Cantina Sociale" is a term that says the wine was produced by a cooperative, with the name of the village accompanying this statement. The Italians have a system to identify the historical production performance of a geographical area similar to the French "Appellation Controlee." Their designation is usually shown on the label as "D.O.C.," standing for Denominazione di Origine Controllata e Garantita (controlled and guaranteed denomination of origin). The Italian denominations do not have the tradition or the restrictions present in the French Appellation, although substantial improvements are being made.

Chianti is the best recognized Italian wine. It is made from the Sangiovese grape. While Chianti is made throughout Italy, Tuscany is recognized as its home and the best wine generally comes from this area. The term "classico" means that the wine comes from a central section of a mature region, typically the best producing area. The older classicos (over three years) can be labeled "Riserva," which are similar to a good Bordeaux. These bottles are numbered and designated as vintages. Labels should also bear the name of the nearest major village.

California. California has produced wine since the days of the early Spanish missionaries. All grape varieties that exist there have been imported primarily from Europe. Today, California stands as the world's leading producer of good quality yet inexpensive wine products. Most of this increase in production and improvement in quality has occurred since the 1960s.

There are three broad classes of wines produced in California: varietals, generics, and jug types. A California varietal must contain at least 51% wine from grapes of the variety shown. A Cabernet Sauvignon must meet this minimum requirement to earn the label. As a matter of fact, most producers use a much higher percentage. If a vintage year is shown, at least 95% of the wine must come from grapes of that year. Cabernet Sauvignon and Pinot Chardonnay are the leading California varietals, although some additional varieties are excellent.

The California generic labels were adopted to copy the more famous French products. There is no variety requirement for California generics. A Burgundy may be made from any red grape in California while a French Burgundy comes from the Burgundy province of France and is most likely made from the Pinot Noir grape. A French Bordeaux is probably a Cabernet Sauvignon while the California equivalent would be bottled as a varietal. The largest volume production in California is in Zinfandel grape, which may be bottled as a varietal or used in generic production.

Jug wines are sometimes pasteurized to retard spoilage; this also hinders development of the wine. Most of these wines are consumed promptly and product consistency is probably more important than any other factor. Jug wine products need to be taste-tested to find one that suits the particular need and then retested regularly to ensure that the product remains consistent.

A California innovation is "bag in a box" wine with packaging similar to that used for years by dairies and tomato catsup processors. Current sizes range from 4 to 18 liters. The advantages claimed are less spoilage from partially used containers, less waste disposal, and lower labor costs. These packages can also be used with automatic metering devices which may offer better portion control for those operators currently using generic wines in the carafe or by the glass. Wine in this packaging must still be checked for quality and verified for shelf life.

Some wineries are also producing canned wine. The current application is small, but some value may be found in using this package, particularly where weight is a problem. Purchasers should be aware that non-traditional packaging does not always meet with the approval of wine connoisseurs, but these innovations appear to meet a market need.

Labels Tell the Story

Labels tell much about the wine in the bottle. Let's look at information typically found on California wine bottle labels and explore their meaning.[2]

Geographic Designation

California: All grapes must be grown in California; the wine must be produced and bottled in California.

Napa Valley (or Sonoma, etc.): 75% of the grapes in the wine must come from this area; the remainder may come from grapes grown anywhere in California.

Generic Labeling (Burgundy, Chablis, etc.)

There is no restriction on the types of grapes used as long as they are from within the state. Generically labeled wines are generally blended for consistency from year to year.

Varietal Labeling

Varietally labeled wine identifies the grape from which it was made and, in California, it is the surest guarantee the buyer has regarding what type of wine to expect. If a wine is labeled a Cabernet Sauvignon, for instance, it must contain a minimum of 51% of the designated grape. The other 49% need not be named. One of the reasons for such a wide range of prices (and qualities) in seemingly similar wines is that some producers may use the minimum (51%) and others may use more. High quality producers often use 100% of the named grape.

Name of Winery

The name of a winery given after some very similar phrases can have very dissimilar meanings. For example:

- "Produced and Bottled by": The winery crushed and fermented at least 75% of the wine; where the remaining 25% was crushed and fermented is unknown.
- "Made and Bottled by": The named winery must have made a minimum of 10% of the wine. The source of the other 90% need not be revealed.
- "Perfected and Bottled by," "Cellared and Bottled by," "Prepared and Bottled by": These phrases indicate that the named winery performed some finishing operations.
- "Bottled by": This is required by federal law and is not very informative.

Vintage Date

The date may be on the label proper or on a separate neck label. If vintage-dated, 95% of the wine must be made from grapes which have been harvested and crushed in the year named. If a varietal wine is vintage-dated, the minimum grape content is raised from 51% to 75%.

Date of Bottling

There is no legal requirement, but a few small producers do put this information on the label. It can be helpful in determining the expected life of some of the better wines.

Estate-Bottled

Such an imposing statement carries great meaning in Germany and France, but it has no legal meaning in California. As in vintage dating, if a wine is varietal and

(continued)

(continued)

> estate-bottled, the minimum grape requirement is increased to 75%. The statement
> has true meaning only in regard to the individual winemaker. It reflects his/her repu-
> tation, policies, and practices.
>
> **Special Terms** (Special Reserve, Private Reserve, Special Selection, Cask #, Lot #,
> Bin #, Cuvee, Special Bottling)
> These terms are without legal meaning and their value depends upon who the maker
> is. They may or may not mean there is anything special about the wine.
>
> **Alcoholic Content**
> The law allows only 1.5% deviation from the stated content. For example, a wine la-
> beled 11% must have at least 9.5% and not more than 12.5%.
>
> **Wine Content**
> Federal law guarantees a standard fill. Imported wines are not subject to this law. The
> rule is so stringent that a slight overfill is generally planned to avoid the risk of any
> short fill products.

The traditional varietal bottle contains 750 milliliters (approximately 21.8 ounces). The current trend is to vary this size, marketing larger and smaller packages to fit customers' needs.

To be classified as cooking wines by the Federal Bureau of Alcohol and Tobacco, salt must be added (by law at least 1.5%). These wines are sold without certain taxes because they are rendered undrinkable by the salt.

Purchasing Alcoholic Beverages

Pricing of alcoholic beverages is subject to a bewildering array of laws and regulations, primarily because of the taxes connected with these products. Some "controlled" states operate distribution and retail outlets with non-negotiable prices. In other "open" states, distribution and retailing are handled by private businesses. There are also states using a combination of suppliers (for example, Montgomery County in Maryland operates distribution and retailing while adjacent Prince Georges County uses private retailers). Other states control the price of liquor at wholesale (distributor) and at retail levels, yet do not perform the selling function themselves. Obviously, buyers must become very familiar with the regulations which affect the jurisdictions in which they operate. These regulations are available from applicable state alcoholic beverage control agencies.

Most liquor distributors change prices monthly whether they are state or privately managed. Price changes received from the distillers and any "specials" are then reflected in the distributor's prices. Generally, price lists are available which show bracket pricing (case prices based upon different purchase quantities) if available in that jurisdiction.

Post-Offs. One fairly common practice of distillers, where permitted, is to offer "post-offs," which are pass-through promotions usually ranging from 5 to 10% of the product's list wholesale price. Post-offs expressed in dollars per case are part of the distiller's annual promotion program and are announced far in advance, sometimes up to one year. They last for varying periods (usually about 30 days) and are available for various brands at different times around the country depending on jurisdiction. Serious buyers plot post-off periods (at least for the major brands) on a calendar and use this information in making purchase decisions.

One common practice is to reduce the inventory of a brand before the scheduled post-off, then buy increased quantities at the reduced post-off rate. Since most post-offs are available at least twice yearly (some more frequently), buyers can take advantage of reduced prices throughout the year. However, the cost of carrying inventory must be calculated into this decision.

Assume that a post-off occurs twice annually for brand "B." The list cost is $100 per case, the post-off is $8, and consumption is 120 cases every 6 months. If the product is bought without a post-off, the total cost for a 6-month period would be $12,000 (120 cases at $100 per case). If a 6-month inventory is purchased with the post-off discount, the cost would be:

120 cases @ $92 ($100 − $8)	= $11,040.00
Average inventory value ($11,040/2)	= 5,520.00

Taking into consideration carrying costs, the total investment and net savings can be calculated as follows:

Basic cost	= $11,040.00
Carrying costs (assume 1% per month)	
$5,520 × 1% × 6 months	= 331.20
Total investment	= $11,371.20

Net savings = $12,000 − $11,371.20 = $628.80

Is the net savings of $628.80 worth the investment, risk, and storage space? Should a smaller inventory be bought? Since it is more difficult to protect a large inventory than a smaller one, will inventory theft reduce the savings? The operator must answer these questions to determine whether the "deal" really is a "deal."

Distribution. Beverages are channeled to the operator through distributors. Beer companies usually handle their own distribution, but wine and spirits are normally handled by local distribution companies. The distillers and vintners seldom appoint exclusive distributors for a city, but not all distributors carry all product lines. The buyer then is generally faced with using more than one distributor unless the volume is so great that the selected distributor agrees to carry the additional items.

Typically, it is best to use as few distributors as possible, even if some modification in the list of brands carried must be made. Buyers must depend on the distributor to help plan post-off purchasing and, in some cases, wine selection. This can be done more effectively with one distributor than with several. Generally, a primary distributor is used, with others used only as necessary.

The selection of the primary distributor is important. Rules for the relationship should be made clear from the onset. For instance, only specified products should

---

Use the Triangle Test to Measure Acceptance

Measuring consumer acceptance of beverage products is always difficult. The triangle test is a good way to measure the acceptability of a new product when compared with that currently in use.

Make up two sets of three samples.

Set 1:   Two samples of the currently used beverage and one of the proposed beverage

Set 2:   Two samples of the proposed beverage and one of the currently used beverage

Convene a panel of five or more people and see if they can independently identify the two like samples within each set. Then determine if they can match the products in sets 1 and 2. Have them state personal flavor preferences. The results should indicate whether there is any discernible difference between the products. If not, the proposed product may be a reasonable substitute.

---

be supplied; no substitutions should be accepted. Delivery times and payment terms must also be established. Of course, pricing must conform to the law of the jurisdiction. Since pricing is largely controlled, there is a tendency to use off-invoice inducements such as free goods to promote sales (where legal). However, the buyer wants the lowest *legal* price and should specify and receive this. The agreement with the distributor should be that any legal discount, whether free goods or cash discounts, accrues to the benefit of the company and that any violation of this policy will result in the termination of the offending employee and discontinuance of the distributor's services.

In addition, the distributor can provide information helpful in planning buying cycles. Buyers can use historical quality and price standards when selecting distributors; service is one of the most important factors to consider.

Under certain circumstances, buyers can deal directly with distillers and vintners. This usually involves a private label for the specific property. In these cases, the distiller or vintner bottles a special formula and determines the selling price. This product flows through the normal distribution chain, whether state or privately managed, the appropriate taxes and distributor markups are applied, and it is then made available to the operation. Chain customers are the primary buyers of these "private label" products. A cost advantage may be likely, since marketing and manufacturing costs are lower, and these savings can legally be passed through to the buyer.

Quality Considerations for Non-Alcoholic Beverages

The remaining sections are devoted to the many non-alcoholic beverages which are required by food service operations. Coffee, tea, cocoa, and carbonated soft drinks are all very profitable items and, therefore, must be properly purchased and managed.

Non-alcoholic beverages are generally formulated in the operation by special machines. Within the operation, quality is usually affected by three factors: water (condition and temperature), ingredient formulas, and equipment condition.

Water is the major physical part of these drinks (approximately 97% in coffee, 85% in carbonated products). Cleanliness, sanitation, and temperature bear on product quality. Water should be filtered to remove impurities. Many operators use activated carbon filters to remove chlorine and other chemicals. Soft water should be used, since hard water affects the flavor of beverages and impedes equipment performance with calcium build-up. Of the several types of water softeners, polyphosphate is one recommended choice for this purpose.

The proper ratio of beverage ingredient to water (or ice) must be maintained. Most coffee today is pre-packaged to accommodate the quantity of water used. Carbonated drink formulas are usually metered automatically.

Coffee

Coffee is imported by the United States, since there is no domestic production of this product (with the minor exception of some Hawaiian coffee). Coffee supplies can be disrupted by weather (freezes), wars, and political upheaval. When these disruptions occur, they often cause dramatic price swings.

Background

Good quality coffee beans are a product of climate and cultivation. Better grades are grown 2,000 feet or more above sea level. Coffee plants need shade from the tropical sun, consistent amounts of moisture, and regular pruning. Picking must be done carefully to protect the unripe beans ("cherries") from damage and to exclude twigs or stones. Colombian coffees, since they meet quality concerns more closely, have long been considered the premium exportable coffee.

Varieties. The coffee bush or tree evolved in the Near East. Today, the Arabica variety forms the basis for the world coffee supply, having successfully adapted to other semi-tropical areas such as Brazil, Colombia, Venezuela, Mexico, and Central America. Two other independent varieties (Robusta and Liberacia) evolved in Africa and comprise about 25% of the world's supply. They are generally considered less desirable than the Arabica types, however. Each producing nation uses its own terminology to identify individual sub-varieties, terms which can confuse the coffee buyer. The discussion which follows applies to the primary exporting nations in South and Central America and Africa.

Buyers must understand some general terms:

- Brazils—Coffees grown in the country of Brazil. They are named after the region in which they are grown or the port through which they are shipped. Santos coffees are shipped through the port of Santos and account for 60% of Brazil's exports.

- Robusta—Coffees which largely come from Africa and are identified by country of origin such as Uganda, Ivory Coast, or the district of growth.

- Milds—Include all other varieties except Robustas and Brazils. Mild coffees are named after the country in which they are grown (e.g., Colombians, Mexicans, and Salvadors).

These terms are much misunderstood among both salespersons and consumers. Brazils, Robusta, or Milds do not describe flavor or quality. For example, a "mild" does not necessarily identify a coffee mild in flavor and lacking bitterness—it simply identifies the country of origin.

Quality and Blending. Two terms that do relate to quality are "rio" and "soft." Rio (river) identifies low-grown (river-grown) coffees which may be of the Arabica variety. Because of the climate in which they are grown, rios sometimes have a harsh flavor and lack other good quality factors. The term "soft" identifies fine-flavored coffees.

While these terms identify coffee characteristics, they do not guarantee good quality or even consistency. Coffee is a product of nature, so qualities vary from one growing season to the next. The length of time in storage also affects quality, since beans can lose moisture or develop mold. Blending beans from various sources is required to produce good coffee.

Commercial or nationally advertised brands are composed of several varieties of coffee. Blends may change annually or even more frequently depending upon the condition of the raw beans. An expert blender is needed to maintain a uniform blend flavor at all times even though the varieties composing the blend may undergo constant change. Coffees used in blends are selected for such characteristics as body, mellowness, sharpness, or filler (inexpensive coffee designed to reduce prices). "Body" is used to describe a brew which has a heavy flavor and aroma, while "thin" applies to a light, almost indistinct flavor and aroma. Sharpness is associated with acidity, which is typically a desirable characteristic in coffee.

Specifications

Roasting, grinding, and packaging specifications are important concerns. Each coffee has a definite character and purpose in the blend. Brazil is thin, sharp, and flavorful. Colombian has a fine coffee flavor and aroma, possessing both body and sharpness; it is mellow yet has noticeable, distinctive traits in comparison to the more bland Brazil. Centrals have much the same characteristics as Colombians, but are not as full-bodied. They are generally less expensive than Colombian and may be substituted for a cost savings. Robustas tend to have less flavor and aroma than American coffees; nonetheless, they do have high levels of soluble solids and are much used in vending and soluble coffee blends.

Grades. There is minimal regulation of coffee shipped into the United States. The New York Coffee and Sugar Exchange has established certain standards to qualify the "chops" (lots of 250 bags) for trading. The FDA has responsibility for determining that the product is wholesome and is traded under its proper name. Grades have been established, but they relate only to allowable defects in the form of extraneous matter such as sticks, stones, and twigs:

Defects Allowed Within Grade	Grade
1–9	#1
10–21	#2
22–45	#3
46–90	#4
91–170	#5
171–348	#6
349–450	#7

For example, a specification calling for "Santos 3-4's" would have an average of approximately 45 defects per bag.

Roasting. Roasting develops flavor in the bean. It releases the volatile oils in the bean and caramelizes the carbohydrates. The type of roast that is "put on" is determined by customer preference. It may be light, medium, heavy, or dark. Usually the roast length and temperature are timed electronically, but in some processing plants it is still done by appearance, roasting to a standard sample for color comparison. Most Americans prefer a light roast, while heavier roasts are more prevalent in foreign countries. The bean loses approximately 16% of its weight during roasting. When it reaches the proper color shade, the roast is "quenched" or "finished" by introducing water into the roast chamber to inhibit further cooking. The water vaporizes to steam and causes a more uniform color.

Grinding. Roasted beans may be purchased and ground at the property. For practical purposes, however, it is generally best to have the coffee ground and packaged by the processor, whose equipment and procedures are better than those found in most hospitality establishments. The specifications should state the grind requirements, which depend upon the type of urn to be used in making coffee.

Each grind contains particles of many sizes. Grinds differ only in the proportions of different particle sizes that they contain. These proportions are measured by shaking samples through a set of graded screens. Two screen sizes are used, 14 mesh and 28 mesh (per inch). The percentages remaining on each screen and in the bottom receptacle should be:

	Regular	Drip	Fine
Remaining on:			
14 mesh screen	33%	7%	none
28 mesh screen	55%	73%	70%
Retained in receptacle:	12%	20%	30%

The finer grinds are used when coffee passes through the coffee bed once, while coarser grinds are used in recirculating urns. In either case, the grind should be uniform.

Brewing. High-yield or high-extraction coffee products are also available. These claim to yield 25% more brewed coffee per pound at a cost just slightly more than the regular product. A special roast and grind are used. Three basic methods may be used to make these types of products:

- Traditional system—A finer grind and a darker roast is used. The product is in traditional crystal form.

- Flake—Coffee crystals are flattened to increase the surface area exposed to the water and to increase extraction.

- Low density/fast roast—The traditional system is used, but the product volume is expanded by introducing water at a crucial point in the process.

How does the purchaser compare prices of high-yield coffees with regular coffee products? Coffee is traditionally brewed at approximately 50 cups per pound (2.5 ounces per 8-cup pot brewer). Suppose that by using a high-yield product, total output of brewed coffee is increased 25%. Assuming regular coffee at $2.50 per pound and high-yield coffee at $2.70, the cost comparison is as follows:

	Cost per lb	Cups per lb	Cost per cup
Regular	$2.50	50	$.05 (2.50/50)
High-Yield	$2.70	62.5*	$.0432 (2.70/62.5)

*50 × 1.25 = 62.5 cups

In this example, better value is achieved by using the high-yield coffee. Of course, this assumes the products are of comparable quality.

Coffee Pricing

Large-volume coffee buyers can profit from a knowledge of market prices. As with other products, coffee prices can be estimated. Currently, the leading market service for coffee prices is *Complete Coffee Coverage*.[3] Another force in the market is the International Coffee Organization (ICO), headquartered in London and engaged in quota assignments to producing nations and promotion to increase consumption.

Exhibit 2 shows pricing formulas for two different coffee blends, but literally hundreds of blends are possible. These pricing formulas can be used to actually specify the coffee types to be blended or they can be used for pricing only, if the buyer leaves the blending in the hands of the roaster. At the very least, they can be used to compare with price offerings from suppliers.

The following steps are suggested to the buyer who wants to obtain the maximum coffee value.

Determine a Specification. If the volume used is large enough (2,000 to 3,000 pounds per week), some contract roasters are willing to experiment with the buyer. They agree to provide a specification that meets the need, and sell on a contract basis similar to the examples presented in Exhibit 2. If this option is not selected, many commercial blends are available. Again, buyers should determine what best suits their needs and test one brand against another using sensory perception: smell first, look for bright sharp odor, sip the brew (black), and check for a flavor which is sharp and acidic, not burnt or bitter.

Establish a Pricing System. There are two basic pricing systems. Buyers may use either a price list or a formula.

Exhibit 2   Pricing Formulas for Coffee

Formula I

60%	Santos 4's @ 2.44		= $1.46/lb
40%	Guatemalan Milds @ 1.63		= .65/lb
100%	Blend		= $2.11/lb
−16%	Roasting loss		
84%	Roasted cost*		= $2.51/lb
Add:	Processing cost	.25	
	Packaging cost (1 lb units)	.05	
	Profit	.15	
	Freight	.05	
Total added cost			.50/lb
Estimated cost to user			$3.01/lb

Formula II

100%	"Other Mild" Arabicas @ 2.29	= $2.29/lb
−16%	Roasting loss	
84%	Roasted cost*	2.73/lb
Total added cost (as above)		.50/lb
Estimated cost to user		$3.23/lb

$$*\text{Roasted cost} = \frac{\text{Raw coffee price}}{100\% - \text{Roasting loss}}$$

Note: The costs given in these formulas are estimates
        used for illustration only.

When using a roaster (or distributor) price list, buyers should realize that prices tend to change less frequently than the cost of raw coffee beans. It is best to have at least two suppliers and to regularly take bids, awarding the business for a fixed period to the low bidder. If only one product is acceptable, the operator depends on the supplier to price fairly.

If a formula pricing system is selected, buyers should establish a spread between reported prices and quoted prices. A fairly sophisticated system was described previously for a large buyer. Smaller buyers can also use a variation of this system. *The Wall Street Journal* carries daily green (unroasted) coffee bean prices in the "Cash Price" section; they were recently quoted at $2.25 per pound. The buyer might receive price quotations on two acceptable products at $3.00 and $3.25 per pound. The difference between *The Wall Street Journal* price and the low bid is $.75 per pound ($3.00 − 2.25 = $.75). The buyer can request that this spread be maintained by the supplier and that new prices be computed on the last Friday of each month for the following month's billing.

Control Receiving and Storage. Check incoming shipments for weight and quality. A sample from a previous shipment should be kept and compared to the quality of the new shipment. Always rotate stocks of coffee. Regardless of packaging, ground coffee should be consumed within two weeks of receipt. Use the FIFO system.

Manage the Brewing Process. Coffee should be brewed at 210°F (99°C) minimum and served at approximately 145°F (63°C). The urn and faucets should be clean. Coffee oils accumulate and become rancid, causing a bitter brew. The spray heads should be checked for proper water dispersal over the coffee bed. Water should be used at the recommended amount per pound of coffee and checked for condition; since hardness adversely effects quality, hard water should be treated with a softener.

Tea

Although tea is important in world commerce and ranks among the top ten internationally traded commodities, it is much less important than coffee as a beverage in the United States. Americans account for one-third of the world's coffee use, but less than one-tenth of the world's tea consumption.

There are three types of tea:

- Green: The leaves have been withered, rolled, and fired immediately; these teas are primarily used by the Chinese and Japanese.

- Black: The leaves have been fermented or oxidized before firing. This class is of primary importance in world trade and is the product generally used in the United States. Major exporting sites are India, Ceylon, Pakistan, Indonesia, and Africa.

- Oolong: These leaves have been partially fermented and are used primarily in blending.

Development of tea bags and "instant" soluble tea (strictly American innovations) has led to some increase in consumption, but it still lags behind population increases. New specialty teas offer a wide range of flavors and are gaining acceptance.

Grades and Quality. There are two basic grades of tea within the classes mentioned—leaf and broken grades. The term "broken" does not denote lack of quality, but rather that the tea is smaller than leaf grades. Broken grades comprise about 80% of the available supply, carry a higher price, and are generally preferred in the United States. Within the leaf and broken leaf grades, there are additional identifications such as Pekoe and Orange Pekoe.

Quality and flavor characteristics vary from one area to another depending upon growing conditions, moisture, cultivation, care in picking, and processing. It is necessary to blend various lots of tea to obtain a uniform, consistent brew. The major tea distributors in the United States have experts who buy from samples and perform this blending function. Some trade designations are explained in Exhibit 3.

Distribution. There are a few major companies in the United States that handle the bulk of tea distribution. Most of these companies import their own leaves and in some cases have buyers in the producing nations. The least expensive way to purchase tea is in 100-pound wooden crates. Blending, packing into bags, or converting to instant soluble tea all add to the price per pound. The buyer's decision regarding these alternatives must take into consideration the operation's volume

Exhibit 3   Black Tea Grades

Term	Abbreviation	Description
Orange Pekoe	O.P.	Thin leaves; some tip leaf; pale liquor
Pekoe	P.E.K.	Shorter leaves; more liquor color
Souchong	S.O.V.	Flat, open leaf; pale liquor
Broken Orange Pekoe	B.O.P.	Broken grade; best quality; small leaves contain tip; liquor is strong; good color
Broken Pekoe	B.P.	Larger than B.O.P.; less color; used as filler
Broken Pekoe Souchong	B.P.S.	Larger than B.P.; less color; used as filler
Fannings	E.N.G.S.	Top grade for tea bag use; smaller than B.O.P.; good brew with good color
Dust	D	Smallest grade; quick brew; strong flavor; used in blends

and ability to brew. Very little bulk tea is used today; in this case, convenience has proven more important than price.

Few companies in the United States have adequate volume to specify their own blend. Private labels are generally a standard acceptable blend, with the user company's tag. Sometimes, economic advantages can be gained by using private labels if the production costs are less. Generally, the processor passes any cost savings on to the buyer.

Pricing. Since tea is not a major U.S. product, pricing is difficult. *The Wall Street Journal* quotes prices on an irregular basis. Tea is quoted regularly on the London Exchange, but most American buyers do not have access to this information or are not in the position to use it. Buyers should perform taste tests and obtain competitive quotes. A broad range of prices exists because the spread between raw tea cost and tea bag price is wide. Tea is available pre-made in tanks, jugs, cans, and many other packagings. Another available form is soluble tea dispensed through machines. All of this convenience increases costs, and the buyer must determine cost per serving. Considering only product costs, the least expensive way to serve tea is to brew bulk tea at the operation.

Cocoa

Cocoa is a product of the cacao tree, which evolved in Central and South America. Of the many varieties of cacao trees, only two are commercially important. The criollo produces a "fine" or "flavor" cocoa. The foraserto yields a "base" or ordinary grade cocoa. Cacao trees flourish only in tropical climates. After harvest, the beans are dried, causing them to turn brown and lose nearly all of their moisture and about half their weight. Most cocoa imported into the United States is in this form.

The candy industry uses the majority of cocoa beans exported to the United States. Upon receipt in the United States, the processor cleans, blends, and roasts the beans; removes the shell; and leaves the meat. The meats are crushed, liquefying the cocoa butter (54% butter content) and forming a "chocolate liquor." In the manufacture of baking chocolate, this fat percentage is maintained. The manufacture of cocoa requires removal of some cocoa butter from the chocolate liquor.

There are generally accepted standards for the percentage of cocoa butter associated with common designations. Breakfast or high-fat cocoa should contain 22% cocoa fat. Cocoa or medium-fat cocoa should have 10 to 22% cocoa fat. Low-fat cocoa should be less than 10% cocoa fat. The cocoa butter removed during cocoa processing is later used in making milk chocolate and fudge topping.

The labeling of chocolate products is sometimes misleading, but, as a general rule, products labeled chocolate must be made from pure chocolate. A product made from cocoa may not be so labeled. For example, chocolate and cocoa are often used to flavor milk. When milk is flavored with chocolate, it may be labeled "chocolate milk." Milk or other dairy drinks made with cocoa should be labeled "chocolate flavored."

The cost of cocoa and chocolate products varies substantially depending on the amount of processing involved. There is no substitution for good specifications, healthy competition, and proper buying, although the buyer's task is still difficult.

Soft Drinks

For hospitality operators, a major source of revenue is flavored drinks, both carbonated and non-carbonated. Colas dominate the flavored drink field, constituting more than 50% of sales. Lemon-lime, orange, root beer, and ginger ale follow in popularity. Diet and decaffeinated products are becoming more popular.

Historical Development

Carbonated drinks have their origins in naturally occurring springs of carbonated water. The Greeks and Romans believed that bathing in these waters was physically beneficial. By the late 1700s, carbonated water was being produced commercially.

The branded carbonated beverage business began in the United States with root beer. Charles Hires established his company in Philadelphia in 1876 and brand identification was born. In 1885 in Waco, Texas, a "Dr. Pepper," who was actually a pharmacist, introduced the drink that bears his name. Coca-Cola was first sold in Atlanta soda fountains in 1886 and, by 1899, the company began franchising, which formed the basis of its early growth. Pepsi-Cola began in New Bern, North Carolina. Another pharmacist developed its formula and the company began bottling operations in 1904.

The formulas for the "cola" flavorings are closely guarded secrets and it is difficult to break down the components. Generally, these flavorings contain sweetener, caramel, acid, and extract from the cola nut. Cola trees are cultivated in Brazil, the West Indies, and west Africa. The nut is high in caffeine, smells like nutmeg, and looks like a horse chestnut.

Low-calorie drinks were introduced in 1952. At the end of the 1960s, Gatorade was marketed as the first product designed specifically to relieve thirst and restore energy by quickly replacing body liquids and salt lost as perspiration.

The use of concentrated syrups in food service operations grew from the original drug store soda fountains. Syrups were purchased by the gallon and combined with carbonated water. By the early 1950s, bottlers developed remote tank systems in conjunction with fountain equipment manufacturers.

Purchasing and Distribution

The carbonated beverage industry is dominated by several major companies. The hospitality buyer can choose among three alternatives in setting carbonated beverage specifications: nationally branded and promoted products, regional or controlled label products, and private label products. The choice depends upon marketing philosophy. Most of the major hospitality chains serve nationally branded products because they believe that this is what the guest wants. The major retail chains offer both branded merchandise and their own private label.

Syrups. Most food service operations use concentrated syrup which is reconstituted at one part syrup to at least five parts carbonated mix. Five-gallon containers are connected in tandem and directed to the fountain through a series of tubes, with carbonated water added at the fountain. Five-gallon pre-mixed product is available from most bottlers. It is ready to use with carbonation and water added by the bottler, and is primarily used with mobile equipment.

Selection of syrup brand establishes the purchasing system used. The major brand companies maintain national price schedules for their distributors and certain classes of direct customers. These schedules are constructed to reflect the cost of performing required services and are available to any customer who meets a standard set of qualifications, which includes size of the shipment, ordering procedures, and payment terms.

Promotion is an important part of the cost structure of manufacturers of syrup products. Customer recognition and acceptance of these branded products is a major part of their stock in trade. To keep their name before the public, the major companies engage in extensive joint advertising and promotion activities with their syrup customers. Syrup is the most profitable way for the soft drink companies to sell their products, which they promote heavily. Promotions vary from glass giveaways to menu or media advertising. The factors necessary to qualify for these programs are now standardized. The essential requirement is that value be received by both parties. Great care is taken so that these allowances are not construed as volume discounts in violation of the Robinson-Patman Act.

Equipment is offered on a lease basis from some syrup manufacturers, generally as part of a promotional package which displays the name or logo of the company. Over the years, the syrup companies have increased their emphasis on promotion activities, which should be a major consideration in the food service operator's selection.

Ready-to-Drink. Ready-to-drink products are of two types. They may be carbonated, then bottled and canned in a variety of sizes. Another form is pre-mixed (generally in five-gallon bulk containers). These products are usually sold on a competitive basis within the regional market. Ready-to-drink products are frequently manufactured by franchise bottlers, although syrup manufacturers operate some plants themselves in certain areas. Depending on the policies of the local franchises and competition, there may be substantial pricing variations by region.

Regional labels offer another alternative to the operator, particularly regarding ready-to-use products. They are generally less expensive than the branded products.

Private Label Products. Private label products offer food service buyers still another option. Flavor and syrup manufacturers have offered their products for years in competition with national brands. For example, the Howard Johnson Company successfully sold its own "HOJO" products. From the viewpoint of product cost, the savings potential is significant. The major ingredient in beverage syrups is sweetener. Liquid sugar costs about $.30 per pound; corn sweeteners are even less expensive. Assuming 5 pounds of sugar per gallon of syrup, the major ingredient then costs about $1.50 per gallon. The cost of syrup to the hospitality operator can easily be three or four times higher than this figure. Buyers and operators should make their own cost comparisons if they feel private label products are a reasonable alternative. While the above costs are only for illustration, a wide spread is likely. A decision has to be made as to how valuable brand identification is to the operation's customers.

Distribution. Distribution may be accomplished through manufacturers, franchised bottlers, or independent distributors. Usually, the size of the shipment determines the method. If purchased from the manufacturer or franchise bottler, the quoted price per gallon usually includes distribution costs. An independent distributor usually sells on a cost-plus basis. Buyers may find it to their advantage, however, to negotiate a fixed amount per tank or case rather than a percentage over cost.

If five-gallon tanks of syrup cost $25, a nominal markup of 10% would yield $2.50. This may be considered relatively high based on the distributor's cost to actually handle the product. Buyers might negotiate a fixed fee per tank for all of their syrup requirements. It should be understood that this negotiation is independent of the promotions sometimes offered by manufacturers of syrups.

Endnotes

1. The remainder of this section is from Donald Bell, *The Spirits of Hospitality* (East Lansing, Mich.: Educational Institute of the American Hotel & Motel Association, 1976), pp. 41–43.

2. Bell, pp. 108–110.

3. *Complete Coffee Coverage* is issued daily by George Gordon Paton & Co., Inc., 161 William Street, New York City, NY.

REVIEW QUIZ

When you feel you have covered all of the material in this chapter, answer these questions. Choose the *best* answer. Check your answers with the correct ones found on the Review Quiz Answer Key at the end of this book.

True (T) or False (F)

T   F   1. In purchasing beverages, the brand itself may serve as the purchase spec- 329 ification. T

T   F   2. Dram shop laws have had little effect upon the hospitality industry. F   329

T   F.   3. There is always a difference between the quality of a call brand and a 330 house brand liquor.

T   F   4. Storeroom par levels should be based on sales. T   330

T   F   5. The quality of beer is primarily governed by the quality of ingredients 331 used and the brewing process.

T   F.   6. In wine terminology, the term "varietal" rates the quality and potential of 333-334 the year's production.

T   F·   7. "Appellation Controlee" is a quality designation for Italian wines. franco 334

T   F   8. One purpose of blending wines is to utilize a product which otherwise 334 might not be marketable.

T   (F·)   9. A California varietal wine must contain at least 75% wine from grapes of 336 the variety shown. 51%

T   F   10. Wines are available in bulk containers so they may be dispensed like beer 333 in hospitality operations. T

T   F   11. Post-offs are special pass-through promotions offered by distillers. 338

T   F· (12.) Beers are normally handled by local distribution companies while wine and liquor companies handle their own distribution. 339

T   F   13. Soft water should be used for making non-alcoholic beverages. 341

T   (F)   14. A "broken" grade of tea indicates that the product lacks quality. smaller than leaf grade   346

T   F   15. Promotion is a major factor in the cost structure of syrup for soft drinks. 349

Multiple Choice

16. Guest preferences for alcoholic beverages are shifting toward:

    a. hard liquors.
    b. wine/wine coolers.
    c. mocktails.
    d. b and c.

Beer companies usually handle their own distribution, wine → handled by local distribution companies

17.   When a customer asks for a specific brand of liquor, it is referred to as a
_____ brand.

    a.   call
    b.   pour
    c.   house
    d.   a or b

18.   Which of the following is/are considered to be top-fermented products?

    a.   lager
    b.   pilsner
    c.   ale
    d.   a and b

19.   The top quality German wines carry the designation:

    a.   QMP.
    b.   Qualitatswein.
    c.   Tafelwein.
    d.   none of the above.

20.   The terms "Robusta" and "Milds" describe coffee on the basis of:

    a.   flavor.
    b.   quality.
    c.   country of origin.
    d.   blending procedures.

Chapter Outline

Capital Equipment
    Capital Equipment Manufacturers
Supplies
    Supply Categories
Services
Miscellaneous Products and Services
Marketing Practices
    Product Delivery Systems

Learning Objectives

1. Define capital equipment and discuss considerations in its purchase.

2. Explain how capital equipment manufacturers market their products.

3. Describe factors considered when specifying supplies.

4. List major supply categories and discuss specific selection factors.

5. Outline the criteria used in contracting for services.

6. Summarize miscellaneous products and services which may be required by hospitality operations.

7. Contrast the traditional and modern distribution systems for equipment and non-food supplies.

8. Describe the primary means by which equipment and non-food supplies are distributed.

9. Define four-tier pricing arrangements.

17

Equipment, Supplies, and Services

THIS CHAPTER DEALS with a vast assortment of purchases which fall outside the food and beverage category. Non-food items, equipment, and services form another category of expense, whose importance is related not only to costs but to the vital contribution they make to the effective operation of a hospitality business.

The three categories covered in this chapter are extremely broad, so an in-depth analysis of every product and service is beyond our scope. Rather, this chapter reviews general categories of equipment (particularly capital equipment), supplies, and services and suggests how they may be purchased. Product delivery systems are also discussed.

With the exception of large-volume operations, buyers are seldom in a position to dictate the specifications for custom-designed equipment and supply items. They generally must select from a limited number of standard or stock products available. This typically presents little problem to buyers, since enough options are generally offered by manufacturers to satisfy the needs of any operation. The aim of this chapter is to assist buyers in identifying points at which improvements in current purchasing practices can be made.

Capital Equipment

The term "capital equipment" describes items having a useful life of more than one year which are expensed through depreciation over their useful life. Examples include ovens, fryers, guestroom furniture, and office equipment such as computers. Equipment purchasing can be a highly technical and time-consuming task.

Equipment is purchased to perform a specific function. How well it performs that function is the key issue prevailing over all others. Other considerations include the length of the equipment's useful life and the amount of "downtime" likely for maintenance and repairs. The buyer should ascertain the *real* needs of the operation and identify equipment which best meets the property's requirements. However, buyers seldom question the proposed need for equipment. Challenging line department decisions is not part of the buyer's traditional role, despite possible benefits to the property. The buyer's role includes offering options to users and clarifying the operation's specific needs. In considering kitchen equipment, buyers may well ask "how often is each equipment item to be used, how will the proposed equipment affect the use of existing equipment, and could two pieces be replaced by one?" Seeking answers to these and related questions can help an operation's personnel define their equipment needs more precisely.

The buyer is involved in equipment purchase at two points: (1) when the specification is established and (2) when the purchase contract is negotiated. The buyer's goal is to have specifications for at least two pieces of equipment approved as interchangeable, thus allowing the buyer to negotiate with more than one supply source. Knowledge of the comparable capabilities of the two pieces of equipment is absolutely necessary. The buyer who wishes to influence the process of developing specifications must invest time and effort in order to be precise and forceful in presenting options.

Problems occur whenever a lack of comparable alternatives reduces the level of supplier competition. This situation is particularly true among equipment manufacturers, where purchasing is frequently limited to negotiation. Usually, buyers work with an equipment specification that restricts the negotiations to a specific manufacturer. In these situations, the basic specification is the brand and model of desired equipment, along with necessary modifications such as fabric type, electrical characteristics, and physical dimensions.

Sometimes, buyers issue bids using an "or equal" approach. In such cases, the supplier is permitted to quote prices on other brands judged to be equal to a specified brand. Of course, the supplier is responsible for proving the "equal" status. This approach can be useful in the initial design phase of a project; however, after blueprints are developed and finalized, substitutions become very difficult.

Capital Equipment Manufacturers

Traditionally, the equipment distributor provided design or layout services to the user when remodeling or installing new equipment. They also contracted to construct fabricated (custom-made) equipment required to complete the job and arranged for its installation. The distributor then sold the products through regular pricing schedules or in response to bid requests.

Product standardization was a major factor in the rapid expansion of hospitality units beginning in the 1950s. As a result, many chains developed internal departments to design their facilities. The next step was to contract centrally with manufacturers to acquire the equipment needed for those facilities. The local distributor, excluded from the planning and sales activity, became a delivery agent.

Responding to this centralized demand, several new types of organizations emerged. Consulting organizations were among them. Consultants initially came from the manufacturing or distributing areas. They were experienced in design, layout, engineering, installation, and budgeting. In other cases, chains developed the capability to perform these functions internally. Out of this development came the "turnkey" operation—a retail unit which is turned over to the operator ready for business. Some of the older equipment distributors have survived these changes by concentrating on replacement business for the chains and orders from independent operators. Others expanded into national organizations.

Manufacturers now market their equipment in three ways:

- Through specialized distributors that act on behalf of large organizations and provide logistical support (design, purchasing, delivery, and installation). They often have the facilities to manufacture specialized equipment such as ventilation hoods, sinks, tables, counters, and other custom-designed items not readily available off the shelf.

- Through traditional local distributors that provide support to smaller local operators.

- Directly to end-users for those large organizations that have the logistic capability to handle the distribution function.

In all three cases, manufacturers sell from price lists that reflect discounts for order size, dollar volume, prompt payment, and related considerations. Year-end volume, special promotions, and other allowances are often part of manufacturers' marketing plans. Buyers should inquire about such opportunities and take advantage of them if possible.

Warranties and service should also be considered. Most manufacturers have a standard published warranty policy. Buyers of equipment should maintain a file of such policies. Some companies offer an additional guarantee in the form of an optional service policy, which buyers may find cost-effective. One caution: warranties and service policies often get attached to invoices, stuck in the paid bill file, and are never seen again. Buyers who pay for these extended warranties should, of course, use them if problems arise.

Many hospitality buyers rate the value derived from energy savings, performance guarantees, and service ahead of price in selecting equipment. All of these factors should be addressed in specifications; most manufacturers strive to provide what their buyers desire in each of these areas.

Supplies

Supplies are consumable products such as paper cups, dishroom soap, guestroom amenities, and adding machine tape. Thousands of consumable supplies are required for operation; most are not a major concern to operators, until they are *not* available when needed or unless cumulative costs create financial problems.

Specifications for supplies are drawn from standard industry products by all but the largest volume buyers. Very few operations are able to have china fired, cloth woven, or flatware manufactured to their specifications. Fortunately, in most of the product areas, a fairly standard set of manufacturer specifications exists. In addition, each manufacturer may have several different quality levels for the same item; purchasers should be careful to compare products of equal quality.

If the organization assigns cost accountability to specific departments, the staff member with budget responsibility generally has specification authority also. The buyer must develop a rapport with this individual in order to make suggestions.

Developing specifications for consumable supplies involves defining the function (utility and/or appearance) of the product. Hospitality organizations, regardless of size, can be divided into public areas (front-of-the-house) and non-public areas (back-of-the-house). Supplies in the "utility" category are normally required by staff in non-public areas, while "appearance only" items are needed by persons working in public areas. Supplies in the "utility and appearance" category are usually shared between personnel in both areas. Emphasis on these two categories

Exhibit 1   Utility and Appearance Considerations in Selecting Supplies

Utility	Utility/Appearance	Appearance
Kitchen aluminum foil	Sandwich foil wrap	Pictures/wall decorations
Kitchen film wrap	Bags, gift/carry-out	Bread service equipment
Cleaning supplies	Salt/pepper shakers	Table top lamps
Forms/office supplies	China	Table linens/napkins
Maintenance supplies	Flatware	
Kitchen utensils/containers	Glassware	
Light bulbs and tools	Bed linens	
	Tray/table liners	
	Tissue, paper towels	

varies with the type of operation, but each product should be reviewed with respect to functional concerns and the relative importance of the function.

For example, trash liners made from polyethylene are used in many operations. The gauge (thickness) of the material is vital. A thin gauge trash liner may cost half as much as a thick variety, yet may be unsuitable for its intended use in a specific property. The only concern is utility: short-term trash storage performed at the least possible cost. The two purchase issues are:

- the proper size to fit the container and

- the proper gauge or thickness to provide required strength.

Both of these issues bear on how much material is used to make the bag; the amount of material, in turn, is the major cost variable. A heavy gauge liner to fit a 55-gallon can will probably cost twice as much as a 33-gallon liner of the same gauge, and may be four times as expensive as a light gauge 33-gallon liner.

On the other hand, items such as tabletop lamps are selected for appearance first and utility second. When the desired lamp is selected, its model number becomes the specification.

By separating supplies into categories based on utility and appearance, operations can identify the determining factors in selecting any given item, thus yielding alternate products and purchasing procedures. Examples of product categories are shown in Exhibit 1. As all products have some level of utility, the classifications are somewhat arbitrary.

Supply Categories

Supplies have traditionally been marketed through distributors for the same reasons that equipment manufacturers used this channel: distributors provided services that both buyers and manufacturers wanted. The supply manufacturers used a territorial franchise system which assured the distributor of credited sales within the territory and provided the manufacturer with exclusive representation in that area.

The same factors which affected equipment manufacturers had an impact on the supply companies as well. The emergence of chain operations resulted in fewer, more efficient distributors. Whenever a distributor did not contribute to the process, a chain organization would try to make direct purchases. The manufacturers were forced to redesign their traditional marketing approaches.

Marketing has been increasingly directed toward the end-user, a trend that will continue as chains gain a greater share of the market. Manufacturers have devised a pricing system that appeals to the large direct user and yields competitive prices through the various distributor channels. Basic elements of the marketing system for some supply items are reviewed for several categories in the following discussion.

China, Glassware, and Flatware. Manufacturers produce these items in a standardized range.[1] Published specifications make it relatively simple to draw comparisons. Buyers can easily obtain price lists, and may obtain further discounts depending on volume. Since freight is a big cost factor, the total weight of individual shipments bears on the price, particularly with less dense (lighter) products.

Manufacturers find value in having products displayed by distributors in the local markets; some manufacturers offer a "stocking discount" when a specified quantity is available at the distributor's showroom. Buyers should be aware of this practice since they may qualify for discounts if, for instance, they carry some inventory in their own warehouses.

Large user organizations, either direct chain buyers or distributors, can have items manufactured to their own specifications. This may or may not have an effect on price lists. In effect, this is a type of bid, with price dependent on such factors as order size, specifications, and the manufacturer's need for the business. Most orders from Asian manufacturers are on a bid basis. If required supplies meet the purchasing specifications and match item requirements, prices normally are lower than for items produced domestically. Lower production costs and subsidized industries are among the reasons for price differences. Potential disadvantages include requirements for large quantity ordering and the long lead times involved.

China. Only a few china manufacturers operate in the United States and all make durable ware. Specifications are usually limited to pattern choices, although large users can obtain special sizes and shapes if the volume is adequate. The average buyer can do little to influence manufacturers' decisions with regard to clay, glaze, or firing time.

Since china is expensive, durability is an important selection factor. In many cases, breakage occurs due to improper handling during washing and storage. Commercial quality china that is fairly resistant to breaking, chipping, and scratching is available from some manufacturers.

Asia is becoming an important site for manufacturing china. Korea, Taiwan, and China have joined Japan as exporters to the United States. Prices for imports can be substantially below domestic cost. Their quality is usually satisfactory, but must be carefully checked. Look for glaze defects, finished bottoms on cups and saucers (which reduces scratching), and decal imperfections. Testing in actual use provides the best indication of product acceptability. Industry grades are select, firsts, seconds, and thirds.

Purchasers should be familiar with other forms of tableware. While disposable dinnerware is unacceptable in many dining room situations, it is used almost exclusively by fast-food, take-out, and delicatessen operations. Managers may find stoneware and earthenware acceptable alternatives to china in some instances.

Glassware. Many of the same factors important in purchasing china also apply to glassware. Breakage is certainly a factor because of replacement costs. Like china, glassware must be compatible with the theme and atmosphere of the property. Shape and size of glassware varies with intended use.

Common glass is made from silica, soda, and lime. The addition of lead oxide adds to its strength and appearance. Repeated heating adds more strength, but also increases costs. Most glass is machine-molded and is weakest at the fusion points. There are only a few glass producers in the United States; products are specified by manufacturer's item number.

Flatware. Flatware is available in a range of prices and styles to suit almost any requirement. Silverplate and stainless steel are standard flatware materials; true silverware is prohibitively expensive for almost all food service operations.

Stainless steel is by far the most common choice in flatware. Stainless flatware is produced by stamping or grade-rolling. Grade-rolling produces the best flatware, since the sheet thickness is varied to accommodate individual items. Stainless flatware should be 12-gauge at a minimum and its finish should be smooth and polished. Chrome-nickel steel has long been used and an 18-8 formula (18% chrome, 8% nickel, and 74% steel) is usually considered a good specification. The chrome adds luster to the flatware's appearance, but ultimately becomes rusty or pitted.

Asian countries producing china also manufacture stainless flatware, some of it very good. (These countries also produce other stainless steel products such as steam table pans, ladles, and cream pitchers.) Buyers should specify gauge, alloy, and finish; samples should be examined for strength and quality.

Silverplate is produced by electroplating a nickel and copper "blank" (unfinished, non-plated form) with silver. Nickel adds strength. Depending on the amount of silver used, silverplate is designated as heavy, triple, or standard. Historically, a teaspoon was used as the standard and all other pieces were required to have an identical depth of silverplate. Heavy weight has eight ounces of silver per gross (12 dozen) of teaspoons, triple weight has six ounces, and standard weight has five ounces. If teaspoon blanks weigh 132 ounces per gross, the blank to silver ratio is 16.5 to 1 for heavy weight silverplate:

$$\text{Blank:Silver} = \frac{\text{Weight of blank}}{\text{Weight of silver}}$$

$$\text{Blank:Silver} = \frac{132 \text{ oz blanks}}{8 \text{ oz silver}}$$

$$\text{Blank:Silver} = 16.5$$

This approximate ratio should be maintained for other flatware items. There are only a few U.S. silverplate manufacturers and specifications are usually by silver weight, total weight, and pattern.

Paper Products, Napkins, Cups, Foil, Film, and Towels. Manufacturers of these items operate in a manner similar to the producers of china, glass, and silverware.

However, there is more bidding and contracting for fixed quantities over a specified time period. Most manufacturers maintain price lists and discount from those lists. Specially designed and printed merchandise is widely used. Printing is normally priced from an established schedule.

In choosing aluminum foil products, the thickness of the foil is a decisive factor since gauge is the major cost factor and affects intended use. If special printing is needed, the buyer has different negotiation concerns than if generic printing or non-printed products are used. Specifications are fairly standardized among manufacturers; standard sizes are less expensive than special sizes.

Chemicals and Cleaning Supplies. There are a few large national manufacturers and hundreds of small regional producers of these supplies. National companies have product lines that are broad and deep. They have traditionally been direct marketers and sellers, heavily oriented toward service. Prices are based on total volume and delivery size, with the potential for significant savings as delivery size increases. Marketing is based on close contact with the end-user. Small manufacturers produce a more limited line of products, usually at a lower cost.

Chemical products are reasonably easy to manufacture. Literally hundreds of companies make these products, but the hospitality market is dominated by a few large organizations that focus on service as well as on products. Product performance is an important measure in determining value; how a product is used is often more important than what is used.

Suppliers of these products may also provide service arrangements. The types of services offered include employee training in proper product use, quantity control, and, in some instances, inspection and maintenance of equipment used in the cleaning activity. Although these products may be purchased without service arrangements, most properties find the increased level of service worth the added cost. Otherwise, the buyer's organization must assume responsibility for maintaining and supervising equipment that often requires specialized attention.

Specifications are typically brand-name products from major companies. Controlled, comparative tests of products over a period of time can help identify the best products. The operator should keep records and restrict use of products to their intended use. At least two products from competing companies should be used to solicit prices. Because service is often a component of product cost, frequent changes in suppliers are not practical. Some buyers specify only one company and negotiate a fixed term with a fixed price.

Linens. The number of domestic linen manufacturers has declined as less expensive imports gain a greater share of the market. While list prices with volume discounts are available, most purchases are bid or negotiated. Such negotiations may be based on a specific volume, usage over a specific time, or both. Prices and product quality can vary substantially, so good specifications are a prerequisite to buying. Some manufacturers protect their distributors and require all but the largest volume buyers to deal through this network. Most of these companies manufacture primarily for retail sales, with the hospitality industry as a secondary customer. The buyer should identify the manufacturer and attempt to learn something about the company's pricing practice. Beyond that, an open bid with good specifications helps maintain competition.

Other Supplies. The vast majority of forms and office supplies are priced off-the-shelf from a schedule graduated by volume. Specially designed and printed merchandise may be listed on a price schedule or may be purchased through bidding.

While buyers may expect few discounts on items such as equipment parts, there may be significant reductions for other items such as light bulbs, paint, and auto tires. Direct buying depends on the specific policy of the manufacturer; some protect their distribution network and do not sell directly to hospitality organizations.

Services

Services are jobs performed by outside contractors. They may be provided when equipment is purchased or leased where preventive maintenance is part of the agreement (for example, cash-handling equipment and heating, ventilating, and air-conditioning systems). Money collection, landscaping, and roofing repair involve the purchase of services only. The recent trend toward using outside contractors relieves operations of duties that were traditionally performed by hotel staff.

The purchase of services, with or without equipment, is often a neglected area since it generally falls between areas of individual responsibility. Some examples of activities covered in this category include:

- Copy machine leasing and maintenance

- Cash-handling equipment leasing

- Money pick-up services

- Pest control services

- Office machine maintenance

- Refrigerator service

- Kitchen hood and duct cleaning

These are just a few of the services required by hospitality operations. Most of these activities are labor-intensive, with the number of hours involved determining the charge. Level of service is the key factor. How often is the service needed and to what extent? What equipment is necessary? Costs of computer services are often difficult to manage because of an inability to accurately measure the tasks to be done.

Considerable up-front analysis must be applied to the purchase of all services. For example, an operation considering pest control services should begin by answering some basic questions.

- Does the pest control company carry out an audit of pest populations in order to pinpoint problems?

- What kinds of pesticides will be used and how will applications be scheduled?

- What equipment will be used to apply the selected pesticides?

- How will program effectiveness be monitored?

Establishing specifications need not be a long and involved process. However, the amount of money to be spent on a service always bears on how much time should be spent in its study. Establishing performance requirements for contract services is always more effective than merely asking a group of suppliers to detail their capabilities.

Miscellaneous Products and Services

The typical hospitality operation requires many other capital equipment items, consumable supplies, and services in addition to those already described.

Vending Products. A first concern is whether to buy the machines or to contract for their use with a vending company. A simple bid should determine the competitiveness of commission rates. Buyers can obtain product costs from local vending distributors or directly from manufacturers if the purchase volume is adequate. A cost-benefit analysis can be undertaken after consideration of such expense categories as equipment, maintenance, and labor. Vending product distributors obtain high turnovers and are able to work on relatively low margins. They often gain part of their margins on manufacturer's promotions and rebates, which are partially passed through to the end-user.

Buyers often find that different market segments have different price schedules: the price of products intended for vending use may differ greatly from that of products intended for general counter or shelf sales. This is justified primarily on the basis of competition. Since they essentially operate on a cost-plus system, how well these vendors buy in large part determines their gross margin. Concerns to address with distributors include markup percentages, commission percentages, and the quality of vended items.

Periodicals. Most buyers find little competition in this area. Magazines, paperback books, and similar items are usually pre-priced, have only one distributor, and generally have a non-negotiable cost. However, publishers compete intensely among themselves for shelf space. Publishers may offer some reduction for displaying their items and for sales volumes. The distributor often performs the stocking function, which involves removing and crediting old items and stocking popular sellers. Distributors should be able to provide information about promotional allowances, as well as sales rankings of periodicals (regular lists published on a geographical basis). The top sellers should certainly be available.

Tobacco and Candy. These products may also be included in the vending products just discussed. Regardless of how these items are purchased, the buyer should have some contact with the manufacturers. The industry leader in each category tends to set the marketing strategy, which, in addition to price, includes new products, sizes, and advertising. Buyers should try to stay up-to-date on all of these factors, but price remains the first priority. Companies tend to change prices on a fairly predictable annual schedule. Candy companies promote on this basis;

promotions usually coincide with a price increase. The tobacco companies do not promote in this manner, but depend more on direct consumer advertising. Both industries offer permanent allowances for point-of-sale displays of their products, which are even more generous for tobacco than for candy.

Bracket pricing is important for candy items. Some companies have five or more delivery brackets beginning with less than one thousand pounds ranging up to truckloads. The difference between the bottom and top brackets is fairly moderate (usually less than 10%) and is partly a function of freight costs, which can vary. Cigarettes are sold in high volumes and are generally distributed in at least half truckloads by manufacturers. Other tobacco items may be shipped in smaller volumes.

Cigarettes have relatively consistent costs around the country. Federal excise taxes are collected by the manufacturer and are reflected in the distributor's invoice cost. Local taxes are generally collected by the distributor (or first receiver), who applies stamps to the packages, includes this tax in their cost, and passes the cost through to buyers. Distributors then pay the tax to the local taxing jurisdiction, receiving some compensation. Not all distributors perform this tax collection function. Some firms buy from a first distributor/receiver to avoid the extra work and then become sub-distributors. Since these transactions may lead to greater markups, buyers should know the class of their distributor.

Markups on cigarettes are low due to large turnover and very high volume. Some states, however, regulate the distributor's price. Most often this regulation is in the form of a minimum price which can be charged. Other tobacco products carry a higher markup. Part of the distributor's markup comes from cash discounts, which are relatively high for cigarettes since the manufacturer wants to generate adequate cash flow. Successful distributors take maximum advantage of these discounts. Buyers should know the amounts of such discounts and thus negotiate a better price, provided they promptly pay the distributor.

Price lists are published by both tobacco and candy manufacturers. Buyers should examine these lists periodically to measure the distributor's performance.

Electronic Games. Electronic games are a potential source of income. Large-volume buyers may deal directly with manufacturers. However, use of local specialized distributors is the key for most users. There are a few points to look for in selecting a company:

- Does it have currently popular games? Revenue per machine depends on a number of factors, but sales for popular games can exceed those for slow games by several times.

- Will the distributor install the machines? What service levels can be expected? Does the distributor have adequate service personnel to keep the machines operating?

- What is the revenue split between the buyer's organization and the distributor company? Various splits are possible depending on service level, parts ownership, and collection practices. The agreement should clearly spell out these arrangements.

- Who counts the money and how is the cash reconciled with the number of plays?

Hospitality operations that purchase machines can develop their own service capabilities through a standard risk/reward calculation. Popular games can return their cost in a few months, but others may never return their costs. Buyers should present the options to line operating managers.

Marketing Practices

Prior to the rapid chain expansion in the 1950s and 1960s, manufacturers primarily used local distributors to deliver their products. There were three general distributor categories:

- Equipment distributors who often held exclusive sales rights to equipment lines in their territory. Generally, these distributors also represented manufacturers for lines of glassware, silverware, smallwares, and china. On occasion, they also stocked paper and/or chemical products.

- Supply distributors who held exclusive sales rights from paper manufacturers and occasionally inventoried smallwares and/or chemical products.

- Specialized distributors who generally represented manufacturers of technical equipment such as air conditioners, building elevators, and lighting fixtures. These distributors provided a combination of products such as office forms, linens, and maintenance items.

Manufacturers traditionally preferred the specialized distributor system for delivering their products, since these distributors offered customers such advantages as:

- Providing service after the sale

- Maintaining floor stock of products

- Assisting with sales efforts

- Helping to collect amounts due the manufacturer

With the expansion of chain operations, tremendous purchasing power became consolidated, leading to changes in this system.

Product Delivery Systems

The response of distributors to the emergence of chain operations has been in three directions:

- Mergers and consolidations gave the distributor organization greater geographical span and access to more customers.

- Product line specialization enabled the distributor to provide valuable services to larger operators.

- Product line expansion permitted larger sales per delivery and spawned the term "one-stop shopping."

Another outcome is that some chains established their own distribution systems and, in some cases, solicited business outside their own companies, thus becoming the competitors of distributors.

These developments have provided more options to buyers, who may now choose from among the following distribution sources.

Local Equipment and Supply Distributors. Many of these companies still remain despite the impact of chain operations. They are restricted to local or fairly narrow regional areas, succeeding primarily on the basis of service. The trend has been toward consolidation within a region, with distributors expanding their product lines as fewer companies survive. To maintain service, distributors have historically stocked large inventories with low turnover, resulting in a low return on investment. To reduce inventory investments, distributors may buy in minimum delivery quantities, which raises unit costs. They operate scheduled deliveries and the average dollar sales per order is often low. These factors have contributed to high markups.

Much of their business is generated by salespersons working on commission. However, many distributors now actively solicit program accounts in which the customer (such as the hospitality operator) and distributor reach agreement on service, specification, and pricing policy. The customer guarantees the business and the distributor finds ways to reduce costs and markups.

Equipment and supply distributors generally use a four-tier pricing arrangement:

- Street business is generated by salespersons and results in the highest markup.

- Program business represents guaranteed sales and typically has the second highest markup.

- Drop shipments are direct deliveries from the factory to the user—the distributor only handles the paperwork. This alternative yields a relatively low markup.

- Package orders are high-volume orders for new or remodeled installations, generally involving a large quantity of equipment/supplies and often fabricated equipment. The distributor is usually required to consolidate the merchandise for delivery to the operating unit. The merchandise is priced either on a cost-plus basis or by a fixed amount. This method typically produces the lowest markup; street business markups may be two or three times the markup on drop shipment and package order business.

In terms of inventory, distributors of paperware, cleaning supplies, and similar items usually have less investment and faster turnover and, consequently, may require lower markups. These distributors use the same four-tier pricing arrangements as equipment companies, although package orders are not as important. All of these companies have expanded their product lines to generate sales; some supply distributors have added food items.

What type of buying system works best when purchasing from equipment and supply distributors? The answer depends upon a number of factors. For example, a buyer for a chain requiring a limited number of items probably maintains contact with the manufacturer, making it possible to follow costs to the distributor. The buyer need only negotiate the markup or handling fee.

A buyer for a multi-unit organization needing many items could negotiate a markup with the distributor, then track a selected group of items through the system to assess distributor compliance. The items evaluated should be changed regularly.

A buyer for a small organization with many items should occasionally use an open bid, since manufacturers' costs may be inaccessible. Even if the distributor promises no more than a 20 or 30% markup, small buyers have no way to measure compliance. Taking two or more bids for selected items provides some measure of control.

Buyers should keep the following factors in mind when negotiating distributor prices:

- Most distributors apply a markup percentage to their costs to arrive at a selling price; their effectiveness in buying is crucial in determining the buyer's cost.

- When the item being purchased is equipment, buyers should give such purchases careful thought and make clear agreements regarding service arrangements.

- Should good customers get lower prices? A good customer is one who is loyal to the seller, plans for minimum deliveries, requires fewer emergency deliveries, and pays bills on time. However, even a good customer should not *expect* to get good prices without negotiating for them.

Regional and/or National Distributors. These distributors carry a wide variety of items (including food products) in response to the customer's demands. The items carried are generally consumables, although a few also sell equipment packages. The large number of items and resulting high investment costs create problems for these companies, but competition compels them to provide a wide selection. Many utilize sophisticated techniques in data processing, warehousing, and scheduling to increase their productivity.

Pricing arrangements with regional/national distributors are similar to those described for equipment and supply distributors, as are the buying systems used. A few points are worth noting when buying non-food items from a distributor whose primary business is in food products:

- Since this is not the company's primary business, it may not buy as well as traditional distributors. When this is the case, higher purchase costs are passed on to the hospitality buyer.

- High inventory levels are of concern to these suppliers; they may be out of stock more frequently.

- Markups should be less. Markups may be substantially reduced if non-food items are combined with food purchases from these distributors.

Specialized Distributors. We have discussed specialized distributors that handle technical equipment and products. Buyers are in contact with many of them. They may also have contact with distributors providing the following services.

1. Some distributors provide packages of merchandise for new or remodeled installations. While primarily involved in furniture, fixtures, and equipment (FF&E), some companies also provide architectural design, installation, construction, and financing services. The services they offer compete directly with similar programs provided by equipment distributors and the in-house staffs of some large chains. They generally require only a few staff members who handle the administration and so, in general, have a low overhead. The labor and products required for a specific job are generally contracted as the jobs are received.

2. Some distributors provide consumable supplies to end-users. This has been most successful in fast-food applications. Food and consumable supplies are frequently supplied by a company that has only a few customers (sometimes just one).

Turnkey package suppliers of FF&E merchandise offer a least-effort system for operators to obtain required merchandise and/or services; pricing is on either a bid or a cost-plus basis. The consumable supplies distributor provides a guaranteed supply program on an agreed-upon price system, usually cost-plus. In both cases, markups are generally less than they would be from a local, regional, or national distributor. Prompt payment by the customer is part of the agreement so that these low markups can be maintained.

Direct to End-User. In these situations, the user, in a sense, replaces the distributor in buying from the manufacturer directly. Storage and transportation must be provided, product shipments scheduled, installation arranged (if needed), service maintained, and bills paid. Hospitality organizations choosing this system must invest in technically competent people and adequate facilities to perform the function.

Organizations considering this option should carefully analyze their requirements to determine if a distribution department will be fully utilized, as considerable expense is involved in its establishment and maintenance.

Endnotes

1. For details about the quality and purchase of china, glassware, and flatware, see Anthony Rey and Ferdinand Wieland, *Management of Service in Food and Beverage Operations* (East Lansing, Mich.: Educational Institute of the American Hotel & Motel Association, 1985), pp. 73–81.

REVIEW QUIZ

When you feel you have covered all of the material in this chapter, answer these questions. Choose the *best* answer. Check your answers with the correct ones found on the Review Quiz Answer Key at the end of this book.

True (T) or False (F)

T F 1. Drop shipments are direct deliveries from the factory to the end-user.

T F 2. Capital equipment has a useful life of more than one year and is expensed through depreciation.

T F 3. The buyer may help to clarify an operation's need for proposed equipment.

T F 4. Specifying equipment on an "or equal" basis is a poor method of purchasing.

T F 5. A turnkey operation is one in which a retail unit is turned over to the operator ready for business.

T F 6. Manufacturers sell their equipment only through specialized distributors or local distributors.

T F 7. Warranties and service are insignificant factors in purchasing equipment.

T F 8. After design blueprints are developed and finalized, equipment items can be more easily substituted.

T F 9. In most product areas, a fairly standard set of manufacturer specifications exists along with various quality levels.

T F 10. Products in the "utility" category are more likely to be used in front-of-the-house operations than products in the "appearance" category.

T F 11. Only china manufactured in the United States is considered acceptable in hospitality operations.

T F 12. Reheating of glass and addition of lead oxide increases the strength of glass.

T F 13. Intended use is the major factor in selecting gauge of aluminum foil.

T F 14. When purchasing chemical products, frequent changes of suppliers are practical and advisable.

Multiple Choice

15. Warranties for equipment should be:

    a. maintained in a separate file.
    b. attached to the invoice.
    c. kept in the paid bill file.
    d. retained on the underside of the equipment.

16. All of the following are considered to be consumable supplies *except*:

    a. paper cups.
    b. dishwashing machines.
    c. guestroom amenities.
    d. cleaning soaps.

17. Which of the following categories has the highest markup in a four-tier pricing system?

    a. program business
    b. drop shipments
    c. package orders
    d. street business

18. Which type of distributor usually provides packages of merchandise for new or remodeled installations?

    a. local distributor
    b. specialized distributor
    c. regional/national distributor
    d. end-user distributor

19. Which is *not* a commercial grade of silverplate?

    a. heavy
    b. triple
    c. commercial
    d. standard

360

Appendix

Trade Organizations and Government Agencies

Agri-Commodities, Inc.
Two Dundee Park
Andover, MA 01810

American Frozen Food Institute
1700 Old Meadow Road
McLean, VA 22102

American Institute of Food
  Distribution
28-12 Broadway
Fair Lawn, NJ 07410-3913

American Meat Institute
P.O. Box 3556
Washington, D.C. 20007

California Avocado Commission
17620 Fitch, Second Floor
Irvine, CA 92714

California Tree Fruit Agreement
P.O. Box 255383
701 Fulton Avenue
Sacramento, CA 95825

Florida Citrus Commission
Florida Department of Citrus
P.O. Box 148
Lakeland, FL 33802

Florida Tomato Exchange
P.O. Box 20635
Orlando, FL 32814

Institute of Food Technologists
221 North La Salle Street, Suite 2120
Chicago, IL 60601

Livestock Business Advisory
  Services, Inc.
10261 Santa Fe Drive
P.O. Box 12916
Overland Park, KS 66212

National Association of Meat
  Purveyors
252 West Ina Road
Tucson, AZ 85704

National Fisheries Institute
2000 M Street, N.W.
Washington, D.C. 20036

National Food Processors Association
1401 New York Avenue, N.W.
Washington, D.C. 20005

National Frozen Food Association
604 West Derry Road
Hershey, PA 17033

National Institutional Food
  Distributors Association
P.O. Box 19936
Atlanta, GA 30325

National Live Stock and Meat Board
444 North Michigan Avenue
Chicago, IL 60611

Northwest Food Processors
2828 S.W. Corbett
Portland, OR 97201

Produce Marketing Association
Food Service Division
700 Barksdale Plaza
Newark, DE 19711

Sunkist Growers, Inc.
P.O. Box 7888
Van Nuys, CA 91409

United Fresh Fruit and Vegetable
  Association
1019 19th Street, N.W.
Washington, D.C. 20036

United States Department of
  Agriculture
Economic Research Service
Agricultural Marketing Service
Washington, DC 20250
(For specific information about meats,
poultry, dairy products, fresh and pro-
cessed fruits and vegetables, and other
items)

Washington State Apple Commission
P.O. Box 18
Wenatchee, WA 98801

Washington State Fruit Commission
1005 Tieton Drive
Yakima, WA 98902

References and Suggested Readings

U.S. Government Publications

(Unless otherwise stated, most U.S. publications are available from the U.S. Government Printing Office, Washington, D.C. 20401)

Department of Agriculture

Cattle on Feed Report, published four times per year.

Cheese Varieties and Descriptions. Agr. Handbook No. 54, revised 1969.

Dairy Inspection & Grading Services. Bulletin #48.

Dairy Market News, Madison, Wis. (Eastern/Southern and Central Areas), or Minneapolis, Minn. (Central/Western Areas).

Dairy Products—Annual Summary.

Federal and State Standards for the Composition of Milk Products. Agr. Handbook 51. Food Safety and Inspection Service. January 1980.

Foreign Plants Certified to Export Meat to the U.S. Food Safety and Inspection Service (published annually).

Fresh Fruit and Vegetable National Shipping Point Trends. Agricultural Marketing Service, Fruit and Vegetable Division, Philadelphia.

Institutional Meat Purchase Specifications: General Requirements; Fresh Beef (Series 100); Fresh Lamb and Mutton (Series 200); Fresh Veal and Calf (Series 300); Fresh Pork (Series 400); Cured, Cured and Smoked and Fully-cooked Pork Products (Series 500); Cured, Dried and Smoked Beef Products (Series 600); Edible By-products (Series 700); Sausage Products (Series 800); and Portion-Cut Meat Products (Series 1000).

Labels on Meat and Poultry Products. Information Bulletin #443. Food Safety and Quality Service, 1981.

Meat and Poultry Inspection. Food Safety and Quality Service Fact Sheet #18. February, 1981.

Poultry Market News Report, Edison, N.J.

Regulations Governing the Grading of Shell Eggs and U.S. Standards, Grades, and Weight Classes for Shell Eggs. 7CFR Part 56. Agricultural Marketing Service, Poultry Division. 26 December 1978.

Regulations Governing the Inspection of Eggs and Egg Products. 7CFR Part 59. Agricultural Marketing Service, Poultry Division. 8 May 1980.

Regulations Governing the Voluntary Inspection and Grading of Egg Products. 7CFR Part 55. Agricultural Marketing Service, Poultry Division. 26 December 1978.

Department of Commerce, National Marine Fisheries Service

Approval List of Sanitary Inspected Fish Establishments, published semi-annually.

Fishery Market News Report (The Green Sheet). New York.

Fishery Market News Report (The Blue Sheet). Boston.

Institutional Purchasing Specification for the Purchasing of Fresh, Frozen and Canned Fishery Products. Written by Jack Dougherty.

Regulations Governing Processed Fishery Products, Title 50 and U.S. Standards for Grades of Fishery Products. 1 October 1977.

Other Publications

Agri-Commodities, Inc. *Meat Price Outlook.* Andover, Mass.

American Dry Milk Institute. *Sanitary/Quality Standards Code for Dry Milk.* Chicago, 1970.

————. *Standards for Grades of Dry Milks.* Chicago, 1971.

American Institute of Food Distribution, Inc. *The Food Institute Report.* Fair Lawn, N.J.

Blue Goose, Inc. *The Buying Guide for Fresh Fruits, Vegetables, Herbs, and Nuts.* Fullerton, Calif., 1976.

Edward Judge & Sons. *The Almanac of the Canning, Freezing, and Preserving Industries.* Westminster, Md. (published annually).

The Erkins Seafood Letter, Bliss, Idaho.

The Meat Sheet, Inc. *The Meat Sheet.* Elmhurst, Ill.

National Association of Meat Purveyors. *Meat Buyers Guide.* Tucson, Ariz., 1976.

————. *The N.A.M.P. Guide to Quality Assurance.* Tucson, Ariz., 1978.

National Dairy Council. *Newer Knowledge of Cheese and Cheese Products.* Rosemont, Ill., 1980.

National Dairy News, Inc. *National Dairy News.* Madison, Wis.

National Frozen Food Association. *Frozen Food Institutional Encyclopedia.* Hershey, Pa., 1977.

National Institutional Food Distributors Association. *Canned Goods Specifications Manual.* West Lafayette, Ind.: Purdue Research Foundation, 1985.

————. *Frozen Foods Specifications Manual.* West Lafayette, Ind.: Purdue Research Foundation, 1986.

National Live Stock and Meat Board. *Meat Evaluation Handbook.* Chicago, 1969.

————. *Meat in the Food Service Industry.* Chicago, 1975.

————. *Merchandising Beef Loins.* Chicago, n.d.

————. *Merchandising Beef Ribs.* Chicago, n.d.

————. *Merchandising Beef Rounds.* Chicago, 1974.

————. *Merchandising Pork Legs.* Chicago, n.d.

————. *Merchandising Pork Loins.* Chicago, 1980.

————. *Merchandising Pork Shoulders.* Chicago, 1978.

The National Provisioner, Inc. *Daily Market and News Service ("The Yellow Sheet").* Chicago.

Pedderson, Raymond B. *SPECS: The Comprehensive Foodservice Purchasing and Specification Manual.* Boston: CBI, 1977.

Potter, Frank E. *Purchasing Dairy Products for Food Service.* Amherst, Mass.: University of Massachusetts, College of Agriculture, Leaflet #15.

Produce Marketing Association. *The Foodservice Guide to Fresh Produce.* Newark, Del., 1983.

Urner Barry Publications, Inc., *Seafood Price-Current* and *Price-Current.* Toms River, N.J.

Index

HOSPITALITY PURCHASING MANAGEMENT

REVIEW QUIZ ANSWER KEY

The numbers in parentheses refer to the page(s) where the answer may be found.

Chapter 1	Chapter 2	Chapter 3	Chapter 4
1. F (8)	1. T (21)	1. F (37)	1. T (52)
2. F (9)	2. F (17)	2. T (43)	2. T (56)
3. F (3)	3. T (22)	3. F (39)	3. T (51)
4. T (6)	4. T (18)	4. T (39)	4. F (58)
5. F (4)	5. T (22)	5. F (42)	5. T (63)
6. F (9)	6. T (27)	6. F (35, 41)	6. F (58)
7. T (13)	7. F (28)	7. T (44)	7. T (63)
8. b (14)	8. T (25)	8. T (45)	8. d (58–59)
9. d (7–9)	9. d (21–22)	9. d (40–41)	9. c (66)
	10. a (22)		10. d (59–60)
	11. c (23)		11. a (63)

Chapter 5	Chapter 6	Chapter 7	Chapter 8
1. T (75–76)	1. T (95)	1. T (108)	1. T (123)
2. F (79–80)	2. F (94)	2. F (110)	2. T (123)
3. F (74)	3. T (97)	3. T (109)	3. F (124)
4. F (74)	4. F (98)	4. F (111–112)	4. T (124)
5. T (86)	5. T (98–99)	5. T (113)	5. T (125)
6. T (72)	6. T (101)	6. F (114)	6. F (125)
7. F (85)	7. F (101)	7. T (117)	7. T (125)
8. T (72)	8. F (103)	8. d (111–116)	8. F (126–127)
9. F (73–74)	9. d (91)	9. d (117–118)	9. F (127–128)
10. T (79)	10. c (91–92)		10. T (127)
11. F (82)	11. c (103)		11. T (128)
12. T (84)			12. T (135)
13. T (82)			13. F (134)
14. d (75)			14. F (129)
15. c (76)			15. a (124)
16. d (71–72)			16. c (125)
			17. b (127)
			18. b (131)
			19. d (139–140)

Chapter 9	Chapter 10	Chapter 11	Chapter 12
1. F (146–148)	1. F (174)	1. T (212)	1. T (236)
2. T (145–146)	2. T (187)	2. F (212–214)	2. F (235–236)
3. T (146)	3. F (183)	3. T (207–208)	3. F (240)
4. F (151–152)	4. T (185)	4. T (210)	4. F (238)
5. F (152)	5. T (180)	5. F (211)	5. T (242)
6. F (153–154)	6. T (180)	6. F (224)	6. T (236)
7. T (155)	7. F (173)	7. F (224)	7. T (239)
8. F (156)	8. T (179)	8. d (210)	8. c (237)
9. F (156)	9. T (181)	9. b (209)	
10. T (157–158)	10. T (184)	10. d (224)	
11. F (162)	11. T (183)	11. a (224)	
12. F (162)	12. F (183)		
13. F (167)	13. T (188)		
14. F (167)	14. T (188)		
15. c (146)	15. T (196)		
16. a (150)	16. b (185)		
17. b (165)	17. a (186)		
18. d (167, 169)	18. c (179)		
19. d (169)	19. a (181)		
	20. d (179)		

Chapter 13	Chapter 14	Chapter 15	Chapter 16
1. T (280–282)	1. F (293)	1. F (315, 316)	1. T (329)
2. T (253)	2. F (293)	2. T (318)	2. F (329)
3. F (254)	3. T (294)	3. a (319)	3. F (330)
4. T (254)	4. T (296)	4. b (320)	4. T (330)
5. T (254)	5. F (297)		5. T (331)
6. F (260)	6. T (297)		6. F (333, 334)
7. T (261)	7. F (297)		7. F (334)
8. F (262)	8. T (298)		8. T (334)
9. T (270)	9. T (300)		9. F (336)
10. F (268)	10. T (303)		10. T (333)
11. F (267)	11. T (303–304)		11. T (338)
12. T (272)	12. T (305)		12. F (339)
13. F (272)	13. T (307)		13. T (341)
14. T (278)	14. T (308)		14. F (346)
15. F (282)	15. F (309)		15. T (349)
16. b (254)	16. b (294)		16. d (329)
17. b (259)	17. a (295)		17. d (330)
18. c (269)	18. d (298)		18. c (331)
19. d (279, 282)	19. b (306)		19. a (335)
20. a (284–285)	20. c (307)		20. c (341–342)

Chapter
17

1. T (366)
2. T (355)
3. T (355)
4. F (356)
5. T (356)
6. F (356–357)
7. F (357)
8. F (356)
9. T (357)
10. F (357)
11. F (359)
12. T (360)
13. T (361)
14. F (361)
15. a (357)
16. b (357)
17. d (366)
18. b (367–368)
19. c (360)